History Made Conscious

GEOFF ELEY has taught at the University of Cambridge and the University of Michigan. His books include *Forging Democracy: The History of the Left in Europe, 1850-2000; Nazism as Fascism: Violence, Ideology, and the Ground of Consent in Germany, 1930-1945*; and, with Keith Nield, *The Future of Class in History: What's Left of the Social?*

History Made Conscious

Politics of Knowledge, Politics of the Past

Geoff Eley

VERSO

London • New York

First published by Verso 2023
© Geoff Eley 2023

1 3 5 7 9 10 8 6 4 2

Verso
UK: 6 Meard Street, London W1F 0EG
US: 388 Atlantic Avenue, Brooklyn, NY 11217
versobooks.com

Verso is the imprint of New Left Books

ISBN-13: 978-1-83976-813-2
ISBN-13: 978-1-83976-814-9 (UK EBK)
ISBN-13: 978-1-83976-815-6 (US EBK)

British Library Cataloguing in Publication Data
A catalogue record for this book is available from the British Library

Library of Congress Cataloging-in-Publication Data

Names: Eley, Geoff, 1949- author.
Title: History made conscious : politics of knowledge, politics of the past
  / Geoff Eley.
Other titles: Politics of knowledge, politics of the past
Description: London ; New York : Verso, 2023. | Includes bibliographical
  references and index.
Identifiers: LCCN 2023013095 (print) | LCCN 2023013096 (ebook) | ISBN
  9781839768132 (trade paperback) | ISBN 9781839768156 (US EBK) | ISBN
  9781839768149 (UK EBK)
Subjects: LCSH: Historiography. | Social history. | Civilization—History
Classification: LCC D13 .E45 2023 (print) | LCC D13 (ebook) | DDC
  907.2—dc23/eng/20230419
LC record available at https://lccn.loc.gov/2023013095
LC ebook record available at https://lccn.loc.gov/2023013096

Typeset in Minion by Biblichor Ltd, Scotland
Printed and bound by CPI Group (UK) Ltd, Croydon CR0 4YY

Contents

Acknowledgements

Most of this book's treatments began in talks and conference papers presented before many varieties of audience, chiefly during the recent two decades. Some chapters indicate particular lines of indebtedness, but a true and full accounting would be far too voluminous to hope to include here. I simply record my immense appreciation for the countless discussions with colleagues, students, and friends, in Cambridge, Ann Arbor, and the wider intellectual cosmopolis, that made my thinking possible.

I especially thank everyone at Verso, notably Sebastian Budgeon, for taking the book on; Jeanne Tao, for guiding it through production; and Charles Peyton, for his consummate copy-editing. With his unfailing astuteness and efficiency, Ken Garner helped prepare the final manuscript, including its overall coherence and general framing. Richard Bachmann compiled the index. My essential interlocutors should be clear from the citations in particular chapters. To my terrible sadness, several of the very best, including Karl Pohrt, Keith Nield, Alf Lüdtke, and Lauren Berlant, died before the book found its final fruition. Incomparable thanks go to Kathleen Canning, Jane Caplan, Erica Carter, Rita Chin, Jessica Dubow, Atina Grossmann, Kali Israel, Jennifer Jenkins, Marjorie Levinson, Bob Moeller, Dirk Moses, Bill Schwarz, Peggy Somers, Scott Spector, Ron Suny, Julia Thomas, and of course Gina Morantz-Sanchez.

Each of the following chapters is a reworked and updated version of an earlier publication, sometimes condensed, sometimes expanded.

'Is All the World a Text? From Social History to the History of Society Two Decades Later', in *The Historic Turn in the Human Sciences*, ed. Terrence J. McDonald (Ann Arbor: University of Michigan Press, 1996), 193–243.

'Between Social History and Cultural Studies: Interdisciplinarity and the Practice of the Historian at the End of the Twentieth Century', in *Historians and Social Values*, ed. Joep Leerssen and Ann Rigney (Amsterdam: Amsterdam University Press, 2000), 93–109.

'The Profane and Imperfect World of Historiography', *AHR* Forum on Geoff Eley's *A Crooked Line*, *American Historical Review* 113: 2 (April 2008), 425–37.

'Nations, Publics, and Political Cultures: Placing Habermas in the Nineteenth Century', in *Culture/Power/History: A Reader in Contemporary Social Theory*, ed. Nicholas B. Dirks, Geoff Eley, and Sherry B. Ortner (Princeton: Princeton University Press, 1993), 297–335.

'Politics, Culture, and the Public Sphere', *positions* 10: 1 (Spring 2002), 219–36.

'Labor History, Social History, Alltagsgeschichte: Experience, Culture, and the Politics of the Everyday – A New Direction for German Social History?', *Journal of Modern History* 61: 2 (1989), 297–343.

'Conjuncture and the Politics of Knowledge: The Center for Contemporary Cultural Studies (CCCS), 1968–1984', in *Cultural Studies 50 Years On: History, Practice, and Politics*, ed. Kieran Connell and Mathew Hilton (London: Rowman and Littlefield, 2016), 25–47.

'Imperial Imaginary, Colonial Effect: Writing the Colony and the Metropole Together', in *Race, Nation and Empire: Making Histories, 1750 to the Present*, ed. Catherine Hall and Keith McClelland (Manchester: Manchester University Press, 2010), 217–36.

'Empire by Land or Sea: Germany's Imperial Imaginary, 1840–1945', in *German Colonialism in a Global Age*, ed. Bradley D. Naranch and Geoff Eley (Durham, NC: Duke University Press, 2014), 19–45.

'Historicizing the Global, Politicizing Capital: Giving the Present a Name', *History Workshop Journal* 63 (Spring 2007), 154–88.

'Stuart Hall, 1930–2014', *History Workshop Journal* 79 (Spring 2015), 303–20.

Introduction: Lowering History's Defences

The thinking behind these essays occurred over a thirty-year period. They serve as both an archaeology and extension of the book I published at the mid-point of that time, *A Crooked Line: From Cultural History to the History of Society*.[1] Some essays preceded that book and enabled its writing; others came well afterwards and carried its arguments further. *A Crooked Line* traced my particular passage through the excitements and travails of the discipline of history since the 1960s, beginning with my student days at Oxford when I encountered the British Marxist historians and the debates surrounding their work. In addition to Edward Thompson, Eric Hobsbawm, Victor Kiernan, and the others, Raymond Williams was a particular inspiration, as were Perry Anderson, Tom Nairn, and their contemporaries writing in *New Left Review*. As I moved into graduate studies at the University of Sussex in the early 1970s, I then added the French *Annales* school and historical sociologies of the English-speaking world to my influences. Those three historiographical streams flowed together to shape my sensibility as a historian and informed the optimism of my outlook – the conviction that social history in particular could help in the processing of the political possibilities of that era.

If my undergraduate education drew me towards dissenting views of the British past, I pursued my graduate studies at Sussex in a different

---

1   Geoff Eley, *A Crooked Line: From Cultural History to the History of Society* (Ann Arbor: University of Michigan Press, 2005).

field, namely German history. At that time, West German historians like Hans-Ulrich Wehler and Jürgen Kocka were actively modernizing German historical studies by means of a self-consciously designed 'historical social science' that embraced multiple sub-disciplinary fields in the interests of an integrated account of the German past. German history at the time was also the scene of huge disputations with highly charged political implications, including the Fischer controversy and the so-called *Sonderweg* debate, which proposed powerful arguments about the origins of Nazism and what was thought to be the exceptional, distorted course of German history when measured against the history of the West. These debates were another major inspiration, leading to my earliest published interventions. However, the 'learning process' they helped provoke – especially by their handling of the complexities of the relationship between social history and politics – made me increasingly hesitant about the possibilities and limits of social explanation, whether for historical work or as a ground of politics.

A further influence on my historian's outlook – a source simultaneously of inspiration and trouble – came directly from politics and the changes acting on the Left's sensibility and thought in the 1970s. One strand was feminism, whose challenge compelled changes at many different levels, although, as I described in *Crooked Line*, a long and complicated process was required before these worked their way through my historical writing. Closely related was a re-theorizing of questions of ideology, consciousness, and subjectivity, partly inside the Marxist tradition, but increasingly breaking from the latter altogether – especially towards psychoanalytic theory, theories of language, and a rich array of approaches to the study of culture. Helping enormously with that open-ended turmoil of revision was the reception into the English-speaking world of the ideas of Antonio Gramsci. My best guide through all of those complexities were the writings of Raymond Williams and Stuart Hall. I had the extraordinary good luck during 1975–79 to have been in Cambridge, where I learned from collective conversation with an amazing group of contemporaries.

By the time I arrived at the University of Michigan at the end of the 1970s, the sufficiencies of social history were coming under far-reaching critical review. After a sequence of big-splash polemical interventions, each by an earlier high-profile advocate of social history, the discipline headed during the 1980s for a period of sustained controversy and often bitter disagreement.[2] By the middle of that decade, new approaches were crystalizing around gender theory, the reception of the works of Michel Foucault, studies of sexuality, new historical anthropologies, and what came to be called the linguistic turn. The consequences coalesced under the umbrella of the 'new cultural history'. In Part I of what follows, 'History in Theory and Politics', this volume's first three chapters look back on the contentious shift from social history to cultural history from a vantage point not long after the events concerned.

Chapter 1 reviews the linguistic turn, with particular focus on the pioneering contributions of William Sewell and Gareth Stedman Jones, leading voices among the previously emergent generation of social historians who now proposed other ways of understanding labour and class. Concurrently, another former social historian, Joan Scott, began pressing the necessity of gender as 'a useful category of historical analysis'.[3] This critical landscape opened up new interdisciplinarity possibilities for research and exploration, merging history with anthropology, literary studies, communications and media studies, gender studies, and a novel cross-disciplinary formation calling itself cultural studies. The very richness and diversity of these approaches, however, produced concerns among social historians as to where, in these new culturalist accounts, 'society' still belonged. If all the world was a text, what could any longer be said about context, or (in that earlier language) society? This, in turn, spawned more fundamental conflicts. The very ground of the historical discipline itself seemed at risk. By turning to other disciplines and succumbing to their excitements, many feared, advocates of the new fads undermined the integrity of historical knowledge. Experimenting with other people's topics and techniques – what was now being called the 'cultural turn' – brought the historian's epistemology into doubt. If some entered

---

2 The most important were Elizabeth Fox-Genovese and Eugene Genovese, 'The Political Crisis of Social History: A Marxian Perspective', *Journal of Social History* 10 (1976); Gareth Stedman Jones, 'From Historical Sociology to Theoretical History', *British Journal of Sociology* 27 (1976); Lawrence Stone, 'History and the Social Sciences in the Twentieth Century', in *The Future of History: Essays in the Vanderbilt University Centennial Symposium*, ed. Charles F. Delzell (Nashville: Vanderbilt University Press, 1977). Three years later came Tony Judt, 'A Clown in Regal Purple: Social History and the Historians', *History Workshop Journal* 7 (1979). The context is explored in detail in Chapters 1 and 2, below.

3 Joan Scott, 'Gender: A Useful Category of Analysis', *American Historical Review* 91: 5 (December 1986), reprinted in Joan Wallach Scott, *Gender and the Politics of History* (New York: Columbia University Press, 1988).

this fresh space with curiosity and excitement, in other words, others found only disorder.

Chapter 2 directly considers how 'interdisciplinarity' emerged within academic history departments in the 1980s, along with the resistance it found. After early encounters with both history's conservatism (at Oxford) and its openness (at avowedly interdisciplinary Sussex), I arrived in 1979 in a very different environment, at the University of Michigan, where forms of cross-disciplinary conversation and collaboration were already second nature – whether institutionally in teaching and research, or as a widely diffused sensibility. This generously distinctive intellectual culture helped launch a major local initiative in the Program for the Comparative Study of Social Transformation (CSST), which between the late 1980s and early 2000s became simultaneously a pacesetter for historians' boundary-crossing activities at Michigan and the local version of a far wider ferment of collaboration across the humanities and parts of the social sciences in the United States. In the course of the resulting departures and debates, historians also gave much thought to the character of 'home', to the defining purposes, practices, and epistemological grounds of historical study as such. How were the disciplines produced and shaped? In a boundary-crossing age, how should disciplinary fields of knowledge be defined? How should we think about history's disciplinary core? How far, and in what ways, should it be preserved? Meanwhile, the conflicts of social and cultural historians continued.

That leads, in Chapter 3, to my own thinking behind the writing of *A Crooked Line*. Part of my purpose in that book was to track the complicated passages from social history to cultural history by using my own trajectory as a reference point. I wanted to write a contemporary intellectual history against the grain of the accounts usually provided, with their over-emphasis on clear lines of descent and disagreement, borne typically by a few prominent exemplars and their works in the most visible of classic debates. Instead, I hoped to capture the messiness and provisionalities, the uncertainties and aporia, through which we actually build our knowledge. I wanted to stress the serendipities, the dead ends, and the wrong turnings through which our thinking more commonly travels. In that light, I argued for a 'basic pluralism' – for patience across differences, for bringing the cultural and the social together, for not having to choose between them. Recognizing history's relationship to politics is part of that too. Politics can speak through the historian subtly and indirectly for much of the time, doing its work imperceptibly and unconsciously. But its impact can also be very direct, whether it unsettles or enables, even inspires. I stressed the intrusions of the public worlds of politics in the very widest meaning of those terms, exploring the three-way interconnections between the historiographical, the personal, and the political.

Four chapters make up Part II, 'Rethinking the Political'. Here, I explore the specific political valences of cultural history and interdisciplinarity, while considering some key institutions and practitioners. Chapters 4 and 5 take up the work of Jürgen Habermas and his theory of the 'public sphere'. In Chapter 4, I trace Habermas's formulation of 'public sphere' by tracing it to Enlightenment beliefs about rational communication and procedural politics, before testing it against historiographies of gender and women's history, state formation and politics, and culture. Chapter 5 turns to the ways in which historians have used Habermas's insights to develop new histories of civil society and the public sphere. Moreover, the term itself has political valences critical for connecting everyday life to notions of political agency and action. In other words, despite blind spots and foreshortenings in Habermas's initial formulation in the early 1960s, the 'public sphere' has been deployed for many political purposes and continues to spark many forms of political action. As I note, it 'supplies a means of conceptualizing an expanded notion of the political'.

Chapter 6 considers the emergence of *Alltagsgeschichte*, or the history of everyday life that emerged out of the tension between German 'historical social science' and the emerging culturalist mode of social history arriving from France and Britain in the 1970s, in the shadow of a gathering recognition of the diminishing political agency of the German working class. Not least in light of the history of Nazism, historians sought new means of recovering the everyday lives and culture of working-class Germans. This chapter profiles some of the key practitioners, including Hans Medick, Adelheid von Saldern, and Alf Lüdtke. The scope of their research ranges ambitiously across many periods and themes, including rural society, working-class social history, grassroots activity, and women's history.

Chapter 6 shifts back to Britain and the Centre for Contemporary Cultural Studies (CCCS) at the University of Birmingham, a key pioneering influence on the new cultural history. After tracing the history of CCCS, we need to ask after its continuing relevance in British historiography. For historians at CCCS, the study of culture was vital for the practice of democracy.

The four chapters comprising Part III expand the concerns of the first two sections into broader questions of empire. Chapter 8 considers how British imperialism was lived and experienced in the everydayness of material life. Taking my cues from the work of Paul Gilroy and others, I start with a discussion of how working-class people experienced empire, considering how the 'nation' itself is in fact imperialized space: that is, nations are products of imperial formation and expansion, rather than the other way around. Indeed, imperial conquest created the material culture of modernity.

Moving onto the continent, Chapter 9 explores Germany's 'imperial imaginary', showing that popular understanding of Germany's colonial empire was disseminated through multiple venues from Colonial Society propaganda to pulp fiction, and that some of these artifacts had afterlives during the Nazi and post-war eras. I then go on to consider the presence, or otherwise, of colonialism in post-war German historiography, and especially the idea of 'social imperialism': that the creation of the German Empire was a response to the rapid, unsettling impact of modernization at home. Yet this interpretation of the social role of imperialism, advanced by historians such as Hans-Ulrich Wehler, betrays a rather limited grasp of the relation between colonies and metropole. Recent practitioners of German history have sought out the wider context of the German colonial project: from the pressures of international economic and military competition to emerging notions of transnationalism and Pan-Germanism. These wider expansionary meanings have opened up new ways for historians of Germany to approach the relationship between the imperialist project and broader German society. Nonetheless, much remains to be done: 'we surely need some means of theorizing the long-term domestic consequences of empire – everything generated from the colonial encounter that became assimilated into the metropolitan society's self-understanding with sufficiently potent and pervasive continuity to have helped the later implanting of the "racial state"' (p. 241). Indeed, these are the very understandings of 'race' that continue to texture every aspect of European life in the early-twenty-first century and were first laid down during this classic period of imperialism and the colonial encounter.

Chapter 10 considers globalization in the light of the attacks of 11 September 2001, and the so-called Global War on Terror. Beginning with a contrast between a specifically British vision of a new international liberal order and the American right's assertions of unilateral supremacy, I contend that such distinct conceptions of global power had strong continuities with the pre-9/11 era. 'Globalization' in this sense not only meant 'regime change' and an unleashing of US-led military power in the Middle East, but also functioned as a form of discourse engineering widespread assent to its ubiquity. However, I argue that, just as British imperialism and German colonialism had their own historical trajectories, our present globalized moment needs to be historicized too. In challenging the presumption of globalization's cheerleaders, we need to historicize the 'global'. A good place to begin this task is by tracing out the experiences of labouring peoples in their encounters with capitalist development. 'If we put these two social regimes of labour together – that of the enslaved mass worker of the New World and that of the servile labourers of the households, workshops, and farms of the Old – then we have the makings of a radically different account of the dynamics of the rise of capitalism and the modes of social subordination that allowed it to occur' (p. 262). Through the recovery of these experiences, the narrative of globalization can be re-centred on the primacy of labour. The chapter then considers another dimension of the global in its historical context. What are the distinctive phases of globalization between the years of the post-1945 international order and the acceleration of globalization since the 1970s? How should we understand the consequent breakdown in the barriers between states and societies, and between states and global capital movements? Finally, I consider the political possibilities of contesting the destructiveness of globalization, especially through social movements advocating a 'global civil society'. The exact way in which we frame our understanding of this question conditions the possible meanings of 'globalization' itself: either a project for capitalist domination, or a politics of civil society reasserting itself.

Finally, Chapter 11 looks back at the life of one of the architects of CCCS and cultural studies as a whole, Stuart Hall. Hall believed that popular culture and interdisciplinary collaboration were unavoidable. 'Culture *matters*' for Hall, 'not just for how capitalism secures its stabilities, but for how critique and political resistance will need to be conducted too' (p. 286). As much as anyone, he brought culture to the centre of the concerns of the British Left in the 1960s and since. Even more, he challenged us to examine the relations binding our contemporary understandings to the legacies of empire and the colonial past. Those relations are always-already inflected by the complicated meanings of 'race'.

So, what do I mean by 'lowering history's defences'? The phrase is a friendly rejoinder to Richard Evans's *In Defence of History*.[4] History loses neither its 'identity' nor its efficacy by turning to other disciplines and seeking to learn from them. Opening one's doors and venturing out is not always a life-endangering exercise. By seeking help from elsewhere – in ideas, methods, traditions and genres of inquiry, entire epistemologies – why should history disappear into any threatening miasma of multiple disciplinary approaches? By drawing consciously on the resources of other disciplines, the practice of history more effectively recuperates the past. The resulting broadening of knowledge then helps us to understand and question the present. Interdisciplinarity 'means transgression, it means disobeying, it means rule-breaking, it means making trouble, it means shaking things up, it means being experimental, it means trying new thoughts, taking risks, being courageous in a relationship to new and unfamiliar knowledges, in the imagining of what those might be' (p. 45). Letting in other bodies of thought can only be of help – for historians and their readers – in persuading the past to deliver its interest and guidance, its cautions and incitements.

---

4   Richard Evans, *In Defence of History* (London: Granta, 1997).

PART I
History and Theory in Practice

1

Is All the World a Text?
Social History and the Linguistic Turn

In the Beginning

For Eric Hobsbawm in 1971, it was 'a good moment to be a social histor-ian'.[1] Ten years later, that was still the case, despite a certain fractiousness in the field. As activity proliferated – journals, conferences, sub-disciplinary societies, international networks, new curricula, ever more dissertations – conflicts over direction understandably ensued. But debates over theory and method suggested vitality more than ill health.[2] Ten years further on, though, optimism became harder to sustain. Historical sensibility was shifting from 'social' to 'cultural' history, a change increasingly flagged as the 'linguistic turn'. One good barometer was Gareth Stedman Jones. From his invigorating polemic against the liberal complacencies and positivistic assumptions of British historiography in 1967 to a variety of critical commentaries through the mid 1970s, Stedman Jones argued for a 'non-empiricist' and 'theoretically informed history' that was Marxist, open to other strands of social theory, and naturally materialist, as the

---

1 E. J. Hobsbawm, 'From Social History to the History of Society', *Daedalus* 1001: 1 (1971), 43.

2 Several essays are commonly cited for these polemical disagreements: see footnote 2 of the Introduction above.

unifying impulse of contemporary social history had taken that to mean.

When, in 1983, Stedman Jones embraced a decidedly non-materialist linguistic analysis that called those given assumptions into doubt, many social historians were perplexed and upset. Thereafter, things moved very fast. Those initially rather cautious formulations were left rapidly behind, lost in a polarization between so-called deconstructionists and unrepentant materialists.[3] The social history emerging from the 1960s was never a unitary project. Yet some notion of social determination, conceptualized on the ground of material life, whether in demographic, political-economic, labour-process, class-sociological, or class-cultural terms, generally supplied a tissue of common assumptions. By the end of the 1980s, in contrast, embittering divisions had opened up. On one side, revisionism reached the point of radically subverting the determinative coherence of the social as such. On the other, the integrity of social-historical materialism was obdurately defended.

Social history became one site of an epistemological uncertainty in wide areas of academic-intellectual life in the humanities and social sciences of the late twentieth century. That flux marked some disciplines far more than others – literary studies and anthropology, for example, as opposed to sociology and the 'harder' social sciences. The most pervasive impact occurred where disciplinary traditions could exercise less constraining power – women's studies and a freshly emergent cultural studies, for example, and in the United States African American studies, ethnic studies, and any area concerned with visuality. For many in the avant-garde, theoretical inspiration came from France.

One map of the uncertainty was supplied by Peter Novick's compendious recounting of academic debates among US historians since the late nineteenth century, *That Noble Dream*, which centred purposefully

---

3   See Stedman Jones's essays, 'History: The Poverty of Empiricism', in *Ideology in Social Science: Readings in Critical Social Theory*, ed. Robin Blackburn (London: Fontana/Collins, 1972); 'Class Struggle and the Industrial Revolution', *New Left Review* I/90 (March–April 1975); 'From Historical Sociology to Theoretical History'; 'Class Expression versus Social Control? A Critique of Recent Trends in the Social History of "Leisure"', *History Workshop Journal* 4 (1977). The essay on language appeared in Stedman Jones, *Studies in English Working-Class History, 1832–1982* (Cambridge: Cambridge University Press, 1983), joined by several of the earlier essays. The best guide to the trajectory of his thinking is the introduction to that volume, together with an interview conducted by Stuart Macintyre. See Macintyre, 'Interview with Gareth Stedman Jones', *Red Shift* 4 (1977).

around Thomas Kuhn, Richard Rorty, Stanley Fish, and Clifford Geertz rather than Michel Foucault, Jacques Lacan, Roland Barthes, and Jacques Derrida. But Novick too easily drew debates into his chosen binary opposition between 'objectivism' and 'relativism'. In ascribing history's dissolution as a professionally centred disciplinary project to an ever more elaborate pursuit of academic specialization, he entirely played down the gathering impact of 'contemporary continental thought'. For Novick, interest in the latter, notably the writings of Foucault and Derrida, was confined to a few 'professionally marginal historians whose primary allegiance was to interdisciplinary communities with membership made up largely of literary theorists, cultural critics, and philosophers'.[4] But he badly misrecognized the pulse of the times. So far from having 'little positive resonance within the historical profession, and practically none outside the sub-discipline of European intellectual history', the figures he wanted to dismiss – above all, Hayden White and Dominick LaCapra – were proving the harbingers of far broader intellectual change.

The earliest stocktaking essays, commonly cited to corroborate a 'crisis' of social history in the later 1970s – by Elizabeth Fox-Genovese and Eugene Genovese (1976), Stedman Jones (1976), Lawrence Stone (1977), and Tony Judt (1979) – were indeed remarkably innocent of the poststructuralist theory Novick dismissed. Those essays mostly presupposed an unreflected materialism. Other programmatic statements revealed the same: founding editorials in *Social History* (*SH*) and *History Workshop Journal* (*HWJ*), both launched in 1976, for example, or an omnibus survey of US historical writing edited by Michael Kammen for the American Historical Association (AHA), *The Past Before Us*, whose essays were commissioned during that same intellectual moment. This early stocktaking still channelled social history's post-1960s expansion far more than the later uncertainty and flux, affirming the materialist assumptions rather than querying them. Systematic perusal of older social history journals – *Past and Present* (*P&P*), *The Journal of Interdisciplinary History* (*JIH*), or *The Journal of Social History* (*JSH*), along with mainstream journals with strong social history contents like *The Journal of Modern History* (*JMH*) or *The*

---

4 Peter Novick, *That Noble Dream: The 'Objectivity Question' and the American Historical Profession* (Cambridge: Cambridge University Press, 1988).

American Historical Review (*AHR*) – reveals little trace of any literary or linguistic trespass. Whereas *AHR* and *JMH* began noticing the latter through review essays and forums, the older social history organs kept their distance, as did another journal very much in the vanguard of the exchange between history and social science, *Comparative Studies in Society and History* (*CSSH*).[5]

But change gradually rippled through the newer journals like *HWJ*, *SH*, and *Radical History Review* (*RHR*). *HWJ*'s founding editorials on 'Feminist History', 'Sociology and History', and 'British Economic History and the Question of Work' remained firmly continuous with the critical materialism of the 1960s.[6] But within just a few years an editorial on 'Language and History' marked some new distance.[7] Relaunched as a 'Journal of Socialist and Feminist Historians', and leading with a guide to 'Foucault for Historians' by Jeffrey Weeks, *HWJ* began a stream of striking departures: an editorial on 'Culture and Gender'; new feminist literary criticism in review essays by Mary Poovey and Joan Scott; essays on psychoanalysis by Sally Alexander and then Laura Mulvey and T. G. Ashplant, followed by a full-blown special feature on 'Psychoanalysis and History' with a response by Jacqueline Rose; another feature on 'Language and History', including Peter Schöttler on 'Historians and Discourse Analysis'; and finally, a heavily 'culturalist' feature on the French Revolution in the emergent literary-cum-linguistic sense.

In large degree, this was a process of complex generationally internal revision. Freshly launched journals like *HWJ*, *SH*, and *RHR* – and the refurbishing of others, like *International Labor and Working-Class History* (*ILWCH*) – had seen the arrival of a particular generation, the one trained over the preceding decade: beneath the sign of a restlessly aggrandizing social history, they now claimed their space. In turning to linguistically conceived forms of cultural history, moved by mixtures of political exigency and theoretical engagement, most sharply registered in feminism and women's history, some now departed that broad

---

5 In *CSSH*, poststructuralist perspectives entered somewhat via anthropology. Historiographically, its contents remained heavily focused on social science, review essays being a partial exception.
6 Sally Alexander and Anna Davin, 'Feminist History', *History Workshop Journal* 1: 1 (1976); Raphael Samuel and Gareth Stedman Jones, 'Sociology and History', *HWJ* 1: 1 (1976); Editors, 'British Economic History and the Question of Work', *HWJ* 3: 1 (1977).
7 Editors, 'Language and History', *History Workshop Journal* 10: 1 (1980).

generational consensus. Tensions exploded into conflicts over theory per se, as in the acrimonious attacks on 'structuralist Marxism' that dominated left intellectual life in Britain for much of the later 1970s.[8] The salience of these particular cohorts and their disputations was magnified by a concurrent reduction in recruits to the profession, which opened a gap in generational transmission. The immediate successors found it harder to register their distinctive voice. This contrasted, yet again, with cohorts qualifying in the later 1980s and early 1990s, who not only had a great deal to say about gender history and cultural studies, but also pressed the radically emergent histories of race, empire, and postcoloniality. The flames of the 1980s and 1990s were fuelled by this complicated generational ecology, in other words.

An intense day-long discussion at the University of Michigan in October 1979, organized by Louise and Charles Tilly, around the theme 'Whence and Whither Social History?' dramatized this generational flux, convening a number of key voices, including James Cronin, David Levine, John Merriman, Joan Scott, William Sewell, and Edward Shorter.[9] It encapsulated the dilemmas of a shared social-historical project just at its point of dispersal. In three consecutive sessions, the meeting addressed precisely those four stocktaking essays mentioned above (Fox-Genovese and Genovese, Stedman Jones, Stone, Judt). Talk kept returning to the deficiencies of 'vulgar Marxism', meaning the quantitative study of everyday experience and material life, as opposed to a 'more sophisticated kind of cultural history'. There was much citing of European theory and British debates (then approaching their chastening climax at the thirteenth History Workshop in December 1979), focused by interventions by the anthropologists present, including

---

8 See E. P. Thompson, *The Poverty of Theory and Other Essays* (London: Monthly Review Press, 1978), and the debate around Richard Johnson, 'Thompson, Genovese and Socialist-Humanist History', *History Workshop Journal* 6 (1978). Other contributions included Perry Anderson, *Arguments within English Marxism* (London: Verso, 1980), and the debate between Stuart Hall, Richard Johnson, and Edward Thompson at the Thirteenth History Workshop in Oxford in December 1979, published in Raphael Samuel, ed., *Peoples' History and Socialist Theory* (London: Routledge & Kegan Paul, 1981). A fourth, feminist, speaker withdrew from that debate on grounds of the tone and terms of the proceedings. See also Susan Magarey, 'That Old Hoary Chestnut, Free Will and Determinism: Culture vs Structure, or History vs Theory in Britain', *Comparative Studies in Society and History* 29 (1987).

9 Brief position papers by Louise Tilly, Edward Shorter, Francis G. Couvares, David Levine, and Charles Tilly were published as 'Problems in Social History: A Symposium', in *Theory and Society* 9: 5 (1980). The only such paper not solicited for the published symposium was my own.

Michael Taussig and Bernard Cohn. Though taken to be Marxist or Marxist-feminist, the desired theory actually involved an emerging antireductionist critique, which would eventually end in dissolving the Marxist problematic as we then knew it. After proceeding in a spirit of notable openness and generosity, finally, the discussions ended in angry hectoring by Charles Tilly, whom the cumulative culturalist advocacy had provoked. In rejoinder, Tilly aggressively upheld 'the harder-edged sociological work' whose primacy the meeting was supposed to defend.[10] Important truths were clearly at stake.

The occasion was portentous. Inside a year, William Sewell's *Work and Revolution in France* had appeared; Joan Scott began a systematic poststructuralist encounter; Charles Tilly held the line. Leading Europeanist progeny of the union of history and sociology, Scott and Sewell now disavowed those earlier roots.[11] Social historians' discourse was starting to become unruly. It outgrew its disciplinary containers, spilling over borders previously thought secure. As Francis Couvares said in his written statement for the Tilly symposium (in oddly gendered language): 'The new harlots of cultural anthropology, "thick description", and semiotics threaten daily to shift the focus, to alter the terms of the discourse.'[12]

The documentary trace shows little of the explosive charge. Charles Tilly acknowledged the challenge of 'anthropological work . . . the study of *mentalités*, and . . . more rigorous Marxist analyses', but believed that existing studies – 'collective biography, quantification, social-scientific approaches, and rigorous studies of everyday behavior' – would continue just as before. The trick was connecting them to 'the established historical agenda' in language historians could understand. His description of social history's 'two callings' was uncontentious: 'asking how the world we live in came into being, and how its coming into being affected the everyday lives of ordinary people; asking what could have happened to everyday experience at major historical choice points, and then inquiring how and why the outcomes won out over other possibilities.'[13]

---

10   In the published account, none of this intensity or concluding explosiveness appears.
11   Each was attached to Charles Tilly in the 1960s – Scott under an SSRC Training Fellowship.
12   Francis G. Couvares, 'Telling a Story in Context; or, What's Wrong with Social History?', *Theory and Society* 9: 5 (1980).
13   Charles Tilly, 'Two Callings of Social History', *Theory and Society* 9: 5 (1980).

But, while cultural constructedness remained absent (and 'everyday experience' and 'ordinary people' were not put into question), the formulation was unlikely to satisfy. Louise Tilly's comments on 'work' ('In order to talk about changes in women's work over time, more rigorous definitions, words, categories are needed') and 'politics' ('Politics must be reconceptualized so we can talk about the politics of those without formal rights') were likewise all to the good.[14] But that rethinking was also applied to familiar sociological ground. In that sense, *Women, Work, and Family* and *Gender and the Politics of History* were separated by more than a matter of years.[15]

Social history had announced its arrival in the 1960s through an eclectic indebtedness to sociology (and sometimes anthropology). But even the most self-conscious social-science historians stressed methodology rather than theory per se, as in demography, family history, mobility studies, urban history, and so on. To that degree, Stedman Jones's essays of 1967–76, urging historians to devise theory of their own, portrayed the relationship accurately.[16] Some historians did indeed take Stedman Jones at his word. That happened in the 1970s partly through a return to Marx – both directly via *Capital*, the *Grundrisse*, and political writings like *The Eighteenth Brumaire*, and indirectly via Gramsci and other heterodox thinkers. Self-conscious critiques of historians' sociological usage certainly occurred, tracking particular concepts like 'social control' or 'community' through their encrusted intellectual histories.[17] A turning to anthropology rather than sociology (such preference being a particular bugbear for the Tillys) was a definite part of this overall process. Already

---

14 Louise Tilly, 'Social History and Its Critics', *Theory and Society* 9: 5 (1980).

15 These titles document the intellectual distance travelled: the first was coauthored by Louise Tilly and Joan Scott, while the second collected Scott's intervening essays.

16 See especially Stedman Jones, 'History: The Poverty of Empiricism' and 'From Historical Sociology to Theoretical History', *British Journal of Sociology* 27, (1976, 295–305). For a particular case, see Terrence J. McDonald, 'The Problem of the Political in Recent American Urban History: Liberal Pluralism and the Rise of Functionalism', *Social History* 10 (1985). At the turn of the 1960s, *P&P*'s Marxist editors turned to non-Marxist social science to broaden their remit. Philip Abrams and Eric Hobsbawm were central to the exchange with sociology, and Jack Goody, Peter Worsley, Keith Thomas, and Hobsbawm for that with anthropology.

17 Stedman Jones, 'From Historical Sociology to Theoretical History'; McDonald, 'Problem of the Political in Recent American Urban History'; Craig Calhoun, '"Community": Toward a Variable Conceptualization for Comparative Research', *Social History* 5 (1980); Peter Gatrell, 'Historians and Peasants: Studies of Medieval English Society in a Russian Context', *Past and Present* 96: 1).

visible in Sewell's *Work and Revolution in France*, it became all the clearer with anthropology's own 'historicizing' process in the 1980s.[18]

But independent theorizing came best where straightforward borrowing was precluded, in fields with a paucity of theory or little pre-existing practice to use – where innovation, initiative, and interdisciplinarity were inscribed more centrally in the very conditions and processes of knowledge production from the start. That applied par excellence to the new and 'un-disciplined' fields of feminist theory/ women's history and cultural studies. Several of the most decisive influences over the longer term – such as Michel Foucault, Judith Butler, and Stuart Hall – were precisely lacking in such ordinary or classical disciplinary affiliation. Was Foucault a historian, or what?

Despite Novick's scepticism, moreover, historians at large were indeed engaging with French poststructuralist theory and its British-American interpreters. Such reception reached past journals like *HWJ* and *RHR* to the central organs of the North American profession, where both *AHR* and *JMH* were giving generous space to the impact of the 'linguistic turn'.[19] That exposure certainly featured those most immediately concerned with language and textuality in the formal sense, namely intellectual historians by sub-disciplinary affiliation. But the ideas circulated far more extensively, inflecting the intellectual practice and certainly the rhetoric of large areas of social and political history. Before the 1990s, the modern German field was hardly distinguished by its methodological and theoretical radicalism, for example, even if radicals worked within it. Indeed, one notable attempt to build an ambitious theoretical argument about the collapse of

18   William H. Sewell Jr, *Work and Revolution in France: The Language of Labor from the Old Regime to 1848* (Cambridge: Cambridge University Press, 1980). See also Bernard S. Cohn, 'History and Anthropology: The State of Play', *Comparative Studies in Society and History* 22 (1980); Cohn, 'History and Anthropology: Towards a Rapprochement?', *Journal of Interdisciplinary History* 12 (1981); Hans Medick, '"Missionaries in the Row Boat"? Ethnological Ways of Knowing as a Challenge to Social History', *Comparative Studies in Society and History* 29 (1987) – originally published in *Geschichte und Gesellschaft* 10: 3 (1984).

19   See the articles by John E. Toews, 'Intellectual History after the Linguistic Turn: The Autonomy of Meaning and the Irreducibility of Experience', *American Historical Review* 92 (1987), and David Harlan, 'Intellectual History and the Return of Literature', *American Historical Review* 94: 3 (1989) – with responses by Hollinger and Appleby; Roger Chartier, 'Texts, Printings, Readings', in *The New Cultural History*, ed. Lynn Hunt (Berkeley, CA: University of California Press, 1989); Robert Darnton, 'The Symbolic Element in History', *Journal of Modern History* 58 (1986); Dominick LaCapra, 'Chartier, Darnton, and the Great Symbol Massacre', *Journal of Modern History* 60 (1988); James Fernandez, 'Historians Tell Tales: Of Cartesian Cats and Gallic Cockfights', *Journal of Modern History* 60 (1988).

the Weimar Republic was quickly silenced.[20] The 'official' organ of North
American Germanists, *Central European History* (*CEH*), seldom surpassed
a reliable middle-of-the-road solidity. Apart from a couple of reviews and
perhaps a few articles, there was nothing of an explicitly Marxist orientation until the Feldman–Abraham exchange in the seventeenth year of
the journal's existence. Apart from a now classic article by Renate Bridenthal in 1973 and three other articles dealing empirically with women,
there was nothing with an explicitly feminist orientation until the journal's
sixteenth year, when two articles appeared by Jean Quataert and Deborah
Hertz (the next five years added only one more, by Quataert again). Even
under the widest definition, the journal's social history content averaged
around one article a year during 1967–87.[21]

In the meantime, the ground shifted markedly. One key driver was the
East Coast–based German Women's History Study Group, whose conference on 'The Meaning of Gender in German History' at Rutgers in April
1986 successfully disturbed the main thinking of the field. A 1988 conference on 'Re-evaluating the Third Reich' at the University of Pennsylvania
kept such influences at bay, but then several events quickly registered the
change: a small Chicago symposium on 'Postmodern Challenges in
Theory and Methodology' (October 1989); a major conference on the
Kaiserreich at the University of Pennsylvania, conceived largely around
gender and the linguistic turn (February 1990); another big conference in
Toronto on 'Elections, Mass Politics, and Social Change' (April 1990),
where similar discussion ensued; and a UCLA event of the same month
on Nazism and the Final Solution ('On the Limits of Historical and Artistic Representation'), where Derrida arrived in person. *CEH* was relaunched
with a special issue containing the papers from the Chicago symposium.[22]

---

20 See David Abraham, *The Collapse of the Weimar Republic: Political Economy and Crisis* (Princeton: Princeton University Press, 1981), and the exhaustive exchange with his persecutor-in-chief, Gerald D. Feldman, in 'Debate: David Abraham's "The Collapse of the Weimar Republic"', *Central European History* 17: 2–3 (1984). There is a good presentation in Novick, *Noble Dream*, 612–21.

21 See Renate Bridenthal, 'Beyond *Kinder, Küche, Kirche*: Weimar Women at Work', *Central European History* 6 (1973); Deborah Hertz, 'Intermarriage in the Berlin Salons', *Central European History* 16 (1983); Jean H. Quataert, 'The Politics of Rural Industrialization: Class, Gender, and Collective Protest in the Saxon Oberlausitz in the Late Nineteenth Century', *Central European History* 20 (1987). This judgment is based on the cumulative index to vols. 1–20 (1968–87), in *Central European History* 20 (1987).

22 The *Central European History* relaunch came with vol. 24 (1991), but the Special Issue preceded this, as 'German Histories: Challenges in Theory, Practice, Technique', *Central European History* 22 (1989). Equivalent shifts occurred in the French field, setting new work

The New Landscape

In 1971, Hobsbawm proposed six areas of priority:

1. Demography and kinship
2. Urban studies in so far as these fall within our field
3. Classes and social groups
4. The history of 'mentalities', or collective consciousness, or of 'culture' in the anthropologists' sense
5. The transformation of societies (for example, modernization or industrialization)
6. Social movements and phenomena of social protest.[23]

Two decades later, Hobsbawm's first three categories clearly still pertained.[24] The machinery of historical demography continued grinding out its findings, often with slight relationship to broader questions, but at its best with meticulous grounding in the classic materialist problematic of social change – usually from an eclectically sociological perspective.[25] Likewise, while theoretically urban history remained ill-defined, the urban community study remained the main practical medium for studying class formation.[26] Class itself was studied largely within Hobsbawm's parameters. To studies of the working class were now added a burgeoning literature on peasants and an emergent one on the bourgeoisie and petty bourgeoisie/lower middle class.

---

by William Sewell, Lynn Hunt, and François Furet against the social history they had previously practised. In France itself, the political referents were different, reflecting the vehement anti-Marxism of contemporary French intellectual life. In Furet's case, the advocacy departed from social history for intellectual and political history, but hardly towards gender or language in the sense I am describing.

23   Hobsbawm, 'From Social History to the History of Society', 12.

24   In updating Hobsbawm's survey, Pat Thane and Anthony Sutcliffe's *Essays in Social History* (Oxford: Clarendon, 1986) chose a mélange of topics and trends. A diffuse shift from 'class' to 'culture' seemed their overriding theme.

25   The apogee was E. A. Wrigley and Roger S. Schofield, *The Population History of England, 1541–1871: A Reconstruction* (Cambridge, MA: Harvard University Press, 1981). A new journal introduced in 1986, *Continuity and Change: A Journal of Social Structure, Law and Demography in Past Societies*, did broaden the vision.

26   Specific urban phenomena naturally retained their importance: urban planning, fiscal policies, global urbanization since the 1960s, and the city as crucible of modernism each come readily to mind.

But as a descriptive framework for 'the actual practice of social history', Hobsbawm's list no longer served. For one thing, fresh topics were emerging in force – crime and punishment, medicine and public health, sexuality, popular religion, popular memory.[27] More to the point, social history's entire standing in the discipline had changed, so that earlier boundaries and distinctions no longer worked. What counted as social-historical knowledge was no longer as clear, and this had profound implications for all six of Hobsbawm's categories. Rather than a more elaborate inventory, therefore, aspects of the surrounding flux needed attention.

First, gender theory was transforming the grounds from which we thought about history. Whether as a dimension of analysis or an empirical focus, women's history was absent from Hobsbawm's survey, and to read such older accounts is to register how vast the change has been. If initially controversial, moreover, the conceptual shift from the history of women to the historical construction of sexual difference gradually sapped the discipline's protected central spaces. Extensive research considered sexual representations as such. But major areas – work, class formation, citizenship and the public sphere, popular culture – were all reshaped from gendered perspectives.[28] Though some of the new work on masculinity settled too easily around men alone rather than their relations with women, gender promised to recast understandings of nationalism and fascism too.[29] Change can be overstated, of course. A core of historical demographers and family historians stayed remarkably loyal to a project defined previously.[30] But

---

27 Established areas like social policy and education were oddly missing from Hobsbawm's list.

28 As late as 1986, a prestigious comparative volume on working-class formation could still barely notice gender, while an imposing handbook of international research had no treatment of women among its mainly thematic entries. See Ira Katznelson and Aristide R. Zolberg, *Working-Class Formation: Nineteenth-Century Patterns in Western Europe and the United States* (Princeton: Princeton University Press, 1986); Klaus Tenfelde, ed., *Arbeiter und Aibeiterbewegung im Vergleich: Berichte zur internationalen historischen Forschung (Historische Zeitschrift-Sonderheft, Sonderhefte 15)* (Munich: Oldenbourg, 1986).

29 See above all Renate Bridenthal, Atina Grossmann, and Marion Kaplan, eds, *When Biology Became Destiny: Women in Weimar and Nazi Germany* (New York: Monthly Review Press, 1984); Klaus Theweleit, *Male Fantasies, Vol. 2: Male Bodies: Psychoanalyzing the White Terror*, trans. Erica Carter, Chris Turner, and Stephen Conway (Minneapolis: University of Minnesota Press, 1987).

30 While feminists challenged historians into rethinking the history of the family – see, for example, Michèle Barrett and Mary McIntosh, *The Anti-Social Family* (London: Verso,

recognition of gender as a 'useful category of historical analysis' became ever harder to avoid.[31]

Second, and comparably important, was the impact of Michel Foucault, less as direct instigator or founding inspiration than as slowly dawning realization. His works themselves were quickly translated; but he was entirely absent from pioneering 1970s historiographies of crime, law, and imprisonment. English-language reception began on the academic margins – in *Telos* and *Partisan Review* in the United States, in freshly launched, self-consciously avant-garde journals like *Economy and Society*, *Radical Philosophy*, *Ideology and Consciousness*, and *m/f* in Britain.[32] It was only by the early 1980s that historians explicitly took note.[33] His presence then rapidly became pervasive – for work on sexualities; on prisons, hospitals, and asylums; on social policy and public health; on histories of science and academic disciplines.

Aside from opening new areas, Foucault's reception had vital theoretical effects. It refocused understanding of politics away from institutionally centred ideas of government and the state, along with allied conceptions of class domination, and towards a dispersed conception of power and its 'microphysics'. It helped disclose the subtleties of the interrelationship between power and knowledge, especially the forms of disciplinary and administrative ordering. *Discourse* was not only a means of theorizing the internal rules and regularities of particular fields of knowledge (their 'regimes of truth'). It also addressed the superordinate patterning of ideas and assumptions that delimit what can and cannot be thought and said in particular settings of time and place. It radically challenged historians' thinking about individual and collective agency and their assumed bases of interest and rationality. It stressed instead the

---

1982); Denise Riley, *War in the Nursery: Theories of the Child and Mother* (London: Virago, 1983) – the technical imperatives of a rigorously institutionalized historical demography could seem as compelling as ever. See the rejoinder of Rab Houston and Richard Smith, 'A New Approach to Family History?', *History Workshop Journal* 14 (1982), to Miranda Chaytor, 'Household and Kinship: Ryton in the Late Sixteenth and Early Seventeenth Centuries', *History Workshop Journal* 10 (1980).

31   Scott, *Gender and the Politics of History*, 28–50.

32   Foucault was first translated in 1965, then again in 1970 and 1972. Other works rapidly followed, until by 1990 all were available, including several collections of interviews and essays.

33   Weeks, 'Foucault for Historians'; Rachel Harrison and Frank Mort, 'Patriarchal Aspects of Nineteenth-Century State Formation: Property Relations, Marriage and Divorce, and Sexuality', in *Capitalism, State Formation, and Marxist Theory: Historical Investigations*, ed. Philip Corrigan (London: Quartet, 1980).

contingencies of how subjectivities are made. They are produced within and through languages of identification lying beyond the volition or control of individuals in any classical sense defined by the Enlightenment or reason.

Third, for many social historians during the 1970s, the history of mentalities (*mentalités*) came as a panacea. It seemed a compelling rival for the high-cultural, canonical, and formalistic-exegetical modes of intellectual history; it promised access to past popular culture; it enabled the use of quantitative methods; it invited a turn to anthropology; it contained the seductions of 'total history'. Orchestrated by a few well-placed cognoscenti, the translation and reception of major *Annales* works was virtually uncritical. As one of them declared, 'social history seemed to turn around the *Past and Present–Annales* axis and to be sweeping everything before it'.[34] By the mid 1980s, however, the history of mentalities seemed in recession. If the tone of a symposium launching the journal *Review* in 1978 was still celebratory, a battery of critiques rapidly appeared.[35] As part of this process, Roger Chartier and Dominick LaCapra reaffirmed the value of a textually founded form of intellectual history.[36]

Concentrating on Fernand Braudel and Emmanuel Le Roy Ladurie, such critiques uncovered the reductionist and underspecified determinisms at the core of the *Annales* corpus. Moreover, meticulous commentaries by Chartier and LaCapra left little doubt that intellectual history had recovered much of its lost ground. Neither could compromise the accomplishments of Marc Bloch and Lucien Febvre or preclude further cultural histories in an *Annales* mode. But historians' interest went

---

34   Robert Darnton, 'Intellectual and Cultural History', in *The Past Before Us: Contemporary Historical Writing in the United States*, ed. Michael G. Kammen (Ithaca, NY: Cornell University Press, 1980), 332.

35   Stuart Clark, 'French Historians and Early Modern Popular Culture', *Past and Present* 100 (1983); Samuel Kinser, 'Annaliste Paradigm? The Geohistorical Structure of Fernand Braudel', *American Historical Review* 86 (1981); Gregor McLennan, 'Braudel and the Annales Paradigm', in his *Marxism and the Methodologies of History* (London: Verso, 1981); Michael A. Gismondi, '"The Gift of Theory": A Critique of the *histoire des mentalités*', *Social History* 10: 2 (1985); Patrick Hutton, 'The History of Mentalities: The New Map of Cultural History', *History and Theory* 20 (1981).

36   Roger Chartier, 'Intellectual History or Socio-Cultural History? The French Trajectories', in *Modern European Intellectual History: Reappraisals and New Perspectives*, ed. Dominick LaCapra and Steven L. Kaplan (Ithaca, NY: Cornell University Press, 1982); Dominick LaCapra, 'Is Everyone a *Mentalité* Case? Transference and the "Culture" Concept', in his *History and Criticism* (Ithaca, NY: Cornell University Press, 1985).

increasingly elsewhere, either beyond the classic early modern locations or onto the ground of language, where *Annales* enjoyed far less influence. By the 1980s, feminist theory, a recharged intellectual history, the reception of Mikhail Bakhtin, and literary studies were moving cultural history into very new directions.[37]

Another influence, contemporary cultural studies, initially produced little historical work. This emergent cross-disciplinary formation comprised varying genealogies: sociology, literary studies, and history in Britain (but not anthropology); mass communications, literary theory, and reflexive anthropology in the United States. US initiatives came more from the humanities (for example, the Unit for Criticism and Interpretive Theory at Illinois, Urbana-Champaign, or Comparative Studies in Discourse and Society at Minnesota), whereas the new interdisciplinary programmes in the social sciences showed very little interest. On the other hand, feminist theory played a key role in both Britain and the United States, as did post-Saidian critiques of colonial and racialist forms of thought. Particular influences varied – Gramscian thought and psychoanalysis were each more salient in Britain – but postmodernism, along with the linguistic turn per se, characterized both. As the 'long present' of cultural studies inexorably lengthened, interest among historians also increased. Cultures of consumption; economies of pleasure and desire; visual studies of film, photography, video, and TV; advertising and commodities; comic books and magazines; popular reading genres, including romances, gothic novels, and family sagas; genres of TV (soap operas, detective series, situation comedies) and cinema (film noir, horror, science fiction, melodrama); autobiography and the personal voice; postcolonial critique – all steadily seeped into historical awareness. The memory boom (popular, collective, national), intensifying into the early 1990s, proved especially important for historically related cultural studies.[38]

---

37   Compare Natalie Zemon Davis, *Society and Culture in Early Modern France* (Stanford, CA: Stanford University Press, 1975) and Robert W. Scribner, *For the Sake of Simple Folk: Popular Propaganda for the German Reformation* (Cambridge: Cambridge University Press, 1981) with Tony Bennett, *Formalism and Marxism* (London: Meuthen, 1979), Robert Stam, 'Mikhail Bakhtin and Left Cultural Critique', in *Postmodernism and Its Discontents: Theories, Practices*, ed. Ann Kaplan (London: Verso, 1988), and Peter Stallybrass and Allon White, *Politics and Poetics of Transgression* (Ithaca, NY: Cornell University Press, 1986).

38   Patrick Wright, *On Living in an Old Country: The National Past in Contemporary Britain* (London: Verso, 1985); Raphael Samuel, *Theatres of Memory, Volume 1: Past and*

Finally, we have a paradox. Earlier ambitions for a 'total history' – for writing the history of society in some integral and holistic way – came radically into question. Social history appealed at the end of the 1970s by virtue of 'its new totalizing potential'. All phenomena might be treated in their social dimensions, it was persuasively argued. But the stronger version, trying 'to understand *all* facets of human existence in terms of their social determinations', had now become problematic.[39] That confident materialist projection of social totality, or 'society', in either its Marxist or non-Marxist articulations, was losing its authorizing hold.

Yet a great deal of historical sociology continued as before, organized by established arguments about state-making, the rise of capitalism, comparative political development, revolutions, and so forth.[40] In a new macro-historical genre, reaching from Mesopotamia to the twentieth century, leading British sociologists rebuilt social theory by writing the history of the world.[41] This was an interesting juxtaposition: radical diagnoses of the 'postmodern condition' declared the demise of all master narratives, while the most ambitious historical sociologies centred around . . . a new range of grand narratives.

All the World's a Text

Surveying the intellectual landscape of the human sciences at the close of the twentieth century, it was hard not to be impressed by the power of literary theory, linguistic analysis, and related forms of theoretical address. Whether we look to the revival of intellectual history and the influence of Dominick LaCapra, to the potential convergence of

---

Present in Contemporary Culture (London: Verso, 1994), and *Theatres of Memory, Volume 2: Unravelling Britain* (London: Verso, 1998); Patrick Hutton, *History as an Art of Memory* (Hanover, NH: University Press of New England, 1993); Susannah Radstone and Bill Schwarz, eds, *Memory: Histories, Theories, Debates* (New York: Fordham University Press, 2010).

39   Geoff Eley, 'Some Recent Tendencies in Social History', in *International Handbook of Historical Studies: Contemporary Research and Theory*, ed. Georg G. Iggers and Harold T. Parker (Westport, CT: Greenwood, 1979). Emphasis in original.

40   Charles Tilly, *Coercion, Capital, and European States, AD 990–1992* (Oxford: Basil Blackwell, 1990); Immanuel Wallerstein, *The Modern World-System, Vol. 3: The Second Era of Great Expansion of the Capitalist World-Economy, 1730–1840s* (New York: Academic, 1988).

41   Anthony Giddens, *A Contemporary Critique of Historical Materialism, Vol. 1: Power, Property and the State* (London: Macmillan, 1981), and *A Contemporary Critique of Historical Materialism, Vol. 2: The Nation-State and Violence* (Berkeley: University of California Press, 1987 [1981]).

intellectual historians with literary critics in a 'new historicist' mould, to the enormous impact of Edward Said and then Gayatri Spivak on intellectuals writing in and about the Third World, to the interest of Joan Scott and other feminists in theories of gender and language, to reflexive anthropology and the narrative ordering of the experienced world, to formal analysis of the 'rhetoric' of economics and other apparently non-literary disciplines, or simply to the common currency of terms like *discourse* and *deconstruction* – in all of these areas, there seemed no escape.

A patron saint was Hayden White. At an early stage, his *Metahistory: The Historical Imagination in Nineteenth-Century Europe* (1973) problematized the boundaries between humanities and social sciences by showing how works in the latter are also constructed around particular narrative and rhetorical strategies, even when bound at their most rigorous and single-minded to the rules of evidence and scientific methodology. White mounted this challenge from the older resources of literary criticism and his own idiosyncratic imagination, confronting 'objectivist' history with the moral and aesthetic principles that order and inform its production.[42] The impact on literary studies of (among others) Jacques Derrida and Paul De Man then radicalized the challenge. The complexities of reading (and writing) brought the category of the text and the work of interpretation into question. From focusing on authorial intention and the text's single attainable meaning (a chimera that obscures the indeterminacy and necessary openness of the text, its 'undecidability', its multiplicity of meanings), literary theory sharpened the practice of reading to a point of technical sophistication where meanings could be endlessly disclosed. Breaking into this magic circle of interpretive expertise apparently required a new language of cleverness and gesture. An authorizing of the theorist within a re-professionalized literary calling – a technocracy of the word – seemed sometimes precisely the point.

But such scepticism belied the patently widening impact of this trend. Some version of deconstruction's basic programme – at its simplest, 'a reading which involves seizing upon [texts'] inconsistencies and

---

42   Hayden White, *Metahistory: The Historical Imagination in Nineteenth-Century Europe* (Baltimore: Johns Hopkins University Press, 1973), and *Tropics of Discourse: Essays in Cultural Criticism* (Baltimore, MD: Johns Hopkins University Press, 1978).

contradictions to break up the idea of a unified whole' – became very commonplace.[43] For social historians, in particular, some notion of externality – determination as the setting of limits, in Raymond Williams's notation, or what Derrida called 'the diachronic overdetermination of the context' – necessarily loomed large.[44] That implied two kinds of moves – *back*, to the contexts of the text's production, and *out*, to where its meanings are constructed. Rather than what the text 'means', we need to understand how it 'works'. As Tony Bennett observed, with the characteristic Gramscian inflection of British cultural studies: 'the text is a site on which varying meanings and effects may be produced according to the determinations within which the work is inscribed – determinations that are never single and given but plural and contested, locked in relations of struggle'.[45] That mode of analysis was increasingly extended from written texts in the more conventional sense to all manner of documents, and thence to experience, behaviour, and events as well. From assailing the transparency of the text in the discourse of literary criticism, textuality became a metaphor for understanding the world in general.

Meanwhile, a freshly diffused academic Marxism, flourishing for the first time in the English-speaking universities, embraced various kinds of radically disconcerting but boldly unrelenting antireductionism. The thinkers involved seemed initially to uphold the tradition's classical commitments, whether in Louis Althusser's 'antihumanist' separation of the mature from the young Marx, in the wider structuralist emphasis on modes of production and an economically centred conception of class, in the revival of Marxist economics, in Harry Braverman–inspired studies of the labour process, or in feminist debates over domestic labour. *Capital* was reinstated as the starting point. At the same time, these discussions defined themselves in no uncertain terms as departures, as critical advances on earlier modes of economism. The 'base/superstructure' model of social determination, with its assignment of logical priority to the economic, came under particular attack. Althusser's impact opened a gap in those orthodoxies, through which a host of mainly French

43   'Editorial: Language and History', *History Workshop Journal* 10 (1980), 1.

44   Jacques Derrida, 'Like the Sound of the Sea Deep within a Shell: Paul De Man's War', *Critical Inquiry* 14 (1988), 606.

45   Tony Bennett, 'Text and History', in *Re-Reading English*, ed. Peter Widdowson (London: Meuthen, 1982), 235.

influences – Lacanian psychoanalysis, Saussurean linguistics, the philosophy of science of Gaston Bachelard and Georges Canguilhem, the
aesthetics of Pierre Macherey, semiotics and theories of film, and so
forth – was then able to rush. This freeing of politics and ideology for
'relatively autonomous' analysis, anchored to the economy via 'structural
causality' and 'determination in the last instance', opened the entire
domain of the 'noneconomic' to Marxist view – aesthetics, literature, the
arts, theories of knowledge and the disciplines, intellectual life, popular
culture, sexuality, and so forth – in short, 'culture', as a convergent strain
of British dissenting Marxism was then seeking to define it.[46]

The excitement of those days, the sense of participating in a continuous and unsettling exercise in revision, was extraordinary. The outcomes
both internationalized (or at least Europeanized) a previously parochial
intellectual culture, wrenching it towards openly theorized modes of
exchange while simultaneously questioning earlier terms of address.
That process can easily be narrated as more unified, more coherent, and
more logically continuous than it was (or could have been), with one
move following naturally on another, causally inscribed in the contradictions and insufficiencies of before. Yet intellectual histories are
seldom undertaken as straightforwardly and rationally as that. The
experience was divisive as much as harmonious, driven by conflicts and
disruptions as well as its own logical momentum.

Feminism was, by far, the most important influence – not only as a
disruption, but not as an integral element either. Assimilating feminist
thought smoothly into this narrative as just one element among many,
whether historiographically or in relation to the overall linguistic turn,
would be misleading, indeed disingenuous. Far better to disturb the
narrative and unsettle its coherence by keeping feminism's apartness
and capacity to challenge and make the ideas anew. On the one hand, as
Terry Lovell observed, contemporary feminist writing followed a trajectory quite recognizable in the aforementioned terms:

> The journey begins with Marxist- or socialist-feminist writings (in
> history social science *and* cultural studies), seeking to uncover the

---

46 For this overall context, see Geoff Eley, *A Crooked Line: From Cultural History to the
History of Society* (Ann Arbor, MI: University of Michigan Press, 2005), 115–81; and Razming
Keucheyan, *The Left Hemisphere: Mapping Critical Theory Today*, trans. Gregory Elliott
(London: Verso, 2013).

material conditions of women's oppression under capitalism; it advances with the recognition that certain aspects of that oppression do not yield very readily to Marxist categories and that a more adequate account of feminine subjectivity is required for an understanding of the ways in which that oppression is *lived*, which might be sought in psychoanalysis rather than Marxism. Then, via Lacan and modern theories of language, the journey continues into the 'poststructuralism' and 'deconstructionism' whose luminaries include Foucault, Derrida, and Kristeva. Some travelers continue beyond feminism itself, into a 'postfeminism' and 'postmodernism' which understand both Lacanian psychoanalysis and Marxism to have been mere staging-posts along the way.[47]

On the other hand, it was still sharply apart. In an essay notable among social historians for engaging theoretically with this question, Sally Alexander put this extremely well:

> If feminism has been only one of the detonators of crisis in marxist thought and practice it has been the most insistently subversive because it will not give up its wish to speak in the name of women; of women's experience, subjectivity and sexuality . . . We were asking the impossible perhaps. As a feminist I was (and still am) under the spell of those wishes, while as a historian writing and thinking in the shadow of a labor history which silences them. How can women speak and think creatively within marxism when they can neither enter the narrative flow as fully as they wish, nor imagine that there might be other subjectivities present in history than those of class (for to imagine that is to transgress the laws of historical materialism)?[48]

Such debates played havoc with received forms of Marxist and more generally materialist understanding. The logic of antireductionist critique brought countervailing effects, both the unforeseen consequences of 'post-Marxist' fields of address and widespread dismay over

---

47   Terry Lovell, ed., *British Feminist Thought: A Reader* (Oxford: Basil Blackwell, 1990), 21–2. Emphases in original.

48   Sally Alexander, 'Women, Class and Sexual Differences in the 1830s and 1840s: Some Reflections on the Writing of a Feminist History', *History Workshop Journal* 17 (1984), 127.

the apparent 'retreat from class'.[49] What for some was the feared Pando-
ra's box of uncontrollable heterodoxies remained, for others, a bottomless
bag of tricks, disclosing not only the antireductionist possibilities
mentioned above but the more daring options of postmodernism and
the linguistic turn. That restless probing of limits showed no signs of a
halt. Shibboleths were falling one by one. By ever more sophisticated
readings of Gramsci, Foucault, Voloshinov and Bakhtin, French poststructuralism, British cultural studies, and still diversifying feminist
theory, the antireductionist momentum carried far beyond the intellectual starting-points of the 1960s, bringing the original materialisms
badly into doubt.

As the economy's hold became progressively loosened, along with the
determinative power of the social structure and its causal priorities, the
imaginative and epistemological space for other kinds of analysis grew.
For many taking that route, the classical materialist sureties were severed
once and for all. 'Society' as a unitary object could no longer be sustained. There was no structural coherence deriving easily from the
economy, from the functional needs of the social system and its central
values, or from any other overarching principle of order. Particular
phenomena – an event, a policy, an institution, an ideology, a text – have
particular social contexts, in the sense of conditions, practices, sites
that conjoin for essential aspects of meaning. But there is no underlying given structure to which they can necessarily be referred as its
essential expression or necessary effects. Confidence in the social totality, in its variant Marxist and non-Marxist forms, was the casualty of this
intellectual flux.

The commitment to grasping society as a whole, to conceptualizing its
underlying principles of unity – conventionally described by this time as
the specifically 'modern' or Enlightenment project – had passed into
crisis. For Marxists and others on the left, this bespoke a complex of
political experiences, including the decline of the historic working class
and its traditions; the crisis of Keynesianism, the welfare state, and statist
conceptions of socialism; the economic, political, and moral bankruptcy
of communist systems; the catastrophe of the environment and of the
scientific mastery over nature; and the declining purchase of directly

---

49   Ellen Meiksins Wood, *The Retreat from Class: A New 'True' Socialism* (London:
Verso, 1986).

class-political forms of address. In Jean-François Lyotard's words, the postmodern moment begins with an 'incredulity with regard to master narratives'. History, in that sense, had lost its way. The grand ideals enabling history to be read in a particular direction, as a story of progress and emancipation, from the Industrial Revolution and the triumph of science over nature, to the emancipation of the working class, the victory of socialism, and the equality of women, could no longer persuade. All bets were off. 'There is no single right way to read history. Indeed, history becomes a narrative without a teleology', a story without an end.[50]

This was a dizzying intellectual history. From the axiomatic primacy of social determinations, when social history seemed to capture the discipline's central ground, we entered a new conjuncture in which 'the social' seemed ever less definite and social determinations surrendered their sovereignty. The road from 'relative autonomy' and 'structural causality' (the hard-won gains of the 1970s) to the 'discursive character of all practices' (the poststructuralist axiom of the 1980s) had been rapid and disconcerting. The persuasiveness of the antireductionist logic had been extraordinarily hard to withstand, an escalator going up with no way down.

But if 'society' as a totalizing category was dissolving, had social explanation lost all independent efficacy? There was a sense in which the reception of Foucault and subsequent poststructuralisms had collapsed 'the social' and 'the cultural' entirely together. If the latter now signified the entire discursive domain, then the interconnectedness of the social formation became redefined agnostically as the aggregate of 'discursive practices', as 'equivalent to the non-unified totality of these practices', or as 'a complex, overdetermined and contradictory nexus of discursive practices'.[51] In that case, if social reality is only accessible via language (in the constitutive theoretical sense as well as the common-sense descriptive one most would accept) and 'the social' is only constituted through discourse, then what place is left for specifically social determinations at all?

---

50   Jean-François Lyotard, *The Postmodern Condition: A Report on Knowledge*, trans. Geoff Bennington and Brian Massumi (Minneapolis: University of Minnesota Press, 1984), xiii–xiv; Kate Ellis, 'Stories without Endings: Deconstructive Theory and Political Practice', *Socialist Review* 19 (1989), 38.
51   Stuart Hall, 'Some Problems with the Ideology/Subject Couplet', *Ideology and Consciousness* 3 (1978), 12.

This was the point reached by the 1990s. Relatively few historians took the train to the end of the line, through the terrain of textuality to the land of discourse and deconstruction, to a radical epistemology that 'relativizes the status of all knowledge, links knowledge and power, and theorizes these in terms of the operations of difference'.[52] That journey can be alternately empowering and disabling. Its revelation of the 'non-fixity' of meaning shows how social and political definitions can be questioned: if the terms of the given are always in play, they are accordingly susceptible to challenge, in the present no less than the past. In its most extreme versions, on the other hand, the critique of epistemology disavows historical knowledge as such, reducing the historian's task to more or less elaborate forms of historiographical commentary and exegesis. Rather than labouring in the archive and worrying about what may have happened, postmodernists have argued, historians should join the endless conversation (and contest) over how the past might be approached and invoked. A much larger group of social historians ignored the train altogether, to be sure, continuing much as before, generally aware of the fuss, but indifferent to the theory and wishing it would go away. Then there were the rest, partly there for the ride, curious to see where it went, not at all sure about reaching or remaining very long at the destination.

That intermediate place (not exactly the 'middle ground', as it presumed the basic value and interest of the journey per se – that is, boarding the train in the first place) was a very good one to take. It had important virtues, pluralism salient among them. But it also had costs. It implied vacating the claim to a distinctive historical knowledge, let alone any claim to superiority (as in 'queen of the disciplines'). For history does, in practice, tend towards a definite epistemology, usually some brand of empiricism: the belief in a knowable past, whose structures and processes are distinct and separable from the various strategies – documentary representations, conceptual and political appropriations, historiographical discourses – that try to construct them. By the 1990s, the epistemological critique of that naive practice was becoming well established.[53]

---

52   Scott, *Gender and the Politics of History*, 4.
53   More radically, epistemology itself came under critique – as 'a theoretical domain that tries to state a mechanism of correspondence between a discourse and objects existing outside discourse which can be specified and made the measure of it'. See Paul Q. Hirst, *Marxism and Historical Writing* (London: Routledge & Kegan Paul, 1985), 128.

But this does not make history pointless or undoable. Rejecting a correspondence theory of truth does not make history completely arbitrary: the historian cannot invent documents at will or discard rules of evidence – fears typically voiced by the linguistic turn's opponents. Criteria for truth do have to be thought very differently. Knowledge becomes as 'good' or as 'bad' as the quality of the questions that constitute it: 'Historical knowledge works by posing, re-posing, and displacing questions, *not* by accumulating "evidence" independently of them. Facts are not given, it is only relative to a question that we can begin to assess the value of those materials which are to constitute evidence for the answer to it.'[54]

As Stedman Jones said in his 1976 article, 'history like any other "social science" is an entirely intellectual operation which takes place in the present and in the head'; and: 'The fact that the "past" in some sense "happened" is not of primary significance since the past is in no sense synonymous with history.' Indeed, the 'real' past is beyond retrieval. Instead, the historian both evaluates documentary residues by the technical procedures of the profession and assigns them relevance through the construction of a significant problem. Accordingly, the common distinction between 'history' and 'theory' makes no sense: 'The distinction is not that between theory and non-theory, but between the adequacy or inadequacy of the theory brought to bear.'[55] The test of history's knowledge (its 'truth') is not some general rule of epistemological probity (i.e. 'truth-in-general') but the particular criteria of adequacy and appropriateness that history, no less than any other particular field, has tended to devise – from biblical scholarship to automobile mechanics. Moreover, those criteria will always themselves be subject to varying degrees of consensus and disagreement.

Furthermore, history is simply unavoidable. It is constantly in play in both everyday understanding and the formal discourses affecting social, economic, cultural, and political exchange. It is invoked and appropriated as a matter of course either implicitly or explicitly in order to make arguments. And, for such arguments to be made (or countered) effectively, due attention is owed to the evidentiary conventions of history as a discipline. But such conventions should not be mistaken for a viable

54   Ibid., 54. Emphasis in original.
55   Stedman Jones, 'From Historical Sociology to Theoretical History', 296–7.

epistemological claim. History's value is not as an archive or a court of 'real experience'. It is as a site of difference, a context of deconstruction – partly because it is indeed always being fought over (invoked and appropriated in contestatory ways), partly because it supplies contexts in which the ever-seductive unities of contemporary social and political discourse, the naturalizing of hegemonies, can be upset. History is distinctive not in revealing earlier stages in our own story or as an unapproachable realm of the exotic, but in enabling that very notion of a single coherent and unified story to be unpicked: 'If [history] does not consist merely in the vindication of our own views of ourselves or in triumphalist accounts of modernity, it is because some historians can recognize that the past is different, not merely an earlier stage of our "story", but a means of unsettling ourselves and investigating, however partially, what we *are*.'[56]

Turning to History

This is all very well, the profession's hard-bitten realists will say, patrolling our practice against these suggestions, but what difference does it make? Worse, they continue, all this endless theorizing, the self-sustaining, self-referential industry of critique, deflects from more concrete and sustained engagements with the past, whose pursuit remains the mundane rationale for specialized departments of history. If such scepticism usually pre-empts the theorizing concerned, instead of considering it seriously, the point is well taken. If earlier assumptions of social history no longer hold, if older notions of social totality and social determination lose their conviction, then how can a critical social history – in dissertation and monographic form, as against the essay-critique – be recharged?

One way is to historicize the category of 'society' itself by exploring the terms of its own social, political, and intellectual history. By tracing those genealogies, we can see how 'the social' first became abstracted into an object of theory-knowledge, a target of policy, and a site of

---

56 Hirst, *Marxism and Historical Writing*, 28. Hirst's essays, mostly produced between the late 1970s and early 1980s, are a valuable guide through these questions. Emphasis in original.

practice, so that the material bases on which 'society' could be convincingly represented as an ultimately originating subject became gradually composed.[57] Here, 'the social' refers not to the universal analytical category of 'society' in the received social-science sense, but to the historically located methods, techniques, and practices enabling such a category to be built in the first place. The impetus for such a project comes unmistakably from Foucault.

Foucault's concept of the disciplinary society directly implicates this process. At one level, it profoundly shifts our understanding of politics, carrying treatments of power away from the core institutions of the state in the national-centralized sense towards the emergence of new individualizing strategies 'that function outside, below and alongside the State apparatuses, on a much more minute and everyday level'.[58] But it was precisely through such individualizing strategies that *society* ('the social' or the 'social body') came to be located, constituted, and elaborated as the main object of science, surveillance, policy, and power. Population (fertility, age, mobility, health), economics, poverty, crime, education, and welfare became not only the main objects of governance but also the measure of cohesion and solidarity in the emerging nineteenth-century social order.

To grasp the latter, it is to the new social-science and medico-administrative discourses, and their technologies and effects, that we must look – to the new knowledges 'concerning society, its health and sickness, its conditions of life, housing and habits, which served as the basic core for the "social economy" and sociology of the nineteenth century'.[59] As we enter the early twentieth century, the repertoire of power-producing knowledges then further expands: psychiatry and psychology, social work and the welfare state, youth policy, industrial relations, public health, social hygiene, eugenics, and so forth. As

---

57   While indebted to Foucault, this approach suggests both the 'keywords' method of Raymond Williams and the *Begriffsgeschichte* of Reinhart Koselleck. See Raymond Williams, *Keywords: A Vocabulary of Culture and Society*, 2nd edn (New York: Oxford University Press, 1983); Otto Brunner, Werner Conze, and Reinhart Koselleck, eds, *Geschichtliche Grundbegriffe*, 5 vols (Stuttgart: Klett-Cotta, 1972–89); Keith Tribe, 'The *Geschichtliche Grundbegriffe* Project: From History of Ideas to Conceptual History', *Comparative Studies in Society and History* 31 (1989).

58   Michel Foucault, *Power/Knowledge: Selected Interviews and Other Writings 1972–1977*, ed. Colin Gordon (Brighton: Harvester, 1980), 60.

59   Ibid., 176.

Jacques Donzelot and others have argued, the family especially draws such interventions and expertise. As feminist scholars and Foucault's own final works have shown, sexuality is an especially rich field for showing such power relations under construction.[60]

This 'discursive' move, from assuming an objective 'society' to studying how the 'the social' came to be thought, was paradigmatic in many areas during the 1980s, for which two cases in particular may serve – histories, respectively, of working-class formation and the growth of citizenship ideals.[61] In the wake of Edward Thompson's impact (to take the first of these), it became ever harder to see working-class formation as the natural consequence or logical unfolding of an economic process and its necessary effects at the levels of social organization, consciousness, and culture. Detailed awareness of the complexities of working-class composition expanded hugely in the meantime, concerning sectional diversity across industries; internal hierarchies of seniority, status, and skill; cultural segmentation by gender, religion, ethnicity, and race. But disaggregation of these elements cannot alone suffice. To grasp class in its manifest political dimensions, we need to go further by accepting the intractable difficulties, methodologically and theoretically, in explaining the rise of labour movements and socialist parties through economically located class interests and social-structural positions. If labour movements are scarcely imaginable *without* capitalist industrialization, nor can they be derived *directly from* the latter and its mechanisms of accumulation and exploitation.

In this sense, class as a political and cultural *postulate* (the assertion of a particular model of social identity) was just as crucial to the process of class formation as the existence of class as a demonstrable social fact (the creation of new social positions defined by their relationship to the means of production or some other material criteria). The *ideology of class*, the

---

60   Jacques Donzelot, *The Policing of Families: Welfare Versus the State* (New York: Pantheon, 1979); Frank Mort, *Dangerous Sexualities: Medico-Moral Politics in England since 1830* (London: Routledge & Kegan Paul, 1987); Antony Copley, *Sexual Moralities in France, 1780–1980: New Ideas on the Family, Divorce, and Homosexuality: An Essay on Moral Change* (London: Routledge, 1989).

61   See especially Margaret R. Somers, 'Workers of the World, Compare!', *Contemporary Sociology* 18 (1989) and 'Narrativity, Narrative Identity, and Social Action: Rethinking English Working-Class Formation', *Social Science History* 16 (1992); Kathleen Canning, 'Gender and the Politics of Class Formation: Rethinking German Labor History', *American Historical Review* 97 (1992) and 'Feminist History after the Linguistic Turn: Historicizing Discourse and Experience', *Signs* 19 (1994).

insistence that class supplied the organizing principle for the social order in emerging capitalist societies, along with the practices and relations developing around that insistence (like trade unions and socialist parties), becomes a better starting point for the study of class formation than the classical one of economics and social structure, because it was at this discursive level that the operational collectivity of class – who got to be included, who set the tone, and who received the recognized voice – was defined. In these terms, the history of a class is inseparable from the history of the category. Class emerged as a set of discursive claims about the social world that sought to reorder that world in terms of those claims.

Such a move frees analysis from the teleology of a class-consciousness causally inscribed in the given patterns of class interest and class-collective experience – and from the need for special explanations when class consciousness fails to appear. Indeed, it converts 'interest' itself into a question, a discursive effect of complex histories rather than a given and causally prior basis for action. Instead of asking which working class interests were reflected in which organizations and forms of action (seeing working-class consciousness as expressively derived), we should examine how varying ideas of working-class interest were produced, how particular practices and institutions encouraged or hindered those ideas, and how one very specific set of images came to be so convincingly entrenched. 'Interest' is far more an effect than a cause.

The treatment of class as a structuring and motivating category in this way brings the partialities and indeterminacies of class formation better into view. As well as the collective dynamics of coalescence, moreover, we can see the mechanisms and spaces of exclusion helping its solidarities to grow. In the task of grasping the always-incomplete histories of construction shaping class as an operative phenomenon, the fissures and limitations mattered just as much as any unifying and homogenizing impulse. The languages of class disclosed not just regularities and underlying coherence, but elements of fracture and difference too. Such language is 'multi-layered, complex, fractured, composed of incoherences and silences, as well as the smooth flow of would-be authoritative public discourses', and should be read for its exclusions as well as for its unifying appeals.[62] The biggest and most continuous exclusion involved women.

---

62   Robert Gray, 'The Deconstruction of the English Working Class', *Social History* 11: 3 (1986), 367.

Working-class identity as elaborated during the nineteenth century – the ideal of the skilled male worker in industry – required dichotomous understandings of what it meant to be a woman or man. Those assumptions aligned men with the practical world of work and the public domain of politics, women with the family and the private realm of domesticity – the one a site of control and rationality, the other a site of affect and subordination. Inscribed in the language of class were distinctions of masculinity and femininity that strictly impeded 'women's access to knowledge, skill, and independent political subjectivity'.[63] So gender, family, and sexuality were constitutively present in the politics of working-class formation. In severing the privacies of family from the public worlds of politics and work, the social construction of sexual difference powerfully shaped how working-class identity came to be understood. Moreover, the fixing of class identity in this way – the gendering of class formation – presumed the suppression of other possibilities. It required the silencing of alternative meanings that might exceed its terms. Materially distributed and discursively secured, 'class' marginalized the roles of women through these fixities of identification. Given those structures and mechanisms, with all their resulting solidities, all the ways in which class became naturalized, where might politics begin? How might the unities be upset?

Mobility and non-fixity are the other side of the coin. Whether as collective agency or individual subjectivity, identity is made from the unstable and unfinished ordering of multiple possibilities. Managed discursively through language, the resulting coherence can only ever be provisional, formed from incompletely realized covenants of difference. This indeterminate multiplicity of identity vitally shapes how class can be encountered historically, including its processes and relations of exclusion. Further, class forms just one especially crucial nexus of significant relations, practices, and meanings among a more dispersed array of sites and connections through which people negotiate some workable coherence for their social and cultural lives. There are always many different forces acting on our everyday lives and the given narratives of selfhood. Amid that disorderly babble of interpellation, we recognize ourselves in varying ways. How we see ourselves as a basis for action, how we become addressed as a particular kind of public, is not fixed. We

---

63   Alexander, 'Women, Class and Sexual Difference', 137.

recognize ourselves variously – as citizens, as workers, as consumers, as parents, as lovers and sexual beings, as enthusiasts for sports and hobbies, as audiences for music and film, as believers in religious and other creeds, as generations, as objects of policy and surveillance, as subjects of race and nation, and so forth. Such recognitions are structured by power relations of various sorts. They are gendered by assumptions placing us as women or men.

This fragmentary, complex, non-fixed quality of identities or subject positions has become a commonplace of contemporary identity talk. But politics is nonetheless conducted *as if* identities were stable and fixed. The operative questions then become: How does identity settle and congeal? How is it worked upon? How does it acquire continuity over time? How is it fashioned into concentrated, resolute, or reasonably reliable shapes? How do some forms of identity get to coalesce into more generalized and presumed forms of collective self-recognition, while others stay inchoate or unassimilable? That is, how is *agency* produced? Under what circumstances, in particular places and times, can identity's non-fixity become provisionally fixed, so that individuals and groups can think of themselves and behave as a particular kind of collective agency, political or otherwise? How do people find themselves shaped into acting subjects, understanding themselves in justified or possible ways? Politics in these terms is the attempt to 'domesticate the infinitude' of identity, giving it strong programmatic form.[64] If identity is decentred, politics becomes the *effort to make a centre*.

The strength of the socialist tradition from the late nineteenth century to the 1970s was its ability to harness popular identities to a strong conception of the working class – by building popular political agency around the discourse of class in its classic gendered, skilled, nationally bounded, industrial sense. In all periods and places, socialist parties were always more complex in their sociology than this, whether in membership, support, or appeal. Even in the restrictive definition, they drew workers highly unevenly. They always inspired broader popularity around the male, skilled, religious, and ethnic core, whether those other constituencies were working class in the fuller sociological sense (women, the unskilled, national minorities, migrants) or not

---

64   Chantal Mouffe, 'Rethinking Pluralism', Comparative Studies of Social Transformations (CSST) Lecture, University of Michigan, Ann Arbor, 21 September 1989.

working class at all as typically understood (dissenting intellectuals, parts of the professions, clerical and other white-collar workers, shop-keepers, and other tradesmen in working-class neighbourhoods). Socialist parties were always active in 'non-class' ways, working through public rhetorics of democratic citizenship, social justice, and egalitari-anism as well as through socialist language per se.

Programmatically, this centring around class was clear enough. But such concentration of identity had its costs. It involved a *reduction* to class. It entailed exclusions and neglects. Positive orientation towards the working class presumed aversions against others – not just other classes, but other kinds of workers too: the unorganized, the rough and unre-spectable, the criminal, the frivolous, the religiously devout, the ethnically different, and of course the female. Socialists struggled with other elements of subjectivity, including anything not easily disciplined into a highly centred notion of class-political agency. Neglecting that space of these 'other' identities gave openings to other labours of construction, whether by the state, political competitors, the churches, or commercial entertainments.

Though posited through the analysis of production and its social relations, the ideal 'unity' of the working class was a never-attainable object of construction, a fictive agency, a mobile contingency of shift-ing political action. 'Citizenship' may be similarly deconstructed. The basic gendering of modern political thought has long been a com-monplace of feminist critique, particularly in those Enlightenment settings where liberal and democratic ideas were first composed. The constitutive moment of modern political understanding was itself constituted by newly conceived or rearranged assumptions about 'woman' and 'man': this was visible not only in constitutions, legal codes, and political mobilizations, but in the ordering of the higher philosophical discourse around universals of reason, law, and nature as well, grounding agentive claims in ideologically arranged differ-ences in gender.

The freshly idealized virtue of the 'public man' was imagined in elab-orate contradistinction to 'femininity', whose relation to domesticity became rationalized into a formal claim about woman's 'nature'. Specific constructions of 'womanness' defined the quality of being a 'man', while the *natural* connotations of the feminine helped enable the *social* and *political* meanings of masculinity. Modern politics was constituted in that sense *as* a relation of gender.[65] During the 1780s and 1790s, reason was counterposed rhetorically against 'femininity, if by the latter we mean (as contemporaries did) pleasure, play, eroticism, artifice, style, politesse, refined facades, and particularity.'[66] In the concentrated circumstances of the French Revolution, women were then silenced to give full rein to masculine speech – in the language of reason. Together with class, race, ethnicity, religion, and age, gender and sexuality delivered the powerful exclusions from which the modern political subject came to be formed. They enabled the very idea of reasoned subjectivity to emerge.

Particular discursive formations – class, citizenship, subjectivity – were themselves centrally implicated in social history. Rather than being predicated on 'experience' or following expressively from a social cause, such ideas helped shape the basic categories of operative understanding, and thus the social, cultural, and political environment where people sought to act and think. Nineteenth-century thinking about citizenship, no less than related conceptions of class-collective identity, involved immensely complex and powerful formations of that type, finely order ing the possibilities for what could and could not be politically thought. Gender was vital not only to the patterning and containment of a class-related identity, but to the endowment and delimitation of political capacities too. Feminist theory has decisively exposed the procedures and assumptions regulating access to political voice. Patriarchy emerges as a continuous figure of European political thought from Hobbes through Locke to the Enlightenment and beyond. Women are essentially confined within the household: 'Within this sphere, women's functions of child-bearing, child-rearing, and maintaining the household are deemed to correspond to their unreason, disorderliness, and "closeness" to nature. Women and the domestic sphere are viewed as inferior to the male-dominated "public" world of civil society and its culture, property, social power, reason and freedom.'[67] Amid the huge political cataclysm of the French Revolution, which otherwise radically enlarged the ideal of human emancipation, this pattern of subordination was then recharged. The nascent liberal model of rational political

---

65   Joan B. Landes, *Women and the Public Sphere in the Age of the French Revolution* (Ithaca, NY: Cornell University Press, 1988), 204.

66   Ibid., 46.

67   John Keane, ed., *Civil Society and the State: New European Perspectives* (London: Verso, 1988), 21.

exchange was not just vitiated by persisting patriarchal structures of an older sort. The very inception of the liberal public sphere was itself shaped by a new exclusionary discourse directed against women.

In highlighting the exclusionary treatment of women, such work subverts the given terms of the story. It not only retrieves previously neglected factors, but delivers insights that fundamentally transform the whole. No less than the nineteenth-century presence of the working class, for example, classical bourgeois society and politics also resulted from processes of class formation that were highly gendered. Thus, gender was constitutively vital in the ordering of the middle-class social world through distinctive patterns of marriage, parenting, and domesticity, inside particular styles of sociality and consumption. At the same time, it shaped the reciprocal relations across this private sphere and the public sphere of associational life and politics, where the latter both reflected and actively reproduced the gendered distinctions of class identity generated between home and work.[68] The remarkable associational cultures of the early nineteenth century strictly demarcated women's and men's roles by means of a mobile repertoire of ideologies and practices, assigning women consistently to a nonpolitical private sphere, with 'at most a supportive role to play in the rapidly expanding political world of their fathers, husbands, and brothers'.[69] Bounding the masculine realm of public activity from the feminine space of the home certainly did not preclude their finely articulated and carefully managed integration. Indeed, precisely the interconnectedness between business and household engendered the prevailing culture of public and private for the emergent nineteenth-century bourgeoisie. An equivalent separation of spheres – between the masculine realm of public activity and the feminine space of the home – was replicated among the working class, as studies of Chartism and nineteenth-century socialist movements, as well as the social history of the working class, have amply shown.[70]

~

---

68   See especially the pioneering study by Leonore Davidoff and Catherine Hall, *Family Fortunes: Men and Women of the English Middle Class, 1780–1850* (Chicago: University of Chicago Press, 1987).

69   John Hall, *Powers and Liberties: The Causes and Consequences of the Rise of the West* (Oxford: Basil Blackwell, 1986), 11.

70   Alexander, 'Women, Class and Sexual Difference'; Sonya O. Rose, *Limited Livelihoods: Gender and Class in Nineteenth-Century England* (Berkeley, CA: University of California Press, 1991).

In taking stock of the shifts between the social and the cultural during the last third of the twentieth century, I have suggested some main directions. While the 1970s revealed a sense of forward movement borne by the unlimited power of social explanation, the 1980s brought a mood of uncertainty and flux. This was partly a generational story. One part of the ascendant social history cohort detached itself from the previous materialist consensus to pursue the antireductionist logic of structuralist and poststructuralist theory. Another part seemed in considerable disarray: some dogmatically reaffirming older, 'classically materialist' positions; some choosing a more eclectic and anthropologically inclined cultural history; many more continuing in the hard-won social-historical practices of the 1970s. Among English-speaking social historians responding to the linguistic turn, I saw two main tributaries: one was the large corpus of British post-Althusserian Marxist and post-Marxist critique, including a separate but convergent feminism; the other was the remarkable North American impact of deconstructive literary theory, also increasingly mediated through self consciously feminist discussion. Where that left the specifically anthropological contribution appeared less clear; but the radical pressure of feminist theory seemed primary.

Left critics of the so-called linguistic turn and their mischievous right-wing counterparts happily reduced this to a therapeutic effect: the self-indulgence of left-wing intellectuals who had lost their way, constructing seductive but self-serving rationalizations for their own ivory-tower isolation. In theorizing gender, identity, and subjectivity, they sought substitutes for a working class that refused their ministrations, sadly losing their nerve for the well-tried but arduous radical projects.[71] Links to politics were by the 1990s clear enough. The social and political histories of the late twentieth century induced widespread scepticism that earlier ideas of class-political agency were any longer a primary or sufficient basis for understanding and acting on the world. In light of those disappointments, the so-called 'cultural turn' held much appeal for those seeking some viable ground for re-elaborating a progressive politics from the contemporary wreckage of state-socialist

---

71   Above all, see Wood, *Retreat from Class*, and Bryan D. Palmer, *Descent into Discourse: The Reification of Language and the Writing of Social History* (Philadelphia, PA: Temple University Press, 1990).

traditions. The constructive possibilities of the theoretical perspectives described above for a politics more adequate to the complexities of collective identity on the threshold of the twenty-first century were definitely important. Alongside the linguistic turn was also an emergent social analysis – of post-Fordism, postmodernity, and the transnational restructuring of the global capitalist economy – that promised to ground a politics of 'new times'. But the sociology of the intellectual history recounted above is extraneous to its theoretical and epistemological challenge. It cannot be invoked as a normalizing materialist move.

The exact relationship between intellectual life – here the impact of theoretical change on the doing of history – and general social and political conditions is anything but clear. One of my purposes is to stress the difficulties of bringing them causally together. Calling the argument back to an earlier conception of the social would be perverse – an act of materialist faith, disabling the very questions it sought to raise. At all events, social history in its amorphous but aggrandizing guise of the 1970s no longer exists. It lost both its coherence as an intellectual project and its prestige as the bearer of the more radical, innovative, and experimental tendencies of the discipline, particularly among the generations currently being recruited. Its place has been taken by the 'new cultural history'.

This was neither a crisis nor cause for regret. Yet, in one book-length reflection, Bryan Palmer saw the linguistic turn as an adversarial attack against historical materialism and social history – a 'hedonistic descent into a plurality of discourses that decenter the world in a chaotic denial of any acknowledgment of tangible structures of power and comprehensions of meaning'; a 'reduction of analysis and theory to the puns and word games of scholastic pretension'; and 'a messianic faddism' that has disastrously captured the imagination of social historians.[72] Palmer veered abruptly from careful and sympathetic exegeses of post-structuralist contributions to swingeing indictments. The linguistic turn was in the end 'a kind of academic wordplaying with no possible link to anything but the pseudo-intellectualized ghettoes of the most self-promotionally avant-garde enclaves of that bastion of protectionism, the University'.[73] But, rather than an intellectual police action ('These are refusals that must be made, and made clearly' – but

---

72 Palmer, *Descent into Discourse*, 188.
73 Ibid., 199.

according to what authority?), we need a critically observed pluralism. Whether, as individuals, we take the linguistic turn or not, there will always be a diversity of histories in the profession. Short of driving opponents from the field and burning their books, debates will never be finally settled. The best we can ask for is openness and seriousness in the exchange. Understanding advances through conflict and the polemical clarification of difference; but the differences will remain.[74]

---

74 This essay was written during the summer of 1990, and reflects both the state of disciplinary discussion and my own thinking at that time. During the intervening years an enormous amount of publication, debate, and clarification has occurred, though arguably not a huge change in the basic epistemological landscape it describes. More historians have begun to explore the excitement of the new perspectives, but probably an equal number continue to rail against the pernicious effects of a demonized 'postmodernism', and the field of difficulty continues much as before. Rather than trying to bring my citations up to date (an entire project in itself), I have left the text and footnotes mostly in their original form as a kind of snapshot of a history still in motion. I am profoundly indebted to still-continuing conversations with Kathleen Canning and Margaret R. Somers More generally, I would like to thank my friends and colleagues in the Program for the Comparative Study of Social Transformations (CSST), who provided the context of intellectual generosity and exploration that allowed these thoughts to cohere. I owe a particular debt to Nick Dirks, Mike Kennedy, Sherry Ortner, Bill Sewell, and Peggy Somers, but especially Terry McDonald, whose intellectual friendship and intelligence has been a vital part of my Michigan years. For an indication of developments immediately following 1990, readers may wish to consult the introduction to Nicholas B. Dirks, Geoff Eley, and Sherry B. Ortner, eds, *Culture/Power/History: A Reader in Contemporary Social Theory* (Princeton: Princeton University Press, 1994), 3–45; and Geoff Eley, 'Playing It Safe. Or: How Is Social History Represented? The New Cambridge Social History of Britain', *History Workshop Journal* 35 (1993).

2

Lack of Discipline: Social History, Cultural Studies, and 1968

Thinking Across Disciplines

By the end of the 1990s, the crossing of traditional boundaries of knowledge production, in a conversation across disciplines, was the strongest contemporary force acting on historians' sense of themselves inside the academy in the United States. If originally it was contentious, often roiling departments, fields, professional meetings, and sub-specialisms very divisively, the following two decades brought high measures of acceptance, even institutionalization, as historians sampled their colleagues' wares, acquired other people's methods, and educated themselves theoretically, while scholars from elsewhere responded in turn. But, even when registered in new programmes, centres, institutes, and curricular initiatives, the resulting space was still ambiguously defined. Here is the feminist legal scholar Patricia Williams, one of the most transgressively creative scholars writing from inside a rebellious interdisciplinarity:

> As I write, my editor at Harvard University Press is waging something of a struggle with the people at the Library of Congress about how this book is to be categorized for cataloguing purposes. The librarians think 'Afro-Americans – Civil Rights' and 'Law Teachers' would be nice. I told my editor to hold out for 'Autobiography', 'Fiction', 'Gender

Studies', and 'Medieval Medicine'. This battle seems appropriate enough since the book is not exclusively about race or law but also about boundary. While being black has been the powerful social attribution in my life, it is only one of a number of governing narratives or presiding functions by which I am constantly reconfiguring myself in the world. Gender is another, along with ecology, pacifism, my peculiar brand of colloquial English, and Roxbury, Massachusetts. The complexity of role identification, the politics of sexuality, the inflections of professionalized discourse – all describe and impose boundary in my life, even as they confound one another in unfolding spirals of confrontation, deflection, and dream . . .[1]

This quotation eloquently describes the multifaceted practice of what I will loosely call 'cultural studies' in the academic scene of the contemporary United States: its use of the personal voice; its ironies and playfulness; its movement back and forth between academic knowledge, public spheres, and the practical encounters of everyday life; its self conscious politicizing of academic discussion; its very strong idea of the situatedness of knowledge; its invoking of a range of different disciplines only to call into question their conventional boundaries. It calls our attention to the politics of knowledge unavoidably required of leading African American and other minority scholars in the universities of the United States today.

In some respects, Patricia Williams enjoys a privileged place in the public sphere of US higher education. She commands impressive cultural capital of a traditional kind, teaching for many years at one of the most prestigious private universities (Columbia) and publishing with another (Harvard). In common with other leading African American scholars, she enjoys acknowledged celebrity status. Relative to given assumptions about what counts as legitimate and creative scholarship and allowable debate, she has extraordinary freedom. Here, the interdisciplinary impulse is intimately joined to political imperatives and their associated knowledge claims, reflecting the bitterly conducted and partially successful struggle to open the universities to previously marginalized groups. One decisive consequence of disciplinary formations

---

1   Patricia J. Williams, *The Alchemy of Race and Rights: The Diary of a Law Professor* (Cambridge: Harvard University Press, 1991), 256–7.

of knowledge as we encounter them during the twentieth century – the traditions, professional hierarchies, vested interests, and institutional forms of the academic disciplines – is their capacity for delimiting the questions that can and cannot be asked, their ability to ensure certain kinds of silencing, so that certain stories have rarely, if ever, been told. Some questions are not easily answerable under the terms of particular disciplines; others cannot even be asked. In that sense, interdisciplinarity creates spaces of fresh possibility, however trammelled and incomplete.

Indeed, access to the undisciplined benefits of that kind of freedom has remained both limited and invariably highly disputed. During the 1980s and 1990s, it became the object of depressingly familiar politics inside the academy, those of the so-called 'culture wars', with all of the notorious and much-debated contentiousness expressed by the term 'politically correct' (PC). Because some parts of the institutional world of US higher education were showing themselves relatively responsive to calls for affirmative action on the juridically designated grounds of gender and race, just as the given regimes of knowledge in some disci-plinary fields were being broken down and opened up, Patricia Williams acquired more latitude precisely from being African American, and, to some extent, from being a feminist woman. But the emergent and rela-tively autonomous spaces – inside disciplines, fields, institutions – remained fragile and small. They were confined to certain universities, certain departments, certain fields and sub-fields of study, certain parts of the undergraduate curriculum, certain graduate programmes, certain jour-nals, certain research foundations, certain publishing houses. Any idea that universities were somehow ruled by a culture of 'PC-ness', or that multiculturalism had dramatically or pervasively recast the content and practices of university life, was both tendentious and extremely naive.

From a vantage-point at the turn of the century, enormous inertia and conservatism prevailed in the institutional arenas where most aca-demic life took place – and among the old-established subject-disciplines, history was more resilient than most. The major US history depart-ments where cultural studies or similar interdisciplinarity had secure standing could be counted on the fingers of one hand. Whereas the public profile of the profession, the visible landscape of interests in the *American Historical Review* and the annual meetings of the American Historical Association (AHA) and other parts of its public sphere, and the main inflections of graduate student interest had all shifted, the main institutional coordinates of historical culture in the universities remained the same. That could be seen in the character of the undergraduate curriculum (notably in US and European history undergraduate survey courses) and the structure of graduate training. Even my own department at the University of Michigan, which gained some notoriety for its supposed radicalism in these regards (described by one departing colleague as a 'department of gender history and cultural studies'), retained both an impeccably orthodox undergraduate curriculum and practices of graduate training that came straightforwardly from the 1960s and 1970s.

In my own university significant changes occurred during my first two decades after joining its History Department in 1979. Aside from long-term reductions in public funding generally afflicting US higher education, which hit Michigan with a vengeance just as I arrived (in the crisis of the automobile industry and severe budgetary cuts in 1980–81), the most far-reaching reforms attended a dramatic and shocking crisis around racism in spring 1987, coinciding with a change of leadership in the university's central administration. The incoming president announced three new programmes that shaped the institution's central priorities across subsequent years: (1) the so-called Michigan Mandate, intended to make Michigan 'the multicultural university of the twenty-first century', comprising a profusion of central initiatives, including especially the systematic furtherance of minority recruitment of students and faculty; (2) a Women's Agenda to promote affirmative action around gender; and (3) 'internationalizing the University' to re-equip it for the demands of globalization. Together, these initiatives required substantial restructuring of institutional priorities and central reallocation of resources. By the early 1990s, they were transforming the public culture of my local institution.

I participated modestly in this process, both administratively and intellectually, whether in the wider sphere of the university or inside the life of my own department. During 1991–94, I served a three-year term on the elected executive committee of the College of Literature, Science, and the Arts (LSA). There, I played some part in the decisions enabling the creation of the university's International Institute in 1994–95, under whose umbrella the area studies centres became concentrated, together with a variety of interdisciplinary programmes, including a freshly created Advanced Studies Center. Across the same period, a variety of existing programmes were proactively strengthened, including Women's Studies, African American Studies, American Culture, Film and Video, and so on. From the later 1980s, in common with most other major universities in the United States, Michigan also acquired a generously endowed Humanities Institute. An Institute for Research on Women and Gender was also added. During my tenure on the LSA executive committee, the bulk of intellectual discussions – for the setting of academic priorities through the allocation of appointments, the reviewing of units, the supporting of new initiatives, and discussions of pedagogy – concerned the balance between interdisciplinarity and the integrity of already constituted disciplinary traditions, especially in the humanities – but also, to some extent, on the boundaries between humanities and social sciences.

Concurrently, I also directed the key intellectual initiative of an interdisciplinary kind (coinciding, as it happened, with that same change of university leadership in 1987), the programme for the Comparative Study of Social Transformations (CSST). This programme's trajectory mirrored the main shift in interdisciplinary keenness among historians during these years, from the social sciences to a hybrid space on the borderlands with the humanities, best described as cultural studies. Beginning as a consortium of historians, anthropologists, and sociologists, CSST quickly reconfigured into a more heterogeneous constituency, exchanging some of the original sociologists and historians for a miscellany of recruits from political theory, communications, and literary studies, with heavy representation from existing interdisciplinary programmes like American Culture and Women's Studies, and a broad presence internationally in each of the area studies centres. Numbers expanded in the process from thirty faculty to some seventy-five. This interdisciplinary energy massively influenced the structure and quality of intellectual life, enabling continuous conversation across units for the first time, focusing the priorities of a variety of smaller groups drawn from participating departments, energizing graduate studies through a flourishing graduate organization (including a joint PhD programme in History and Anthropology), sponsoring a series of conferences, and changing the manner in which faculty and students thought about and practised their work. In History, it drew the interest of roughly half the department during its peak years from 1987 to the mid-1990s.

These local histories of the reorganizing of knowledge within particular universities are vital to an understanding of contemporary
intellectual life. They resonate with larger national and international
debates over academic freedom and useful knowledge, just as they
respond to initiatives of government and foundations for promoting
policy-related objectives and setting public priorities, such as the post-
Communist and future organization of area studies. These political
processes generate tremendous opportunities for creative interdisciplinary work, whether in particular institutions or the wider public
culture of our intellectual lives, while simultaneously activating strong
institutional resistance. Finding the space between these two forces,
the possibilities and constraints, is no easy matter. Not accidentally,
many of the boldest innovations developed from the fundamentally
*un*disciplined fields of women's studies, African American studies,
ethnic studies, gay and lesbian studies, film studies, cultural studies, and
more. But these are still 'minor' knowledges inside the university's
institutional precincts. How exactly such creativity might achieve
continuity remains anything but clear.

In the absence of institutional supports, individuals can still make
much headway. Subcultures and enclaves may certainly form in the
interstices of an institution's dominant or official culture, along with
the wider counter-networks of an immediate field or specialism. A
sympathetic political climate can also deliver essential reinforcement.
But without change in the immediate institutional environment inside
departments and universities, the collective and everyday settings for
sustained collaborative and cross-disciplinary work can be harder to
grow. Degrees of personal isolation can be demoralizing. I have been
lucky enough to experience successive places and times where supports
were exceptionally strong; I have just described Michigan. Before 1979 I
was in Cambridge, where a happy synergy of younger faculty, graduate
students, and intellectual subcultures occurred in the margins of official
life. I was a DPhil student at recently founded Sussex, where interdisciplinarity was built into curriculum and institutional structures. I was an
undergraduate during 1967–70, when intellectual and political radicalism inspired us to experiment.[2]

---

2   I discussed some of this in Geoff Eley, *A Crooked Line: From Cultural History to the
History of Society* (Ann Arbor, MI: University of Michigan Press, 2005), 1–12, 90–102.

Disciplinary traditions of academic knowledge have always seemed insufficient to me – a lasting disposition acquired from the late sixties and early seventies. The great forcing-time for out-of-the-box intellectual creativity, those years were the crucible for our contemporary interdisciplinary sensibility, the inception point for the long present stretching into the new century. As a student in Oxford, eventually joining the History Faculty Reform Movement and editing the *Oxford Historian* (where I won my most prized undergraduate distinction: to have been denounced to the Faculty Board by Hugh Trevor-Roper), it was entirely clear that History was not enough, that it needed 'theory', that for the purpose other disciplines were required, meaning principally sociology and political science, perhaps anthropology, but at all events the rich repertoire of critical social science. This challenge also meant that great incitement to cross-disciplinary, or perhaps pan-disciplinary knowledge – namely, Marxism. In becoming a fully credentialed member of the historical profession, I failed to outgrow my earlier sense. I kept adding to the 'extra-historical' theoretical knowledges and other disciplinary influences I needed to make History sufficient – state theory; theories of ideology; Antonio Gramsci, Raymond Williams, and Stuart Hall; feminism; Michel Foucault; other post-structuralisms; psychoanalytically influenced theories of subjectivity; film theory; literary theory; and the long-evolving field of cultural studies. This vitally influenced – continues to influence – how I read and write and think, the colleagues I seek, the way I organize my teaching, the kind of graduate students I help advise, and the general principles guiding what seems intellectually, pedagogically, and politically most important in what I do. Whatever modest virtues I possess as a historian arise from the degree to which I have followed this very unhistorianly practice – the degree, that is, to which I am not a historian.

But it seems silly to minimize differences between actually constituted disciplinary modes of understanding – between the diverse epistemological cultures and associated intellectual histories around which the disciplines have coalesced, the pluralities of outlook and practice composing each of those disciplines, and the multiplicity of variously composed agendas that necessarily contribute to any interdisciplinary coalescence. Such disjunctions (including those between national intellectual practices) are both an impediment and an incentive to interdisciplinary exchange. They frequently get in the way, yet supply an ideal basis for exchange – not for the purpose of subsuming differences or homogenizing understanding, but so as to grasp and specify their reach. Different people are interested in different things; at one level such diversity is irreducible. But why should those differences of topic and orientation be marked only or mainly along *disciplinary* lines, as against seeing them inside a variety of cross-disciplinary problematics? In principle, as much may unite practitioners in one discipline with cognate groups in another as may characterize the cohesion of the disciplines as such. This emerges clearly from a focus on significant problems – such as cultural studies, state-making, the study of everyday life, sexuality, the labour process, and so forth. How, then, to preserve a definite disciplinary core? The given disciplinary boundaries hardly describe any homogeneous intellectual space. But nor are they devoid of useful meaning.

So, what do we mean – what do *I* mean – by interdisciplinarity? For me, it means much of the outlook fashioned in the originary and turbulent circumstances of the sixties it means transgression, it means disobeying, it means rule-breaking, it means making trouble, it means shaking things up, it means being experimental, it means trying new thoughts, taking risks, being courageous in our relationship to new and unfamiliar knowledges, in the imagining of what those might be. It means finding spaces of possibility on the other side of what we already do. This is all to do with the addressing of difference, with stepping outside our familiar regimes of intelligibility, with defamiliarizing them, with unsettling our customary conditions and habits of understanding, with the release of meaning rather than its predictable accumulation. When we go to another discipline, or another field of knowledge (because this concerns the crossing of cultural difference, or of historical time, as much as the traversing of disciplinary boundaries per se), we are entering a site of difference in this way, a context of deconstruction, a context where the ever-seductive unities of established and familiar discourse, the naturalizing of hegemonies, may be upset. This is a way of challenging the given centrings of knowledge and the silencings and suppressions, the marginalizations, these entail.

This feels like a fundamental philosophical condition, a prerequisite of seeing myself as an intellectual in some justified and useful way, as trying to think inside an engaged intellectuality that sees itself in some meaningful and effective relationship to what we sometimes call the real world. It is the difference between the security of established practice, the security of what we already do and know, and the excitements and risks of self-extension, of venturing onto ground where our thinking can be organized anew. The difficulty, of course, in the destabilizing of certainties is to allow ourselves sufficient confidence to imagine making fresh positives in their stead. But, in the end, interdisciplinarity is for me all about the critical recognition of established fixities, about exploring how the openings and closures of knowledge and understanding can occur, about examining the categories through which we construct our relationship to the world, about disturbing familiar assumptions and allowing ourselves to see the absences and non-necessities of closure, the horizon of a different possibility, the lineaments of another way.

Three Phases

Present encouragements towards interdisciplinary work have a much longer history, going back to the 1960s. That intellectual backstory can be separated into three phases

The first phase saw the intellectual prestige of the social or behavioural sciences (especially sociology), usually in some framework of modernization theory, reaching its climax in the late 1950s and early 1960s. Driven by the research boom of the post-war capitalist prosperity, this was further aided by Marxism's atrophy as an intellectual tradition in the English-speaking world after the crisis of Stalinism in 1956. For historians, the main sites of this early conversation were a number of journals: *Past and Present* in Britain, which turned to the dialogue with non-Marxist sociology and anthropology; and three new journals in the United States, *Comparative Studies in Society and History*, *Journal of Interdisciplinary History*, and the *Journal of Social History*.[3] The turning to sociology was eclectic and dependent: historians 'learned' theory from sociology. The most self-conscious borrowings focused on methodology rather than theory per se, most successfully through the use of sophisticated quantitative techniques in areas like

---

3 Several other journals, including *Theory and Society* and *Politics and Society*, had less specifically historical content (by authors' disciplinary affiliation), but shared this same moment.

historical demography, family history, mobility studies, migration, urban history, and so forth.[4]

In a second phase, social historians escaped the tutelage of those social-science paradigms. The later 1970s brought a series of stock-taking essays – by Elizabeth Fox-Genovese and Eugene Genovese, Gareth Stedman Jones, and Tony Judt – as well as some new journals, including *Social History* and *History Workshop Journal* in Britain and *Radical History Review* in the United States.[5] Younger scholars trained in the 1960s and early 1970s were claiming their space, flying the banner of a restlessly aggrandizing social history. Freshly confident in its own knowledge claims, this field was now sceptical of the social sciences and their authority. The new generation embraced the project of a 'non-empiricist' and 'theoretically informed' history, guided by an unproblematic materialism that was frequently Marxist, open to other forms of social theory, and sure in its own pedagogy. The social history emerging from the 1960s was never unitary. But some notion of social determination, conceptualized on the ground of material life, moved by the ambition to grasp 'society as a whole', was a common framework of conviction.[6]

The third phase, gathering pace between the mid 1980s and early 1990s, dislodged social history as the acknowledged source of radical-ism in historical studies, while making the 'new cultural history' the fresh site of interdisciplinary exchange. Beginning from the popularity of an anthropologically oriented cultural history, inspired by Clifford Geertz, Natalie Zemon Davis, and Edward Thompson, this bore the imprint of an antireductionist Anglo-Marxism, further extended by the reception of Michel Foucault and the challenge of feminist theory.[7]

---

4   See Terrence J. McDonald, 'What We Talk about When We Talk about History: The Conversations of History and Sociology', in *The Historic Turn in the Human Sciences* (Ann Arbor, MI: University of Michigan Press, 1996).

5   See the detailed citations in Chapter 1, p. 5, above. For my own commentary of the time, see Geoff Eley, 'Some Recent Tendencies in Social History', in *International Handbook of Historical Studies: Contemporary Research and Theory*, ed. Georg G. Iggers and Harold T. Parker (Westport, CT: Greenwood, 1979), and Geoff Eley and Keith Nield, 'Why Does Social History Ignore Politics?', *Social History* 5: 2 (1980).

6   Hobsbawm's 1971 essay, much cited, translated, and reprinted, gave the characteristic lead: 'From Social History to the History of Society', *Daedalus* 100: 1 (1971).

7   See Lynn Hunt, ed., *The New Cultural History* (Berkeley/Los Angeles: University of California Press, 1989). For fuller detail, see Chapter 1, above, as well as Dennis Dworkin, *Cultural Marxism in Postwar Britain: History, the New Left, and the Origins of Cultural Studies* (Durham, NC: Duke University Press, 1997).

By the later 1980s, historians were speaking the language of 'cultural constructionism', drawing increasingly on the remarkable impact in North America of French literary theory and British cultural studies, each sharply mediated by feminism. As 'race' calibrated the terms of social anxieties and political exchange ever more pervasively, it joined 'gender' as a central category of historical analysis, not least under the aegis of postcolonial studies.[8] The result was an extremely mobile 'culturalism', not indifferent to social analysis necessarily, but drawn far more to 'meaning'. This helped revive the flagging morale of intellectual history. More to the point, it pulled history towards literary theory, linguistic analysis, history of art, studies of film and visuality, reflexive anthropology, and theories of cultural representation. This opened the agenda of possible histories in remarkable ways. A range of new journals again appeared, all of them interdisciplinary (or perhaps adisciplinary) but with strong historical content, whether or not the authors were historians by disciplinary affiliation: *Representations*, *Critical Inquiry*, *Social Text*, *New Formations*, *Public Culture*, and more.[9]

This last phase arrived through a fracturing of generational consensus, in a series of confrontational debates and reorientations whose tones roiled the profession as bitterly as earlier battles over social history. These conflicts were sometimes over theory per se, as in the attacks on 'structuralist Marxism', whose acrimony dominated British left-intellectual life in the later 1970s, or similar animus against Foucault and other poststructuralisms in the United States. But the turn to linguistically conceived forms of cultural history, within wider fields of cross-disciplinary exchange, also mirrored shifts in the political climate. Career paths also brought tenured security and institutional influence, along with new access to graduate students and the chance to shape the policies of journals. The salience of this generational voice was magnified by the relative paucity of successors. Drastic reductions in history PhDs left the

---

8   See, emblematically, Joan Wallach Scott, *Gender and the Politics of History* (New York: Columbia University Press, 1988), and David R. Roediger, *The Wages of Whiteness: Race and the Making of the American Working Class* (London: Verso, 1991).

9   See Peter Novick, *That Noble Dream: The 'Objectivity Question' and the American Historical Profession* (Cambridge: Cambridge University Press, 1988); McDonald, *Historic Turn in the Human Sciences*; Robert F. Berkhofer Jr, *Beyond the Great Story: History as Text and Discourse* (Cambridge: Cambridge University Press, 1995). Berkhofer's book marked exactly the distance from the first phase of interdisciplinarity. See his earlier *A Behavioral Approach to Historical Analysis* (New York: Free Press, 1969).

cohorts qualifying in the 1980s very thin in number. This contrasted with those from the early 1990s, who gained tenured security by the 2000s: moved by the challenge of the linguistic turn and its politics of knowledge, they had much to say about gender history and cultural studies.

Theory and Society ran a symposium in 1980, at an early stage in this transition, on current directions in social history. Deriving from a meeting convened by Louise and Charles Tilly at the University of Michigan the year before, under the title 'Whence and Whither Social History?', this published version comprised statements by Edward Shorter, Francis G. Couvares, David Levine, and the Tillys themselves. The meeting had ended in some acrimony when Charles Tilly assailed his close associate William Sewell in the closing session, while moderator Joan Scott, another close follower, uncomfortably looked on. Mentored by Tilly as junior scholars in the 1960s, at the height of the union between history and sociology, Sewell and Scott were now arguing for a cultural turn, with much talk of the insufficiencies of 'vulgar Marxism' and quantitative studies of material life, and of the need instead for a 'more sophisticated kind of cultural history'. While Sewell, Scott and others worried productively over the limitations of the existing materialist paradigm, Tilly battled angrily for 'the harder-edged sociological work' the meeting was called to defend.[10]

In his published remarks, Tilly noted the challenge of 'anthropological work . . . the study of *mentalités*, and . . . more rigorous Marxist analyses', but thought the existing social history project ('collective biography, quantification, social-scientific approaches, and rigorous studies of everyday behavior') should prevail. It simply needed linking more effectively to 'the established historical agenda' in language historians could understand. His description of social history's 'two callings' was unexceptionable, as far as it went: 'asking how the world we live in came into being, and how its coming into being affected the everyday lives of ordinary people; asking what could have happened to everyday experience at major historical choice points, and then inquiring how and why the outcomes won out over other possibilities'.[11]

But so long as cultural construction was ignored, and categories like 'everyday experience' and 'ordinary people' not subjected to scrutiny,

10   See Chapter 1 above, footnote 9.
11   C. Tilly, 'Two Callings of Social History', *Theory and Society* 9:5 (1980), 681.

questions would be begged.[12] Likewise, Louise Tilly's reflections on 'work' ('to talk about changes in women's work over time, more rigorous definitions, words, categories are needed') and 'politics' ('Politics must be reconceptualized so we can talk about the politics of those without formal rights') were all to the good.[13] But she, too, kept to the given sociological ground. In that sense, Louise Tilly's collaboration with Joan Scott, *Women, Work, and Family* (1978), and Scott's own *Gender and the Politics of History* (1988) were separated by far more than just years.[14]

In my earlier reflections on these developments, in the years 1987–90, I saw US historical studies entering a time of flux. In the modern German field, for example, habits were being challenged in a variety of ways – by the East Coast German Women's History Study Group; by a series of major conferences; and by a new porousness of disciplinary boundaries under the pressure of gender perspectives, the ferment around poststructuralist theory and 'postmodernism', and the excitements of cultural studies. Since then, things have moved much further along. Gender history is fully established: if in its first twenty years the flagship journal, *Central European History*, ran only four explicitly feminist articles and three more dealing empirically with women, in the next ten years there were *sixteen* on women and gender, nine in the two volumes for 1995–96.[15] The various conference-volumes brought the arguments to the centre ground of German historiography.[16] New approaches were debated in the main forums – annual meetings of the German Studies Association (GSA), sessions sponsored by the Conference Group in Central European History at the AHA, and so on.[17] With

---

12   For the consequences of taking 'everyday life' seriously, see Chapter 6, below.

13   Louise Tilly, 'Social History and its Critics', *Theory and Society* 9: 5 (1980), 670.

14   Louise Tilly and Joan Scott, *Women, Work, and Family* (New York: Holt, Rinehart & Winston, 1978); Scott, *Gender and the Politics of History*.

15   See Jean H. Quataert, 'Introduction 2: Writing the History of Women and Gender in Imperial Germany', in *Society, Culture, and the State in Germany, 1870–1930*, ed. Geoff Eley (Ann Arbor, MI: University of Michigan Press, 1996); Lynn Abrams and Elizabeth Harvey, eds, *Gender Relations in German History: Power, Agency, and Experience from the Sixteenth to the Twentieth Century* (London: UCL Press, 1996).

16   See the special issue of *Central European History*, 'German Histories: Challenges in Theory, Practice, Technique' 22: 3–4 (1989); Eley, *Society, Culture, and the State in Germany*; Saul Friedlander, ed., *Probing the Limits of Representation: Nazism and the 'Final Solution'* (Cambridge, MA: Harvard University Press, 1992).

17   See the response of Geyer and Jarausch to Barkin's polemic against 'postmodernism', originally delivered at the 1994 AHA in San Francisco: Kenneth Barkin, 'Bismarck in a Postmodern Age', *German Studies Review* 18: 2 (1995); Michael Geyer and Konrad H. Jarausch,

Scott Denham, Irene Kacandes, and Jonathan Petropoulos's *German Studies as Cultural Studies: A User's Manual*, cultural studies definitively arrived in the modern German field.[18]

Turning to Culture

Cultural studies, as a now-instituted cross-disciplinary formation of the English-speaking world, contains a varying miscellany of eclectic streams – sociology, literary studies, and social history in Britain (but interestingly rather few anthropologists), and mass communications, film studies, literary theory, reflexive anthropology in the United States, with a heavy presence of women's studies, American culture, ethnic studies, African American studies, and so on. The main US impulse comes from the humanities, with far less interest from social scientists, which had their own interdisciplinary programmes. British initiatives took the contrary tack, although the strength of qualitative sociologies also blurred the humanities/social science divide. Feminist theory had radical effects on both sides of the Atlantic, as did post-Saidian critiques of colonial and racist legacies of thought in Western civilizational traditions. Specific patterns vary across the Atlantic divide, but both the linguistic turn and postmodernist fascinations enabled national discussions to converge. Most empirical studies in either country preferred the 'long present' of cultural studies since 1945, where transfers to historians easily occurred.

Culture comprises notoriously disorderly ground. As Edward Thompson observed, it is 'a clumpish term, which by gathering up so many activities and attributes into one common bundle may actually confuse or disguise discriminations that should be made between them.'[19] Its usage extends from the arts, letters, and aesthetics, through the generalized life of the mind, to wider analytical domains. That includes institutional treatments of such themes in the public sphere

'Great Men and Postmodern Ruptures', *German Studies Review* 18: 2 (1995). This exchange led to extensive discussion on the H-German list during summer 1995, climaxing in a panel at the Chicago German Studies Association in October 1995.

18 Scott Denham, Irene Kacandes, and Jonathan Petropoulos, eds, *German Studies as Cultural Studies: A User's Manual* (Ann Arbor, MI: University of Michigan Press, 1997).

19 Edward P. Thompson, *Customs in Common: Studies in Traditional Popular Culture* (New York: Free Press, 1993), 13.

of artistic and intellectual activity, the educational system, other institutions of higher learning, and so forth (broadly speaking, the 'high-cultural' tradition of scholarship); the realm of symbolic and ritual meaning for a society's cohesion and overall ethos (the anthropological field of approaches); and what Terry Eagleton calls 'the whole complex of signifying practices and symbolic processes in a particular society' addressed by cultural studies.[20] Even these distinctions entail a gross clumping of approaches, so a full survey would include social-science theories of action too. Sociologists treat culture more often discretely, either by bracketing culture altogether (as in rational-actor models, or in resource-mobilization theory and other sociologies of collective action) or by placing it in a separable domain of study (as in forms of systems theory, including recent Habermasian conceptions of the lifeworld). For one symposium, 'culture in history' meant neo-institutional approaches, rational-actor models, and ideas of consumer preference: 'culture' was acknowledged as 'a fundamental part of the distribution of resources and the relations of power in a society'; but for most of the ensuing volume it receded from the forefront of analysis, except as the 'values' which 'inform the strategic calculations which people make about their interests' and support or inhibit particular paths of development.[21]

Moreover, when 'culture' is added or counterposed to 'structure' as an answer to the latter's over-objectified materialism, it can often reinscribe structural history's familiar analytic, with an underlying logic of long-term determination. If we approach culture differently, not as an empirically separable domain, but as the production and construction of meaning in any area or dimension of social life, we open far better space analytically for instabilities, contradictions, contingencies, and change. This requires no mutually exclusive choice. Rather, we need ways of theorizing the two approaches together: both the regularities and instabilities of culture, its unifying as well as fragmenting tendencies. If we step back from trying to theorize the relations of 'the social' and 'the cultural' in the most globally abstract of ways – that is, at the meta-level of the history and structure of whole societies – and seek some intermediate ground, then the conversation-impeding hyper-abstraction and schematizing may be

---

20   Terry Eagleton, *Ideology: An Introduction* (London: Verso, 1991), 28.
21   Joseph Melling and Jonathan Barry, eds, *Culture in History: Production, Consumption, and Values in Historical Perspective* (Exeter: Exeter University Press, 1992), 18–19.

easier to avoid. By more modestly thematizing culture's importance, we edge closer to its specific valency in historical analysis, as in the various couplets so generative during the past two decades – culture and custom, culture and production, culture and consumption, culture and colonialism. In each case, cultural analysis transformed our understanding, particularly in relation to politics, as a vital dimension of how different forms of politics can and cannot take place. Indeed, cultural analysis decisively expanded the very category of the political.

Combining potently with events in the world, 'theory' effectuated a long-maturing crisis of confidence in the forms of social understanding that so confidently marked the 1960s. Here, 'events in the world' signifies everything from globalization, the post-Fordist restructuring of the capitalist economy, de-industrialization, and the recomposition of class to the collapse of Communism, the end of the Cold War, and the dialectics of markets and democracy during the post-socialist transition. For many historians, this conjunction of theoretical flux and structural transformations severely damaged the persuasiveness and viability of the classic materialist analytics of both Marxist and non-Marxist sociologies. 'Society' as a unitary object became much harder to attain. Structural coherence was no longer easily derived from the economy, from the functional needs of the social system and its central values, or from some other overarching principle of social order. Particular phenomena – an event, a policy, an institution, an ideology, a text – have *particular social contexts*, in the sense of the conditions, practices, and sites that conjoin to produce an essential part of their meaning. To that degree, 'structural' or 'social' analyses remained indispensable. But there was no underlying given structure of the economy or the social system from which they necessarily derived in some clear materialist, causal, or expressive sense.

The major casualty of that intellectual flux or uncertainty was the traditional notion of social totality in its variable Marxist and non-Marxist forms. That commitment to grasping society as a whole – to conceptualizing its underlying principles of unity – now conventionally described as the specifically 'modern' or Enlightenment project, passed into disarray. This was commonly called the crisis of grand narratives. Even so, the most widely diffused notations of this predicament – of scepticism about 'Western civilization' and the cultural superiority of the West, disillusionment with science and its authority, disbelief in the inevitability of progress and the long-term possibility of universal improvement, the experience of localism, fragmentation, and loss of coherence – retained a commitment to general analysis. Fredric Jameson's 'cultural logic of late capitalism' and David Harvey's 'condition of postmodernity' sought alike to combine readings of specific cultural phenomena with an overarching structural argumentation, historicized within some developmental framework. Indeed, many who found post-modernist critiques provocative or persuasive precisely *did not* abandon societal analysis altogether. For my own part, I continued thinking in terms of capitalism, class, the nation, the social formation. But I acquired far more caution and uncertainty about what exactly these grand con-cepts might allow me to discuss or explain, including the level of abstraction at which it made sense to do so.

In particular, I understood more clearly how all of those terms are heavily laden with contexts of meaning, which as historians we try to uncover, specify, and locate. This does not require some exclusive stress on intellectual history or language in either the formal or straight-forwardly referential sense. It means recognizing that our categories are culturally constructed *as well as* socially produced. Even more, the social circumstances of material life are always worked upon and shaped in historically specific ways to affirm and enact certain forms of under-standing as against others. In principle, this approach – problematizing, deconstructing, and historicizing our most familiar categories of analy-sis and social understanding, while deploying the copious resources of the particular interdisciplinarity called cultural studies for the purpose – can be extended to other major issues revisited under the impact of contemporary cultural theory. Reopening the question of modernity while historicizing a viable concept of modernism supplies one example of these. Work on nationalism and nationhood would be another. Popular memory would be a third. In each case, cultural studies chal-lenged historians to translate its questions into projects amenable to the normal protocols of evidence and argument. In deciding how to do cultural history, moreover, it matters not only which body of cultural theory is acknowledged and adopted, but why.

3

No Need to Choose: The Profane and Imperfect World of Historiography

I wrote my book *A Crooked Line* in 2003–04 in a rush of urgency and optimism.[1] The urgency came from the parlous political state of the world. I found myself reflecting not only on the changing bases of intellectual dissent since the 1960s, but on the current difficulties in bridging the gap between what we do in our scholarly lives and what counts as history in the public sphere. For any historian whose calling included an ethics of political involvement – whether directly, more modestly through the politics of knowledge, or simply by recognizing the salience of political meanings – these were dispiriting times. Yet my optimism came from a sense of opportunity inside the discipline. The angry contentiousness of some years before, during history's own versions of the culture wars, was giving way to more collegial and constructive conversations, both field by field and in the discipline overall. Younger generations with less of the old baggage were now being heard.

Historiographically, I wanted to take stock, tracking the complicated passages between social history and cultural history since the 1970s to see what had been gained and what might be lost. But my second goal was to reflect at length on history's relation to politics. This can be treacherous ground. I refused any straightforward or instrumental transmission between the two, and took great pains in tackling the

---

1 Geoff Eley, *A Crooked Line: From Cultural History to the History of Society* (Ann Arbor, MI: University of Michigan Press, 2005).

complexities. Rather than any one-to-one equivalence, I stressed the gaps and disjunctions, the tensions in history's connectedness to the public worlds of politics, and the necessary spaces of difficulty. I wanted to show the subtle and disguised entrance of political meanings into historians' practice – sometimes willingly invited, but just as often guardedly rebuffed. Such meanings are frequently unwelcome intruders. If, for much of the time, politics is inscribed indirectly and imperceptibly, at other times its presence is powerful and very direct, troubling historians' practice as much as inspiring it. There is also an interior politics of knowledge, involving everything from the institutional settings where history is practised (departments, institutes, universities, classrooms, conferences, journals, networks, associations) to the rules and protocols defining its boundaries and the widest debates over its methods, its archives, its schools and traditions, its forms of theory, and its epistemologies. Finally, I wanted to discuss how ideas and assumptions about the past tend to circulate in popular terms more widely across the public culture. All these are aspects of history's politics.

In addressing these matters, I made modest use of my own story. I am struck not only by the messy and uneven entrance of political changes into my own thinking, but also by their time-lagged, bumpy relationship to how I approached my immediate historical work. The resulting non-synchronicity can be very disconcerting. No one likes confessing inconsistencies, least of all in one's fundamental principles or most valued ethical commitments. We see our own thought more commonly as the unfolding of maturity or the arrival at understanding – as a seamless progression, as growth and enlargement, as consciously working a problem through to its necessary solution. Yet we seldom actually experience change in so straightforwardly directed and self-conscious a way. In practice, problems creep up on us. They register their presence slowly and partially, taking up residence in hidden or shrouded corners, doing their work behind our backs. Often, they ambush our understanding and take us by surprise. In other cases, we notice them unexpectedly through chance encounters (a seminar we attend, a controversy we observe, a book we happen to read). Many of these experiences have to accumulate before receptiveness to their shared meaning accrues. Where ideas threaten or challenge what we think we already understand, resistance and evasions probably result. Before change can be consummated, a great deal of wrestling has to occur. The change itself brings much elaborate redescription. Consistency and coherence will be rediscovered and projected backward in time. Belatedly, we realize what we had really wanted to think.

In pondering how my own thinking changed, I wanted to write an intellectual history of the present open to these elements of unexpectedness and contingency. I wanted to honour the difficulties, confusions, and resistances through which fundamental changes of thought usually occur, particularly when unconscious or only partially understood. Moreover, we already possessed a detailed intellectual accounting of the so-called cultural turn.[2] Those histories quite properly centre on the principal theoretical and epistemological issues, emphasizing the major personalities, along with the resulting controversies and debates. These are now captured in a profusion of guides, commentaries, anthologies, forums, new journals, and much continuing discussion. Instead of retelling that story one more time, I looked for other ways of writing the intellectual history.

In discussing the 1980s, for example, I sought a series of emblematic books whose impact transcended fields and disciplines, around which variegated interest converged, and which did something to accumulate the readiness for change. Often preceding the most commonly cited texts, those works had their own prehistories of gestation too – in seminars, conferences, pedagogical settings, and varieties of collaboration cutting across field and disciplinary boundaries. They captured the oblique effects of new departures somewhat removed from one's immediate scholarly work – in other fields, other periods, other parts of the world, other disciplines – whose pertinence was not so easily apparent, but whose unsettling or enabling potentials registered nonetheless. Feminist critiques and the slow-burning consequences of women's history supplied one primary instance; a second was the advent of race theory and postcolonial studies in the 1990s, for which 'whiteness' and subaltern studies were my twin markers.

---

2   Especially Elizabeth A. Clark, *History, Theory, Text: Historians and the Linguistic Turn* (Cambridge, MA: Harvard University Press, 2004); Miguel A. Cabrera, *Postsocial History: An Introduction*, trans. Marie McMahon (Lanham, MD: Lexington, 2004); Gabrielle M. Spiegel, 'Introduction', in her *Practicing History: New Directions in Historical Writing after the Linguistic Turn* (New York: Routledge, 2005); Ann Curthoys and John Docker, *Is History Fiction?* (Ann Arbor, MI: University of Michigan Press, 2005), esp. 137–237. In addition to the two preceding chapters, I addressed these questions in Geoff Eley, 'Problems with Culture: German History after the Linguistic Turn', *Central European History* 31 (1998).

Using my own story was a way of coming closer to how changes actually happened – by showing something of the confusions, false starts, dead ends, and wrong turnings needed along the way. Capturing such complexity required a particular kind of contextualizing, which a personally grounded narrative hoped to convey. If writing an intellectual history of contemporary historiography relies on the published traces of explicit debate around which key departures could crystallize, then we also need the messier histories that those recognized texts presuppose. The framework I devised honoured two complementary priorities: close attention to explicating the texts as such (all the pertinent bibliography of the linguistic and cultural turns); but an equally searching analysis of the social circumstances behind them, including the philosophical underpinnings of the relevant historiographical practices, the very specific institutional histories involved, and whichever political dynamics may have impinged. Each purpose is vital to the fullest historiographical understanding – that is, both the careful and critical exegesis of the major texts themselves and the dense thickets of discussion and practice through which those texts had eventually emerged. We might call this the profane and imperfect world of historiography.[3]

Confined to certain nuts and bolts of narrative reconstruction – the story of who said what to whom and when – this might seem banal. Yet a fuller account of the sites and settings of intellectual debates, especially in their institutional and eventful dimensions, brings us closer to the stakes involved. It exposes the local and mundane micro-dynamics of how ideas are formed, along with their wider cultural politics. That, in turn, delivers more complicated and unexpected genealogies for the historiographical present. We would understand far more about the enabling consequences and possible limitations of Joan Scott's embrace of poststructuralism in the early 1980s if we knew more about the trajectory from *Glassworkers of Carmaux* (1974) through *Women, Work, and Family* (1978) to *Gender and the Politics of History* (1988). Scott's transition from teaching women's history at the University of North Carolina to directing the Pembroke Center for Teaching and Research on Women at Brown University would

---

3   Gabrielle M. Spiegel, 'France for Belgium', in *Why France? American Historians Reflect on an Enduring Fascination*, ed. Laura Lee Downs and Stéphane Gerson (Ithaca, NY: Cornell University Press, 2007), which describes the 'social logic of the text' (97). See also Spiegel, 'Revising the Past/Revisiting the Present: How Change Happens in Historiography', *History and Theory* 46 (2007).

be especially revealing, not least for the influence of Denise Riley, who collaborated with Scott at Brown, and whose book '*Am I That Name?*' was one of my emblematic texts.[4] Through Riley, we loop back into British feminist debates of the later 1970s. So, far from mere storytelling, such details are essential to a careful sociology of knowledge. They hardly diminish theoretical commentary, but rather supplement and thicken it. Modestly pooling historians' own stories, less as autobiography than as autocritique, could be very illuminating. In drawing on my own experience, I was tempting others into doing the same.

With respect to the particularities of my standpoint (and some attendant points of neglect), Gabrielle Spiegel rightly called for a deepening of the specifically French background to the intellectual departures of the 1970s. As she says, structuralism and poststructuralism had each been 'intellectually motivated by a rejection of phenomenology', which, in Michel Foucault's case, went back to his attendance at Maurice Merleau-Ponty's lectures in the late 1940s.[5] This clearly has bearing on how we see the early critical impetus for much of the linguistic turn, no less than on the intervening range of subsequent second thoughts. Yet the wider English-language borrowings of 'ideas from France' in the 1970s and 1980s were far more eclectic and disorderly than Spiegel allows, with an uncertain relation to the suggested ground of 'post-phenomenological' disputation. Her urging of a 'neo-phenomenological' direction for the emergent revisions of the 'post-linguistic turn' likewise proposes far greater coherence than those new critiques can bear.[6] In

---

4   See Denise Riley, '*Am I That Name?*': *Feminism and the Category of 'Women' in History* (Minneapolis: University of Minnesota Press, 1988). For Scott's three works, see Joan Wallach Scott, *Glassworkers of Carmaux: French Craftsmen and Political Action in a Nineteenth-Century City* (Cambridge: Cambridge University Press, 1974); Louise Tilly and Joan Scott, *Women, Work, and Family* (New York: Holt, Rinehart & Winston, 1978); Joan Wallach Scott, *Gender and the Politics of History* (New York: Columbia University Press, 1988). See also Elaine Abelson, David Abraham, and Marjorie Murphy, 'Interview with Joan Scott', *Radical History Review* 45 (1989), which sheds light on the early years but not the 1980s.

5   See Gabrielle M. Spiegel, 'Comment on *A Crooked Line*', *American Historical Review* 113: 2 (2008), 410; David Macey, *The Lives of Michel Foucault: A Biography* (New York: Vintage, 1995), 31–6.

6   'Ideas from France' comes from the title of an emblematic volume on the impact of French theory across the academic disciplines and the arts in Britain, originating in a discussion series on 'French Legacies' at the Institute of Contemporary Arts in November–December 1984, marking Foucault's death. It was followed in 1985 by a conference on 'Crossing the Channel'. See Lisa Appignanesi, ed., *Ideas from France: The Legacy of French Theory – ICA Documents* (London: Free Association Books, 1989).

each case, the discursive heterogeneity exceeds Spiegel's more tightly drawn account. Indeed, as *A Crooked Line* took great pains to point out, distinct tendencies in the history of ideas too easily become conflated into a single shift, in this case blurring the 'new cultural history' into the more specific purposes of the 'linguistic turn':

> Writing the . . . history of that extraordinarily complex intellectual upheaval – in a manner commensurate with all its unevenness . . . and with all the broader cultural, social, and political forces partially explaining it – has so far eluded most commentators. It becomes ever clearer that the favored shorthand descriptions – 'cultural turn', 'linguistic turn', and 'postmodernism' – were coined in the heat of relatively short-lived, but extremely polarizing, initial battles, disguise as much as they clarify, and conflate manifold variations . . . Turning to 'culture' was the rather vague common denominator for heterogeneous discontents.[7]

On a broader front, William Sewell took *A Crooked Line* to task for ignoring 'the macrosocial environment in which the historiographical changes took place'.[8] Yet the destructive social and political fallout from capitalist restructuring was in fact an essential referent for how I tried to deal with the complicated back-and-forth between politics and historiography.[9] Certainly, I did abstain from treating extensively either of the two big conjunctures concerned, the post-war capitalist boom and

---

    7   Eley, *Crooked Line*, 156. Another of my relative neglects was the degree of epistemological indebtedness of the 1980s departures 'to the reception of structuralist semiotics from France in the early 1970s and the extension of Saussurean and post-Saussurean semiotic models into historical and sociological analysis'. See Manu Goswami, 'Remembering the Future', *American Historical Review* 113: 2 (2008), 419. Encountering a severely structuralist Marxism on arriving in Cambridge in January 1975, as it happens, I committed many hours of dogged self-education to semiotics. In describing what it meant to 'think like a Marxist', I gestured towards that extraordinarily intense initiation, but, in the interests of economy, left much of the detail out. Eley, *Crooked Line*, 18.
    8   William H. Sewell Jr, 'Crooked Lines', *American Historical Review* 113: 2 (2008), 410.
    9   'The dispiriting political experiences associated with the crisis of a class-centered socialist tradition from the late 1970s, under the combined effects of capitalist restructuring, deindustrialization, class recomposition, and right-wing political assaults . . . profoundly shaped how I'm able to think about the kinds of history I do. [T]he cultural turn was appealing because its implications translated across these different sites – not only my teaching and writing, but also my political knowledge and social understanding, including the everyday settings of personal life' (Eley, *Crooked Line*, 187).

the post-Fordist transition that followed. That was deliberate. I wanted to model a different way of writing the intellectual history of the present by examining the three-way reciprocities between the historiographical (or more broadly intellectual), the political, and the personal. If contemporary transformations of capitalism were explicitly coded into my understanding of what the category of the political entailed, then, for the purposes of that particular book, I consciously abstained from the detailed sociology of knowledge Sewell wished I had supplied. Undertaking the careful and elaborate analysis needed to refer 'the epistemic practices of historians' convincingly to the post-Fordist 'transformation of the social forms of world capitalism' would surely have exceeded my bounds.[10] My own discussion occurred elsewhere, partly in my history of the Left in Europe, but especially in the book I authored with Keith Nield, *The Future of Class in History*, conceived as a companion to *A Crooked Line* and directly addressing the relationship between historiography and the real worlds of capitalism.[11]

Beyond those practical constraints, there was a principle involved too. By calling the prevailing Marxist idiom of 'base and superstructure' into question, Raymond Williams and other thinkers of the later 1960s had begun a decades-long wrestling with problems of materialist explanation that supplied the red thread for my own treatment of the relationship between 'the social' and 'the cultural'. In light of the heavily diminished confidence in social analysis, and the resulting anti-reductionist reticence, the very possibility of explaining extremely particular changes of academic life in terms of 'the changing macrosocial forms and fortunes of world capitalism' has become far more difficult to accomplish, or even imagine.[12] In the abstract, Sewell's postulates may certainly suggest plausible analytical projects. There might

---

10   Sewell, 'Crooked Lines', 401. The desirability of such analysis was nonetheless clear: 'That crisis of "class-political understanding" bespoke an actually occurring sociopolitical transition of genuinely epochal dimensions. [T]ogether with the larger political and theoretical rethinking it connoted, the cultural turn represented a necessary struggling with contemporary problems, for which the loyal reaffirming of classical materialist positions afforded little help.' See Eley, *Crooked Line*, 277, n. 6.

11   Sewell's 'macrosocial' analytic is vital for many purposes, but not for what *Crooked Line* wanted to do. See Geoff Eley, *Forging Democracy: The History of the Left in Europe, 1850–2000* (New York: Oxford University Press, 2002), 337–490, and Geoff Eley and Keith Nield, *The Future of Class in History: What's Left of the Social?* (Ann Arbor, MI: University of Michigan Press, 2007).

12   Sewell, 'Crooked Lines', 400.

well be 'a certain elective affinity' between the 'general epistemic uncertainty' observable 'all across the human sciences' in the late twentieth century, and the 'heightened "flexibility" that is one of the hallmarks of the new global economic order'. The earlier but now 'reified categories of the previous intellectual era' may also have aligned with a preceding Fordist regime of regulation. Carefully done, such a sociology of knowledge under the sign of the post-Fordist transition is one I can also find appealing. *Crooked Line* gestures several times in that direction.[13] But arguments about 'the condition of postmodernity' or the 'cultural logic of late capitalism' work best at a certain level of theorized generality.[14] The language of 'homologies', 'affinities', and 'correspondences' brings us only so far. To show an explanatory relationship between changes in the material worlds of capitalism and the shifting interests of an academic discipline, the changing paradigms in a field of knowledge, and radical departures in the intellectual practices of historians, something more will be needed. The aggregation of developments that coalesced into what we call the cultural turn occurred in extraordinarily disparate ways, field by field and institution by institution, with widely varying local histories, and according to very complicated temporalities. To capture those complexities, a particular method of detailed reconstruction would be needed.

Much depends, therefore, on how Sewell's 'macrosocial' perspective (his 'deeper social causes') can be shown to have translated into forms of action or patterns of thought on the ground, whether among intellectuals working in universities or for other social categories of actors.[15] Sewell

---

13   Eley, *Crooked Line*, 151–2, 188–9, 96–7. For Sewell's more detailed explication, see his 'The Political Unconscious of Social and Cultural History, or, Confessions of a Former Quantitative Historian', in *Logics of History: Social Theory and Social Transformation* (Chicago: University of Chicago Press, 2005). See also the following essays by George Steinmetz: 'Scientific Authority and the Transition to Post-Fordism: The Plausibility of Positivism in US Sociology since 1945', in *The Politics of Method in the Human Sciences: Positivism and Its Epistemological Others* (Durham, NC: Duke University Press, 2005); 'The Epistemological Unconscious of US Sociology and the Transition to Post-Fordism: The Case of Historical Sociology', in *Remaking Modernity: Politics, History, and Sociology*, ed. Julia Adams, Elisabeth S. Clemens, and Ann Shola Orloff (Durham, NC: Duke University Press, 2005); 'Regulation Theory, Post-Marxism, and the New Social Movements', *Comparative Studies in Society and History* 36 (1994).

14   See David Harvey, *The Condition of Postmodernity* (Oxford: Basil Blackwell, 1989); Fredric Jameson, *Postmodernism, or, The Cultural Logic of Late Capitalism* (Durham: Duke University Press, 1991).

15   Sewell, 'Crooked Lines', 399.

linked the rise of social history in the 1960s to the post-1945 prevalence in the West of 'so-called "Fordist" or state-centered capitalism'. As he put it, 'the epistemological optimism of social history – its faith in the possibility of reconstructing a history of the social totality – was made plausible in large part by the specific form of capitalist development that characterized the great worldwide postwar capitalist boom'.[16] But the causal links from one to the other – from Fordist economics to new kinds of historical thinking – are rarely direct or straightforward. If 'the "structure of experience" generated by postwar capitalism underwrote the plausibility of social history, whether in its Marxist, Annaliste, or social-scientific form', then the primary impulse was less the distinctive patterns of Fordist accumulation per se, however directly they enabled the expansion of universities. Rather, the intelligibility of social history as a knowledge formation, as well as its intellectual appeal linked to wider sociopolitical aspirations, came far more from the *political* climate – from the legacies of 1945 and the distinctive public culture of the long post-war, including the emancipating possibilities of upward mobility and a broadly egalitarian ethic of social improvement. That is, between the shifting configurations of the 'endless accumulation of capital' and their resonance for politics, culture, and ideas, a great deal of mediation and articulation had to occur – whether for the assembling of organized agency inside the polity, or the appeal of social history to particular generations of students in universities.

Why 'class' and the 'endless accumulation of capital' need setting *against* each other, making one the more fundamental category of analysis over the other, remains unclear. In this macrosocial explanatory ambition to relate changes in the ideas of historians to an underlying logic of capitalism, moreover, there is a hint of that old 'final instance' syndrome of structural causality. But ideas usually change in response to other ideas, or at least to the institutional cultural and political forms through which they are rendered. Thus, to the political and cultural legacies of 1945, as Sewell indeed acknowledges, were linked extraordinarily resilient traditions of class-centred collectivist politics, whose cohesion and purchase began falling apart after the 1960s under the impact of what we would each call the post-Fordist transition. I am not sure how Sewell would conceptualize the possibilities for politics other

---

16   Ibid.

than through the forms of collective agency, for which the concept of class remains a helpful theoretical category. Emphasizing the importance of class requires no diminution of the 'endless accumulation of capital' and its shifting 'configurations of political power, spatial relations, class struggles, intellectual forms, technology, and systems of economic regulation'.[17] Both grounds are surely essential to any analysis on the societal scale: not only the reconfigurations of capitalism as Sewell presents them, but also the bases of organized action and collective agency inside society, for which the changing dynamics of class formation remain one key place to begin. Grasping the ways in which class is now being remade will be vital to understanding capitalism's latest social imaginary.[18]

'Between social history and cultural history', I urged in *A Crooked Line*, 'there is really no need to choose'.[19] That insistence had two purposes: it was strategic, in that I argued for the possibility of fruitful conversation across sometimes irreducible yet mutually respectful differences; but it was more specifically historiographical, marking the growing success of historical work that transcended earlier demarcations and sub-specialisms. 'New hybridities' was my term for the resulting forms.[20] Neither Sewell nor Spiegel liked this stance. They saw it as a lack of clarity, a 'weak' or poorly developed grasp of theory, and a lack of ambition, a recidivism – the practising historian's bad old habits of trusting the virtues of imaginative empirical work and simply 'muddling through'. For Sewell, the choice was clear after all: facing up to theoretical difficulties *versus* avoiding them; doing the hard work of theory *versus* merely striking an attitude; taking theory seriously *versus* 'set[ting] theory aside and get[ting] on with a wide range of interesting empirical work'.[21]

But the alternatives are not 'theory' *versus* 'no theory', I have to insist. My conclusion may not lay out a fully elaborated theoretical perspective

---

17   Ibid., 404.

18   This is the argument in Eley and Nield, *Future of Class in History*, esp. 139–201.

19   Eley, *Crooked Line*, 181.

20   Ibid., 201. Whereas I took pleasure in the growing redundancy of traditional divisions between discrete regions of study (like social history and cultural history), Sewell took me to be describing 'hybridity' as the decisive characteristic of the 'new cultural history'. But what I actually wrote was that, by the 1990s, many former social historians 'now moved increasingly freely across the old distinctions between the social, the cultural, the political, the intellectual, and so forth, allowing new hybridities to form'. See Sewell, 'Crooked Lines', 403.

21   Sewell, 'Crooked Lines', 403.

of the kind Sewell wants to see, and which the final chapter of his own recent book supplies so impressively. But, within the many particularities of its discussions, *A Crooked Line* is nonetheless saturated with theory. My decision not to pull this together programmatically at the end of the book as a clarion call for the future was a deliberate one. Partly, I wanted not to overburden the text; partly, I wanted to observe my conciliationist purpose, as mentioned above – the desire, that is, to abstain from insisting on the superior virtues of 'one authorizing form of theory against another'. I certainly have my own preferences, which so far from being weakly developed are laid out pretty clearly in my book. But I do also think, as a matter of principle, that no one set of theories and methodologies can serve as an answer to each and every question historians are now trying to ask.

I called here for a 'basic pluralism'. This was not a wishy-washy eclecticism and fudging of theoretical debates. I argued, rather, that there are different ways of seeing the world, none sufficient alone for every possible analytical or interpretive purpose. There are biographical dimensions here too, involving contingencies of origin, generation, schooling, cultural formation, political conjuncture, and so forth. We each enter the stream or get on the train at different points along the way, with different destinations in mind (or different imaginings of what the destination might be), having missed earlier stretches of the journey which for others were the really formative part. Spiegel's explication of the phenomenological backstory to the structuralist Marxist departures of the 1960s and 1970s (when my own self jumped on the train) described one such itinerary. So too did her very acute characterization of current commentaries on the cultural turn's insufficiencies. Yet her actor-centred perspective and neo-phenomenological approach seem best fitted for her own preferred kind of history – mainly intellectual and cultural, less concerned with state formation, social movements, collective action, and other areas where different approaches might be deployed. Her proposal offered far less help for Sewell's macrosocial problematic or for satisfying Manu Goswami's interest in comparative capitalism. But we each have our own likings; and for various kinds of questions, different kinds of theory are called for.[22] Who is to say, really,

---

22 Those preferences can make us impatient with how others do their work. It is simply not the case that either an 'empirically grounded social history' or an acknowledgment of the

that one tradition is 'better' than another? Frankfurt School as opposed to post-Althusserian Marxism? Gramsci as opposed to phenomenology? Habermas rather than Foucault? I have my own very strong preferences for certain kinds of theory over others, relative to the questions I want to ask. But if some of my colleagues hold equally coherent but differing views for other types of questions, this ought not to impede all collaboration. Those are the terms of my plea: mutually respectful coexistence, building of coalitions, reasoned intellectual exchange.

Spiegel was right to wonder whether methodological and epistemological pluralism can be 'a genuinely theoretical position'.[23] But in proposing it I was not ducking the hard choices. Nor was I trying to give everyone their own thing. 'Basic pluralism' meant the politics of collaboration through respect for differences – differences of theoretical outlook, differences of epistemology, differences of intellectual biography, differences of project. However rigorously we explicate our positions, those differences will always remain. Colleagues may pursue modes of inquiry using methodological approaches and theoretical frameworks we find profoundly wrongheaded, theoretically antithetical, or epistemologically flawed. But that does not preclude fruitful conversation. We can still form collaborations at a variety of institutional and intellectual levels. We can still find common enemies. Nor does that absolve us from being clear and consistent in the standpoints we prefer.[24] Martin Jay expresses this principle with characteristic generosity:

> Any given analysis, if it is sincerely pursued, produces the necessity of its alternatives. Every particular approach, whether it is hermeneutic or theoretical or narrative or experiential, will be ultimately inadequate. You will reach a point where it will fail to do justice to the complexity of the phenomena. What is really required is a nimble way to move from one mode of analysis to another without expecting them to necessarily cohere in a definitive way. In this sense, the image of a force-field or constellation, which I've always found so useful in my

importance of structures 'implicitly reverts to that "noble dream" of an objective basis for historical investigation'. See Spiegel, 'Comment on *A Crooked Line*', 413.

23   Ibid.

24   And it implies no aversion to conflict, no blanket opposition to polemical exchange, no shying away from genuine differences when they appear. These are limits to possible collaborations too.

work, captures the inexhaustible variety of our interface with the world better than any single unified approach.[25]

Goswami rightly criticizes the new cultural history's reticence about 'future-oriented' thinking – its seeming reluctance to replicate social history's earlier commitment to a vision of social transformation that could both frame the effort to appropriate the past and encourage 'the prospect of a radically other future'. Such a vision would need to contain 'the potential of mediating between the past and the present, the actual and the possible'.[26] If my own discussion emphasized more the 'space of experience', Goswami rightly affirms the 'horizon of expectation' too. And here she detects a quietude: cultural historians seem uninterested in shaping their projects according to any radically transformative image of a future that lies anywhere beyond the current hegemonies of a permanently unfolding neoliberal present.[27] Much of that critique seems justified. 'The organizing premises of cultural history', which Goswami lists as 'contingency, episodic ruptures unmoored in immanent social contradictions, undecidability, difference, fragmentation', can encourage a backing away from 'whole society' analysis. This tendency expressed not just a pragmatics of adjustment, but often a conscious choice in times of terrible defeat and disappointment, when the palpable exhaustion of large-scale projects of remaking the social world seemed to make small-scale reconstructions the only viable ethical course.[28] In this sense, social history and cultural history sustained highly distinct forms of political subjectivity.

This returns me to my starting point: if I stay optimistic about reactivating certain kinds of conversation beyond the divisiveness of earlier historiographical differences, then my sense of continuing political endangerment also retains its urgency – that sense of no longer knowing

---

25   Douglas J. Goodman, 'Dream Kitsch and the Debris of History: An Interview with Martin Jay', *Journal of Consumer Culture* 3 (2003), 119.

26   Goswami, 'Remembering the Future', 420.

27   See Reinhart Koselleck, '"Space of Experience" and "Horizon of Expectation": Two Historical Categories', in *Futures Past: On the Semantics of Historical Time*, trans. Keith Tribe (Cambridge, MA: MIT, 1985) – originally published as *Vergangene Zukunft. Zur Semantik geschichtlicher Zeiten* (Frankfurt: Suhrkamp, 1979); David Scott, *Conscripts of Modernity: The Tragedy of Colonial Enlightenment* (Durham, NC: Duke University Press, 2004), 23–57.

28   The turning away from 'whole society' analysis during the 1980s characterized above all historians working in and on the European and North American West, as opposed to many of those writing from 'an extra-European vantage-point'. See Eley, *Crooked Line*, 197.

where the grounds of any future-oriented optimism about the directions of change in the actually existing worlds of capitalism might yet be found. Writing the intellectual history of the present has to involve not only a degree of political self-consciousness, but also a willingness to explore the material or structural conditions of possibility that helped sustain the generalized turning to cultural history across so many different fields during the late twentieth century. However mediated and complex, 'only a framework attuned to the dynamic interchange between social transformations and categories of perception' can help ground the accomplishments of cultural history in the most generative of ways.[29] Yet it is only now – and precisely because the cultural turn has been accomplished – that we can begin to bring these broader contextual fields into focus: those 'new histories of society' I called for at the end of my book, or those 'forms of historical totalization' which Goswami describes cultural historians as having first needed to reject.[30] If we write our own histories, it might be said, then we do so with theoretical approaches, types of methodology, and general historiographical supports not always of our own choosing. We only set ourselves the questions we know can be answered.

Nonetheless, I disagree that cultural historians as a body 'either overtly celebrate or uncritically reflect the absence of a systemic alternative to the predominant social and cultural forms of the present'. Even if the cultural turn sometimes impedes new histories of society, to call this 'the corral of culturalism' takes the polemic too far.[31] The nuances are important. I intended neither a 'celebration of contemporary cultural history' nor its blanket 'endorsement'.[32] But nor do I see the terrain left by the cultural turn as merely a 'shapeless bazaar' where younger historians are simply 'muddling through'.[33] As my book set out to argue, the turning *away* from Marxisms, materialisms, and macro-historical ambitions registered a real crisis in those given forms of understanding, just as the turning *towards* culturalisms of various kinds enabled some real gains and solutions. If I say that social history 'simply isn't available

---

29   Goswami, 'Remembering the Future', 422.
30   Ibid. See Geoff Eley, 'Historicizing the Global, Politicizing Capital: Giving the Present a Name', *History Workshop Journal* 63 (2007).
31   Goswami, 'Remembering the Future', 424.
32   Ibid., 418, 420.
33   Sewell, 'Crooked Lines', 403. That remark does younger historians a serious injustice.

anymore', I am referring to social history 'in the form of the original project'. Obviously, there are forms of recuperable social analysis.[34] Divested of earlier expectations, while taking on board all we can learn through the cultural turn, new histories of the social will certainly be written. But, likewise, if I uphold the gains that cultural history enabled, in the ways I used Carolyn Steedman's work to exemplify, that does not mean I believe everything about it can be 'uncritically' accepted. Let us sit down together and think about the various ways, some large and some small, in which these differing projects might be joined. For the sake of *that* conversation, we should precisely not be required to choose.

---

34 See Eley, *Crooked Line*, 189, where I spell out the terms of that original project: 'Its coherence derived from the sovereignty of social determinations within a self-confident materialist paradigm of social totality, grounded in the primacy of class.'

PART II
Rethinking the Political

4

Nations, Publics, and Political Cultures: Placing Habermas in the Nineteenth Century

By 'the public sphere' we mean first of all a realm of our social life in which something approaching public opinion can be formed. Access is guaranteed to all citizens. A portion of the public sphere comes into being in every conversation in which private individuals assemble to form a public body. They then behave neither like business or professional people transacting private affairs, nor like members of a constitutional order subject to the legal constraints of a state bureaucracy. Citizens behave as a public body when they confer in an unrestricted fashion – that is, with the guarantee of freedom of assembly and association and the freedom to express and publish their opinions about matters of general interest. In a large public body this kind of communication requires specific means for transmitting information and influencing those who receive it. Today newspapers and magazines, radio and TV are the media of the public sphere. We speak of the political public sphere in contrast, for instance, to the literary one, when public discussion deals with objects connected to the activity of the state. Although state activity is so to speak the executor, it is not a part of it . . . Only when the exercise of political control is effectively subordinated to the democratic demand that information be accessible to the public, does the political public sphere win an institutionalized influence over the government through the instrument of law-making bodies.[1]

The public sphere, for Habermas, is a normative ideal forever unattained. History provides only partial realizations, whether at the inception, when the participant public meant only the bourgeoisie, or with later transformations, when this 'bourgeois ideal' of informed and rational communication receded still further from universal completion. In *Strukturwandel der Öffentlichkeit*, Habermas unfolds an immanent critique, tasking the liberal ideal of the reasoning public with the actuality of its own particularism and long-term disempowerment. He wrote in the late 1950s from a declensionist pessimism, 'etching an unforgettable portrait of a degraded public life, in which the substance of liberal democracy is voided in a combination of plebiscitary manipulation and privatized apathy, as any collectivity of citizenry disintegrates'.[2] But his book was not just a story of decay. It carefully explored a distinct historical moment through which certain possibilities for human emancipation were unlocked. Ordered for Habermas around the 'central idea of communicatively generated rationality', these became the leitmotif for his own life's work.[3]

In a nutshell, the public sphere means 'a sphere which mediates between society and state, in which the public organizes itself as the bearer of public opinion'. Its growth began in the later eighteenth century with the widening of political participation and the crystallizing of citizenship ideals. It eventuated from the struggle against absolutism (in Britain from the securing of constitutional monarchy), which turned arbitrary rule into rational authority, beneath the scrutiny of citizens organized into a public body under the law. It was joined to representative government and a liberal constitution, along with basic civil freedoms

---

1   Jürgen Habermas, 'The Public Sphere', *New German Critique* 3 (1974), 49. Habermas originally developed his argument in *Strukturwandel der Öffentlichkeit* (Neuwied: Hermann Luchterhand, 1962), which was translated as *The Structural Transformation of the Public Sphere: An Inquiry into a Category of Bourgeois Society*, trans. Thomas Burger (Cambridge: MIT, 1991).

2   Perry Anderson and Peter Dews, in their interview with Habermas, 'A Philosophico-Political Profile', in *Autonomy and Solidarity: Interviews with Jürgen Habermas*, ed. Peter Dews (London: Verso, 1986), 178.

3   Rick Roderick, *Habermas and the Foundations of Critical Theory* (Basingstoke: Macmillan, 1986), 43.

before the law (speech, press, assembly, association, no arrest without trial).

But Habermas was less interested in this more familiar process of state-centred governance and overtly political change. For the public sphere presumed prior changes in social relations, their condensing into new institutional arrangements, and the generating of new social, cultural, and political discourse around this changing environment. Conscious and programmatic *political* impulses formed most strongly where such underlying processes were reshaping social communication. The public sphere presupposed this larger accumulation of sociocultural change. It was linked to the growth of urban culture, both metropolitan and provincial, as the novel arena of a locally organized public life (meeting houses, concert halls, theatres, opera houses, lecture halls, museums); to a new infrastructure of social exchange (press, publishing companies, other literary media); to the rise of a reading public (language societies, subscription publishing, lending libraries); to improved transportation; and to adapted centres of sociability (coffeehouses, taverns, clubs). It bespoke a new universe of association.

More effect than cause, the conscious actions of reformers were only partially responsible. The public sphere derived rather from longer-term societal transformations located by Habermas between the late Middle Ages and the eighteenth century: namely, a trade-driven transition from feudalism to capitalism, powered by capital accumulation from long-distance commerce and the steerage of early modern mercantilism. As a category of social life, 'the public' was the unintended consequence of underlying socioeconomic change. It crystallized from the aspirations of a self-consciously successful bourgeoisie, whose economic functions and social standing implied an accruing agenda of desirable innovation. Habermas sees a causal homology of culture and economics in this sense, growing from 'the traffic in commodities and news created by early capitalist long-distance trade'.[4]

On the one hand, commercialization undermined the earlier household-based economy, reoriented productive activity 'toward a commodity market that had expanded under public direction and supervision', and reconstituted state–society relations through a new distinction between private and public. On the other hand, the flow of international news

---

4   Habermas, *Structural Transformation of the Public Sphere*, 15.

attending the trading networks brought a new category of public knowledge and information, particularly during the seventeenth-century
wars and intensified rivalry between 'nations' in the mercantilist sense,
creating a new medium of formal exchange and the press. This model of
change, where both new cultural possibilities and new political forms
emerge from an accumulating structural transformation, can be extended
to industrialization too. Nineteenth-century growth of local government
owed much to an improvised grappling with the immense challenges of
an urbanizing society, from poverty, housing, and policing, through
lighting, transportation, and sewage, to commercial licensing and
revenue creation. Indeed, the local state was even *constituted* by the
practical associational initiatives of a citizenry-in-the-making – not as
the strategic outcome of any coherent design, but as the unintended,
rolling effect of structurally invited interventions.

Habermas is interested less in these realized political dimensions of
the public sphere than in abstracting a strong ideal for gauging its subsequent forms. Ever the ambivalent Frankfurt School legatee, he resumed
the critique of mass culture in the wake of the Christian Democratic state
and the post-war boom, while upholding a progressivist Enlightenment
ideal. The urgency of this standpoint, with its sense of a compromised,
uncompleted modernity, shaped the book's motivating problematic.
Habermas affirmed the critique of the present (consciousness industry,
commodification of culture, manipulation and manipulability of the
masses), while specifically retrieving the past (Enlightenment as founding moment of modernity). His conception of the public sphere had an
avowedly double function. In Peter Hohendahl's words, 'It provides a
paradigm for analyzing historical change, while also serving as a normative category for political critique.'[5] Moreover, while Habermas sees the
public sphere as crucial to politics in any full democratic sense (as the
enlargement of human emancipation), it remains anterior to politics of
the parliamentary or institutional kind. Parliamentary defence of liberty
mattered less than the larger grounds of rational and unrestricted discourse it presupposed. 'Publicness' began from reading, thought, and
discussion, from reasonable exchange among equals. It resided in acts of
speech and circuits of exchange:

---

5   Peter Uwe Hohendahl, 'Critical Theory, Public Sphere, and Culture: Jürgen Habermas
and His Critics', *New German Critique* 16 (1979), 92.

> The truly free market is that of cultural discourse itself, within, of course, certain normative regulations . . . What is said derives its legitimacy neither from itself as message nor from the social title of the utterer, but from its conformity as a statement with a certain paradigm of reason inscribed in the very event of saying.[6]

How far Habermas saw his ideal of rational communication, predicated on free and equal participation, actually realized by classical liberalism is unclear. Sometimes, he concedes its class- and property-bound limitations, but not to the point of compromising his basic claim. However, the public sphere's 'structural transformation' then brought a narrowing over the longer term that forms the starting point for his book. From the late nineteenth century, the growing contradictions of a capitalist society – the passage of competitive into monopoly or organized capitalism, the regulation of social conflicts by the state, the rational public's fragmentation into an arena of competing interests – eroded the independence of public opinion and the legitimacy of its institutions. In the cultural sphere proper, from the arts to the press and mass entertainment, the logics of commercialization and rationalization increasingly target the individual consumer, while eliminating the mediatory roles of reception and rational discussion. The public sphere's classic bases disappear: a clear distinction between public good and private interest; the principled demarcation of state and society; a participant citizenry, free of domination, defining public policy and its terms through reasoned exchange. Relations between state and society are reordered, to the advantage of the former and the detriment of a 'free' political life.

Remarkably, given Habermas's wider impact during the 1970s and 1980s, the public-sphere argument drew little interest in the English-speaking world until the book was finally translated in 1989.[7] In what

---

6 Terry Eagleton, *The Function of Criticism: From the Spectator to Poststructuralism* (London: Verso, 1984), 15.

7 For the subsequent reception, see Chapter 5 below. *Strukturwandel* was strikingly absent from English-language commentaries on Habermas's work: Thomas McCarthy, *The Critical Theory of Jürgen Habermas* (Cambridge: MIT Press, 1978); David Held, *Introduction to Critical Theory* (Berkeley: University of California Press, 1980); Roderick, *Habermas and the Foundations of Critical Theory*; Anthony Giddens, 'Jürgen Habermas', in *The Return of Grand Theory in the Human Sciences*, ed. Quentin Skinner (Cambridge: Cambridge University Press, 1985); John B. Thompson and David Held, eds, *Habermas: Critical Debates* (Cambridge: MIT Press, 1982). Though avowedly inspired by Habermas's idea, John Keane, *Public Sphere and Late Capitalism: Toward a Socialist Theory of Democracy* (Cambridge:

follows I will consider Habermas's argument against a corpus of intervening historiography, including: (1) a range of literatures confirming
the fruitfulness of the concept of the public sphere per se; (2) treatments
of gender and the impact of women's history and feminist theory; (3)
studies of the state and politics in the strict sense; and (4) treatments of
popular culture.

The Findings of Social History

Habermas's approach has been strikingly confirmed by social histories
across a wide variety of fields. Indeed, his claims have proved remarkably well grounded, given the thinness of historiography available at the
time. Bearing a notable affinity with Raymond Williams in his freshly
published *Culture and Society, 1780–1950* (1958), Habermas had built
from similar definitional foundations by tracking shifts in the connotations for 'public' in English, German, and French between the late
seventeenth and late eighteenth centuries.[8] The very method of moving
from the 'world of letters' to the structure of society mirrored Williams's
purposes. In charting the public sphere's degenerative transformation,
Habermas also anticipated *The Long Revolution* (1961) and *Communications* (1962), where Williams examined the long-term diminishing of
popular access and control in the cultural realm.[9] At the same time,
Williams's later work on mass media always stressed the democratic
potentials of new communications technologies. His view of film, radio,
TV, popular fiction, and popular music departed markedly from the

---

Cambridge University Press, 1984) omitted any direct treatment or contextual discussion, as
did Keane's *Democracy and Civil Society: On the Predicaments of European Socialism, the
Prospects for Democracy, and the Problem of Controlling Social and Political Power* (London:
Verso, 1988), and his companion anthology, *Civil Society and the State: New European
Perspectives* (London: Verso, 1988). Hohendahl's *Institution of Criticism* (Ithaca, NY: Cornell
University Press, 1982) was a vital exception (see also note 4, above), as was Joan B. Landes,
Women and the Public Sphere in the Age of the French Revolution (Ithaca, NY: Cornell Univer-
sity Press, 1988). See also Richard Sennett, *The Fall of Public Man: On the Social Psychology of
Capitalism* (New York: W.W. Norton, 1976).

    8   Habermas, *Structural Transformation of the Public Sphere*, 1–26.

    9   See ibid., Chapter 18: 'From a Culture-Debating Public to a Culture-Consuming
Public', and Chapter 20: 'From the Journalism of Private Men of Letters to the Public
Consumer Services of the Mass Media', 159–74, 181–95. See also Raymond Williams, *Culture
and Society, 1780–1950* (London: Chatto & Windus, 1958), *The Long Revolution* (London:
Chatto & Windus, 1961), and *Communications* (Harmondsworth: Penguin, 1962).

Frankfurt School's critique of mass culture, popular taste, and commodity fetishism.[10] Interestingly, Williams had no entry for 'public' in his *Keywords* (1976).[11]

A variety of major historiographies provide especially strong evidence for the Habermasian approach:

- an abundance of eighteenth-century British social history that confirms and elaborates the framework without explicitly citing Habermas himself;[12]
- studies of nineteenth-century British popular liberalism, including the politics and moral campaigning of provincial Dissent;[13]
- social histories of German liberalism from Enlightenment to unification;[14]

10   See especially Raymond Williams, *Television: Technology and Cultural Form* (London: Fontana, 1974), and 'Culture and Technology', in *The Year 2000* (New York: Pantheon, 1983).

11   The entry for 'Private' ignores the public/private distinction. See Raymond Williams, *A Vocabulary of Culture and Society*, 2nd edn (New York: Oxford University Press, 1983), 242–3.

12   See esp. J. H. Plumb, 'The Public, Literature, and the Arts in the Eighteenth Century', in *The Emergence of Leisure*, ed. Michael Robert Marrus (New York: Harper & Row, 1974); Neil McKendrick, John Brewer, and J. H. Plumb, *The Birth of a Consumer Society: The Commercialization of Eighteenth-Century England* (Bloomington, IN: Indiana University Press, 1982); Peter Borsay, 'The English Urban Renaissance: The Development of Provincial Urban Culture, c. 1680–c. 1760', *Social History* 5: 2 (1977), Angus McInnes, 'The Emergence of a Leisure Town: Shrewsbury 1660–1760', *Past and Present* 120 (1988); John Brewer, *Party Ideology and Popular Politics at the Accession of George III*, (Cambridge: Cambridge University Press, 1976;); Linda Colley, 'Whose Nation? Class and National Consciousness in Britain 1750–1830', *Past and Present* 113 (1986); John Money, *Experience and Identity: Birmingham and the West Midlands 1760–1800* (Montreal: McGill-Queen's University Press, 1977); Nicholas Rogers, 'The Urban Opposition to Whig Oligarchy, 1720–1760', in *The Origins of Anglo-American Radicalism*, ed. Margaret C. Jacob and James R. Jacob (London: Allen & Unwin, 1984).

13   Classically in John Vincent, *The Formation of the British Liberal Party 1957–68* (Harmondsworth: Penguin, 1972). See also Patricia Hollis, ed., *Pressure from Without in Early Victorian England* (London: Edward Arnold, 1974); Eileen Yeo and Stephen Yeo, eds, *Popular Culture and Class Conflict 1590–1914: Explorations in the History of Labour and Leisure* (Brighton: Harvester, 1981). Emblematic monographs include Stephen Yeo, *Religion and Voluntary Associations in Crisis* (London: Croom Helm, 1976); Paul McHugh, *Prostitution and Victorian Social Reform* (London: Croom Helm, 1980).

14   See, for example, Franklin Kopitzsch, 'Die Aufklärung in Deutschland: Zu ihren Leistungen, Grenzen und Wirkungen', *Archiv fur Sozialgeschichte* 23 (1983); Otto Dann, ed., *Lesegesellschaften und bürgerliche Emanzipation: Ein europäischer Vergleich* (Munich: Beck, 1981); Thomas Nipperdey, 'Verein als soziale Struktur in Deutschland im späten 18. und frühen 19. Jahrhundert', in his *Gesellschaft, Kultur, Theorie: Gesammelte Aufsätze zur Neueren Geschichte* (Göttingen: Vandenhoeck & Ruprecht, 1976); Gert Zang, ed., *Provinzialisierung einer Region: Regionale Unterentwickiung and liberale Politik in der Stadt and im Kreis Konstanz im 19. Jahrhundert: Untersuchungen zur Entstehung der biügerlichen Gesellschaft in der Provinz* (Frankfurt: Syndikat, 1978); Geoff Eley, *Reshaping the German Right: Radical*

- disparate literatures on political socialization in peasant societies, stressing the passage of parochial identities into national
  political cultures;[15]
- historical sociology of communications, focused on the press
  and other media, the rise of a reading public, popular literacy,
  and mass communications.[16]

The last two of these literatures resonate especially strongly through
the scholarship on nation-making and nationalist movements. One
fundamental point of departure is Karl Deutsch's classic 1954 study of
nationalism and social communication, imaginatively adapted by Czech
historian Miroslav Hroch for his comparative treatment of the nineteenth-century emergence of smaller nationalities. In large parts of
southern and eastern Europe in the later nineteenth century (and in the
extra-European colonial world in the twentieth), the shaping of nationality (that is, the growth of a public for nationalist discourse) was
simultaneously the emergence of a public sphere. That codetermination
makes a large body of the literature on nationalism relevant to historical
uses of Habermas's idea.[17]

These historiographies share a focus on associational activity as the
main medium of public communications. If publicness presumed a
prior transformation of social relations, then voluntary association serves
as an indicator of social progress in Habermas's sense. The confluence of
older eighteenth-century associations (reading and literary societies,

---

Nationalism and Political Change after Bismarck, 2nd edn (Ann Arbor, MI: University of
Michigan Press, 1991 [1980]).

15   *Journal of Peasant Studies* remains the best general guide. For a particular region, see
Grant Evans, 'Sources of Peasant Consciousness in South-East Asia: A Survey', *Social History*
12: 2 (1987). French historiography is especially rich: Peter McPhee, 'Recent Writing on Rural
Society and Politics in France, 1789–1900', *Comparative Studies in Society and History* 30: 4
(1988); Edward Berenson, 'Politics and the French Peasantry: The Debate Continues', *Social
History* 12: 2 (1987); Ted Margadant, 'Tradition and Modernity in Rural France during the
Nineteenth Century', *Journal of Modern History* 56: 3 (1984).

16   James Curran, Michael Gurevitch, and Janet Woollacott, eds, *Mass Communication
and Society* (London: Edward Arnold, 1977); George Boyce, James Curran, and Pauline
Wingate, eds, *Newspaper History from the Seventeenth Century to the Present Day* (London:
Constable, 1978).

17   Miroslav Hroch, *Social Preconditions of National Revival in Europe: A Comparative
Analysis of the Social Composition of Patriotic Groups among the Smaller European Nations*
(Cambridge: Cambridge University Press, 1985) – a combined edition of two earlier books in
German (1968) and Czech (1971); Gale Stokes, 'The Social Origins of East European Politics',
East European Politics and Societies 1: 1 (1987).

patriotic clubs, political discussion circles, Freemasonry, other secret societies) with the nascent political ambitions and desire for social prestige of an emergent bourgeoisie produced a more evident push for social leadership and dominance. Throughout early-nineteenth-century Germany, the urban and small-town bourgeoisie crystallized their claims by way of an exclusive social club, under names like Harmony, Concordia, Resource, or Union. Such clubs supplied the matrix for convening a local elite. They acquired their own buildings, recruited only the sturdiest pillars of local society (a few dozen businessmen, merchants, lawyers, doctors, civil servants), admitted others only by careful election, and offered a reading room and other social facilities, while staging balls, concerts, banquets, and lectures. Natural venues for political conversation, they sponsored philanthropic, charitable, and recreational opportunities for residents at large. The Heilbronn Harmony in south-west Germany owned its own building with club-rooms, reading rooms, library, and the adjoining Shareholders' Garden. A fine web of informal activity radiated outwards into local society. Visible performance of civic standing was vital to moral authority in the town, whether by serving on charitable or philanthropic committees, improving public amenities, patronizing the arts, promoting education, organizing public festivals, or commemorating great events.[18]

This centrality of associational initiatives for civil society (*bürgerliche Gesellschaft*) in nineteenth-century Germany was intimated but not concretely elaborated in Habermas's text. Voluntary association was the medium of civic emancipation and bourgeois self-affirmation. By form and intent, the practice of association abjured older principles of corporate recognition, with their ascriptive protocols of hereditary and legal estate. The new principle of association promised instead an independent *public* space where opinion could be expressed and taste formed, beyond the status prescriptions of absolutist monarchy. Sociologically, associationism reflected the growing density of social, personal, and family ties among the educated and propertied bourgeoisie (*Bildung und Besitz*). It described a public arena where bourgeois precedence could naturally run. It was the constitutive form of a new force for cultural and political change: the societal prestige and self-consciously

---

18 See Eley, *Reshaping the German Right*, 32–6, 150–5. For Heilbronn, see Theodor Heuss, *Preludes to Life: Early Memoirs* (London: Deutsch, 1955), 34–5.

civilized values of a bourgeoisie imagining itself as a general or universal class. Voluntary association was the primary setting of bourgeois aspirations to the exercise of general leadership in nineteenth-century society. It was here that the underlying principles of bourgeois life – economic, social, moral – were publicly acted out and consciously institutionalized into an ideal to be emulated, especially by the petty bourgeoisie and working class, the natural objects of philanthropy and cultural edification.[19]

In British historiography, this interconnectedness between bourgeois-driven societal progress and liberal political success emerges especially clearly. For many years during the 1960s and early 1970s, J. H. Plumb remained one of the few voices holding open such broader social analysis of eighteenth-century politics, as against the narrow interest-based conception of high politics that had come to dominate that field.[20] Over time, he carried this further by exploring the cultural changes enabling something like a free political life to materialize. Those contributions fall definitively inside the Habermasian framework, emphasizing the growth of a reading public, the commercialization of leisure, expanding educational provision, the transition from private to public entertainment, and the general spreading of such processes from the capital city into the provinces. Plumb demonstrated the gradual coherence of a self-conscious middle-class public, which wore its provincialism less as an embarrassment than as a proud assertion of creativity.[21]

Plumb inspired a much wider corpus, including above all John Brewer's study of politics in the 1760s, which emphasized not the self-sealing, interest-oriented, place-seeking solipsism of Westminster, but the extreme porousness of that parliamentary arena. In analysing the press, Brewer examined the entire institutional fabric of public debate,

---

19   See esp. David Blackbourn, 'The Discreet Charm of the Bourgeoisie: Reappraising German History in the Nineteenth Century', in David Blackbourn and Geoff Eley, *The Peculiarities of German History: Bourgeois Society and Politics in Nineteenth-Century Germany* (Oxford: Oxford University Press, 1984), and 'Politics as Theatre: Metaphors of the Stage in German History, 1848–1933', in *Populists and Patricians: Essays in Modern German History* (London: George Allen & Unwin, 1987). In its cultural dimensions, Blackbourn's is the classic Habermasian analysis.

20   See J. H. Plumb, *The Growth of Political Stability in England, 1675–1725* (London: Oxford University Press, 1967). For the principal inspiration behind that interest-based high-political model, see David W. Hayton, *Conservative Revolutionary: The Lives of Lewis Namier* (Manchester: Manchester University Press, 2019).

21   See Plumb's works cited in note 12, above.

including the nature of literacy, media of publication (newspapers, periodicals, pamphlets, squibs, handbills, songs), complexities of literary production (as in the seasonality and varied media of circulation), discrepancies between circulation and actual readership, the role of 'bridging' ('transmission of printed information in traditional oral forms', as in ballads), the social universe of coffeehouse and club, and the expanding infrastructure of postal and turnpike communications. He added a reading of the ritual and symbolic aspects of crowd behaviour during the Wilkite manifestations that deepened George Rudé's classic treatment of popular politics in the 1760s while stressing the nascency of its emergent forms. Brewer's 'alternative structure of politics' had major democratic and oppositional implications, particularly for the coming conjunctures of the 1780s and 1790s. How far this represented the emergence of the Habermasian public sphere – sociologically, organizationally, ideologically – remains moot. But a novel understanding of publicness and the 'public' was certainly in play.[22]

John Money's study of the West Midlands, likewise influenced by Plumb, makes a related contribution. Studying the transition from a rural to a mainly urban-industrial society, Money explored the cultural adaptations that absorbed much of the potential for social conflict in the new manufacturing centre of Birmingham. In this reading, Birmingham's social, economic, and political integration within the wider Warwickshire community was enhanced rather than fractured by urbanization between the 1760s and 1790s, enabling a new regional identity to form. This claim was grounded in a careful sociology of local notables – Birmingham merchants and manufacturers – who preserved their links with county landowners through projects like the Birmingham General Hospital and societies like the Bean Club and the masonic lodges, while defining a separate identity against London and other regions. This regional development hardly lacked tensions. Money gave much space both to religious disagreements and to the rise of a more popular radicalism. But neither the rivalries of Anglicans and Dissenters nor urgencies of reform and the challenge of Jacobinism could tear the fabric of regional community.[23]

---

22   See Brewer, *Party Ideology and Popular Politics*, and 'Commercialization and Politics', in McKendrick, Brewer, and Plumb, *Birth of a Consumer Society*; George Rudé, *Wilkes and Liberty: A Social Study of 1763 to 1774* (Oxford: Oxford University Press, 1962), and *The Crowd in History: A Study of Popular Disturbances in France and England, 1730–1848* (New York: Wiley, 1964).
23   See Money, *Experience and Identity*.

Money's book concretely dissected regional political culture. With Brewer, he shared intimate knowledge of the concrete details of public discourse – not just the press, but the public spectacle of music and stage, the associational milieu of 'taverns, coffee houses, and clubs', and the literary world of 'printing, publishing, and popular instruction'. He called this 'the means of communication and the creation of opinion'. The possibilities for a free political life, exactly a public sphere in Habermas's sense, flourished in this wider cultural domain, enabling a self-confident middle class to coalesce. The foundations were laid between the 1680s and 1760s in an 'English urban renaissance'. The growth of towns, new patterns of personal consumption, expanding demand for services, proliferating professions, expanding luxury trades, and commercialization of leisure all converged into a new culture of organized recreation, public display, improved amenities, and urban aesthetics.[24] But the political fruits came only later in the century, with commercialization and 'the birth of a consumer society'. The resulting differentiation brought the self-consciousness of a 'middling sort of bourgeoisie'. Comprising some 'million of the nation's nearly seven million' inhabitants, these 'men of moveable property, members of professions, tradesmen, and shopkeepers' strove for an independent space between the 'client economy' of the aristocracy and the dependence of the labouring poor.[25]

Money tracks this flourishing in very practical ways. The extension of formal culture to the provinces presumed public places where performances and concerts could be held: hence the assembly room built by private subscription, where 'society' could gather for balls, music, lectures, and theatre, in a 'transitional stage between private and fully public entertainment'.[26] Assemblies were sustained by associational action, reaching in Birmingham from Freemasons and other secret rings to the establishment Bean Club, exclusive intellectual circles like the Lunar Society, and sundry reading societies. From this came a wider cultural and political identity, for which the Birmingham General Hospital, built in 1765–79 by private subscription, became the seal. The hospital's triennial music festivals gathered the region's leading

---

24   See work by Borsay cited in note 12, above.
25   Brewer, 'Commercialization and Politics', 197.
26   Plumb, 'The Public, Literature, and the Arts', 32.

families, drawing their patronage and realizing the city's cultural ambitions.[27] New communication networks were equally important, easing not just exchange of ideas and information but institutional impetus for politics. Canal building hugely solidified the new regional and national identities. The elaborate repertoire of initiatives entailed in floating a canal scheme – creating new regional networks, cultivating public opinion, joining national parliamentary institutions, lobbying the private and public interests – led eventually to calls for rationally expediting the whole unwieldy process. Duplication of projects amid the anarchy of particularisms fuelled this urgency, increasingly justified by a larger 'national interest'. Parliament was called in 'as mediator between the public interest on the one hand and private property and enterprise on the other'.[28] Road building was eased by the invention of the turnpike trust. A short-lived response in 1785–87 to government fiscal measures that was indifferently successful outside the West Midlands and Manchester, the General Chamber of Manufacturers of Great Britain further solidified these regional networks, while pointing them towards national institutions, whether existing (parliament) or notional (a national market).

The formation of political cultures, in this sense, was integral to capitalist development. Emergent liberal values of the later eighteenth and early nineteenth centuries presupposed definite developmental processes of class formation and social growth: the transition from feudalism to capitalism in Habermasian notation, with concomitant coalescence of the bourgeoisie. For Brewer no less than Habermas, a particular ideological structure or cultural formation proved the complex, uneven effect of underlying socioeconomic transformation: liberalism, the ideal of emancipation grounded in rational communication, the Enlightenment discourse of freedom, on the one hand; the rise of capitalism, commercialization, and the birth of a consumer society, on the other. This whole process was mediated by the novel institutional

---

27 Here, see Borsay, 'English Urban Renaissance', 590–3, for the growth of towns as a new type of social centre and cement. He picks out four main instances: health resorts (Bath, Tunbridge, Scarborough, Buxton, Harrogate, Cheltenham); county towns and other administrative hubs (diocesan centres like Lichfield or other legal centres like Preston, Lancashire, for the Duchy Courts); 'travel towns' such as Stamford; and new industrial towns (Birmingham, Manchester, Liverpool, and Bristol). For a dissenting view, see McInnes, 'Emergence of a Leisure Town', which adds to Borsay's picture rather than supplanting it.

28 Money, *Experience and Identity*, 29.

complex of the public sphere.[29] In that way, Habermas showed how the genesis of the liberal tradition could be grounded in a particular social history. Treatments like Brewer's or Money's vividly concretize the argument.

What are the problems? Habermas stayed too strictly with the bourgeoisie. On grounds of its dominance, he specifically confined himself to 'the *liberal* model of the bourgeois public sphere', addressing neither 'the plebeian public sphere' of the Jacobin phase in the French Revolution, subsequently manifest in Chartism and continental labour movements, nor 'the plebiscitary-acclamatory form of regimented public sphere characterizing dictatorships in highly developed industrial societies' – namely, fascism.[30] The plebeian version was in any case 'suppressed in the historical process' while effectively tethered to 'the intentions of the bourgeois public sphere'. But this is far too restrictive. 'Publicness' was no emanation from the sociocultural dynamism of the bourgeoisie alone. It could originate beyond the transactions of a polite and literate middle class. Despite the latter's best efforts at asserting exclusive ownership, 'private people putting reason to use' was also happening elsewhere.[31]

1. The liberal faculty of reasoned exchange was successfully exercised by non-bourgeois subaltern groups, from the radical intelligentsia of Jacobinism and its successors to wide sections of the peasantry and working class. Whether in literary or political terms, from the production and diffusion of ideas to the adoption of constitutions and liberties under the law, plebeian voices aspired to the equivalent emancipatory language. Those positive values quickly acquired democratic resonance through the collective cultures of impressively inventive popular movements, which shaped their own variants of a public sphere. If sometimes

---

29 Habermas is silent on the grand question of causality, i.e., the specific mechanisms and relations between, on the one hand, longer-run societal development and, on the other hand, the growth of specific ideologies, traditions of thought, and cultural patterns, or between each of these and specific political events, whether on the global scale of the French Revolution or the smaller scale of local political conflicts. The bourgeoisie's collective agency is not addressed. For my own reflections, see Geoff Eley, 'In Search of the Bourgeois Revolution: The Particularities of German History', *Political Power and Social Theory* 7 (1988).

30 Habermas, *Structural Transformation of the Public Sphere*, xviii. Emphasis in original.

31 Ibid., xviii.

derivative (as Habermas assumed), they had their own dynamics of emergence and forms of interior life. The evidence is by now plentiful, whether for Owenism, Chartism, and British popular politics or for political sociability in the French countryside.[32] 'A child of the eighteenth century',[33] Chartism was bound to a dominant model, with its inherited languages of radicalism and political opposition, yet also formed in its own specificity.[34] Habermas's oppositions of 'educated/uneducated' and 'literate/ illiterate' simply do not work. His liberal public sphere was challenged in the very moment of its inception not only by a 'plebeian' public that was easily disabled and suppressed, but also by a more coherently radical one that was both combative and highly educated and literate.

2. Under the French Revolution's transnational impact, liberal ideals of publicness entered many regions in Europe ahead of the long-run social transformations that gave Habermas his western European starting-point. All over east-central and southern Europe, speaking for barely more than themselves, circles of intellectuals responded to the French example with their own claims to nationhood and civic belonging. French Revolutionary events gave them an inspiringly novel political vocabulary, a structured aspirational discourse of political self-government and individual rights into which they could exuberantly insert themselves. The revolutionary encounter inspired reflections not just on the political bonds of dependency, but on the associated socioeconomic handicaps too. Indeed, intellectuals in the Mediterranean, the Balkans, and east-central Europe took from the French Revolution an ability

---

32 For the former, see Geoff Eley, 'Edward Thompson, Social History and Political Culture: The Making of a Working-Class Public, 1780–1850', in *E. P. Thompson: Critical Debates*, ed. Harvey J. Kaye and Keith McClelland (Cambridge: Polity, 1990); Eileen Yeo, 'Some Practices and Problems of Chartist Democracy', and James Epstein, 'Some Organizational and Cultural Aspects of the Chartist Movement in Nottingham', both in *The Chartist Experience: Studies in Working-Cass Radicalism and Culture, 1830–1860*, ed. James Epstein and Dorothy Thompson (London: Croom Helm, 1982); Barbara Taylor, *Eve and the New Jerusalem: Socialism and Feminism in the Nineteenth Century* (New York: Virago, 1983). For the latter, see the essays by McPhee, Berenson, and Margadant cited in note 15, above.

33 Habermas, *Structural Transformation of the Public Sphere*, xviii.

34 See Gareth Stedman Jones, 'Rethinking Chartism', in his *Languages of Class: Studies in English Working-Class History, 1832–1982* (Cambridge: Cambridge University Press, 1983).

to see their circumstances as 'backwardness' in the first place. It interpellated them through the new forms of nationalist political address. Armed with this self-confident outlook, they set about constituting a national public sphere in all the above-mentioned ways – from literary societies, subscription networks, the press, and a national reading public to the gymnastic and sharpshooter clubs, and the popular reading rooms that carried their words to the countryside. But there were differences. The impetus came from the outside, not from endogenous societal development, in response to backwardness rather than progress. It was consciously expansive rather than narrowly restrictive, proselytizing among the people rather than closing ranks against them.[35]

3. 'Publicness' was, from the outset, plural and contested. *Competing* publics were present not just later in the nineteenth century, when Habermas saw the classic liberal model fragmenting, but at each earlier stage in the public sphere's history. As suggested immediately above, emancipatory initiatives might originate in ways not encompassed by Habermas's model, whether in popular peasant and working-class movements or among early nationalist intellectuals. His approach is needlessly restrictive in other ways too. By overlooking the public sphere's elitism, which wilfully blocked any broader participation, he idealizes its bourgeois character. He ignores other sources of an emancipatory impulse, from the popular Dissenters studied by Edward Thompson and Christopher Hill to the Wilkites and assorted neo-Jacobin radicals of the later eighteenth century, who forged vigorous public spheres of their own.[36] By subsuming all into his 'liberal model of the bourgeois public sphere', Habermas misses

---

35 See Geoff Eley, 'Nationalism and Social History', *Social History* 6: 1 (1981), and 'Remapping the Nation: War, Revolutionary Upheaval, and State Formation in Eastern Europe, 1914–1923', in *Ukrainian–Jewish Relations in Historical Perspective*, ed. Peter J. Potichnyj and Howard Aster (Edmonton: Canadian Institute of Ukrainian Studies, University of Alberta, 1988).

36 Classically in E. P. Thompson, *The Making of the English Working Class* (London: Gollancz, 1968); and Christopher Hill, *The World Turned Upside Down: Radical Ideas During the English Revolution* (London: Temple Smith, 1972). See also Barry Reay, 'The World Turned Upside Down: A Retrospect', in *Reviving the English Revolution: Reflections and Elaborations on the Work of Christopher Hill*, ed. Geoff Eley and William Hunt (London: Verso, 1988).

this diversity. More to the point, publicness was always-already constituted through conflict. Its emergence was never defined solely by struggles against absolutism and traditional authority, but materialized from popular containment too. The classic model was subverted from the very point of its formation, as subalterns contested the meaning and extent of the 'citizenry'. What made the London Corresponding Society any less impressive as a context of 'public reasoning' than, say, the Birmingham Lunar Society (let alone the Birmingham Bean Club)? Rather than the class-specific accomplishment of the bourgeoisie in some sufficient and organic sense, the public sphere makes far more sense as the structured setting in which cultural and political contestation or negotiation among a variety of publics was able to occur. I will return to this point below.

4. Finally, Habermas was entirely inattentive to the exclusions of gender and race. Each, in their respective ways, defined the most sharply drawn and least permeable of the boundaries shaping permissible membership in the imagined or juridical collectivity of the public sphere. During the later eighteenth and early nineteenth centuries, both citizenship and legitimate political agency were strictly confined to a white-skinned confraternity. I take up the question of gender in detail in the section that follows. But 'race' proved a far longer-lasting ideational and structural impediment not just in the deeper sociopolitical histories of popular access and participation, but in the social theorist's and historian's operative understanding. Thus, even as popular movements in Europe and North America – peasants, workers, plebeians, *menu peuple*, early nationalist intellectuals – banged on the doors of civic identity and political recognition, compelling debate over the meanings of political personhood, those boundaries remained implacably closed against black and brown people, whether colonized or transplanted, free or enslaved. Only since the late twentieth century have social and cultural historians begun to see the perduring consequences of those exclusions. If speech and the other civic freedoms were deemed foundational to the pursuit of liberty by later eighteenth-century Enlightenment thought, marking the faculties of civilization and even humanity itself,

then elaborate repertoires of racial exclusion, endlessly renewed
and redeployed, have remained active ever since. In its axiomatic
Eurocentrism, Habermas's thinking in *Strukturwandel* unsurprisingly observed the prevailing patterns of understanding of
the time. But the intervening historiographies of slavery and
emancipation, colonialism and postcoloniality, themselves
compelled into existence only by the transformed politics of the
1970s and 1980s, took a very long time to coalesce. Only very
recently have historians begun to map the historic contours of
black and brown political agency among subaltern peoples who
were entirely beyond the European and North American public
spheres. Thinking globally, whether about the pre-democratic
settings of the eighteenth and nineteenth centuries or the
dynamics of popular politics in our contemporary worlds,
profoundly changes perspectives on the public sphere.[37]

Gender and the Public Sphere

For Habermas, publicness possessed a doubled meaning, at once historical and normative. As the organizing category for an avowedly liberal
view of the transition to the modern world, it supplied ideal grounds for
the conduct of intellectual and political life. The argument was holistic:
a 'subjectivity originating in the interiority of the conjugal family',
became conscious first of itself and then of a wider domain of communicative human relations, travelling next into an associational arena of
literary-intellectual exchange and rational-critical debate, before

---

37   I explored the historiographical impact of the new politics of race and postcolonialism in the 1980s ('Two Disruptions') in Geoff Eley, *A Crooked Line: From Cultural History to
the History of Society* (Ann Arbor, MI: University of Michigan Press, 2005). My own awareness of their importance failed to register in the earliest version of this chapter, which was
composed in the late 1980s. In the meantime, our knowledge of black political thought and
action under slavery and after emancipation, both in the Caribbean and the United States, has
grown immeasurably. Among the vast literatures, see above all Julius S. Scott, *The Common
Wind: Afro-American Currents in the Age of the Haitian Revolution* (London: Verso, 2018);
Vincent Brown, *Tacky's Revolt: The Story of an Atlantic Slave War* (Cambridge: Harvard
University Press, 2020); Miles Ogborn, *The Freedom of Speech: Talk and Slavery in the Anglo-
Caribbean World* (Chicago: University of Chicago Press, 2020); Paul Gilroy, *The Black
Atlantic* (Cambridge: Harvard University Press, 1993).

replicating itself in a political public sphere of property-owners.[38] But this model of political conduct – deliberative politics forged in communicative reason – was far too idealized an abstraction from the political cultures actually materializing around 1800. Whether in the associational networks of the West Midlands, the elite clubs of German small towns, or the literary societies of nineteenth-century east-central Europe, the process of becoming public involved not just reasoned communication, but disparities of interest, prestige, and power. In its classical liberal guise, the public sphere was partial and narrowly based, constituted from fields of contest, adversarial meanings, and exclusion.

The most consistent of the partialities – both preceding and outlasting (for example) the public sphere's bounding by class – is the exclusion by gender. 'Society' for Habermas consists in a complex relationality of structures: on the one hand, the systematically integrated domains of economy and state; on the other, the socially integrated domains of the lifeworld, including both the privacy of family and the publicness of citizenship. Each forms a distinct context of action, requiring processes of material and symbolic reproduction respectively: functionally driven transactions secured through money and power in one case; value-driven interactions focused through intersubjective consensus in the other. Running continuously within and through these basic categories of social analysis and their separations, as Nancy Fraser classically observed, is a 'gender subtext'. The economic and state systems are simultaneously 'disengaged or detached from the lifeworld' and then 'related to and embedded in it', where they operate 'in a context of everyday meanings and norms'. For that purpose, the lifeworld is itself distributed into two 'complementary environments': 'the "private sphere" or modern, restricted, nuclear family . . . linked to the (official) economic system' through the medium of monetary exchange; and 'the "public sphere" or space of political participation, debate, and opinion formation . . . linked to the state-administrative system' through the exchange medium of power. Once added, however, the gender perspective cuts through this elaborate structure of distinctions:

> Once the gender-blindness of Habermas's model is overcome, however, all these connections come into view. It then becomes clear

---

38 Habermas, *Structural Transformation of the Public Sphere*, 51.

that feminine and masculine gender identity run like pink and blue threads through the areas of paid work, state administration and citizenship as well as through the domain of familial and sexual relations. This is to say that gender identity is lived out in all arenas of life. It is one (if not the) 'medium of exchange' among all of them, a basic element of the social glue that binds them to one another.[39]

The ramifications are huge. Cumulative feminist critique reveals the very structure of modern political thought to have been gendered. The constitutive moment of modern political understanding in the Enlightenment and French Revolution was itself formed by freshly conceived or rearranged assumptions about 'woman' and 'man'. This was registered not only in the practical accomplishments of constitutions, legal codes, and political mobilization and their forms of justification, but also in the higher philosophical discourse around the universals of reason, law, and nature. Each disclosed discursively ordered systems of difference in gender. The elaborations were complex. Earlier continuities notwithstanding, the forms of women's exclusion from political participation and civil rights can be convincingly historicized to the French Revolution. Constructed through a series of oppositions to 'femininity', the novel category of the 'public man' and his 'virtue' mobilized older conceptions of domesticity and women's place while rationalizing them into an epistemological claim concerning women's 'nature'. Particular constructions of 'womanness' defined the quality of being a 'man'. Establishing sexuality and desire as natural properties of the feminine enabled the social and political construction of masculinity. Rhetorics of the 1780s and 1790s counterposed reason to 'femininity, if by the latter we mean (as contemporaries did) pleasure, play, eroticism, artifice, style, politesse, refined facades, and particularity'.[40] The silencing of women, given this mannered frivolity, granted masculine speech – in the language of reason – full rein.

---

39 Nancy Fraser, 'What's Critical about Critical Theory? The Case of Habermas and Gender', in *Feminism as Critique: Essays on the Politics of Gender in Late-Capitalist Society*, ed. Seyla Benhabib and Drucilla Cornell (Minneapolis: University of Minnesota Press, 1987), 41, 45.

40 Landes, *Women and the Public Sphere*, 46. Landes sees this opposition as a backlash against the salons of aristocratic women during the *ancien régime*. Generalized hostility against the 'unnatural' prominence of women in public life made femininity a general repository for the vices that republican virtue would overcome.

Women's absence from the political realm 'has not been a chance occurrence, nor merely a symptom of the regrettable persistence of archaic patriarchies', but an outcome of the revolutionary era itself. Alongside all the other radical departures, modern politics was constituted 'as a relation of gender'.[41] The very breakthrough to constitutional legality – with the reordering of social relations around distinctions of public and private, by principles of right, citizenship, and property – forced the issue of woman's place, because the codification of participation brought conceptions of gender difference necessarily into play. As Landes says, this occurred through 'a specific, highly gendered bourgeois male discourse that depended on women's domesticity and the silencing of "public" women, of the aristocratic and popular classes'. And: 'the collapse of the older patriarchy gave way to a more pervasive *gendering* of the public sphere.'[42]

Habermas saw both the patriarchy of family relations and women's exclusion from the nineteenth-century polities.[43] But he assigned each to the widening discrepancy between ideal and reality in the nineteenth-century public sphere, reflecting a deeper difficulty of his argument: the abstraction of an ideal of communicative rationality from historical appearances that were always-already imperfect. Critique of women's subordination can proceed at two levels. Patriarchy was, on the one hand, a continuous feature of European political thought from Hobbes through Locke to the Enlightenment and beyond. Women are confined essentially to the household: 'Women's functions of child-bearing, child-rearing and maintaining the household are deemed to correspond to their unreason, disorderliness and "closeness" to nature. Women and the domestic sphere are viewed as inferior to the male-dominated "public" world of civil society and its culture, property, social power, reason and freedom.'[44] But, on the other hand, this pattern of subordination became potently recharged amid the major political cataclysm, the French Revolution, whose effects radically enlarged the vision of human emancipation. In other words, Habermasian rational communication was vitiated not just by a persisting patriarchy of an older sort; the

---

41 Ibid., 204.
42 Ibid., 2. Emphasis in original.
43 Habermas, *Structural Transformation of the Public Sphere*, 43–56, 132.
44 John Keane, introduction to *Civil Society and the State: New European Perspectives* (London: Verso, 1988), 21.

very inception of the public sphere was itself shaped by a new exclusionary ideology aimed against women. As Carol Pateman puts it, 'In a
world presented as conventional, contractual and universal, women's
civil position is ascriptive, defined by the natural particularity of being
women; patriarchal subordination is socially and legally upheld throughout civil life, in production and citizenship as well as in the family. Thus
to explore the subjection of women is also to explore the fraternity of
men.'[45]

The story of associational activity may likewise be retold in gendered terms. Explaining women's exclusion in terms of older
patriarchal structures is again too easy. If middle-class men, too, were
excluded from the English political process before the turn of the
nineteenth century, then the marginalizing of middle-class women
from the radical reform movements that culminated in 1832 will
require further explanation. Why did attacks on Old Corruption, the
unreformed polity, and traditional values stop short of patriarchy?[46] As
the historically specific structuring of sexual difference, gender was
constitutive not only for the ordering of the middle-class social world
through particular patterns of family, domesticity, and consumption,
but also for the reciprocal interactions between this private domain
and the public sphere of associational life and politics. The resulting
back-and-forth both reflected and actively reproduced the gendered
distinctions of class identity generated across the home–work border-
line.[47] During a time of enormous socioeconomic and political
disorder (from the 1790s to the 1840s), the middling propertied layers
(farmers, manufacturers, merchants, professions), impatient with
persisting aristocratic predominance, sought ways of converting their

---

45   Carole Pateman, 'The Fraternal Social Contract', in Keane, *Civil Society and the State*,
121. See also Carole Pateman, *The Sexual Contract* (Cambridge: Cambridge University Press,
1988); Jean Bethke Elshtain, *Public Man, Private Woman: Women in Social and Political
Thought* (Princeton: Princeton University Press, 1981); Ellen Kennedy and Susan Mendus,
eds, *Women in Western Political Philosophy: Kant to Nietzsche* (New York: St Martin's, 1987);
Dorinda Outram, *The Body and the French Revolution: Sex, Class, and Political Culture*
(London/New Haven: Yale University Press, 1989). For a dissentient view, see Sylvana
Tomaselli, 'The Enlightenment Debate on Women', *History Workshop Journal* 20 (1985).
46   Catherine Hall, 'Private Persons versus Public Someones: Class, Gender, and Politics
in England, 1780–1850', in *Language, Gender and Childhood*, ed. Carolyn Steedman, Cathy
Urwin, and Valerie Walkerdine (London: Routledge & Kegan Paul, 1985), 11.
47   Leonore Davidoff and Catherine Hall, *Family Fortunes: Men and Women of the
English Middle Class, 1780–1850* (Chicago: University of Chicago Press, 1987).

growing economic importance into 'moral and cultural authority . . . not only within their own communities and boundaries, but in relation to other classes'. Their means of doing so was that same associational trajectory that brought Habermas's public sphere concretely into existence. Such activity reached from informal circles of family and friendship to networks of business and religion; from clubs and coffeehouses to lodges, guilds, and prestigious societies; from scientific, cultural, and educational societies to business-, professional-, and property-related associations; and from moral campaigning into national political movements.

This creativity strictly demarcated the roles of men and women in a mobile repertoire of ideologies and practices that consistently assigned women to a nonpolitical private sphere, where they had 'at most a supportive role to play in the rapidly expanding political world of their fathers, husbands and brothers'.[48] Davidoff and Hall present this gendering of the public sphere in remarkable richness of detail:

Middle-class men's claims for new forms of manliness found one of their most powerful expressions in formal associations. The informal, convivial culture of eighteenth-century merchants, traders and farmers was gradually superseded by the age of societies. Men organized themselves in myriad ways, promoting their economic interests, providing soup kitchens for the poor, cultivating the arts, reaching into populated urban areas and rural outposts. This network of association redefined civil society, creating new arenas of social power and constructing a formidable base for middle-class men. Their societies provided opportunities for the public demonstration of middle-class weight and responsibility; the newspaper reports of their events, the public rituals and ceremonials designed for their occasions, the new forms of public architecture linked to their causes. The experience of such associations increased the confidence of middle-class men and contributed to their claims for political power, as heads of households, representing their wives, children, servants and other dependents. This public world was consistently organized in gendered ways and had little space for women. Indeed, middle-class women in the second half of the nineteenth century focused many of their

---

48   Hall, 'Private Persons versus Public Someones', 11.

efforts on attempting to conquer the bastions of this public world, a
world which had been created by the fathers and grandfathers.[49]

This separation of spheres – between the masculinities of public action
and the feminine realm of the home, with their many subtle reciprocities – was replicated among the working class.[50] In democratic
movements of the early nineteenth century, with the significant exception of utopian socialism, popular sovereignty was a male preserve.
Chartism's famous Six Points for democratizing the constitution (1837–
38) expressly omitted votes for women. While individuals raised the
issue intermittently thereafter, the enduring consensus (shared by
Chartist women no less than the men) gave women's suffrage low priority. This was clearer still for movements of peasants, shopkeepers, and
artisans, where the gendered division of labour in small-scale household
production gave women a necessary but subordinate place. By the
1890s, European socialist parties flew women's political symbols proudly
on their standards. But by 1914 female suffrage was showing meagre
gains. Women had the vote in parts of the North American West and
just four parliamentary states: New Zealand (1893), Australia (1903),
Finland (1906), and Norway (1913).[51]

Sustaining such entrenched discrimination were ideas about the
'naturalness' of woman's place and the social ordering of sexual difference. Women lacked autonomous standing in prevailing theories of
government and representation. As Sally Alexander says, 'The legal,
economic, and political subject in radical popular speech reaching back
to the seventeenth-century Levellers, was the propertied individual, and
the propertied individual was always masculine – whether head of
household, skilled tradesman or artisan whose property was his labor.'
Inscribed in the language of radical democracy was a clear distinction
between the public world and a domestic-cum-communal sphere, where
patriarchal 'notions of labor, property, and kin' structured 'women's
access to knowledge, skill, and independent political subjectivity'.
Women were highly active in Chartism and comparable agitations of
the time. But they spoke only behind the walls of the embattled

---

49   Davidoff and Hall, *Family Fortunes*, 416.
50   Davidoff and Hall are excellent on the complex imbrication of family and economics:
Family Fortunes, 195–315.
51   All frontier societies in one way or another.

popular community. Speaking to the outside world, 'in the first person for the community as a whole', fell to the men. Public discourse, including the whole field of socioeconomic discontents, campaigns for civil freedoms, struggles over the law, and demands for the vote, was closed to women. It was 'a dialogue of negotiation between the men of the communities and the ruling class – "capitalists and lawgivers"'.[52]

For radical working men – 'the small master craftsmen, the displaced domestic worker, the artisan and mechanic, the skilled factory operatives' at the core of Chartism and related movements – the household's integrity anchored political identity. However complementary the household division of labour, the family contained a regime of domestic authority centred on masculine privilege. In angrily resisting capitalist industry, which undermined their skills and pulled wives and children to the factory, radical artisans defended their own family privilege: 'their status as fathers and heads of families was indelibly associated with their independence through "honourable" labour and property in skill, which identification with a trade gave them'. Women lacked such access to independence. Excluded from most trades in their own right, they practised a craft by virtue of male kin. Usually they 'assisted' the latter. Woman's 'skill' rested in the household, her 'property in the virtue of her person'. If 'separated from the home, her family, and domestic occupations, or outside the bonds of matrimony, a woman was assured of neither'. A woman's political identity was held by the man. The rare Chartists advocating women's suffrage limited themselves to 'spinsters and widows', because wives and husbands were deemed to be one.[53]

Such thinking adapted easily to industrialization. By the 1830s and 1840s, demands for 'protective' laws were especially clamorous. Defending women and children against the degradations of the new mills bespoke an idealized notion of family, hearth, and home, where the 'natural differences and capacities' of women and men ordered the household economy under benign patriarchy. When the husband-father was workless or his wages depressed, driving wives and children to the

---

52   Sally Alexander, 'Women, Class and Sexual Differences in the 1830s and 1840s: Some Reflections on the Writing of a Feminist History', *History Workshop Journal* 17 (1984), 136, 137, 139. The quotations that follow are from the same source.

53   See Dorothy Thompson, *The Chartists: Popular Politics in the Industrial Revolution* (New York: Pantheon, 1984), 125, citing pamphlets by Manchester Chartist Reginald John Richardson and London Chartist John Watkins.

factory, that natural order was upset. Aggravating this breakdown in moral authority (the 'unsexing of the man', in Engels's phrase) were the effects of women's cheap labour, whose widening use spelled loss of jobs, status, and skill for the respectable workingman. This fusion of economic and ideological anxieties – resistance to capitalist reorganizing of industry, desire to quarantine the family's moral regime – proved a compelling motivation for those skilled workers with enough bargaining power.[54] Under the post-1850 prosperity and political stability, they came into their own.

The outcome was a recharged familial ideology of masculine precedence, confined in practice to those skilled workingmen able to support a wife and children by their own earning power alone. Where work was casual, irregular, and seasonal, with low wages and weak organization, male earnings required whatever the rest of the family could bring, usually from casualized, sweated, or home-based employment and the informal economy. Measured by the bulk of working-class experience, accordingly, the skilled craftsman's ability to keep his wife in domesticated non-employment conferred definite privilege – not just over women, but over the mass of the male unskilled. Pre-1890s trade unionism was predicated on such exclusions: the putative norm of the 'family wage' distinguished a unionized craft elite from the generality of the working poor. Not only did this outlook affirm the skilled worker's material advantage; it disparaged women's employment as exceptional and undesirable. It justified 'keeping women in their place'. It demoted women drastically in trade-union terms. It had traction far beyond the ranks of labour aristocrats themselves, pervading workers' views of women's political status. Thus, the backbone of pre-1914 socialist parties, the staunchest proponents of women's *political* rights, were skilled workers practising the worst craft exclusiveness against women. The socialist tradition's official endorsement of female suffrage concealed practical indifference to the recognition of women's interests in the movement's agitation. Such political neglect reflected attitudes and practices materially embedded in working-class

---

54 Capitalist transformation of the labour process and dissolution of family controls were 'the two themes which spurred all visions of a new social order' in early-nineteenth-century Britain: the idea that 'labor, as the producer of wealth and knowledge, should receive its just reward'; the belief that 'kinship was the natural and proper relation of morality, authority and law'. See Alexander, 'Women, Class, and Sexual Differences', 138. For Engels's phrase, 'The Condition of the Working Class in 1844', see Karl Marx and Friedrich Engels, *On Britain* (Moscow: Foreign Languages Publishing House, 1962), 179.

everyday life – at work, in the neighbourhood, and at home. Behind this labour-movement indifference were historically transmitted patterns of masculinist behaviour and belief that trade unionists and left-wing politicians consistently overlooked.[55]

How and when do these public–private borderlands become the ground of politics? Like the related couplet of state and civil society, the distinction in any case remains permeable. Nor can the autonomies of the private realm easily be separated and defined. Where is the economic in that three-way schema of state, civil society, and private sphere? How far does morality transcend all three? How does the Habermasian public sphere align with an older 'civil society' lineage of thought?[56] The public realm itself can be variously defined. Is it a purely 'political' context in the narrower sense of government and public administration, or does politics extend to other more 'private' spheres like the economy, recreation, the family, sexuality, and interpersonal relations? Among progressivist traditions of thought, until the late twentieth century, there were three main answers:

- a *democratic* one, stressing political rights and a clear separation of the public from the private sphere, in which the constitution guarantees strong autonomy for the latter through civil freedoms, freedom of conscience and religion, property rights, rights of privacy, and so forth
- a *socialist* one, which extends the public sphere of democracy to the economy through nationalization, an expanded public sector, trade unionism, a welfare state, and other socialized provision for healthcare, social insurance, education, recreation, and so forth
- a *utopian* one, in which democracy expands to social relations *tout court*, embracing personal life, domestic living arrangements, friendship, and child raising, usually through some form of communitarianism.

---

55 For instance, Richard J. Evans, 'Politics and the Family: Social Democracy and the Working-Cass Family in Theory and Practice before 1914', in *The German Family: Essays on the Social History of the Family in Nineteenth- and Twentieth-Century Germany*, ed. Richard Evans and W. R. Lee (London: Croom Helm, 1981).

56 See John Keane, 'Remembering the Dead: Civil Society and the State from Hobbes to Marx and Beyond', in his *Democracy and Civil Society*, esp. 35–6.

Since the late 1960s, a fourth may be added: the *feminist* one, which enters
the private sphere in a qualitatively different way. By politicizing the
personal aspects of social relations in terms of family, sexuality, self, and
subjectivity, it upsets and transforms earlier forms of the public–private
distinction. Contemporary feminism is not without antecedents. Relative
to the staid preoccupations of subsequent socialists, early-nineteenth-
century utopians politicized the personal sphere in strikingly radical ways.
Strong commitments to reproductive rights and liberated sexuality developed on the margins of the Left between the 1880s and 1914, and more
extensively during 1917–23. But only since the last third of the twentieth
century have the classical public sphere's gendered confinements fully
fallen to critique – via theories of sexuality and subjectivity, by identify-
ing ideologies of motherhood, by tackling the sexual division of labour in
households, and by critiques of family as such. As Pateman says,

> The meaning of 'civil society' . . . has been constructed through the
> exclusion of women and all that we symbolize. To create a properly
> democratic society, which includes women as full citizens, it is neces-
> sary to deconstruct and reassemble our understanding of the body
> politic. This task extends from the dismantling of the patriarchal
> separation of private and public, to a transformation of our individu-
> ality and sexual identities as feminine and masculine beings. These
> identities now stand opposed, part of the multifaceted expression of
> the patriarchal dichotomy between reason and desire. The most
> profound and complex problem for political theory and practice is
> how the two bodies of humankind and feminine and masculine
> individuality can be fully incorporated into political life. How can the
> present of patriarchal domination, opposition, and duality be trans-
> formed into a future of autonomous, democratic differentiation?[57]

State Formation and the Public Sphere

Despite the richness of Habermas's account of (west) European political culture, it contains little about either the state per se or specific
political histories, despite extensive commentaries on the law. His

---

57   Pateman, 'Fraternal Social Contract', 123.

purpose was legitimately different, to be sure, focused on the 'free space' of society rather than a state-centred architecture of public authority or political development. Conversely, treatments of comparative political development since the late 1960s were remarkably silent on the public sphere and political culture in Habermas's sense. Thus, Immanuel Wallerstein was only secondarily concerned with political, as against economic, history; Perry Anderson dealt with state–society relations, but for an earlier period; Theda Skocpol tackled the state as a central nexus of government institutions. Charles Tilly's work on collective action and state formation came closer to political culture, but focused on 'the extractive and repressive activities of states'. Barrington Moore approached comparative political development through the contests of social forces ('lord and peasant in the making of the modem world'), with little attention to either the shaping of a public sphere or the role of urban classes. Neither Michael Mann nor Anthony Giddens had anything to say about the public sphere as such; the latter's discussion of 'Class, Sovereignty, and Citizenship' was bizarrely perfunctory, adopting an entirely 'administrative' perspective.[58] Each paid little mind to political culture, to the state's wider impact in society through modalities of popular consent and opposition, or to the social processes grounding politics. In sharp contrast, Habermas shifted discussion brilliantly onto sociocultural terrain, especially for his time of writing.

As a theorist of political development, though, Habermas had his limitations. By approaching the rise of liberalism and the constitution-alizing of arbitrary authority through an argument about communicative rationality, and by stressing the shift to a more interventionist state under advanced capitalism, he implied a *weak* state during the public

---

58　See Immanuel Wallerstein, *The Modern World System, vol. 1: Capitalist Agriculture and the Origins of the European World-Economy in the Sixteenth Century* (New York: Academic, 1974), *The Modern World System, vol. 2: Mercantilism and the Consolidation of the European World-Economy, 1600–1750* (New York: Academic, 1980), and *The Modern World-System, vol. 3: The Second Era of Great Expansion of the Capitalist World-Economy, 1730–1840s* (New York: Academic, 1988); Perry Anderson, *Lineages of the Absolutist State* (London: New Left Books, 1974); Charles Tilly, ed., *The Formation of National States in Western Europe* (Princeton: Princeton University Press, 1975); Theda Skocpol, *States and Social Revolutions: A Comparative Analysis of France, Russia, and China* (Cambridge: Cambridge University Press, 1979); Barrington Moore Jr, *Social Origins of Dictatorship and Democracy* (Boston: Beacon, 1966); Michael Mann, *The Sources of Social Power, vol. 1: A History of Power from the Beginning to AD 1760* (Cambridge: Cambridge University Press, 1986); Anthony Giddens, *A Contemporary Critique of Historical Materialism, vol. 2: The Nation-State and Violence* (Berkeley: University of California Press, 1987), 198–221.

sphere's initial rise. But was the liberal state really so uninterested in regulating the private sphere or so strongly non-interventionist in tackling social and political conflict? Habermas himself stressed the legal reforms needed to secure the changing bases of property; as Karl Polanyi insisted, the road to laissez-faire was paved with state intervention. That was true for sociocultural and political, no less than economic, freedoms: to deregulate society and confirm a protected space for the public, an entire regulative programme was required.[59]

Similarly, Habermas idealized rational discourse in the formation of the public sphere, neglecting the founding of its institutions on sectionalism, exclusiveness, and repression. In eighteenth-century Britain, parliamentary liberty and the rule of law were inseparable from the attack on customary rights, popular liberties, and nascent radical democracy.[60] Participants in the bourgeois public always faced two ways in this sense: *forward* against the old aristocratic and royal authorities, but also *backward* against the popular/plebeian elements already in pursuit. The ambiguities of the liberal departure – in the consolidation of the public sphere during 1760–1850 – expressed the fragility of liberal commitments and the fraught nature of contestation. Only by extending Habermas in this direction – towards the wider public domain, where authority is not only constituted as rational and legitimate, but where its terms may also be contested and modified (and occasionally overthrown) – can we grasp this complexity.

For this purpose, Antonio Gramsci's concept of 'hegemony' may be needed. In Gwyn A. Williams's early definition, this signifies 'an order in which a certain way of life and thought is dominant, in which one concept of reality is diffused throughout society in all its institutional and private manifestations, informing with its spirit all taste, morality, customs, religious and political principles, and all social relations,

---

59   See Karl Polanyi, *The Great Transformation: The Political and Economic Origins of Our Time* (Boston: Beacon, 1944), 146–7; Fred Block and Margaret Somers, 'Beyond the Economistic Fallacy: The Holistic Social Science of Karl Polanyi', in *Vision and Method in Historical Sociology*, ed. Theda Skocpol (Cambridge: Cambridge University Press, 1984), esp. 52–62.

60   Edward P. Thompson, 'The Moral Economy of the English Crowd in the Eighteenth Century', *Past and Present* 50 (1971), 'Patrician Society, Plebeian Culture', *Journal of Social History* 7 (1973–74), *Whigs and Hunters: The Origins of the Black Act* (London: Allen Lane, 1975), and 'Eighteenth-Century English Society: Class Struggle without Class?', *Social History* 3: 2 (1978). For my own commentary, see Geoff Eley, 'Re-Thinking the Political: Social History and Political Culture in 18th and 19th Century Britain', *Archiv für Sozialgeschichte* 21 (1981).

particularly in their intellectual and moral connotation'.[61] 'Hegemony' here is not interchangeable with 'ideology' or 'ideological domination' *tout court*, in a perspective stressing the 'manipulations' or 'social control' exercised by a ruling class. In Raymond Williams's words, hegemony comprises 'not only the conscious system of ideas and beliefs [i.e., "ideology" in a commonly accepted sense] but the whole lived social process as practically organized by specific dominant meanings and values', 'a sense of reality for most people in the society, a sense of absolute because experienced reality beyond which it is very difficult for most members of the society to move, in most areas of their lives'. Hegemony should be seen

as in effect a saturation of the whole process of living – not only of political or economic activity, nor only of manifest social activity, but of the whole substance of lived identities and relationships, to such a depth that the pressures and limits of what can ultimately be seen as a specific economic, political, and cultural system seem to most of us the pressures and limits of simple experience and common sense. Hegemony is then not only the articulate upper level of 'ideology', nor are its forms of control only those ordinarily seen as 'manipulation' or 'indoctrination'. It is the whole body of practices and expectations, over the whole of living: our senses and assignments of energy, or shaping perceptions of ourselves and our world.[62]

This sense of pervasiveness and externally structured experience, of 'the wholeness of the process' by which a given social order holds together and acquires its legitimacy, is the most compelling feature of Gramsci's idea.[63]

But, contrary to some older commentaries, Gramsci's was not a 'totalitarian' concept.[64] He used it to distinguish elements of pluralism and competition, persuasion and consent, from authoritarian and repressive modes of rule. He certainly saw how the state acted coercively against society to suppress opposition, contain dissent, and manipulate

---

61 Gwyn A. Williams, 'The Concept of "Egemonia" in the Thought of Antonio Gramsci: Some Notes on Interpretation', *Journal of the History of Ideas* 21: 4 (1960).

62 Raymond Williams, *Marxism and Literature* (Oxford: Oxford University Press, 1977).

63 Ibid., 108.

64 For example, H. Stuart Hughes, *Consciousness and Society: The Reorientation of European Social Thought 1890–1930* (New York: Vintage, 1958), 96–104.

educational, religious, and other ideological agencies for imposing popular compliance. But he expressly linked hegemony to a domain of public life relatively independent of such controls (he called this 'civil society', but it might also be the 'public sphere'), seeing its achievement as a far more contingent process. In winning supremacy, Gramsci argued, a dominant class not only *imposes* its rule via the state but performs its 'intellectual and moral leadership' too. This requires the arts of persuasion, a continuous labour of creative ideological intervention. The capacity 'to articulate different visions of the world in such a way that their potential antagonism is neutralized', rather than simply suppressing those visions beneath 'a uniform conception of the world', encapsulates hegemony in Gramsci's thinking.[65] By the same quality, hegemony is susceptible to change and negotiation: it proceeds not just through consent under conditions of pluralist competition (however partial), but also by patterns of dominance and subordination. Structured by class inequality, this process involves contradictory and opposing interests.

Hegemony is characterized by uncertainty, impermanence, and contradiction. It 'is not a fixed and immutable *condition*, more or less permanent until totally displaced by determined revolutionary action, but is an institutionally negotiable *process* in which the social and political forces of contest, breakdown and transformation are constantly in play'.[66] In that sense, hegemony is always under construction, because bringing it finally to closure would entail either a utopia of social harmony or its replacement by coercive rule. Hegemony remains open to modification. Under specific circumstances, it may be radically transformed or even break down altogether. Civil society offers chances for *contesting* as well as *securing* the system's legitimacy. Hegemony has 'to be won, secured, constantly defended'. It requires 'a struggle to win over the dominated classes in which any "resolution" involves both *limits* (compromises) and *systematic contradictions*'.[67] Societal dominance is continually renegotiated, varying with the fluctuating economic, cultural, and political dispositions of subaltern classes.

---

65   Ernesto Laclau, *Politics and Ideology in Marxist Theory* (London: New Left Books, 1977), 161.

66   Geoff Eley and Keith Nield, 'Why Does Social History Ignore Politics?', *Social History* 5: 2 (1980), 269. Emphases in original.

67   Stuart Hall, Bob Lumley, and Gregor McLennan, 'Politics and Ideology: Gramsci', in *On Ideology*, ed. Centre for Contemporary Cultural Studies (London: Hutchinson, 1978), 68.

Gramsci's distinction between 'hegemonic' and 'coercive' forms of rule has a historical dimension. He directly contrasts developed capitalist polities whose legitimacy rests on a fairly stable 'equilibrium of hegemonic and coercive institutions' with an older type of state lacking such vital reciprocity:

> In the ancient and medieval state alike, centralization, whether political-territorial or social . . . was minimal. The state was, in a certain sense, a mechanical bloc of social groups . . . The modern state substitutes for the mechanical bloc of social groups their subordination to the active hegemony of the directive and dominant group, hence abolishes certain autonomies, which nevertheless are reborn in other forms, as parties, trade unions, cultural associations.[68]

The passage from one type of rule to another presumes processes of social change enabling new political ambitions to crystallize. For Gramsci, these consist of three moments: the growth of corporate solidarities; their organization into a larger class collectivity; and their translation onto the highest political plane of 'universal' interest. With that final step, hegemonic construction has begun, with a new 'national-popular' dimension to public life, and a new claim to 'intellectual and moral leadership' in society overall. The institutional scaffolding for civil society gradually takes shape. In an oft-cited passage, Gramsci hinted at comparative possibilities:

> In Russia the state was everything, civil society was primordial and gelatinous; in the West there was a proper relation between state and civil society, and when the state trembled a sturdy structure of civil society was at once revealed. The state was only an outer ditch, behind which there stood a powerful system of fortresses and earthworks.[69]

If, for Gramsci, this explained Bolshevik success in the Russian Revolution, it equally disclosed the contrasting exigencies for revolutionary change in Western Europe, where the greater complexity of the social

---

68 Antonio Gramsci, *Selections from the Prison Notebooks* (London: Lawrence & Wishart, 1971), 54. The earlier quoted phrase, 'equilibrium . . .', comes from Eric J. Hobsbawm, 'Great Gramsci', *New York Review of Books* 21: 5 (April 1974), 42.
69 Gramsci, *Selections from the Prison Notebooks*, 238.

fabric, the liberal traditions of citizenship and constitutionalism, and the polity's functioning pluralism made authority far harder to identify and isolate. Power there was diffused intangibly through a diversity of non-official practices and organizations, rather than being physically located in a central institutional core in the capital city. In Russia, the backward-ness of civil society left the state an isolated citadel, vulnerable to being stormed. But, in the West, society's structures were more complex, requiring a long-term war of position, not the insurrectionary war of movement. In those terms, nineteenth-century Russia was an excellent counter-case for the public sphere. It showed the absence of the condi-tions that *Öffentlichkeit* presupposed, especially the emancipatory, free-associational impulse. Under Tsarism, this was precluded by a combination of social backwardness and repressive state authority.

Popular Culture and the Public Sphere

For Gramsci, civil society was not the neutral setting for rational political discourse that Habermas imagined. It was an arena of contestation, where distinct – and opposing – publics jockeyed for space, and specific publics (women; subordinate peoples; popular classes like the urban poor, working class, and peasantry) might be excluded altogether. Contestation was more than negotiated political coexistence or a straight-forward pluralism of tendencies and groupings. It came from class-divided societies structured around inequality, so domination – power, in its multiple socioeconomic, cultural, and political dimensions – was also involved. Hegemony, as the harnessing of public life to the interests of one particular grouping in a social bloc shaped around the dominant classes, had to be systematically pursued, whether consciously and pro-grammatically (as in the early stages) or as the 'natural' and unreflected administration or reproduction of a given way of doing things. *Intellec-tuals* in Gramsci's schema – as a broadened social category, including journalists, party officials, teachers, priests, lawyers, technicians, and other professionals, as well as writers, professors, and intellectuals in the stricter sense – were the functionaries of this process.

That quality of conflict – the public sphere's fractured, contested character – defined exactly the constitutive dynamics described by Habermas for late-eighteenth-century Britain, but in ways that require substantial recasting of his case. Thus, reworking part of Edward Thompson's *Making of the English Working Class*, Günther Lottes found a key source of the new publicness in the heated reciprocities of an oppositional intelligentsia and plebeian public.[70] In the 1770s–1780s, radicals initially sought constitutional renewal through popular education and parliamentary reform, challenging the governing system's corruption and besetting factionalism with an extraparliamentary campaign of public enlightenment. But at that stage the popular links remained external rather than organic, asserted through principle and propaganda, not yet through new forms of communication and participation. Those intellectuals were also notables, drawn from three overlapping upper-class categories: landowners, merchants, and other prosperous businessmen; lawyers, Nonconformist clergy, and other academic professions; and literati in the narrower sense, freshly coalescing from the nascent literary marketplace. Their activity was loosely structured around London's coffeehouse society, in discussion circles like the Robin Hood Society, the Speculative Society, and the Debating Society in Coachmakers' Hall. Provincial counterparts were, if anything, more ramified, certainly in Manchester, Birmingham, and other major centres. At the apex was the Society for Constitutional Information (SCI, founded 1780), the radical intelligentsia's principal forum before the London Corresponding Society (LCS) was launched in 1792. Thus far, the account fits nicely into what Habermas had argued.

Expressly imagining an extraparliamentary public, this reform movement broke the mould of legitimate politics. By educating the populace into citizenship, pre-Jacobin radicals broached universal manhood suffrage and broke with 'the previously uncontested dogma of political theory that property alone justified a claim to political participation.'[71] But the SCI still stopped short of directly mobilizing the people. Openly agitating the masses came only with a second stage: English Jacobinism proper. As the agency of this breakthrough, the LCS had two distinguishing features. Its leadership came from less prestigious circles: not only recognized intellectuals like merchant's son Maurice Margarot and Unitarian minister Jeremiah Joyce, or lawyers Felix Vaughan, John Frost,

---

70 Günther Lottes, *Politische Aufklärung and plebejisches Publikum: Zur Theorie und Praxis des englischen Radikalismus im späten 18. Jahrhundert* (Munich: Oldenbourg, 1979).
71 Ibid., 14. My translations.

and John Martin, but also 'not yet arrived or declassed marginal deni-
zens of the London literary-journalistic scene'. These included John Gale
Jones, Joseph Gerrald, William Hodgson, the Binns brothers (John and
Benjamin), and John Thelwall ('the prototype of the literatus from a
modest background who tried vainly for years to find a foothold in the
London artistic and literary scene'); numerous small publishers and
book dealers; and the 'first representatives of an artisan intelligentsia'
like shoemaker Thomas Hardy, silversmith John Baxter, hatter Richard
Hodgson, or tailor Francis Place.[72] Still more tellingly, these new Jacobins
went directly to the masses themselves, braving the plebeian rowdiness.

The key to LCS's originality was this engagement with the ebullient
but pre-political culture of the urban masses – what Lottes calls 'the
socio-cultural and institutional context of the politicization of the petty
and sub-bourgeois strata'.[73] In espousing the democratic axiom of
'members unlimited', the LCS embraced not just popular participation,
but 'confrontation with the traditional plebeian culture', to which it
brought big misgivings: 'The Jacobin ideal of the independent, well-
informed and disciplined citizen arriving at decisions via enlightened
and free discussion stood in crass contradiction with the forms of
communication and political action characteristic of the plebeian culture'.[74] Riot, revelry, and rough music would give way to the pamphlet,
committee room, resolution, and petition, aided by the disciplined
democracy of an orderly open-air demonstration. Lottes elaborates
the practicalities of this departure – the LCS's meticulous constitutionalism, the climate of reasoned debate, the critique of the 'mob', the ideal
of 'enlightenment praxis'. A 'plebeian public sphere' grew from the
intense political didacticism of the LCS sections, nourished on a rich
diet of pamphlets, tracts, political magazines, and the theatrical pedagogy of Thelwall's *Political Lectures*. Unlike earlier radicals, Jacobins
wanted *direct* relations with their public, in non-manipulative and non-
demagogic ways.

Jacobin radicalism was no mere footnote to the grander narrative of
parliamentary reform. Nor was it just a precursor of the later labour
movement. In the global context of the 'Atlantic Revolution', defined by

---

72   Ibid., 223–32.
73   Ibid., 109.
74   Ibid., 337.

the dynamics of parliamentary reform, the complex sociology of an intelligentsia, and the political economy of London and provincial handicrafts, it was a programme for educating the masses into citizenship. Jacobins hoped to supplant the protest rituals and riotous traditions of 'the crowd' with 'a political movement equipped with firm organization, a middle- and long-term strategy, and a theoretically grounded programme'.[75] The LCS wished to educate the tradesmen, shopkeepers, and mechanics into political knowledge not just to ensure 'their more effective participation in politics', but 'to rid society of the turbulence and disorder which was then often inseparable from the ventilation of popular grievances'.[76]

They faced insuperable limits. The Jacobins' advanced democracy presupposed the very sophistication it was meant to create. Political pedagogy was hard to join to the demands of effective organization, creative leadership, and maximum participation, particularly once state repression intensified after 1793. It was hard to confront popular 'backwardness' without compromising either the resonance of radical propaganda or the movement's democratic credentials. Jacobins were further confined by the tenacity of prevailing eighteenth-century oppositionism: a potent combination of 'Country' ideology and natural-rights thinking that stressed the degeneration of a once-healthy constitution and impeded Tom Paine's sharper break with English constitutional tradition. Still in thrall to the 1780s, Jacobin radicalism only partially escaped those limits.[77]

Here is the main point: eighteenth-century pursuit of communicative rationality through the public sphere revealed far richer social histories than Habermas's conception of bourgeois emancipation allowed. By seeing *Öffentlichkeit* in those terms, he altogether obscured contending histories of popular-democratic mobilization happening entirely *beyond* that classical liberal framework of civil society. My chosen rubrics – the findings of social history, questions of gender, state formation, and popular politics – are not the only grounds for critique. Nineteenth-century nationalist movements, communications, and mass culture would each equally serve. The 'linguistic turn' and the 'new cultural

---

75 Ibid., 14.
76 Albert Goodwin, *The Friends of Liberty: The English Democratic Movement in the Age of the French Revolution* (Cambridge, MA: Harvard University Press, 1979), 157.
77 Lottes, *Politische Aufklärung*, 263–334.

history' could also cast Habermas in an interesting critical light. The claim to *rational* discourse was simultaneously a claim to *power* in Michel Foucault's sense. But none of this diminishes the value of *Strukturwandel der Öffentlichkeit*, whose impact only grew in the wake of its translation.

5

Politics, Culture, and the Public Sphere: What a Difference Habermas Made

For some three decades after its original German edition in 1962, Habermas's book had virtually no impact on historians in any language or national field.[1] Indeed, the international resonance of its author's other works among social scientists was achieved largely independently of the standing of this earlier book. In the English-speaking world, his reception was defined far more by his renewal of critical theory in *Knowledge and Human Interests* and *Theory and Practice* (published in English in 1971 and 1973); by his polemic against the West German student movement, *Toward a Rational Society* (translated 1970); by his analysis of the state under late capitalism, *Legitimation Crisis* (translated 1975); and finally by his mature general theory broached in *Communication and the Evolution of Society* (1979) and culminating in the two-volume *The Theory of Communicative Action* (1984). These works moved from the original German into English with growing rapidity.[2]

---

1 See Jürgen Habermas, *The Structural Transformation of the Public Sphere: An Inquiry into a Category of Bourgeois Society*, trans. Thomas Burger (Cambridge: MIT Press, 1991), originally published as *Strukturwandel der Öffentlichkeit* (Neuwied: Hermann Luchterhand, 1962).

2 See the following works by Habermas: *Toward a Rational Society: Student Protest, Science, and Politics*, trans. Jeremy J. Shapiro (Boston: Beacon, 1970); *Knowledge and Human Interests*, trans. Jeremy J. Shapiro (Boston: Beacon, 1971) – originally published as *Erkenntnis und Interesse* (Frankfurt: Suhrkamp, 1968); *Theory and Practice*, trans. John Viertel (Boston: Beacon, 1973) –originally published as *Theorie und Praxis* (Frankfurt: Suhrkamp, 1963); *Legitimation Crisis*, trans. Thomas McCarthy (Boston: Beacon, 1975) – originally published

Thereafter, translations appeared virtually simultaneously, from his disputes with French poststructuralists and an important collection of interviews to the many volumes of the philosophical-political writings and the major theoretical treatise, *Between Facts and Norms*, and beyond.[3] Even among the rising generation of historians in West Germany itself, who were self-consciously fashioning a new 'historical social science' partly under Habermas's influence, *Strukturwandel der Öffentlichkeit* also mattered far less than the various works of critical epistemology, which during the 1970s were invoked with talismanic regularity.[4]

For many years, access to *Strukturwandel* through the English language was gained mainly via the translation of a short encyclopaedia article on 'The Public Sphere' in an early issue of *New German Critique*,

as *Legitimationsprobleme im Spätkapitalismus* (Frankfurt: Suhrkamp, 1973); *Communication and the Evolution of Society*, trans. Thomas McCarthy (Boston: Beacon, 1979) – originally published as two separate volumes: *Sprachpragmatik und Philosophie* (Frankfurt: Suhrkamp, 1976) and *Zur Rekonstruktion des Historischen Materialismus* (Frankfurt: Suhrkamp, 1976); and *The Theory of Communicative Action*, 2 vols, trans. Thomas McCarthy (Boston: Beacon, 1984) – originally published as *Theorie des Kommunikativen Handelns* (Frankfurt: Suhrkamp, 1981). This is by no means an exhaustive listing of Habermas's works.

3 See Peter Dews, ed., *Autonomy and Solidarity: Interviews with Jürgen Habermas* (London: Verso, 1986); and the following works by Habermas: *The Philosophical Discourse of Modernity: Twelve Lectures*, trans. Frederick G. Lawrence (Cambridge: MIT Press, 1987) – originally published as *Der Philosophische Diskurs des Moderne: Zwölf Vorlesungen* (Frankfurt: Suhrkamp, 1985); Shierry Weber Nicholsen, ed. and trans., *The New Conservatism: Cultural Criticism and the Historians' Debate* (Cambridge: MIT Press, 1989); *The Past as Future*, interviewed by Michael Haller, trans. Max Pensky (Lincoln, NE: University of Nebraska Press, 1994); *A Berlin Republic: Writings on Germany*, trans. Steven Rendall (Lincoln, NE: University of Nebraska Press, 1997) – originally published as *Die Normalität einer Berliner Republik* (Frankfurt: Suhrkamp, 1995); *The Inclusion of the Other: Studies in Political Theory*, ed. Ciaran Cronin and Pablo De Greiff, trans. Ciaran Cronin (Cambridge: MIT Press, 1998) – originally published as *Die Einbeziehung des Anderen. Studien zur politischen Theorie* (Frankfurt: Suhrkamp, 1996); *The Postnational Constellation: Political Essays,* ed. and trans. Max Pensky (Cambridge: MIT Press, 2001) – originally published as *Die postnationale Konstellation: Politische Essays* (Frankfurt: Suhrkamp, 1998); *Between Facts and Norms: Contributions to a Discourse Theory of Law and Democracy*, trans. William Rehg (Cambridge: MIT Press, 1996) – originally published as *Faktizität und Geltung. Beiträge zur Diskurstheorie des Rechts und des demokratischn Rechtsstaats* (Frankfurt: Suhrkamp, 1992). For these and subsequent publications, see Matthew Specter, *Habermas: An Intellectual Biography* (Cambridge: Cambridge University Press, 2010).

4 See especially the various works of Hans-Ulrich Wehler, especially *Bismarck und der Imperialismus* (Cologne: Kiepenheuer & Witsch, 1969); *Historische Sozialwissenschaft und Geschichtsschreibung: Studien zu Aufgaben und Traditionen deutscher Geschichtswissenschaft* (Göttingen: Vandenhoeck & Ruprecht, 1980), as well as Hans-Ulrich Wehler, ed., *Moderne deutsche Sozialgeschichte* (Cologne: Kiepenheuer und Witsch, 1968). The flagship journal of this generational grouping is *Geschichte und Gesellschaft*, subtitled *Zeitschrift für historische Sozialwissenschaft* ('Journal of Historical Social Science'), which began publishing in 1975.

a journal that also pioneered the earliest discussions of Habermas's idea.[5] In the book-length English commentaries on Habermas's work appearing from the end of the 1970s, for example, *Strukturwandel* remained notable by its absence. Surprisingly, it was no more visible during the 1980s in the flourishing discussions of 'civil society', which in many ways stood in for the idea of the public sphere.[6] A French translation was published in 1978 as *L'espace public: archéologie de la publicité comme dimension constitutive de la société bourgeoise*, whose title managed to imply both a Foucauldian inflection to the book's intellectual history and the more directly class-based social history than it actually contained.[7] Otherwise, a younger West German historian, Günther Lottes, published an avowedly Habermasian and highly original account of English Jacobinism and its relationship to the 'pre-procedural' turbulence of the eighteenth-century plebeian public.[8] The appearance in 1972 of Oskar Negt and Alexander Kluge's New Left theoretical tract, *Öffentlichkeit und Erfahrung*, also established a critical West German counterpoint to Habermas's idea.[9]

In my own early work on political change in Germany between the 1890s and the First World War, I used the concept of the public sphere

---

5   Jürgen Habermas, 'The Public Sphere', *New German Critique* 3 (1974). See also Peter Uwe Hohendahl, 'Critical Theory, Public Sphere, and Culture: Jürgen Habermas and His Critics', *New German Critique* 16 (1979).

6   See Thomas McCarthy, *The Critical Theory of Jürgen Habermas* (Cambridge, MA: MIT Press, 1978); David Held, *Introduction to Critical Theory* (Berkeley, CA: University of California Press, 1980); Rick Roderick, *Habermas and the Foundations of Critical Theory* (Basingstoke: Macmillan, 1986); Anthony Giddens, 'Jürgen Habermas', in *The Return of Grand Theory in the Human Sciences*, ed. Quentin Skinner (Cambridge: Cambridge University Press, 1985); John B. Thompson and David Held, eds, *Critical Debates* (Cambridge, MA: MIT Press, 1982). For the civil society debates of the 1980s, see two volumes edited by John Keane: *Democracy and Civil Society: On the Predicaments of European Socialism, the Prospects for Democracy, and the Problem of Controlling Social and Political Power* (London: Verso, 1988), and *Civil Society and the State: New European Perspectives* (London/New York: Verso, 1988).

7   See Habermas, *L'espace public: archéologie de la publicité comme dimension constitutive de la société bourgeoise* (Paris: Payot, 1978).

8   Günther Lottes, *Politische Aufklärung and plebejisches Publikum: Zur Theorie und Praxis des englischen Radikalismus im späten 18. Jahrhundert* (Munich: Oldenbourg, 1979).

9   Oskar Negt and Alexander Kluge, *Öffentlichkeit und Erfahrung: Zur Organisationsanalyse von bürgerlicher und proletarischer Öffentlichkeit* (Frankfurt: Suhrkamp, 1972), equally belatedly translated as *The Public Sphere and Experience: Toward an Analysis of the Bourgeois and Proletarian Public Sphere*, trans. Peter Labanyi, Jamie Owen Daniel, and Assenka Oksiloff (Minneapolis: University of Minnesota Press, 1993). See also Miriam Hansen, 'Unstable Mixtures, Dilated Spheres: Negt's and Kluge's *The Public Sphere and Experience* Twenty Years Later', *Public Culture* 5 (1993).

from the start of the 1970s. It proved invaluable for thinking about the changing circumstances of political mobilization during the nineteenth century, and for placing the rise of German liberalism and its subsequent crises in a broader meta-analytical frame. This was true of a number of Habermas's specific themes, especially the circulation of news and growth of the press, the rise of a reading public, the organized sociability associated with urban living, the distinctive institutional infrastructure of social communication accompanying the development of capitalist markets, and the spread of voluntary associations, all of which helped connect the mid-nineteenth-century coalescence of liberal parties to an emergent social history of the German bourgeoisie. At a time when German historiography provided little support for doing so, Habermas's book encouraged me to think conceptually about the changing dynamics of state–society relations and the shifting space for political action in the new constitutional polities of the later nineteenth century. It gave me a handle for understanding what happened next, when the prevailing liberal approaches to the organizing of public life started to break down.

In looking back through my first book, *Reshaping the German Right* (1980), I am struck by how little explicit trace of Habermas it reveals, although one of my main theses – concerning popular mobilization, the dissolution of an older pattern of politics during the 1890s, and a general broadening of the political nation – was heavily indebted to his argument about the public sphere.[10] In the companion study I published with David Blackbourn in 1984, *The Peculiarities of German History*, which explored the relationship between political forms and the cultural manifestations of a self-confident bourgeois society, that indebtedness was far more visible.[11] Moreover, in parallel work I was doing in the late 1970s and early 1980s on the social history of European nationalism and the growth of political culture, the public sphere was certainly one of the organizing ideas.[12] I was always aware that Habermas's idea could not

10   Geoff Eley, *Reshaping the German Right: Radical Nationalism and Political Change after Bismarck*, 2nd edn (Ann Arbor, MI: University of Michigan Press, 1991).

11   David Blackbourn and Geoff Eley, *The Peculiarities of German History: Bourgeois Society and Politics in Nineteenth-Century Germany* (Oxford: Oxford University Press, 1984).

12   Geoff Eley, 'Nationalism and Social History', *Social History* 6: 1 (1981), and 'State Formation, Nationalism, and Political Culture: Some Thoughts on the German Case', in *Culture, Ideology and Politics: Festschrift for Eric Hobsbawm*, ed. Raphael Samuel and Gareth Stedman Jones (London: Routledge, 1983).

deliver the theoretical goods alone, but needed to be combined with other approaches to the cultural complexities of political change. For me these centred on the concept of civil society, theories of ideology, and the ideas of Antonio Gramsci, whose reception in Britain was then in full spate, converging in important ways with the influence of Raymond Williams.[13] In 1981, I published a long essay on social history and political culture in eighteenth- and nineteenth-century Britain bringing all of this together. Among other things, it considered Edward Thompson's writings within an explicitly Habermasian framework, which I further reformulated in Gramscian terms.[14]

During that period, to my recollection, virtually no historians were writing in consciously Habermasian ways. The literary scholar Peter Hohendahl, who introduced Habermas's book into the English-speaking world through the pages of *New German Critique*, was a vital exception, publishing in 1982 a key study of the shaping of a German national literary tradition.[15] But, otherwise, even the advocates of Habermas's centrality to critical theory showed little interest in his historical arguments about the growth and transformation of the public sphere as such. Remarkably enough, John Keane's *Public Life and Late Capitalism* (1984), which was avowedly inspired by a reading of Habermas, included no extended reference to the historical substance of *Strukturwandel* itself. Similarly, Keane's two volumes on the discourse of civil society in the 1980s, which strategically captured the political momentum of that extremely important European discussion, made no connection to notions of the public sphere.[16]

In the 1990s this suddenly changed. A first sign was Joan Landes's stimulating book on women and the public sphere in the French

---

13   Geoff Eley, 'Reading Gramsci in English: Observations on the Reception of Antonio Gramsci in the English-Speaking World, 1957–1982', *European History Quarterly* 14 (1984). There are strong affinities between Habermas's argument in *Strukturwandel* and the early works of Raymond Williams published at around the same time. See Raymond Williams, *Culture and Society, 1780–1950* (London: Chatto & Windus, 1958), *The Long Revolution* (London: Chatto & Windus, 1961), and *Communications* (Harmondsworth: Penguin, 1962).

14   Eley, 'Re-Thinking the Political: Social History and Political Culture in 18th and 19th Century Britain', *Archiv für Sozialgeschichte* 21 (1981).

15   Peter Uwe Hohendahl, *The Institution of Criticism* (Ithaca, NY: Cornell University Press, 1982) – originally published as *Literaturkritik und Öffentlichkeit* (Munich: R. Piper, 1974). See also Hohendahl, 'Critical Theory, Public Sphere, and Culture'.

16   John Keane, *Public Sphere and Late Capitalism: Toward a Socialist Theory of Democracy* (Cambridge: Cambridge University Press, 1984). See also Keane, *Democracy and Civil Society*, and *Civil Society and the State*.

Revolution, which, by adding feminist critiques of political theory to
Habermas's historicized framework, excited widespread interest and
debate. Around the same time, Leonore Davidoff and Catherine Hall
published *Family Fortunes*, searchingly problematizing the public–
private distinction in a gendered analysis of the making of the English
middle class.[17] But the real impetus came from the belated translation of
Strukturwandel der Öffentlichkeit itself in 1989, powerfully reinforced by
the published proceedings of an accompanying conference.[18] From that
point, Habermasian discussions blossomed all over the map.

The most elaborate concentrations of work can be found in territories
originally mapped by Habermas's book: eighteenth- and nineteenth-
century British history; the background to the French Revolution;
formations of bourgeois civility and associational culture in Germany.
Specific topics easily follow: the steady accretions of an urban way of life
in both provincial and metropolitan settings; civic arenas of action and
display in the form of meeting houses, concert halls, theatres, opera
houses, lecture halls, and museums; the spread of pedagogy, science,
and philanthropy; the flourishing of print culture in the press, publishing, and other literary media; the rise of a reading public through salons
and reading societies, subscription publishing and lending libraries;
new spaces of sociability in coffee houses, taverns, and clubs; and the
general universe of voluntary association. All these areas of social and
cultural history have been booming since the 1980s.[19] Not all historians

---

17   Joan B. Landes, *Women and the Public Sphere in the Age of the French Revolution*
(Ithaca: Cornell University Press, 1988); Leonore Davidoff and Catherine Hall, *Family
Fortunes: Men and Women of the English Middle Class, 1780–1850* (Chicago: University of
Chicago Press, 1987).

18   See the published proceedings: Craig Calhoun, ed., *Habermas and the Public Sphere*
(Cambridge, MA: MIT Press, 1992).

19   Exhaustive citations would be inappropriate here, but see especially the following:
Dena Goodman, 'Public Sphere and Private Life: Toward a Synthesis of Current Historio-
graphical Approaches to the Old Regime', *History and Theory* 31 (1992); Jon Cowans,
'Habermas and French History: The Public Sphere and the Problem of Political Legitimacy',
French History 13 (1999); Colin Jones, 'The Great Chain of Buying: Medical Advertisement,
the Bourgeois Public Sphere, and the Origins of the French Revolution', *American Historical
Review* 101 (1996); Anthony J. LaVopa, 'Conceiving a Public: Ideas and Society in Eighteenth-
Century Europe', *Journal of Modern History* 64 (1992); Ian McNeely, 'The Intelligence Gazette
(*Intelligenzblatt*) as a Road Map to Civil Society: Information Networks and Local Dynamism
in Germany, 1770s–1840s', in *Paradoxes of Civil Society: New Perspectives on Modern German
and British History*, ed. Frank Trentman (New York: Berghahn, 2000); Belinda J. Davis,
'Reconsidering Habermas, Gender, and the Public Sphere: The Case of Wilhelmine Germany',
in *Society, Culture, and the State in Germany 1870–1930*, ed. Geoff Eley (Ann Arbor, MI:

working in them are directly inspired by Habermas's ideas, but the reception of *Strukturwandel*'s translation shaped the environment in which they now have to think. Moreover, beyond these immediate domains, ideas of the public sphere permeate discussion in a wide diversity of transnational and cross-disciplinary fields, linking literary scholars, historians, and theorists of art and architecture, film specialists, sociologists, anthropologists, political theorists, and anyone placing themselves in the disorderly and un-disciplined field of cultural studies.

In the process, the concept has migrated a long way from its original usage. Aside from its general currency among historians and across the humanities and social sciences as a term of theory, 'public sphere' has become adaptable for widely varying purposes. After the early 'proletarian public sphere' proposed by Negt and Kluge, we now have the black public sphere, the feminist public sphere, professional public spheres, the 'phantom public sphere', the global public sphere, the 'indigenous public sphere', the intimate public sphere, the electronic public sphere, and so forth.[20] The burgeoning new journals in cultural studies have aired these discussions, mobilizing work across the disciplines from literature to anthropology, philosophy to musicology, history to communications: they include *Critical Inquiry* (founded 1974), *Media, Culture, and Society*

University of Michigan Press, 1996); John Brewer, 'This, That, and the Other: Public, Social, and Private in the Seventeenth and Eighteenth Centuries', in *Shifting the Boundaries: Transformations of the Languages of Public and Private in the Eighteenth Century*, ed. Dario Castiglione and Leslie Sharpe (Exeter: University of Exeter Press, 1995); David Zaret, *Origins of Democratic Culture: Printing, Petitions, and the Public Sphere in Early Modern England* (Princeton, NJ: Princeton University Press, 1999); Margaret C. Jacob, 'The Mental Landscape of the Public Sphere: A European Perspective', *Eighteenth-Century Studies* 28 (1994).

20   See the theme issue on 'The Black Public Sphere', *Public Culture* 7 (1994), republished as *The Black Public Sphere: A Public Culture Book* (Chicago: University of Chicago Press, 1996). See also Joan B. Landes, ed., *Feminism, the Public, and the Private* (Oxford: Oxford University Press, 1998); Bruce Robbins, ed., *The Phantom Public Sphere* (Minneapolis: University of Minnesota Press, 1993); John Hartley and Alan McKee, *The Indigenous Public Sphere: The Reporting and Reception of Aboriginal Issues in the Australian Media* (Oxford: Oxford University Press, 2001); Lauren Berlant, ed., *Intimacy* (Chicago: University of Chicago Press, 2000); Douglas Kellner, 'Globalization from Below? Toward a Radical Democratic Technopolitics', *Angelaki: Journal of the Theoretical Humanities* 4 (1999); Lincoln Dahlberg, 'Cyberspace and the Public Sphere: Exploring the Democratic Potential of the Net', *Convergence* 4 (1998); and 'Extending the Public Sphere through Cyberspace: The Case of Minnesota E-Democracy', *First Monday* 6 (2001), firstmonday.org. See also the 'Public Sphere Project' of the Computer Professionals for Social Responsibility (CPSR) Initiative, launched by the CPSR Symposium on 'Shaping the Network Society: The Future of the Public Sphere in Cyberspace', Seattle, Washington, 20–23 May 2000.

(1978), *Social Text* (1982), *Representations* (1983), *Cultural Critique* (1985), *Cultural Studies* (1987), *New Formations* (1987), *Public Culture* (1988), *International Journal of Cultural Studies* (1998), *European Journal of Cultural Studies* (1998), and more. Even the most casual visit to the internet revealed an extraordinary wealth of activity around the term, ranging across national and linguistic borders, inside the academy and out, and across all manner of disciplines and fields, from poetry to psychoanalysis, law to markets, television to cybernetics.

In contemporary discourse, 'public sphere' came to signify the general questing for democratic agency in an era of declining electoral participation, compromised sovereignties, and frustrated or disappointed citizenship. The term was called upon wherever people came together for collective exchange and expression of opinion, aiming both for coherent enunciation and the transmission of messages onward to parallel or superordinate bodies, whether these were the state, some other institutional locus of authority, or simply the dominant culture. Such publics might be local and extremely modest, as in the public sphere of a particular institution like a company or university, or in the actions of citizens in a special part of their lives, such as parents mobilizing at school boards. Or they might be spatially quite indefinite, as in the novel and aspirational publics of cyberspace, transnational diasporas, and globalization.

Where does this profusion leave us? First, and most obviously, the term has become decisively disengaged from its author's original purpose. Arguments can certainly still be made for the public sphere's embeddedness in the consequences of those large-scale societal transformations between the late Middle Ages and the eighteenth century, where Habermas began his account. In *Strukturwandel*, he linked an emergent political logic of transition to a complexity of long-run changes in that way, from trade-driven processes of capital accumulation and the reconfiguring of state–society relations to the dissolving of the household economy and the coalescence of the bourgeoisie into a new and dynamic social force. But the term's value has been emancipated from those more particular beginnings. Habermas himself now deploys the concept in relation to citizenship and 'democratic legitimation' more generally, using it to express the 'equal opportunity to take part in an encompassing process of focused political communication' and the need to fashion a resilient 'communicational infrastructure' towards that end.[21] It now functions as a mobile theoretical term analogous to state or society, and thereby lends itself quite appropriately to contexts other than the western European ones Habermas originally discussed, such as the Japanese, South Asian, and various postcolonial settings readily encountered across a variety of academic disciplines.[22]

Second, at a time of extreme uncertainty among social historians, when the so-called linguistic turn and the 'new cultural history' were placing them uncomfortably on the defensive during the 1990s, *Strukturwandel* offered an account of democracy's cultural prerequisites that remained grounded in highly materialist ways. It begins with a particular model of the formation of commercial society for understanding the transition from feudalism to capitalism, embracing all the institutional innovations presupposed in the organization of markets, of communications, of the creation of newspapers, and so on, linking the circulation of ideas to a new infrastructural environment of social organization and exchange. For its time, this account was impressively based on the social-historical scholarship then available.[23] It always implied a social history rather than just an argument about ideas. Its beauty was to have theorized the emergence of modern politics in a way that was precisely grounded in materialist social history and a broader conception of public action. In that sense, the suggestion that its appeal in the 1990s was 'the result of the slow decline of unreconstructed social history and the linguistic and cultural turns in the discipline' is very wide of the mark: on the contrary, it allowed key social bearings and lines of social explanation to be preserved while so many voices were casting them out.[24]

Third, there is more ambiguity to *Öffentlichkeit* than much of the English-language discussion allows. An unwieldy aggregation of terms

---

21 Jürgen Habermas, 'Why Europe Needs a Constitution', *New Left Review*, II/11 (September–October 2001), 17.

22 For a valuable review of this changing theoretical valency, see Margaret R. Somers, 'Narrating and Naturalizing Civil Society and Citizenship Theory: The Place of Political Culture and the Public Sphere', *Sociological Theory* 13 (1995).

23 Given the paucity of pertinent historiography at the time, Habermas's book offered an extraordinarily creative synthesis, whose challenge remained long unmet. West German scholarship was shaped more by the state-centred perspective of Koselleck's magisterial *Preußen zwischen Reform und Revolution: Allgemeines Landrecht, Verwaltung und soziale Bewegung von 1791 bis 1848* (Stuttgart: Ernst Klett Verlag, 1967).

24 Despite cavalier dismissal of the wider value of the concept of the public sphere, the author gave a rich treatment of the coffeehouse milieu, with excellent guidance to wider literature. See Brian Cowan, 'What Was Masculine about the Public Sphere? Gender and the Coffeehouse Milieu in Post-Restoration England', *History Workshop Journal* 51 (2001), 129.

like *publicness, publicity, public culture,* and *public opinion* captures the
term perhaps more accurately than the customary 'public sphere', which
manages a rather clumsy and unsatisfactory approximation of the
complex German meaning. The latter connotes something more like
'the quality or condition of *being public*', making space for a set of ethical
and philosophical desiderata in addition to the more distinctly institutional arena of political articulation foregrounded in most English
discussions. The changing coordinates of political life become more
intelligible once we consider them within this rather different horizon,
rather than confining ourselves to the institutional approach. Politics
since the 1960s is simply not graspable, for example, using only a framework of constitutional liberalism, parliamentary politics, and reasoned
public debate, any more than the 1960s turbulence was itself assimilable
by the consolidated political culture of the post-war moment. Instead,
violence, direct-action militancy, street demonstrations, the politics of
memory, visual culture, the mass circulation of images, and the com-
mercialized and mass-mediated domain of popular culture all demand
a different analytic from the one Habermas classically supplied. These
aspects of 1968 exploded the terms of established political discourse.
Theoretically speaking, they also expose some crucial difficulties at the
centre of the Habermasian public sphere.

Whenever we grapple with questions of conflict, disputation, and pluralization in that way, we necessarily complicate the framework proposed
by *Strukturwandel,* with its classic grand narrative of bourgeois emancipation between the Enlightenment and later nineteenth century, followed
by twentieth-century degeneration and decline. Habermas's idealized
picture of the rational political agency of a bourgeois citizenry, however
flawed by exclusions and however vulnerable to empirical critique, retains
its normative appeal for democratic theory, with its protected space of
procedural deliberation and reasoned political exchange, intermediate
between state and civil society. But to grasp our contemporary problems
of democratic articulation, we need to engage the thesis of the public
sphere's decline and fall – the 'structural transformation' of the book's title.[25]

There is here an irony to Habermas's critique of the Federal Republic's degraded public sphere as he saw it from the early 1960s. This 1962
lament for the supposedly vanished public sphere of classical liberal

---

25   See my summary of the argument in Chapter 4, above.

modernity was actually part of a sustained contemporary plea to create that ideal in West Germany in the first place. *Strukturwandel* drew its impetus from a gathering political discussion of the early 1960s among the so-called '1945ers' – journalists, writers, social commentators, TV pundits, academics, and other public intellectuals born roughly between 1921 and 1933, who as teenagers or young adults experienced Nazism's defeat as their decisive life-defining event, embraced reconstruction and the opening towards 'the West', and were now calling for the further strengthening of the Federal Republic's liberal democracy. Growing confidently into its prosperous stabilities, while openly reclaiming deeper German virtues and traditions, Konrad Adenauer's 'CDU state' seemed by the early 1960s troublingly continuous with an earlier author- itarian past. The sociopolitical patterns and proclivities so favourable to the rise and success of Nazism had not been as honestly and effectively disavowed as supporters of West German democracy had hoped. The increasingly vocal 1945ers urged an altogether more candid and encom- passing reckoning with this still-unmastered past. They wanted a new climate of polite pluralism, national civility, and reasoned public exchange, in a thoroughgoing politicization of the public discourse.[26]

This commitment to securing the conditions of public reasoning was very much the ideal animating Habermas's 1962 book. But what figured there as a *nostalgia* for something that once existed but had now been lost was actually the newly voiced *disideratum* of a vigorously maturing generational critique, seeking to fashion such a public sphere for the first time. In other words, so far from standing alone as the generative theoretical text for a new and original line of analysis, as *Strukturwandel* later came to resemble, Habermas's book was actually just one inter- vention among very many. Its author joined an extremely dense and much broader existing debate about the desirable meanings of public- ness – *Öffentlichkeit* – for West German democracy. That debate was about the urgency of building on the post-1945 foundations by facing up to Germany's earlier anti-democratic traditions.

If the earlier 1960s had presaged concrete and attainable progress towards a fragile but functioning pluralism, then the radicalism of the

---

26 See especially A. Dirk Moses, 'The Forty-Fivers: A Generation between Fascism and Democracy', *German Politics and Society* 17: 1 (1999); Christina A. Hodenberg, *Konsens und Krise. Eine Geschichte der westdeutschen Medienöffentlichkeit, 1945–1973* (Göttingen: Wallstein Verlag, 2006).

later rupture of 1968 becomes far easier to understand. For the vehemence of the 1968ers' critique was directed against precisely the perceived hollowness of the new culture of public civility the 1945ers were so assiduously trying to create. During 1967–68 the passions of the West German student movement were fuelled not only by the excesses of Franz-Jozef Strauss, the CDU-CSU, and the far Right, but also by the equally crude authoritarianism of the West Berlin SPD – supposedly the best support for a progressivist West German future. Thus both of Willy Brandt's successors as mayor of that city, Heinrich Albertz and Klaus Schütz, treated the escalating student activism of the Socialist German Students (SDS) and Extra-Parliamentary Opposition (APO) with a completely unbending disdain, mouthing the nostrums of parliamentary legality and constitutional defence while inflaming the worst intolerance against the new dissent. The public climate became brutalized into angry adversarialism, the opposite of Habermasian proceduralism and reasoned exchange. In other words, the very champions of the liberal-democratic political culture Habermas hoped to see more effectively instituted were feeding the generational enmity, fuelling the anti-APO hysteria, and inciting the police to excess. The language of constitutional democracy (the 'free democratic basic order') was not only reified, but even converted into a weapon, turned unforgivingly against student radicals. Exercising the classic civil freedoms was no longer applauded, but demonized.

In the most painful of ironies, the apostles of authority and order spoke for precisely those political groupings whose political advance Habermas and his fellow advocates expected to realize their reforming hopes. But politics had gone out of doors. Once that happened, with all the resulting misbehaviour and commotion – direct-action turbulence, shocking irreverence, scandalous experimentation, stylistic provocation, sheer ill-mannered rebellion – the political energies and purposes necessarily outgrew the existing boundaries of acceptability, and sometimes blew them violently apart. The 1968ers had scant patience for the protocols of comportment and civility the 1945ers wanted to preserve. While the proceduralist rules of parliamentary democracy had to be upheld, they needed equally to be complemented by participatory energies and responsiveness to the grass roots: by 1968, the committee room needed the streets. Yet, in the event, the aggressive obstinacy of nearly all SPD and liberal proceduralists in the face of this civic exhortation – making citizenship manifest through activism – confirmed New Left critics in their increasingly militant disaffection. The self-serving narrowness of the existing system seemed to be exposed. In the minds of extraparliamentary radicals, the democratic potential of public-sphere proceduralism was already negated by the confining rules of the polity. To establish a genuinely democratic publicness, radical extensions were needed.

These questions, and the related West German conflicts of the 1950s and 1960s, have obvious resonance for histories elsewhere, whether in Europe or globally. In those societies emerging from fascism or other dictatorships during the mid 1940s – not only Italy, Germany, and Japan, but also their various satellites and, in a different way, those societies under fascist military occupation and accompanying collaborationist regimes – similar challenges of coming to terms with a difficult or delegitimized recent past continued to complicate post-war politics for decades to come. Likewise, decolonizing societies had their own challenge of establishing the conditions for democratic public life after periods of coercively intolerant and exclusionary political rule. In those cases, moreover, colonial annexation and subsequent state-making had commonly occurred well in advance of the developmental histories Habermas thought so essential to the possibility of the public sphere in western Europe, violently disrupting those already existing societies with their dispersed sovereignties and fragmented polities. During the construction of postcolonial national states after 1945, publicness was as much superimposed on those societies as crystallizing organically within them.

In other post-fascist cases, intellectuals, activists, and citizens all struggled with issues analogous to those confronted by West German intellectuals in the wake of the Third Reich: How could democratic political culture be reconstituted in societies severed from the normal resources of continuity and tradition, in which the national past per se had lost its authorizing legitimacy, or seemed to have been entirely disqualified? If these individual thinkers inevitably diverged in many specific ways from Habermas and other West German counterparts, then the structural syndromes of these other 'post-wars' remain nonetheless comparable, and the specific differences can be as illuminating in that respect as the similarities. Thus, Japanese instances of the 'localization' and pluralization of the public sphere during the 1960s provide evident points of convergence with the West German protest movements of the same period, whose comparative possibilities cycle back through the *Bürgerinitiativen* (Citizens' Initiatives), the new social movements, and eventually the Greens between the late 1960s and early 1980s. The fields of tension between these new direct-action militancies and Habermas's adamant defence of communicative and proceduralist reasoning showed clear similarities with the counterpart conflicts in Japan.

The classical framework of proceduralist *Öffentlichkeit* seems particularly ill-fitted for the new types of publicness that erupted in the 1960s and 1970s, a disjunction dramatically and poignantly illustrated by the conflicts Habermas directly solicited with the West German New Left.[27] This applies most blatantly to the counter-cultural radicalisms of 1968, where Japanese events again invite another fascinating plane of potential comparison, ranging across the official spectacle of the Tokyo Olympiad, the potential counter-public imagined by the documentarists, and the avant-garde interventionism developing around the remarkable 'Model 1,000-Yen Incident'. For example, in the West German context, we know something about the Situationist and avant-garde precursors of *Kommune I* and other counter-cultural groups, and during the 1960s a variety of bohemian and hedonistic subcultures in major cities like Munich, Frankfurt, Hamburg, and West Berlin were crystallizing alternative publics of some long-term importance. Across the North Sea in Britain, analogously, it is also clear that the worlds of jazz and R&B, poetry in pubs, folk music, little magazines, and art schools were just as basic to 1968's prehistories as the Campaign for Nuclear Disarmament and the New Left Clubs. In given treatments of the public sphere, the contributions of stylistic dissidence, aesthetic radicalism, and the associated cultural politics remain both seriously neglected and a potential source of extremely fruitful comparison.[28]

---

27 See Oskar Negt, ed., *Die Linke antwortet Jürgen Habermas. Mit Beiträgen von Wolfgang Abendroth et al.* (Frankfurt: Europäische Verlagsantalt, 1969); Jürgen Habermas, *Protestbewegung und Hochschulreform* (Frankfurt: Suhrkamp, 1969); and Habermas, *Toward a Rational Society*.

28 See Dick Hebdige, *Subculture: The Meaning of Style* (London: Methuen, 1979), and *Hiding in the Light* (London: Comedia, 1988). See also Peter Wollen, 'The Situationist International: On the Passage of a Few People Through a Rather Brief Period of Time', in his *Raiding the Icebox: Reflections on Twentieth-Century Culture* (Bloomington: Indiana University Press, 1993), and 'Global Conceptualism and North American Conceptual Art', in *Global Conceptualism: Points of Origin, 1950s–1980s*, ed. Luis Camnitzer, Jane Farver, and Rachel Weiss (New York: Queen's Museum of Art, 1999).

Finally, the most important of the counter-publics generated by the new conflicts of the 1960s has been the feminist one. Feminist critiques have also been the most far-reaching of the responses to Habermas in the decade since the translation of *Strukturwandel* appeared.[29] As both history and idea, these have argued, the public sphere was constructed around a system of gendered meanings, whether in the formal intellectual discourse of politics, citizenship, and rights, in the institutional arenas of publicness and publicity, in the associational universe of civic engagement and sociality, or in the personal sphere of family life. More generally, whether in theory or politics, feminists have turned the relationship of the personal and the political completely inside out. Since the explosions of the late 1960s and early 1970s, the connections between everydayness and political life have been entirely remade, whether in the family or the workplace, in sexuality and personal relations, or in all the situations where pain and pleasure are produced.

The notion of the public sphere has proved an excellent means of connecting these settings of everyday life to an idea of political agency and action. It opens a space for talking about political action without subsuming it into the conventional institutional assumptions about how politics occurs. Those narrower understandings have been especially common for many workaday historians, who might be very sophisticated in their handling of empirical-analytical work, but recalcitrantly anti-intellectual when assumptions are to be explicated or theory put to use. Politics can be all too easily located in the political process narrowly understood – in parties, in legislatures, in government. This continues to characterize contemporary common-sense understandings too. As a theory term taken from Habermas, 'public sphere' supplies a means of conceptualizing an expanded notion of the political. It forces us to look for politics in other social places.

---

29   This friendly feminist critique was presaged in the later 1980s. See Nancy Fraser, 'What's Critical about Critical Theory? The Case of Habermas and Gender', and Isis M. Young, 'Impartiality and the Civic Public', both in *Feminism as Critique: Essays on the Politics of Gender in Late-Capitalist Society*, ed. Seyla Benhabib and Drucillla Cornell (Minneapolis: University of Minnesota Press, 1987); Landes, *Women and the Public Sphere*; Mary P. Ryan, *Women in Public: Between Banners and Ballots, 1825–1880* (Baltimore: Johns Hopkins University Press, 1990); *Civic Wars: Democracy and Public Life in the American City during the Nineteenth Century* (Berkeley, CA: University of California Press, 1997); Landes, *Feminism, the Public, and the Private*.

Its uses are not only historical. It activates a sense of ordinary and efficacious citizenship today. The 'public sphere' in that sense is the space between state and civil society in which political action may acquire wider resonance, whether in terms of its local effects or in building a sense of political agency, or in behaving ethically in one's social relations and allowing some notion of collective goods to be posed, and thereby contributing to wider processes of political mobilization. It supplies one means of making connections between what we think and do in everyday life, including the personal sphere, and the world of politics at a time when such extreme and debilitating scepticism has accumulated about the purpose and potency of such action. When in popular perceptions 'politics' degenerates ever more cynically into a synonym for corruption, self-interestedness, and machineries of privilege beyond realistic popular control, the 'public sphere' offers a way of restoring intelligibility to the political process. Politics can be reclaimed for a realistic discourse of democracy.

At a time of such depressingly extensive political disbelief – of disaffection and disablement around one's agency as a citizen – the term 'public sphere' becomes an excellent starting point for thinking again about what politics is, about where it takes place, and about how it can function as a space available to ordinary people, not just official or career politicians. It allows one to imagine – modestly and realistically – how a sense of citizenship might be re-engaged, whether in the public sphere of particular institutions like universities or professions; in some local setting like a school board, a workplace, or a community campaign; or in the new political communities of cyberspace. It may even infiltrate the political process more conventionally understood, in relation to parties and elections, the articulation of 'interests', and the presentation of demands in government. This is clearly linked also to notions of civil society, as the ground on and from which political actions arise. So, if I argue that the public sphere makes more sense as a structured setting in which contestation and negotiation can occur, this is what I have in mind, whether in relation to the late eighteenth and early nineteenth centuries, to Japan and Western Europe since 1945, to the 1960s, or to the present.

6

Labour History – Social History – Alltagsgeschichte: Experience, Culture, and the Politics of the Everyday; Or, New Ground for German Social History

Labour History and Its Boundaries

The most arresting departure in West German historiography during the late twentieth century was *Alltagsgeschichte*, or the history of everyday life. Beginning around the mid 1970s, the term quickly gained currency as the watchword for a new historical sensibility. Invariably locally based, the resulting enthusiasm reached far beyond the academy into museums, exhibitions, adult education, and local government cultural offices, along with popular media, local publishing, and self-organized amateur research. It was as much a lay as a professional movement, not least because so many recent PhDs lacked university jobs, or at best kept only a foothold in the profession. Loosely grouped from early 1980s in the *Geschichtswerkstatt* (History Workshop) movement, these 'barefoot historians' coincided with the peace movement and the Greens. An early peak came in 1980–81, when the President's Prize for German History in Schools was assigned the theme 'Daily Life under National Socialism'. After earlier iterations on 'Movements of Freedom' in one's own locality (1974–76) and 'The Social History of

Everyday Life' (1977–79), this third competition drew some 12,000 entries, amid widespread public controversy.[1]

One sign was a flood of literature seeking a wider-than-academic readership: memoirs, oral histories, diaries, and 'eyewitness accounts'; anthologies of documentation, pictures, and commentary; local histories; exhibition catalogues; handsomely illustrated coffee-table books. Nazism was strongly featured: one composite 1986 review by Detlev Peukert collected over fifty works on the Third Reich.[2] Public enthusiasm ranged very widely across the past: witness the remarkable popularity of the 1977 Stuttgart exhibition on the culture of the Staufen period (1150–1250), or the prestigious West Berlin Prussia exhibition ('Prussia: Attempt at a Balance') four years later.[3] The new public history appealed all across the political spectrum, attracting the Historical Commission of the SPD no less than the post-1982 commemorative agenda of Helmut Kohl's governing CDU. Palpably linked to a 'normalizing' vision of German history – in a healthy national past untainted by Nazism – Kohl's proposals for a Museum of German History in West Berlin and a House of History of the Federal Republic in Bonn were also hotly contested.[4] Public controversy exploded in the mid 1980s around the *Historikerstreit*, in disputes over the museum projects, in antifascist vigilance against sweeping Nazism under the carpet, in the mushrooming of community histories, and in the take-off of women's history. In all these respects, *Alltagsgeschichte* acquired definite political traction.[5]

---

1   See 'Ein kraftiger Schub für die Vergangenheit: Spiegel-Report über die neue Geschichtsbewegung in der Bundesrepublik', *Der Spiegel* 23 (6 June 1983). For schools' competition materials, see Dieter Galinski and Ulla Lachauer, eds, *Alltag im Nationalsozialismus 1933–1939: Jahrbuch zum Schülerwettbewerb Deutsche Geschichte um den Preis des Bundespräsidenten* (Braunschweig: Westermann, 1982); Dieter Galinski, Ulrich Herbert, and Ulla Lachauer, eds, *Nazis und Nachbarn: Schüler erforschen den Alltag im Nationalsozialismus* (Reinbek bei Hamburg: Rohwolt, 1982); Dieter Galinski and W. Schmidt, eds, *Die Kriegsjahre in Deutschland 1939–1945: Ergebnisse u. Anregungen aus d. Schülerwettbewerb Deutsch Geschicte um d. Preis d. Bundespräsidenten 1982/83* (Hamburg: Verlag Erziehung & Wissenschaft, 1985).

2   Detlev J. K. Peukert, 'Das "Dritte Reich" aus der "Alltags"-Perspektive', *Archiv für Sozialgeschichte* 26 (1986).

3   For the wider context, see Geoff Eley, 'Nazism, Politics and the Image of the Past: Thoughts on the West German *Historikerstreit*, 1986–87', *Past and Present* 121 (1988).

4   See Jacob S. Eder, *Holocaust Angst: The Federal Republic of Germany and American Holocaust Memory since the 1970s* (New York: Oxford University Press, 2016).

5   See Heide Gerstenberger and Dorothea Schmidt, eds, *Normalität oder Normalisierung? Geschichtswerkstätten und Faschismusanalyse* (Münster: Verlag Westfälisches Dampfboot, 1987); Geschichtswerkstatt Berlin, ed., *Die Nation als Ausstellungsstück: Planangen, Kritik*

Most of the coffee-table genre eschewed politics.[6] Hermann Glaser, long-time cultural officer for Nuremberg city and leading popularizer of cultural history, was a good example. Coming from an older tradition of museum-based pedagogy, he broadened its charge to previously disregarded topics, notably the lives, manners, and morals of the working class, for which *Industriekultur* (industrial culture) then supplied an organizing frame. Though progressive and humane, this stopped short of *Alltagsgeschichte* per se. It remained a catchall for the texture of social life in industrial society. After co-authoring volumes on mechanization, the impact of railways, Nuremberg in the machine age, and nineteenth-century social life, all generously illustrated in large format, Glaser launched a series on *The Industrial Culture of German Cities and Regions.*[7]

Wolfgang Ruppert, based in 1978–81 at Glaser's Centre for Industrial Culture, before moving to a Bielefeld chair of cultural history, was one bridge into *Alltagsgeschichte.* His splendidly produced 1986 anthology *Die Arbeiter* exemplified the more popular genre.[8] Comprising thirty specially commissioned contributions, its five thematic sections (work, daily life, collective hopes for change, the institutions of workers' culture, political and trade-union organization) surveyed working-class history during 1860–1933. Like most of the commercially produced publications, it presumed a contemporary closure in which the 'world of the

---

and Utopien zu den Museumsgründungen in Bonn and Berlin (Hamburg: VSA-Verlag, 1987).

6 For example, the series *Fotografierte Zeitgeschichte* launched by Düsseldorf publisher Droste: R. Italiaander, ed., *Wir erlebten das Ende der Weimarer Republik: Zeitgenossen berichten* (Düsseldorf: Droste, 1982); Klaus-Jörg Ruhl, *Brauner Alltag: 1933–1939 in Deutschland* (Düsseldorf: Droste, 1981); George Holmsten, *Kriegsalltag: 1939–1945 in Deutschland* (Düsseldorf: Droste, 1982); Robert Fritzsch, *Nürnberg unterm Hakenkreuz: Im Dritten Reich 1933–1939* (Düsseldorf: Droste, 1983).

7 Hermann Glaser, Wolfgang Ruppert, and Norbert Neudecker, eds, *Industriekultur in Nürnberg: Eine deutsche Stadt im Maschinenalter* (Munich: C. H. Beck, 1980); Hermann Glaser and Walther Pützstück, eds, *Ein deutscher Bilderbuch 1870–1918: Die Gesellschaft einer Epoche in alter Photographien* (Munich: C. H. Beck, 1982). See also, Jochen Boberg, Tilman Fichter, and Eckhart Giller, eds, *Exerzierfeld der Moderne: Industriekultur in Berlin im 19. Jahrhundert* (Munich: C. H. Beck, 1982); Volker Plagemann, ed., *Industriekultur in Hamburg: Des Deutschen Reiches Tor zur Welt* (Munich: C. H. Beck, 1984). Glaser was first known for his classic *Spiesser-Ideologie: Von der Zerstörung des deutschen Geistes im 19. und 20. Jahrhundert* (Freiburg: Rombach, 1964), translated as *The Cultural Roots of National Socialism*, transl. Ernest A. Menze (London: Croom Helm, 1978).

8 Wolfgang Ruppert, ed., *Die Arbeiter: Lebensformen, Alltag and Kultur von der Frühindustrialisierung bis zum 'Wirtschaftswunder'* (Munich: C. H. Beck, 1986).

worker', the labour movement, and a self-consciously distinctive work-ing-class culture were all consigned to the past. It opened a window onto a strange and vanished world, appealing to family-based curiosity but with little purchase on the present, whether building from the material privations or from the utopian values and class solidarities. The purpose was fascination: engaging the readers' human sympathy but not their politics. From the book overall, a critical edge was missing.[9]

Ruppert's volume synthesized a mountain of new research on German working-class history, which flourished remarkably in these years. Much reflected labour history's classic priorities – less studies of the SPD itself than of unions, strikes, and particular industries, as in another imposing anthology of the time comparing pre-1914 unionization in Germany and Britain.[10] One pair of essays there analysed strike patterns in the two countries (James Cronin, Friedhelm Boll), while another consid-ered relations between unions and party (Jay Winter, Hans Mommsen). But the book then turned to salient themes, drawing on contributors' monographic research. On the German side, this embraced the evolving dynamics of localism, craft unionism, and industrial unionism (Klaus Schönhoven); the persistence of localism in Berlin (Dirk Müller); early trade unionism up to the 1890s (Klaus Tenfelde); rank-and-file union-ism on the Hamburg docks (Michael Grüttner); Christian unions (Michael Schneider); and the role of the state (Klaus Saul).

Comparison recurred consistently to *politics*. Economics was still primary. Germany's compressed and accelerated industrialization, joined to high levels of industrial concentration, explained its central-ized, industry-wide unionism, as against the gradual industrializing and early craft strengths in Britain, enabled the distinctive mixture of craft, industrial, and general unionism. While noting this structural divergence, German historians then commonly turn to politics: an authoritarian state explained both the German unions' weakness under the law and the workers' greater electoral radicalism, while the employ-ers' anti-union rigidity drew from the same reactionary source. Thus,

---

9   The ninety-four contributions in Volker Plagemann, ed., *Industriekultur in Hamburg: Des Deutschen Reiches Tor zur Welt* (Munich: C. H. Beck, 1984), included no single treatment of the 1892 cholera, whose centrality for the city's sociopolitical history was concurrently examined in the 676 pages of Richard J. Evans, *Death in Hamburg: Society and Politics in the Cholera Years, 1830–1910* (Oxford: Oxford University Press, 1987).

10   Hans Mommsen and Hans-Gerhard Husung, eds, *The Development of Trade Union-ism in Great Britain and Germany 1880–1914* (London: George Allen & Unwin, 1985).

for Tenfelde, the Bismarckian state's repressive policies artificially delayed the arrival of a 'British' pattern of liberalized and accommodative industrial relations. Repression 'disrupted the process of trade union formation' in the 1870s, just as 'the "natural" relationship between conflict and organization' was about to arrive. So, in Germany, the modern patterns of industrial conflict failed to produce the matching forms of collective regulation via a 'responsible' and pragmatic trade unionism.[11] These new social histories certainly studied working conditions, community organization, labour-market dynamics, and workplace sociology. But, in explaining the differential progress of British and German trade unionism, the *German state* did most of the work.[12]

Barring this anti-democratic impedance, labour's ultimate integration was presumed inevitable. Such was the SPD's 'inescapable fate' once the Anti-Socialist Law was repealed, according to Gerhard A. Ritter. That future could be glimpsed in 'the workers' involvement in ever greater areas of practical effectiveness, of which there were thousands of individual manifestations', from the parliamentary moderation of the South German Social Democrats to the service activities of labour secretariats, workers' participation in consultative tribunals, and union leaders' sensible pragmatism.[13] The SPD's revolutionary posturing was just hot air, 'theoretical humbug', in Ritter's view, the gratuitous side-effect of anti-socialist intransigence.[14] German labour's oppositional culture channelled political backwardness – those 'traditional patterns of authority' blinding big employers to the rational case for industrial conciliation. This implies a teleology of 'modern' industrial relations: a pluralist model of equilibrium or 'partnership' between capital and labour that in Germany was abnormally held back. Analysis is pulled upwards to the decisiveness of large-scale political determinations, rather than 'micro' explanations from everyday life.

---

11 Klaus Tenfelde, 'Conflict and Organization in the Early History of the German Trade Union Movement', in Mommsen and Husung, *Development of Trade Unionism*, 213, 204.

12 See here Geoff Eley, 'The British Model and the German Road: Rethinking the Course of German History before 1914', in *The Peculiarities of German History: Bourgeois Society and Politics in Nineteenth-Century Germany*, ed. David Blackbourn and Geoff Eley (Oxford: Oxford University Press, 1984). See also, Gerald D. Feldman and Klaus Tenfelde, eds, *Workers, Owners and Politics in Coal Mining: An International Comparison of Industrial Relations* (New York: Berg, 1990).

13 Gerhard A. Ritter, *Die Arbeiterbewegung im Wilhelminischen Reich 1890–1900* (Berlin: Colloquium Verlag, 1959), 149, 208, 187.

14 Ibid., 127.

Similar teleology shaped a concurrent growth area in social history from the later 1970s: the study of nineteenth-century 'social protest'. Following pioneering accounts in British and French history by George Rudé, Eric Hobsbawm, Edward Thompson, and Charles Tilly, West German scholars produced a dense historiography of their own in remarkably short time.[15] They broadly replicated their predecessors' underlying assumption – namely, that spontaneous and direct popular actions like food riots and similar crowd violence came to be superseded during modernization by rationally organized collective mobilization, such as trade-union-directed strikes. The classic thesis of a transition from 'preindustrial' to 'industrial' protest – 'the "Pilgrim's Progress" of industrial relations', with respectable trade unions at its end – emerged entirely intact.[16]

We can trace this through a third emblematic anthology edited by Heinrich Volkmann and Jürgen Bergmann, in which the 'crowd in history' became the avatar for a society in epochal, structural transition, as popular cultures reacted against modernizing change.[17] Volkmann and Bergmann found a 'type of protest specific to a particular period' from the beginnings of capitalist industrialization to the end of the 1849–73 boom, coinciding with the German unification.[18] This translates to a story of progressive sophistication, as spontaneous, sporadic, uncoordinated, and locally bounded direct actions subsided before the planned, continuous, and supralocal representation of collective interests, increasingly attuned to national politics. Volkmann distributed

---

15   See Eric J. Hobsbawm, *Primitive Rebels: Studies in Archaic Forms of Social Movement in the Nineteenth and Twentieth Centuries* (Manchester: Manchester University Press, 1959); George Rudé, *The Crowd in History: A Study of Popular Disturbances in France and England, 1730–1848* (New York: Wiley, 1964); E. P. Thompson, 'The Moral Economy of the English Crowd in the Eighteenth Century', *Past and Present* 50 (1971); Charles Tilly, *The Vendée* (Cambridge: Harvard University Press, 1964); Charles Tilly, Louise Tilly, and Richard Tilly, *The Rebellious Century 1830–1930* (Cambridge: Harvard University Press, 1975). See *Geschichte und Gesellschaft* 3: 2 (1977), where Heinz-Gerhard Haupt, 'Zur historischen Analyse von Gewalt', and Karin Hausen, 'Schwierigkeiten mit dem "sozialen Protest"', developed critiques of Richard Tilly. See also Robert J. Holton, 'The Crowd in History: Some Problems of Theory and Method', *Social History* 3: 3 (1978).

16   The quoted phrase is Andrew Charlesworth's in Charlesworth, ed., *Atlas of Rural Protest in Britain 1548–1900* (London: Croom Helm, 1982), 64.

17   Heinrich Volkmann and Jürgen Bergmann, eds, *Sozialer Protest: Studien zu traditionaller Resistenz und kollektiver Gewalt in Deutschland vom Vormärz bis zur Reichsgründung* (Opladen: Westdeutscher Verlag, 1984).

18   Heinrich Volkmann and Jürgen Bergmann, 'Einleitung', in ibid., 13.

protests to a fourfold typology – entirely informal, loosely structured, more organized, and preplanned (*regellos, regelhaft, organisiert, geplant*) – while stressing the rationality in their own terms of even the most 'spontaneous' actions.[19] The volume studied the mechanics of this transition, as popular actions faced the combined challenge of social transformation and new political opportunities. The emergent labour movement could build on earlier practices by transcending them. It 'translated them onto a new level by replacing non-legal and spontaneous actions with the legitimizing function of the demand for political power.'[20]

But the teleology remains. For Ulrich Engelhardt, labour history in 1848–70 saw a linear transition 'from "protest" to "strike"', where successive modalities registered changes in the social system: 'Genuinely pre-industrial motives and forms of protest, which also reached into the early stages of industrialization . . . such as food riots, machine-breaking, and so forth, automatically gave way to social interests and methods of action specifically oriented . . . toward the industrial economy.' For labour itself, this imposed a 'learning process' that created the modern labour movement as we know it, with incremental union growth and a 'continual increase in the rationality of strike behaviour.'[21] This invokes once again the distorting effects of reactionary politics on the natural unfolding of a pragmatic and responsible trade unionism: rather than liberalizing labour law as in Britain, the 1860s mobilizations triggered repression, so that a pluralist framework for industrial conflict was never secured. A companion anthology on strikes repeated this same anti-progressivist scenario, in which the passage to legitimate and 'normal' trade unionism was politically cut off.[22] The new German research was defined by the 'modernization of protest', or the 'rationalization of collective behaviour in conflicts.'[23]

---

19 Heinrich Volkmann, 'Kategorien des sozialen Protests im Vormärz', *Geschichte und Gesellschaft* 3: 2 (1977).

20 Arno Herzig, 'Vom sozialen Protest zur Arbeiterbewegung: Das Beispiel des märkisch-westfälischen Industriegebietes (1780–1865)', in Volkmann and Bergmann, *Sozialer Protest*, 280.

21 Ulrich Engelhardt, 'Von der "Unruhe" zum "Strike": Hauptzielsetzungen und -erscheinungsformen des sozialen Protests beim Übergang zur organisierten Gewerkschaftsbewegung 1848/49–1869/70', in ibid., 251, 229–30, 252.

22 Klaus Tenfelde and Heinrich Volkmann, eds, *Streik: Zur Geschichte des Arbeitskampfes in Deutschland während der Industrialisierung* (Munich: C. H. Beck, 1981).

23 Klaus Tenfelde, 'Konflikt und Organisation in einigen deutschen Bergbaugebieten 1867–1872', *Geschichte und Gesellschaft* 3: 2 (1977).

Subsequent critics blurred the sharpness of the transition at either end. In his study of eighteenth-century journeymen's strikes, Andreas Griessinger found everything associated with the later 'modernization': pre-planning, focus on the business cycle, early democratic structures and nascent trade unionism, nonviolence, and supralocal organization.[24] In the early 1900s, Richard Evans and others likewise showed the resilience of 'older' forms (riots, hunger disturbances, violent actions) long after the rationalization of conflict had supposedly extinguished them.[25] As Dick Geary argued, the vaunted norm of the more modern pre-planned and formally organized strike, based on longer-term economic calculations, describes few actual disputes. Explanation of the variable incidence of militancy, including its relation to centralized unionism, required far more than expanding rationalization. In the wider repertoire of protests, riots were less the archaic emanations of 'traditional' or 'pre-industrial' society than the effects of present-generated political breakdown and economic hardship. The years 1916–23 saw popular tumults just as extensive, varied, violent, and direct as those of the 1840s: 'This suggests that there is no unilinear development in which "modernization" necessarily entails the abandonment of violent forms of protest . . . in so far as the nature of food riots changed over time, the concept of "pre-industrial protest" may obscure as much as it reveals.'[26]

The new historiography certainly brought gains. Forms and incidence of pre-1860s popular disturbances were finally mapped, raising German research to the level of the British and French in a sociology of the German crowd and its transactional rationality.[27] The rootedness of popular protests in publicly sanctioned customary culture that

---

24   Andreas Griessinger, *Das symbolische Kapital der Ehre: Streikbewegungen und kollektives Bewußtsein deutscher Handwerksgesellen im 18. Jahrhundert* (Frankfurt: Ullstein, 1981).

25   Richard J. Evans, '"Red Wednesday" in Hamburg: Police, Social Democrats and Lumpenproletariat in the Suffrage Disturbances of 17 January 1906', *Social History* 4: 1 (1979); Dick Geary, 'Protest and Strike: Recent Research on "Collective Action" in England, Germany, and France', in *Arbeiter and Arbeiterbewegung im Vergleich: Berichte zur internationalen historischen Forschung, Historische Zeitschrift-Sonderheft 15*, ed. Klaus Tenfelde (Munich: Oldenbourg, 1986).

26   Ibid., 365–6.

27   See also Rainer Wirtz's pioneering essay, 'Die Begriffsverwirrung der Bauern in Odenwald 1848: Odenwälder "Excesse" und die Sinsheimer republikanische Schilderhebung', in *Wahrnehmungsformen und Protestverhalten: Studien zur Lage der Unterschichten im 18. und 19. Jahrhundert*, ed. Detlev Püls (Frankfurt: Suhrkamp, 1979); Heinz Reif, ed., *Räuber, Volk und Obrigkeit: Studien zur Geschichte der Kriminalität in Deutschland seit dem 18. Jahrhundert* (Frankfurt: Suhrkamp, 1984).

mediated the effects of economic development, shortages, and pauper-
ism (Thompson's 'moral economy') finally trumps the so-called uprooting
thesis, which derived protest directly from social dislocation.[28] Griessinger's critique notwithstanding, German research confirms Hobsbawm's
classic typology, which charts a movement from the crisis-related strike
propensity of early industrialization (strikes as reactions to extreme
distress), through 'classic competition' between the 1850s and 1890s
(workers learning to exploit their labour power by the business cycle), to
the post-1890s era of monopoly or organized capitalism, when growing
centralization of employer and union resources combined with state
intervention to reduce spontaneity in favour of planning and strategic
rationalization.[29] The social protest research sets the stage for the organized oppositional culture of the SPD, linked implicitly to political
development's modernizing effects.[30]

In that progressive scenario, the relation between popular capacities
and state-political authority would be reconfigured into a national
system of political representation, exchanging the customary culture of
locality for the associational arena of civil society and the public realm.
But where does 'culture' itself fit? The broader category of protest sub-
sumes diverse phenomena usually placed by social historians generically
within popular culture, from job-changing, go-slow, and skiving in the
workplace to drinking and other free-time pursuits, popular piety and
religious enthusiasm, popular community rituals, social criminality
(such as wood theft), and social problems like mental illness, alcoholism,
and domestic violence. But this larger cultural domain tacitly disappears
in the passage to associational politics. Defining protest becomes nuga-
tory once Free Trade Unions and SPD have arrived. *Culture* is subsumed
in the political colonization of the social world, ordered around new
agencies from the political realm.

---

28 See the succinct critique in David Crew, *Town in the Ruhr: A Social History of
Bochum 1860–1914* (New York: Columbia University Press, 1979).

29 Eric J. Hobsbawm, 'Economic Fluctuations and Some Social Movements', in *Labour-
ing Men: Studies in the History of Labour* (London: Weidenfeld & Nicolson, 1984) – originally
published in *Economic History Review* 5: 1 (1952). See Freidhelm Boll, 'International Strike
Waves: A Critical Assessment', and James L. Cronin, 'Strikes and the Struggle for Union
Organization: Britain and Europe', in Mommsen and Husung, *Development of Trade
Unionism*.

30 See Charles Tilly's classic essay, 'Britain Creates the Social Movement', in *Social
Conflict and the Political in Modern Britain*, ed. James E. Cronin and Jonathan Schneer (New
Brunswick, NJ: Rutgers University Press, 1982).

But cultures of protest outlasted the arrival of responsible trade unionism and rationalized nation-state politics. Developmental scenarios are a good fit for the organized labour movement, whose architects consciously embraced that rationalizing teleology for themselves. But, for workers at large, unevenness and complexity reigned. As Lothar Machtan and René Ott showed in their reading of the 1873 South German 'Beer Riots', impeccably 'traditional' protests dramatically exceeded any progressive narrative of orderly action. The SPD certainly looked askance, firmly consigning riots to a backward, superseded stage. The labour movement shared in the chorus of disapprobation. Under the shining new constitutional legality of the German nation-state, the predictable military repression was, in any case, reinforced by the novel unanimity of middle-class opinion, which could finally swallow its misgivings about the military and public order. But socialists now distanced themselves from 'excesses' and the 'folly of the masses' too, drawing a sharp line between the respectable workingman's self-improving sobriety and the 'unenlightened' turbulence of the streets beneath. Such disparagement gave the labour movement a fraught relationship to some working-class actualities, reflecting its uneasy ambivalence about major parts of popular culture.[31]

Socialists colluded in the moral policing of working-class existence. Drinking focused their ambivalence. Taverns were vital to working-class sociability and politics, so socialists often soft-pedalled the 'alcohol problem', blaming the social pathology of capitalism: drunkenness came from the latter rather than individual failings or a disordered family. But that easily blurred into denial: firmly wedded to uplift and self-improvement, upstanding Social Democrats deflected the 'problem of drink' onto the disorderly and demoralized poor. If, from the 1890s, the SPD was broadening its support towards the semi-skilled and unskilled working class, party officials looked warily on the 'lumpenproletariat' proper, who were the 'dangerous classes' of socialist imagination. The antithesis of the disciplined, class-conscious proletariat, whose identity the party already claimed, they became an elastic moral container for any feature of

31 Lothar Machtan and René Ott, '"Batzebier!" Überlegungen zur sozialen Protestbewegung in den Jahren nach der Reichsgründung am Beispiel der süddeutschen Bierkrawalle vom Frühjahr 1873', in Volkmann and Bergmann, *Sozialer Protest*. On the period 1844–50, see Werner Blessing, 'Konsumentenprotest und Arbeitskampf. Vom Bierkrawall zum Bierboykott', in Tenfelde and Volkmann, *Streik*.

working-class behaviour socialists disavowed. In valuing dignity, sobriety, frugality, self-improvement, and orderly family life, Social Democrats pursued working-class survival in a demoralizing social environment. But they thereby enacted much the same opposition between respectability and roughness that liberals had earlier pioneered.[32]

Beneath the labour movement's presence remained a popular culture still relatively impervious against appeals to orderliness. Collective violence could burst spectacularly through the integument of Social Democratic representation before 1914, as on Hamburg's Red Wednesday in 1906 or in the Moabit Disturbances of 1910.[33] Social Democrats condemned this lumpenproletarian 'other'. Not all working-class experience belonged comfortably in the labour movement's familiar and approved story; but there was no hard border between the latter and a wider working-class universe. The SPD's representative labours reached far past any immediate membership, particularly for certain purposes at certain times, like an election campaign or a strike. Boundaries were fluid. Yet gaps between formal and quotidian cultures also opened inside the labour movement itself, where officials downplayed or neglected entire areas: namely, 'a broad spectrum of expectations, anxieties, and hopes', or the contradictory fullness of working-class 'lifeworlds', even among card-carrying members.[34] Indeed, empathy for the existential diversities of working-class life could be extremely terse. Precisely this uncertainty about the working class even within the movement's own ranks – affirming and disparaging by turns – gave labour historians their greatest difficulty. This is where *Alltagsgeschichte* came in.

History from Below?

Superficially analogous to 'history from below', *Alltagsgeschichte* had definite West German features. But three moves in English-speaking historiography were pertinent, and each bore Edward Thompson's

---

32 See James S. Roberts, *Drink, Temperance and the Working Class in Nineteenth-Century Germany* (London: Allen & Unwin, 1984).

33 Evans, '"Red Wednesday" in Hamburg'; Helmut Bleiber, 'Die Moabiter Unruhen 1910', *Zeitschrift für Geschichtswissenschaft* 3 (1955).

34 Alf Lüdtke, 'Protest – oder: Die Faszination des Spektakulären: Zur Analyse alltäglicher Widersetzlichkeit', in Volkmann and Bergmann, *Sozialer Protest*.

imprint. One took an institutionally and biographically centred labour history towards the class 'itself', foregrounding 'consciousness', 'culture', and 'ways of life'. The second travelled to a novel territory beyond either politics or work, defined more residually than theoretically in cultural terms, but embracing distinctively New Left themes: community and self-management; popular recreation; madness, criminality, and deviance; youth; the family; and eventually the history of women, sexuality, and gender. Third, this new agenda shifted the standpoint. For many British and North American practitioners, social history meant the history of ordinary people – recovering suppressed alternatives, returning people to their own past, rebuilding the record 'from the bottom up'. Versions of activist democracy were a sustaining motivation, from US Civil Rights and its descendants to the women's movement, or some socialist ideal of working-class emancipation. Shorn of naivety and romanticism, recast by intervening political developments, this remains important. In Thompson's famous words, he wished 'to rescue the poor stockinger, the Luddite cropper, the "obsolete" hand-loom weaver, the "utopian" artisan, and even the deluded follower of Joanna Southcott, from the enormous condescension of posterity'. Or, in the words of another social historian, social history was about 'retrieving European lives'.[35]

When West German social history took off in the mid 1970s, social science directions were uppermost, within a liberal conception of modernizing the discipline, as against the radical-cum-populist outlook in English-speaking historiography ten years before.[36] Only gradually did other perspectives emerge. With his major 1976 article on 'The Proto-Industrial Family Economy', Hans Medick announced a long-term interest in popular culture during transitions from feudalism to capitalism.[37] That

---

35   Edward P. Thompson, *The Making of the English Working Class* (London: Gollancz, 1963), 12; Charles Tilly, 'Retrieving European Lives', in *Reliving the Past: The Worlds of Social History*, ed. Oliver Zunz (Chapel Hill, NC: University of North Carolina Press, 1985), 17–19.

36   The new journal *Geschichte und Gesellschaft* was launched in 1975, subtitled 'Zeitschrift für historische Sozialwissenschaft' (Journal for historical social science).

37   Hans Medick, 'The Proto-Industrial Family Economy: The Structural Function of Household and Family during the Transition from Peasant Society to Industrial Capitalism', *Social History* 1: 3 (1976); Peter Kriedte, Hans Medick, and Jürgen Schlumbohm, *Industrialization before Industrialization: Rural Industry in the Genesis of Capitalism*, transl. Beate Schempp (Cambridge: Cambridge University Press, 1981) – originally published as *Industrialisierung vor der Industrialisierung* (Göttingen: Vandenhoeck & Ruprecht, 1977). See also Hans Medick, 'Plebeian Culture in the Transition to Capitalism', in *Culture, Ideology, and Politics. Essays for Eric Hobsbawm*, ed. Raphael Samuel and Gareth Stedman Jones (London: Routledge, 1983).

same year, Lutz Niethammer and Franz Brüggemeier published a remarkable article on working-class housing under the *Kaiserreich*, exploring
patterns of working-class solidarity beneath the levels of party, trade-
union, and associational life.[38] Then Alf Lüdtke edited an issue of the
journal *Sozialwissenschaftliche Informationen für Unterricht und Studium*
(*SOWI*) on 'Needs, Experience, and Behaviour', suggesting more broadly
what the new perspectives entailed. Jürgen Reulecke and Wolfhard Weber
took this further by showcasing empirical research on 'the social history
of everyday life in the industrial age', covering workplace, family, and
leisure.[39]

Each moved social history away from the aforementioned social-
science terrain. They proposed qualitative readings of ordinary people's
lives, embracing not just material actualities of daily existence ('production and reproduction of immediate life', in Engels's well-worn phrase),
but inner worlds of popular experience at work, at home, at school, and
at play – in short, everything normally assigned to culture. By exploring
social history in these experiential or subjective dimensions, conventional distinctions between 'public' and 'private' might be transcended,
and the elusive connection between 'the political' and 'the cultural'
finally discovered. It was precisely these 'insides' of the 'structures, processes and patterns' of social analysis – 'the daily experiences of people
in their concrete life-situations, which also stamp their needs' – that
were usually left out.[40] *Alltagsgeschichte* wanted to bring them in.

What were its main inspirations?

1. One was the West German New Left, in two particular directions: the heterodox Marxist philosopher, Ernst Bloch, whose
   Principle of Hope informed much of the conscious utopianism;
   and the German student movement's anti-authoritarian critique
   of the repressive and alienated qualities of conventional living,

---

38   Lutz Niethammer and Franz-Josef Brüggemeier, 'Wie wohnten Arbeiter im Kaiserreich?', *Archiv für Sozialgeschichte* 16 (1976).

39   See editorial, 'Bedürfnisse, Erfahrung und Verhalten', *SOWI* 6 (1977); Jürgen Reulecke
and Wolfhard Weber, eds, *Fabrik – Familie – Feierabend: Beiträge zur Sozialgeschichte des
Alltags im Industriezeitalter* (Wuppertal: Peter Hammer Verlag, 1978). See also Dieter Groh,
'Base-Processes and the Problem of Organisation: Outline of a Social History Research
Project', *Social History* 4: 2 (1979). Early hubs were the Universities of Essen and Konstanz
and the Göttingen Max Planck Institute of History.

40   Alf Lüdtke, 'Zur Einleitung', *SOWI* 6 (1977).

typified in Henri Lefebvre's *Everyday Life in the Modern World*.[41] The emblematic text, visible across the emergent literature and uniting sundry late-sixties moments, from the simultaneous revival and critique of the Marxist tradition to concerns with cultural politics, mass consumerism, and the consciousness industry, was Oskar Negt and Alexander Kluge's *Öffentlichkeit und Erfahrung*, with its discursive centring of a 'proletarian life-context' around the category of experience.[42] Interest in a theory of human needs imparted a quality absent from earlier Anglophone literature. Interestingly, Edward Thompson then also turned to this question in the mid-1970s, calling for the 'education of desire', showing a belated interest in such utopian themes.[43]

2. As the best route to everydayness, some voices advocated 'ethnological ways of knowing'.[44] Central here were Hans Medick, Alf Lüdtke, and others at the Göttingen Max Planck Institute of History, where an international conversation across history and anthropology came to be centred. If Medick began from his Swabian village study and interest in proto-industrialization, his anthropological interests took on a life of their own. From

---

41   See Ernst Bloch, *The Principle of Hope*, 3 vols, transl. Neville Plaice, Stephen Plaice and Paul Knight (Cambridge: MIT Press, 1986) – originally published as *Das Prinzip Hoffnung* (Frankfurt: Suhrkamp, 1959); Ernst Bloch, *Heritage of Our Times*, transl. Neville and Stephen Plaice (Berkeley, CA: University of California Press, 1991) – originally published as *Erbschaft dieser Zeit* (Frankfurt: Suhrkamp, 1962). See also Rudi Dutschke, *Die Revolte: Würzeln und Spuren eines Aufbruchs* (Reinbek bei Hamburg: Rohwolt, 1983); Henri Lefebvre, *Everyday Life in the Modern World* (London: Verso, 2014), originated in various texts going back to the 1930s, whose German edition became the two-volume *Kritik des Alltagslebens* (Munich: Hanser, 1973–75).

42   Oskar Negt and Alexander Kluge, *Öffentlichkeit und Erfahrung: Zur Organisationsanalyse von bürgerlicher und proletarischer Öffentlichkeit* (Frankfurt: Suhrkamp, 1972), eventually translated as *The Public Sphere and Experience: Toward an Analysis of the Bourgeois and Proletarian Public Sphere*, transl. Peter Labanyi, Jamie Owen Daniel, and Assenka Oksiloff (Minneapolis: University of Minnesota Press, 1993).

43   See Edward P. Thompson, *William Morris: Romantic to Revolutionary* (London: Merlin, 1977 [1955]), 793. See also Barbara Taylor, *Eve and the New Jerusalem: Socialism and Feminism in the Nineteenth Century* (New York: Virago, 1983); Gareth Stedman Jones, 'Utopian Socialism Reconsidered', in *People's History and Socialist Theory*, ed. Raphael Samuel (London: Routledge & Kegan Paul, 1981); Sheila Rowbotham, *Dreams and Dilemmas: Collected Writings* (London: Virago, 1983), 216–20.

44   Hans Medick, '"Missionaries in the Row Boat"? Ethnological Ways of Knowing as a Challenge to Social History', *Comparative Studies in Society and History* 29 (1987) – originally published in *Geschichte und Gesellschaft* 10: 3 (1984).

the late 1970s, international roundtables produced a series of programmatic anthologies. While travelling a path blazed by Edward Thompson and Natalie Zemon Davis, Medick also learned directly from English-speaking anthropologists like Marshall Sahlins, Sidney Mintz, Clifford Geertz, and Jack Goody. Pierre Bourdieu's 'theory of practical action' was similarly crucial for his work.[45]

3. *Alltagsgeschichte* refused both the telos of modernization and 'objectivist' ideas of macro-historical development – the structures and processes celebrated by West German 'historical social science'. It gave claims to 'progress' a sceptical eye. Interest 'in historical "losers" or in non-establishment views of the processes of change' found natural sympathy among critical anthropologists studying the costs of the Third World's encounter with the West.[46] Shifting focus onto the 'internal costs' of social transformations brought the casualties of progress to the forefront, as Thompson and others so eloquently urged: 'One of the gains from an anthropological approach, which has increasingly been accepted into the social historian's discipline, is increased insight into the costs of modernization and industrialization. We can see in a similar perspective not only the contemporary third and fourth worlds but also all those groups, levels, and classes in European society itself that were in growing measure pauperized, excluded, and frequently also deprived of their rights in the course of the secular upheavals of the sixteenth through nineteenth centuries.'[47] Turning to ethnology also shifted focus from impersonal social processes to the agency of human

---

45   See Robert Berdahl, et al., *Klassen und Kultur: Sozialanthropologische Perspektiven in der Geschichtsschreibung* (Frankfurt: Syndikat, 1982); Hans Medick and David Sabean, eds, *Interest and Emotion: Essays on the Study of Family and Kinship* (Cambridge: Cambridge University Press, 1984); Alf Lüdtke, ed., *Herrschaft als soziale Praxis: Historische und socialanthropologische Studien* (Göttingen: Vandenhoeck & Ruprecht, 1991); Gerald Sider and Gavin Smith, eds, *Between History and Histories: The Making of Silences and Commemorations* (Toronto: University of Toronto Press, 1997). See also David William Cohen, *The Combing of History* (Chicago: University of Chicago Press, 1994), 1–23; Geoff Eley, *A Crooked Line: From Cultural History to the History of Society* (Ann Arbor, MI: University of Michigan Press, 2005), 53, 226–7.

46   Medick and Sabean, 'Introduction' to *Interest and Emotion*, 1.

47   Medick, '"Missionaries in the Row Boat"?', 82–3.

actors: 'If social science had traditionally assumed the existence of objective sets of relationships, the need now was to study the social and cultural world from the perspective of the women, men and children who composed it.'[48] The priority was a social history of subjective meanings drawn from highly concrete microhistorical settings – not to supplant, but to specify and enrich understanding of structural processes of social change. Indeed, an everyday focus would specifically transcend any 'sharp dichotomy opposing objective, material, structural, or institutional factors to subjective, cultural, symbolic, or emotional ones'.[49]

4. Interest in fascism was a further ingredient, vitally driven by debates in and around the journal *Das Argument*.[50] Resonating with concurrent debates about the *Kaiserreich* during the Fischer Controversy, these foregrounded authoritarian continuities tied to the interest-based politics of a dominant-class coalition whose power impeded and undermined democratic growth before 1933.[51] But they also questioned the capacities for domination and resistance inside German society, including the production and persistence of fascist potentials. Niethammer and Lüdtke returned consistently to those questions – Lüdtke by studying state violence in earlier-nineteenth-century Prussia, Niethammer from earlier research on denazification and neo-Nazi survivals to subsequent work on fascism in popular memory.[52]

48   Introduction to Georg Iggers, ed., *The Social History of Politics: Critical Perspectives in West German Historical Writing since 1945* (Leamington Spa: Berg, 1985), 41.

49   Medick and Sabean, *Interest and Emotion*, 2.

50   Relevant issues of *Das Argument* were: 30 (1964); 32 (1965); 33 (1965); 41 (1966); 47 (1968); 58 (1970).

51   For an overview, see Geoff Eley, 'Germany, the Fischer Controversy, and the Context of War: Rethinking German Imperialism, 1880–1914', in *Cataclysm 1914: The First World War and the Making of Modern World Politics*, ed. Alexander Anievas (Leiden: Brill, 2015).

52   For Alf Lüdtke, see: 'Zur Kontinuitätsfrage', *Das Argument* 70 (1972); 'Faschismus-Potentiale und faschistische Herrschaft oder Theorie-Defizite und antifaschistische Strategie', in *Gesellschaft: Beiträge zur Marxschen Theorie 6* (Frankfurt: Suhrkamp, 1976); *Police and State in Prussia, 1815–1850*, transl. Pete Burgess (Cambridge: Cambridge University Press, 1990) – originally published as *'Gemeinwhol', Polizei und 'Festungpraxis': Staatliche Gewaltsamkeit und innere Verwaltung in Preussen, 1815–1850* (Göttingen: Vandenhoeck & Ruprecht, 1982); '"Formierung der Massen" oder: Mitmachen und Hinnehmen? "Alltagsgeschichte" und Faschismusanalyse', in *Normalität oder Normalisierung? Geschichtswerkstätten*

For each, *Alltagsgeschichte* contained earlier intellectual and political commitments.[53]

Approaching *Alltagsgeschichte* obliquely reveals its diverse forms and interests. Each orientation – New Left intellectual legacies, critical anthropologies, sociologies of subjective meanings, experiential histories of fascist potentials – translates very distinctly. Nor is there any shortage of manifestos and programmatic statements.[54] But by the close of the 1980s there were four intermingling streams:

a) historical anthropologies of rural society (Medick) and the working class (Lüdtke), centred on Göttingen and its network, with strong affinities to *Volkskunde* (folklore/ethnology) at the Ludwig Uhland Institute for Empirical Cultural Studies in Tübingen[55]

b) working-class social history using oral sources, with links to unions and the SPD's Friedrich Ebert Foundation in Bonn,

---

und Faschismusanalyse, ed. Heide Gerstenberger, Heide and Dorothea Schmidt (Münster: Verlag Westfälisches Dampfboot, 1987). For Lutz Niethammer, see: *Angepasster Faschismus: Politische Praxis der NPD* (Frankfurt: S. Fischer, 1969); and Lutz Niethammer and Alexander von Plato, eds, *Lebensgeschichte und Sozialstruktur im Ruhrgebiet 1930–1960*, 2nd edn, 3 vols (Bonn: Dietz, 1986).

53   See also Detlev J. K. Peukert's works: *Die Edelweisspiraten: Protestbewegungen jugendlicher Arbeiter im Dritten Reich. Eine Dokumentation* (Cologne: Bund Verlag, 1980); *Inside Nazi Germany: Conformity, Opposition, and Racism in Everyday Life*, transl. Richard Deveson (London: Batsford, 1987); Detlev J. K. Peukert and Jürgen Reulecke, eds, *Die Reihen fast geschlossen: Beiträge zur Geschichte des Alltags unterm Nationalsozialismus* (Wuppertal: Peter Hammer Verlag, 1981).

54   See the debate between Peukert and Lüdtke: Detlev J. K. Peukert, 'Arbeiteralltag – Mode oder Methode?', in *Arbeiteralltag in Stadt und Land*, ed. Heiko Raumann (Berlin: Argument-Verlag, 1982); Alf Lüdtke, '"Kolonisierung der Lebenswelt" – oder: Geschichte als Einbahnstrasse?', *Das Argument* 140 (1983); Detlev J. K. Peukert, 'Glanz und Elend der "Bartwichserei": Eine Replik auf Alf Lüdtke', *Das Argument* 140 (1983). For hostile critiques, see Hans-Ulrich Wehler, 'Alltagsgeschichte: Königsweg zu neuen Ufern oder Irrgarten der Illusionen?', in *Aus der Geschichte lernen? Essays* (Munich: C. H. Beck, 1988); Jürgen Kocka, *Sozialgeschichte: Begriff, Entwicktung, Probleme*, 2nd edn (Göttingen: Vandenhoeck & Ruprecht, 1986), 132–76; Klaus Tenfelde, 'Schwierigkeiten mit dem Alltag', *Geschichte und Gesellschaft* 10: 4 (1984).

55   For the relationship to *Volkskunde*, see Wolfgang Kaschuba, 'Popular Culture and Workers' Culture as Symbolic Orders: Comments on the Debate about the History of Culture and Everyday Life', in *The History of Everyday Life: Reconstructing Historical Experiences and Ways of Life*, ed. Alf Lüdtke (Princeton: Princeton University Press, 1995); Martin Scharfe, 'Towards a Cultural History: Notes on Contemporary *Volkskunde* (Folklore) in German-Speaking Countries', *Social History* 4: 2 (1979).

centred around Niethammer and collaborators in Essen and at the Hagen *Fernuniversitat*, Jürgen Reulecke in Bochum and then Siegen, and Detlev Peukert in Essen and Hamburg

c) a semi-professional grassroots milieu, loosely connected through the History Workshop movement, inspired by a democratic public history, and borne by locally grounded collaborative research, via exhibitions, radical museum projects, local government cultural initiatives, adult education circles, and community histories[56]

d) an emergent field of women's history, whose purposes converged increasingly with *Alltagsgeschichte*, not least via the peace movement, radical ecology, and the Greens.[57]

Alf Lüdtke's advocacy, writings, and activity were central during this emergence. He combined the four strands more completely perhaps than anyone else. Formed in the intellectual culture of the Tübingen New Left and joining post-Fischer debates about the *Kaiserreich* from the margins, he linked historiography explicitly to the fascism debate. He pursued the ethnological turn uncompromisingly into working-class history, as against rural society. And he went furthest in articulating the social theory that microhistories require.[58]

---

56   For the History Workshop movement, see Peter Schöttler, 'Die Geschichtswerkstatt e. V.: Zu einem Versuch, basisdemokratische Geschichtsinitiativen und -forschungen zu "vernetzen"', *Geschichte und Gesellschaft* 10: 3 (1984); Anthony McElligott, 'The German History Workshop Festival in Berlin, May–June 1984', *German History* 2 (1985).

57   Women were notably absent from the early initiatives: none of the contributors to *SOWI*, vol. 6 (1977) or Berdahl et al., *Klassen und Kultur*; two of sixteen in Reulecke and Weber, *Fabrik – Familie – Feierabend*; one of twenty-two in Peukert and Reulecke, *Die Reihen fast geschlossen*; two of fifteen in Gerhard Huck, ed., *Sozialgeschichte der Freizeit: Untersuchungen zum Wandel der Alltageskultur in Deutschland* (Wuppertal: Peter Hammer Verlag,1980). For women's history in the 1980s, see Renate Bridenthal, Atina Grossmann, and Marion Kaplan, eds, *When Biology Became Destiny: Women in Weimar and Nazi Germany* (New York: Monthly Review, 1984); Dorothee Wierling, 'The History of Everyday Life and Gender Relations: On Historical and Historiographical Relationships', in Lüdtke, *History of Everyday Life*.

58   Lüdtke's bibliography is too voluminously rich to be cited completely here. Some early essays were collected as Alf Lüdtke, *Eigen-Sinn: Fabrikalltag, Arbeitererfahrungen und Politik vom Kaiserreich bis in den Faschismus* (Hamburg: Ergebnisse, 1993). He turned later towards everyday life under dictatorship and fascism. See, for example, 'People Working: Everyday Life and German Fascism', *History Workshop Journal* 50 (2000), 'The Appeal of Exterminating "Others": German Workers and the Limits of Resistance', in *Resistance against the Third Reich: 1933–1990*, ed. Michael Geyer and John W. Boyer (Chicago: University of Chicago Press, 1994), 'War as Work: Aspects of Soldiering in Twentieth-Century Wars', in *No Man's Land of Violence: Extreme Wars in the 20th Century*, ed. Alf Lüdtke and Bernd

How did Lüdtke proceed? First, with the call to history from below, with its particular empirical ground: 'At the centre . . . are the lives and sufferings of those who are frequently labelled, suggestively but imprecisely, the "small people" [*kleine Leute*]. [*Alltagsgeschichte*] involves their work and non-work. The picture includes housing and homelessness, clothing and nakedness; eating and hunger, love and hate.'[59] Second came a stress on subjectivity and experience, on the production and construction of meaning, theorized not only in terms of ethnology and anthropology, but also ethnomethodology and symbolic interactionism in sociology. Third, he insisted on the '*systematic decentralization* of analysis and interpretation' by careful construction of historical 'miniatures' to capture ambiguities and contradictions in how workers actually live their lives.[60] Fourth, this was no *retreat* from the big questions of process and structure, but a different means of posing them. Indeed, *Alltagsgeschichte* 'cannot be isolated from the relations of production, appropriation, and exchange, and the related interest structures of a society'[61] Nor, fifth, was politics neglected, as the same microhistorical settings allowed questions of both public and private, the personal and political, to be searchingly addressed. Last, this was avowedly a history of and for the present: grasping the 'otherness' of popular culture in the past permits an understanding of its complexities today.[62]

Lüdtke explored the local, personal, and quotidian settings where capacities for either conformity or resistance can be made. While studies of working-class consciousness had long moved from labour movements alone to more elaborate histories of working-class culture, Lüdtke went further still into the less penetrable territory of workers' daily lives. He found potentials for solidarity in the innumerable small acts through which workers created and defended a sense of self, delimited some

---

Weisbrod (Göttingen: Wallstein, 2006). See also Belinda Davis, Thomas Lindenberger, and Michael Wildt, eds, *Alltag, Erfahrung, Eigensinn: Historisch-anthropologische Erkundungen* (Frankfurt: Campus, 2008). A collection of Lüdtke's essays is planned by the University of Michigan Press.

59   Alf Lüdtke, '"Alltagsgeschichte": Verführung oder Chance? Zur Erforschung der Praxis historischer Subjekte', unpublished paper, 1. Emphasis in original.

60   Ibid., 10, 12.

61   Lüdtke, 'Zur Einleitung', 147.

62   As Lüdtke notes in response to hostile critiques, 'taking the subject seriously' requires neither positive empathy nor uncritical identification. Getting into the skin of Nazis is as vital as recreating the outlook of anti-Nazi workers.

autonomous space, and generally armed themselves against a hostile and limiting world. This was *Eigensinn* – a mixture of self-reliance, self-will, and self-respect, through which alienated social relations might be reclaimed, especially at work, but also at school, in the street, and anywhere else externally shaped by structures and processes beyond workers' immediate control.[63] Such small acts of selfhood may have lacked any self-consciously socialist or anti-capitalist meaning. But, at a visceral, vernacular level, this everyday culture 'in the factory or the office, in the tenement house and on the street' bespoke 'an intense political sensibility and militancy'. Workers' apparent removal from organized politics implied no lack of longing for an alternative society or better life. Rather, such hopes were locked away in a 'private' economy of desires. A vital question arises here: How might connections to 'real' politics be made?[64]

Lüdtke brings that question into view. Only minorities of workers ever joined a socialist party or its unions; still fewer saw the finer points of socialist programmes or their associated outlook. Yet, as the practical terrain where domination and exploitation were directly encountered, everyday life cultivated instincts of solidarity and independence with clear political potentials. Under prevailing class-circumscribed settings of social value and action, where movements actively addressed people in class-conscious ways, *Eigensinn* could be a basis for much broader mobilization. The workers' *Alltag* housed a culture of resistance, which, under circumstances of generalized sociopolitical crisis (such as the revolutionary years 1918–20) or locally bounded turbulence, might acquire fuller political meaning. Then the worlds of politics and the everyday could begin moving together, inside the same time.

---

63   See Alf Lüdtke, 'Organizational Order or Eigensinn? Workers' Privacy and Workers' Politics in Imperial Germany', in *Rites of Power: Symbolism, Ritual, and Politics since the Middle Ages*, ed. Sean Wilentz (Philadelphia: University of Pennsylvania Press, 1985), 305: 'The creative reappropriation of the conditions of daily life implied a striving for time and space of one's own.' He contrasts strategies of self-claiming at the bosses' expense, including 'horseplay' and enjoyable timewasting, from walking around to gossiping and daydreaming, with the formally permitted breaks used practically and soberly for recharging one's energies. Physical horseplay – ritualized practical jokes or initiation acts – was especially important, as it carved a niche of worktime and shop-floor space for workers' self-directed activity. Such demonstrative expressions of 'being-by-oneself and with one's workmates' enabled an independent shop-floor culture to form, one with unpleasant features – masculinist, hierarchical, ageist – as well as democratic, egalitarian ones. See Alf Lüdtke, ibid., 311–15; and Paul Willis, *Learning to Labour: How Working-Class Kids Get Working-Class Jobs*, 2nd edn (New York: Columbia University Press, 1981).

64   Lüdtke, 'Organizational Order or Eigensinn?', 322.

There was nothing natural or predetermined about such a progressive juncture, about the synchrony of working-class parties with the
broader working-class culture of everyday life. On two spectacular
occasions, it failed to happen: August 1914 and early 1933. Here, it was
the growing abstraction of 'the political' in narrower terms – that 'arena
of formalized politics and large-scale political organization' at the level
of the state – into a separate realm far removed from most ordinary
workers, in the 'everyday politics' of *Eigensinn*, that left them so vulnerable to radicalized systems of rule once the democratic openings of
1918–20 had been missed. Under the Third Reich, accordingly, once the
organized machinery of working-class politics was gone, quotidian
forms of solidarity and self-assertion were all that was left. While these
offered vital resources for working-class survival in some private, existential sense, they faced Nazism with no new challenge, but rather
signalled accommodation.[65] Lüdtke's *Alltagsgeschichte* is the opposite of
a workerist romanticism. In *Eigensinn*, he sees precisely 'the ambivalence and ambiguition' of the working-class everyday. In the dialectics of
popular consciousness and formal politics, it was the inner world of
popular experience and the subjective dimension of class relations –
quotidian culture as a generative site of contradiction – that was central.

What social theory corresponds to this historical practice? Negt and
Kluge's *Öffentlichkeit und Erfahrung* functioned as a kind of ür-text,
along with a certain range of anthropological reference and indebtedness to Thompson and other British Marxist historians. Sociologies of
work and industrial relations were less important than phenomenology,
ethnomethodology, and social interactionism, with their stress on the
'social construction of reality' through the meaningful transactions of
the experienced world.[66] Lüdtke took this in a strongly anthropological

---

65 Alf Lüdtke, 'Betriebe als Kampffeld: Kontrolle, Notwendigkeits-Kooperation und
"Eigensinn": Beispiele aus dem Maschinenbau 1890–1940', in *Organisation als soziales System:
Kontrolle und Kommunikationstechnologie in Arbeitsorganisationen*, ed. Rüdiger Seltz, Ulrich
Mill, and Eckart Hildebradt (Berlin: Edition Sigma, 1986), 132. Lüdtke cites Social Democratic skilled workers at Krupp who survived Nazism by withdrawing into precisely such an
informal culture of work, allowing some pride in and on the job. But in wartime they were
sucked inexorably into exercising supervisory and semi-managerial roles over the mass of
forced foreign workers, in whose brutalization they structurally shared. *Eigensinn* meant both
survival and complicity.

66 See Peter L. Berger and Thomas Luckmann, *The Social Construction of Reality: A
Treatise in the Sociology of Knowledge* (Harmondsworth: Penguin, 1971); Alfred Schutz, *The
Phenomenology of the Social World* (Evanston: Northwestern University Press, 1967); Harold

direction via Bourdieu's theory of practice and cultural forms, rein-forced by Paul Willis's ethnographies of British working-class life.[67] The radicalism of Henri Lefebvre, for whom everyday life was 'the time of desire', the real locus of revolutionary contradiction in an alienated social world, resonates powerfully through Lüdtke's work.[68]

Challenges for Social History

Initially, *Alltagsgeschichte* made little impression on social historians at large. Research into labour history, working-class formation, and social protest continued much as before. For Klaus Tenfelde's imposing 1986 guide to the state of international research in labour history, *Alltags-geschichte* barely rippled the surface. That volume gathered its surveys under six rubrics: workers in preindustrial economies of the eighteenth century; comparative social stratification; community, class, and culture; social conflict and trade unions; ideology and politics of the labour movement; scholarship on individual regions. Tenfelde himself glanced at *Alltagsgeschichte* while discussing workers' mentalities during indus-trialization. Several others also took note, notably David Crew in a chapter on community studies in the United States, Britain, Germany, and France. But Vernon Lidtke's essay on 'Workers' Culture in Germany and England' fluffed its chance: everyday aspects were mentioned as such only in relation to DDR historian Jürgen Kuczynski's four-volume compilation, which was hardly typical.[69]

Garfinkel, *Studies in Ethnomethodology* (Englewood Cliffs: Prentice-Hall, 1967); Arbeits-gruppe Bielefelder Soziologen, ed., *Alltagswissen, Interaktion und gesellschaftliche Wirklichkeit*, 2 vols (Reinbek bei Hamburg: Rohwolt, 1973). See also Agnes Helter, *Everyday Life* (London: Routledge, 1984); Patrick Wright, *On Living in an Old Country: The National Past in Contem-porary Britain* (London: Verso, 1985), esp. 1–32; Stuart Hall, 'The Hinterland of Science: Ideology and the "Sociology of Knowledge"', in *On Ideology*, ed. Centre for Contemporary Culture Studies (London: Hutchinson, 1978) – reprinted in *Essential Essays, Vol. 1*, ed. David Morley (Durham: Duke University Press, 2019).

67   See Willis, *Learning to Labour*.

68   Henri Lefebvre, *Everyday Life in the Modern World* (London: Verso, 2014), 61, 182. See also Oskar Negt and Alexander Kluge, *Geschichte und Eigensinn* (Frankfurt: Zweitausend-eins, 1981), transl. Cyrus Shahan, Joel Golb, and Richard Langston as *History and Obstinacy* (Cambridge: Zone, 2014).

69   See Klaus Tenfelde, 'Sozialgeschichte und vergleichende Geschichte der Arbeiter', in *Arbeiter und Arbeiterbewegung im Vergleich*, 13–62; see also Jürgen Kuczynski, *Geschichte des Alltags des deutschen Volkes*, 4 vols (Cologne: Pahl-Rugenstein, 1981–82).

Coalminers are a fine place to begin. Miners are an arresting arche-
type of the oppressed but militant proletariat. Dark, dirty, and dangerous,
their work has always drawn sympathetic social reportage, just as it
pervades labour's own folklore. Separated into self-contained communities, hardened by the dignity and muscular solidarities of exceptionally
difficult labour, miners bear the best aura of the class struggle. Mining
communities attract the more 'culturalist' social history too, magnified
in the British case by geography – in the northerly locations of most
English coalfields and the militancy of South Wales and Scotland. This
romance of the coalfields reached its mythopoeic culmination in the
three great strikes of 1972, 1974, and 1984–85.[70] Miners hold a similar
place in German labour traditions. The 1980s brought a rush of scholarship on the Ruhr, including works by David Crew, Stephen Hickey,
Erhard Lucas, Klaus Tenfelde, and Franz-Josef Brüggemeier. Most
attuned to *Alltagsgeschichte* was the collective oral history initiated by
Lutz Niethammer.[71]

Forged out of nowhere in the later nineteenth century, from a landscape of small towns and open fields, the Ruhr heavy-industrial region
offers a telling laboratory for historiographies discussed in this essay.
Having previously operated under the state-regulated Prussian mining
sector, miners' protections – from the autonomies of work teams underground to the distinctive corporate insurance office of the *Knappschaft*
and privileged access to a paternalist royal bureaucracy – were abruptly
dismantled by liberal deregulation during 1850–65. Assailed by a reck-
lessly untrammelled capitalism, particularly in the post-1873 depression,
miners slowly adjusted their behaviour. Based in royal privileges, nineteenth-century legal precedent, and customary ideas of justice and moral
economy, time-honoured practices of petitioning served initially as a
medium of redress, but by the great strike of 1889 had lost their efficacy

---

70   See Raphael Samuel, ed., *Miners, Quarrymen and Saltworkers* (London: Routledge
& Kegan Paul, 1977); Raphael Samuel, Barbara Bloomfield, and Guy Boanas, eds, *The Enemy
Within: Pit Villages and the Miners' Strike of 1984–5* (London: Routledge & Kegan Paul,
1986).

71   Crew, *Town in the Ruhr*; Erhard Lucas, *Zwei Formen von Radikalismus in der
deutschen Arbeiterbewegung* (Frankfurt: Verlag Roter Stern, 1976), and *Märzrevolution 1920*,
3 vols (Frankfurt: Verlag Roter Stern, 1973–78); Tenfelde, *Sozialgeschichte der Bergarbeiter-
schaft*; Stephen H. F. Hickey, *Workers in Imperial Germany: The Miners of the Ruhr* (Oxford:
Oxford University Press, 1985); Franz-Josef Brüggemeier, *Leben vor Ort: Ruhrbergleute und
Ruhrbergbau 1889–1919* (Munich: Verlag C. H. Beck. 1984). Niethammer and von Plato, eds.,
Lebensgeschichte und Sozialstruktur.

and credence.[72] Miners turned instead to strikes and unions. Petitions intermittently reappeared (for example, surrounding the 1889 and 1905 coalfield strikes), but as mere 'husks of the older forms' filled with 'new contents'. Customary notions of justice succumbed to a new language of rights and social justice focused on the wage, on larger questions of distribution, and ultimately on citizenship and political participation. A *Lernprozess* ('learning-process') brought miners into the modern era of organized protest. Given parallel shifts among other groups of workers, it bespoke a general 'transition to modernity . . . from traditional forms of grievance articulation to modern forms of conflict regulation'.[73]

Miners' corporate practices were swamped by the sheer scale of expansion. The Ruhr mining workforce grew from 12,741 to 394,569 between 1850 and 1914 – Bochum's population from 19,000 to 256,000 in 1855–1910, Hamborn's from 5,300 to 103,000. If 63 per cent of Bochum's residents were immigrants in 1907, 24 per cent from beyond Rhineland-Westphalia, then, for miners, the numbers were still higher, at 84 and 37 per cent respectively. As migrants flocked from far and near, in such startling diversity of linguistic, religious, ethnic, and customary cultures, with such turmoil of local mobility, miners' customary culture lost all purchase.[74] This working class was overwhelmingly freshly arrived – 'not an established, settled, cohesive community . . . but socially disorientated, geographically unsettled, and culturally diffuse'.[75] Tenfelde's *Lernprozess* lacked meaning for these incomers, who suffered very different dislocations of their own. As Brüggemeier notes, 'memory of better times' could hardly 'shape the thinking and behaviour of miners who in 1889 had never experienced those times themselves'.[76]

Disunity was a default condition for the Ruhr working class. From staggering levels of in-migration and continuing local mobility through

72 Some 300 surviving petitions cover the years 1816–1933, with seventy-two concentrated in 1850–71 and a further spike just before 1914. The petitioning of 1858–60 brought a first disillusionment, followed by rejection of the 1867 Essen Miners' Petition, leading to the 1868 strike. See Klaus Tenfelde and Helmut Trischler, eds, *Bis vor die Stufen des Throns: Bittschriften und Beschwerden von Bergleuten im Zeitalter der Industrialisierung* (Munich: C. H. Beck, 1986), 27–31.
73 Ibid., 43, n. 90.
74 Hickey, *Workers in Imperial Germany*, 165–8.
75 Ibid., 35.
76 Franz-Josef Brüggemeier, 'Ruhr Miners and Their Historians', in *Peoples' History and Socialist Theory*, ed. Raphael Samuel (London: Routledge & Kegan Paul, 1981), 329.

housing conditions to the multiply divisive ethno-religious demographics, social life decisively impeded working-class solidarity, quite aside
from working conditions in particular. Catholic and Protestant churches
fostered discrete associational and communal worlds, further fractured
by large subcultures of Poles, Protestant Masurians, and numerous
smaller ethnicities. Neither factor stressed by social historians in the
'making of the working class' elsewhere – artisanal traditions and patterns of working-class community – was relevant for the volatile frontier
societies created at breakneck speed in the pre-1914 Ruhr: 'the fluid,
unstable, and divided character of working-class society and politics'
powerfully trumped any factors fostering 'cooperation and solidarity'.[77]
Culture divided more than it united the working class.

Here is a paradox. The great coal strikes of 1889, 1905, and 1912
vividly demonstrated the miners' militancy. These were general strikes
of the whole coalfield, with peaks of 80 per cent in the first two cases
and some 60 per cent in the third, with multiple disputes in single localities or groups of mines in between (at least seventeen in Bochum in
1889–1914). Miners' militancy stood out against the other major industries – iron, steel, and heavy engineering – where few actions occurred
and unionization was low. The Ruhr's metalworkers were fragmented by
elaborate hierarchies and craft-derived demarcations of skill, endless job
classifications, and the gulf separating skilled worker from labourer. In
comparison, miners shared a cohesive occupational community reinforced by residential apartness.[78]

Yet both the 1889 and 1905 strikes and the bulk of smaller disputes
were launched spontaneously against the union's resistance, with the
younger haulers, as against the more senior face-workers, in the lead.
Indeed, Otto Hué, the miners' leader who emerged in the 1890s, built
union strategy precisely against such spontaneity, impelled by misfired
strikes during 1889–93, when the infant union tried to capitalize on the
existing impetus. For Hué, union strategy proceeded from weakness.
Miners were divided by religion and nationality, with organized Catholic (1894) and Polish (1902) rivals to the SPD. Added to the employers'
centralized resources, organized around workplace authority and
company paternalism, these divisions placed socialist unionism at

77   Hickey, *Workers in Imperial Germany*, 292.
78   Crew, *Town in the Ruhr*, 186–94.

terrible disadvantage. Hué responded with caution, stressing discipline, organizational continuity, and political 'neutrality', conserving resources for the future rather than wasting them in confrontational militancy.

By specifying the structural features of working-class formation in the Ruhr in this way, Hickey delivers a sympathetic materialist account of reformism, based in the real impediments to organizing the coalfield. Hué's reformism was hardly less 'class-conscious' than the militancy of his critics. Given the prevailing ethnic and religious diversity, a genuine 'class' strategy presumed softening socialist hostilities against political Catholicism, as the union needed to surpass its sectionalism in the cause of industry-wide mobilizing. Success in 1889 and 1905 had required cross-confessional and cross-national solidarity between SPD, Catholic, and Polish strikers, whereas in 1912 the stoppage was called by Socialist, Polish, and Liberal unions over Catholic opposition, and collapsed in only a week.

But this was not the whole story. The strategy's hard-nosed 'realism' never compensated for its modest returns: even at its 1905 peak, the SPD union counted only 29.4 per cent of the mining workforce, dwindling to 15.8 per cent by 1913. Its strategy was ill-suited for integrating the localized, sporadic, and often turbulent rank-and-file militancy actually responsible for the union's bitterly won gains. The longed-for reformist breakthrough, whether through recognition by coal owners or sympathetic legislation, might easily prove a poisoned chalice. As the First World War revealed, the union's practical co-optation would deepen the wedge between officialdom and alienated rank and file. In the long run, this conundrum – reconciling the case for centralism with the countervailing demands of intra-union democracy – proved the source of tremendous conflict. How might the gap have been reconciled?

Underneath the miners' formal ties (and the demographics of cultural disunity) were certain informal patterns of solidarity. Miners enjoyed unusual below-ground autonomy, in which small work-teams ('comradeships') organized work and trained newcomers, while handling the functions normally exercised by managers and foremen. That made the wage system all the more vital to managerial control through their power to set the rate and judge the amount and quality of a miner's output. An unbendingly authoritarian view of the managerial prerogative and its harsh disciplinary regime further enhanced miners' everyday solidarity. Anchored by blacklists and company unions, coal-owner paternalism also reached into the social sphere, above all through company settlements, where, by 1914, between a half to two-thirds of all mining employees in the northern Ruhr lived. Isolated, self-contained, and homogeneous, these miners' colonies were meant to create a stable and dependent core of workers loyal to the company on a scale made feasible by the high levels of concentration in this heavy-industrial sector. But this could also backfire, as miners improvised their own systems of self-help in an informal culture of mutuality. The 'half-open family structure' gave 'rootless' young miners bonds of attachment as lodgers (*Schlafgänger*) with mining families: one in five mining house-holds had lodgers at any one time, rising in the northern colonies to one in two. Responding to a chronic shortage of taverns in the new coal towns, miners' drinking clubs (*Schnapskasinos*) filled a vital need for sociability, while hosting SPD and union activity. Flourishing in the wake of the 1889 strike (some 110 clubs with 16,640 members in 1894, concentrated in the coalfield's north), they were banned by a change of licensing laws in 1896.[79]

Here, Brüggemeier not only gets inside the miner's skin by relating cultural forms to the subjective and existential as well as the material circumstances of life in the coalfield. He also shines a light on the labour movement: union and SPD visions of working-class advancement intruded between the miners and their everyday experience in ways that squandered the mobilizing potential of informal solidarity structures. The authorities might rail against *Schnapskasinos* as 'the real hotbeds of drunkenness, malingering, brutalization, domestic ruin, and family distress' that corroded the moral basis of the resistance to socialism.[80] But Social Democrats had prejudices of their own: miners' everyday culture – disorderly, violent, and rough – was something to be remoulded and improved, a source of difficulty and disruption, rather than material for class-conscious militancy.

Much historiography has stressed the vitality of rank-and-file move-ments, notably in the unharnessed democratic potential of workers' councils in the German Revolution of 1918–20. Another rich literature

79 Brüggemeier, *Leben vor Ort*, 52–74, 142–61; Brüggemeier and Niethammer, 'Wie wohnten Arbeiter?'; Lutz Niethammer and Franz-Josef Brüggemeier, 'Schlafgänger, Schnap-skasinos und schwerindustrielle Kolonie', in Jürgen Reulecke and Wolfhard Weber, *Fabrik – Familie – Feierabend*.
80 Brüggemeier, *Leben vor Ort*, 153.

shows the constitutive role for later-nineteenth-century labour movements of artisanal traditions, with craft pride and workshop autonomy
transmuting into later thinking about workers' control. Brüggemeier
deploys these and other arguments, including Crew's stress on miners'
occupational community, while grounding them in the social relations
and social practices of the mining industry and mining communities, of
the miners' *Alltag* in its material and experiential dimensions. Brüggemeier's point is not the higher virtue of the miners' everyday culture.
This is explicitly not a romance of miners' authenticity or their essential
militancy – quite the contrary. He marks, rather, the gaps separating
'informal' and 'formal' regions of the coalfield's collective life. The miners'
everydayness held political capacities whose potential the organized
labour movement neglected to tap; those capacities became removed
from even the miners themselves. In closing with a portrait of a miner
and his wife shortly before the former's death from pneumoconiosis in
1920, Brüggemeier honours that unknown multitude for whom the 1919
socialization drive came too late, raising barely a light on the horizon:

> Their life story showed no upward development; they achieved no
> personal high-point. For them, the optimistic dynamic of my account
> of the miners' history had no or very little meaning. For them, the
> independence and possibilities for action I have described lasted
> only for a short time, and were removed by repeated reverses: at times
> they lived in the bitterest poverty, from which there was no escape.
> Personal hopes they had abandoned long ago – long before the
> miners' collective hopes of early 1919 had been dashed.[81]

A rolling wave of rank-and-file militancy crashing over the union's
officialdom and the SPD's moderation, the socialization campaign
epitomized this tragedy. Imaginative openness to what it might have
achieved quickly became refracted through the leadership's limited,
parliamentary conception of the German Revolution and the ensuing
political history. Yet the movement grew from precisely the informal
solidarity structures Brüggemeier describes: 'Socialization was no mere
utopia or abstract construction, it was also the sum of [the miners']
experiences; not just projection, but also a taking up of elements and

---

81   Ibid., 258.

structures grounded in the everyday; a continuation of the everyday.'[82] This returns us, indeed, to Lüdtke's distinction between an alienated realm of formalized political action and the informal sphere of the everyday. With remarkable ease, Labour leaders assumed the social fears of the Ruhr bourgeoisie, charging the miners not only with lack of discipline and immature consciousness but even with a generalized lack of 'culture'. Their crudities would disappear only as the labour movement organized, educated, and reformed them. Ironically, the miners already had a culture of great resourcefulness, one that in both pit and colony sustained an autonomous social space, a 'semipublic' domain. Where union and party leaders saw only roughness, turbulence, and disorder, without the discipline of a genuinely emancipatory impulse, Brüggemeier finds the unevenly assembled materials of a broader-based and organically rooted popular movement.

The Everyday Life of the SPD

Brüggemeier stops short of examining the SPD itself. But if the labour movement existed in such tension with its intended mass constituency, the quality of its everyday connections should be explored. Primary sources are notoriously elusive, so Adelheid von Saldern's discovery of the Göttingen SPD's local minute-book for 1899–1910 delivers exceptional insight.[83] Göttingen contrasted starkly with the Ruhr: neither big-city SPD bastion (for example, Nuremberg, Hamburg, Berlin) nor major industrialized region, but a medium-sized university town with little industry or popular politics before the SPD arrived in 1891 after the lifting of the Anti-Socialist Law. The local party was modestly sized – 190 members among 30,000 inhabitants in 1908 – with a thinly stretched subculture: a branch of the worker gymnasts dating from 1894 (some forty members in 1906); a loosely connected consumers' cooperative (3,459 members in 1905); a union legal office opened in

---

82   Ibid., 251.
83   Adelheid von Saldern, *Auf dem Wege am Arbeiter-Reformismus: Parteialltag in sozialdemokratischer Göttingen (1870–1920)* (Frankfurt: Materialis Verlag, 1984). By the early 1980s, Saldern had joined Medick, Lüdtke, and Niethammer among leading practitioners of *Alltagsgeschichte*. See also Adelheid von Saldern, *The Challenge of Modernity: German Social and Cultural Studies, 1890–1960*, transl. Bruce Little (Ann Arbor, MI: University of Michigan Press, 2003).

1913 (counselling 406 people, including 191 unorganized); two grievance committees collecting complaints for the construction industry and factory inspectorate; a youth committee formed in 1909; and a child protection committee established in 1914. Some industrialization occurred from the 1890s, including precision tools and optical firms around the university, but only the railway repair shop and a textile factory had over 400 employees; the rest – textiles, various light industries – were small-scale.

For just these reasons, Göttingen typified a certain SPD ecology: smaller semi-industrial provincial towns and country districts whose given societies absorbed industrialization while impeding the labour movement. It contained a university, a Prussian garrison, fragmented industrial enterprise, and many small businesses. In this Social Democratic province supporters were commonly poorly paid craft-workers in small shops, where the ranks of the more successfully self-employed delivered the local leaders: master-shoemaker Wilhelm Stegen and joiner-turned-tobacconist Fritz Wedemeyer. In contrast, the one large linen mill, the railway works, and the better-paid precision engineering plant brought few recruits.[84] In this unpromising environment, the local SPD was thrown back onto its own rather meagre resources, producing the beleaguered mentality familiar from SPD historiography with its stress on the party's self-contained isolation. But the Göttingen SPD lacked the subcultural resources that usually went with a broader base in a larger working class. It found itself reliant instead on the Hanover regional party: aside from the routines of branch life, its public presence was confined largely to regionally and nationally initiated propaganda.

The Hanover SPD was very non-radical in outlook. Yet Göttingen Social Democrats were not themselves straightforwardly 'reformist'. For one thing, that hardly matched their local circumstances. Apart from industrial tribunals and public insurance committees, local workers had no concrete participatory outlets to mitigate the exclusion, while the imperial state's tariff and fiscal policies constantly refreshed the inequities of the existing undemocratic order. This continuously recharged

---

84 Saldern, *Auf dem Wege am Arbeiter-Reformismus*, 290–300, contains an appendix of fifty-four local SPD biographies. In Green-oriented politics, the term *Provinz* implied returning to rural and small-town concerns previously disregarded by the urban Left as 'provincialism'. See Dieter Bellmann, Wolfgang Hein, Werner Trapp, and Ger Zang, 'Provinz als politisches Problem', *Kursbuch* 39 (1975).

sense of injustice fired a critique of the system's class characteristics, for which Kautsky's official centrist ideology – a philosophy of socialist inevitability, fuelled by the logic of capitalist accumulation and crisis – proved a perfect expression. If that outlook formally professed revolution, then the Göttingen party's practical circumstances conduced to reformism. When it came to mobilizing broader popular support, whether before 1914 or in the revolutionary crisis of 1918–20, the local disadvantages sustained a disabling political psychology.

Faced with the town's semi-industrial economy and its social relations, Göttingen Social Democrats turned inward, while paradoxically displacing their main attention onto national priorities. Severely constrained by Göttingen's provincialism, they overcompensated subjectively by borrowing others' advanced outlook, switching energies to larger affairs. While party conversation pulled constantly towards the national and international arenas in that way, the local and provincial receded, slighting the urgency of grassroots grievances and community-based agitation. The Göttingen branch almost entirely neglected municipal concerns, denying itself that local political bridgehead. Rather than growing into a campaigning movement of broader popular range, it shrank to a socializing agency for the already converted. Inside its distinctive local-political imaginary, it favoured grand-historical developments over immediate traditions and centralist control over local accountability. This brought a lack of political self-confidence, which recourse to the authority and expertise of higher party bodies did nothing to overcome.

A key symptom of this was the approach to education. Göttingen activists tried transcending their marginality through a countervailing emphasis on 'culture' as the self-conscious cultivation of progressive values. Given the local thinness of the free-time and self-improvement subculture, that translated to a classical, thoroughly non-subversive vision of uplift or 'reception of existing educational goods'.[85] Belief in academic schooling and emancipation through knowledge, fuelled by the university's presence, can hardly be gainsaid. But such ideas replicated existing notions of value: 'Party activists wanted to live worthy, upstanding, moral, moderate, and disciplined lives: on the one hand, to show the workers who were not yet organized a good example; on the

---

85 Saldern, *Auf dem Wege am Arbeiter-Reformismus*, 235.

other hand, to show bourgeois society that one was up to all tasks, that one deserved good standing and respect.[86] Social Democrats venerated 'high culture', whether as classical literature, theatre, art, and music, or as taste, morality, and sensibility. While the party was still excluded, that bespoke an oppositional stance. But when the constitutional setting changed after 1918 and the SPD won democratic legitimacy, assimilationist tendencies grew less encumbered. The party's radicalism was tempered and often compromised by its conventional cultural outlook – from hesitant or deferential attitudes towards hierarchy and authority, a prevalence of militarist rhetoric, and a fetishization of order and discipline to latent patriotism and patriarchal assumptions about family, child-raising, and the place of women.[87]

The downside of the pursuit of culture was this failure to challenge hegemonic values, whether through a more radically oppositional 'movement culture' or by attracting a much broader dissentient public. The new century was a watershed in this regard. Early years saw some pursuit of larger political momentum, but largely by motivating the core membership – by collective reading of newspaper articles, assignment of political reports, use of a question-box at meetings. But, after 1901–02, even this fell away, with barely a single collective reading per year during 1904–07, as against eight in 1900 and 1901. A wider public was rarely agitated: meetings were held indoors; May Day was an intra-party festivity, not an open rally; meetings occurred around lectures, with little spontaneous exchange; strikes were carefully depoliticized. Party politics were rarely integrated with members' personal lives and everyday circumstances, let alone those of workers at large. Everyday discourse was even consciously depoliticized, most of all affecting family, sexuality, and private life. The political valencies of ordinary life were measured by established precepts, especially the rational ordering of social behaviour. Much working-class conservatism remained intact, particularly regarding gender and generational roles. Those areas were even dignified in terms of the quest for respectability, while other parts of workers' culture – the 'rough' ones beyond the Göttingen party's small

---

86   Ibid.
87   For this contrast between Imperial and Weimar settings, see Saldern, 'Arbeiterkulturbewegung in Deutschland in der Zwischenkriegszeit', in *Arbeiterkulturen zwischen Alltag und Politik: Beiträge zum europäischen Vergleich in der Zwischenkriegszeit*, ed. Friedhelm Boll (Vienna: Europa-Verlag, 1986), 34–5.

domain – were disdained. This spelled neglect of the entire creative and imaginative realm. The party's socialist ideals lacked prefigurative grounding in everyday life.

This returns us to Lüdtke's argument about the often-alienated quality of formally instituted working-class politics. If labour history leapt excitingly forward with social histories of the working class, the latter now themselves required an everyday approach. Through *Alltags-geschichte*, labour's political capacities could be more imaginatively and effectively located in structures and practices of experienced social life – whether by Brüggemeier's stress on informal solidarity structures, by von Saldern's critique of the Göttingen SPD's disconnectedness from ordinary practices of working-class life, or by Lüdtke's insistence on the disjunctive and nonsynchronous relations between formalized political discourse and the everyday politics of *Eigensinn*. These insights help enormously with the basic conundrum of relating working-class formation to working-class politics: How exactly might high degrees of social solidarity, political cohesion, and wider social influence be achieved among wage-earning populations otherwise fragmented around sectional, religious, ethnic, gendered, sexual, and cultural contradictions?

~

Alltagsgeschichte was, and remains, a phenomenon of its time. It began during the late 1970s partly amid the uncertainties of a West German historical profession experiencing a complex conjuncture of method-ological debate, generational politics, university retrenchment, and conservative *Tendenzwende*. It grew historiographically from tensions in the sequential reception of two distinct paradigms: first, the drive for 'historical social science', guided by a Weberian sociology in the mould of post-war US social and political theory at the height of its 1960s influence; second, the culturalist mode of social history of French and British provenance, informed by contemporary Marxisms and radical sociologies, with definite anthropological interest in the inside and underside of social life. If the former explicitly affirmed 'Western' prin-ciples of enlightened modernity, then the latter openly disavowed liberal conceptions of progress and modernization. Finally, underlying the turn to everyday life was a crisis of belief in the progressive political agency of the working class. This came partly from the labour movement's integration and growing distance from past traditions of working-class mobilization, partly from the structural dissolution of the working class itself in any classic sense of the term. Not only had the labour movement withdrawn from earlier visions of cultural emancipation. The working class had ceased to be the self-evident addressee for such a project, even leaving the stage as an obvious social force, let alone an active class-subject. *Alltagsgeschichte* was informed less by the conviction of an earlier labour history in the forward march of the working class than by recognition of its opposite: that by the late 1970s the march had stopped.[88]

The upshot was an encroaching awareness of the finiteness and historical specificity of the working-class culture whose progressive potentials had long motivated social historians on the Left: the aforementioned mixture of historiographical and political factors pushed strongly for rethinking the labour movement's relationship to the working class. The sense of contemporary sociopolitical flux, combined with growing critical distance from an earlier Left historiography, exposed the insufficiency of received nostrums and their underlying economic and sociological assumptions. Classical visions of the progressive agency of the working class came to be decentred, if not entirely set aside. The flourishing of *Alltagsgeschichte* was in that sense an intellectual counterpart to the new social movements. Obversely, the fiercest response to new thinking came unsurprisingly from those most invested in the SPD's liberal-democratic evolution since 1945 – an evolution bringing precisely the alienation of the labour movement's institutional discourse from those mundane perceptions and experiences of ordinary workers in the production and reproduction of their everyday lives that historians such as Lüdtke, Brüggemeier, and von Saldern sought to explore.

In effect, *Alltagsgeschichte* was making a 'third space' *between* the older institutional accounts and the structural approaches to industrialization and working-class formation preferred by social-science historians.[89]

---

88   See Eric J. Hobsbawm et al., *The Forward March of Labour Halted?* (London: Verso, 1981); Rolf Ebbighausen and Friendrich Tiemann, eds, *Das Ende der Arbeiterbewegung in Deutschland? Ein Diskussionsband zum sechzigsten Geburtstag von Theo Pirker* (Opladen: Westdeutscher Verlag, 1984); Michael Schneider, 'In Search of a "New" Historical Subject: The End of Working-Class Culture, the Labour Movement, and the Proletariat', *International Labour and Working-Class History* 32 (1987).

89   The apogee of social-science approaches, published just as culturalist critiques were under way, was Ira Katznelson and Aristide Zolberg, eds, *Working-Class Formation: Nineteenth-Century Patterns in Western Europe and the United States* (Princeton: Princeton

Alltagshistoriker dug beneath organized party, union, and associational activity, where working-class agency and consciousness were taken to reside, to study ordinary working people themselves. Informal settings of everyday working-class life, they argued, in families, households, streets, neighbourhoods, bars, and free-time spaces, as well as the many different kinds of workplace, specifically spawned subjectivities and patterns of sociability that vitally shaped possible forms of politics. If those other contexts – understood culturally and ontologically, as well as spatially – were carefully and imaginatively recovered, the fields of differences separating labour movement from working class could come properly into focus.

Given the generally progressive inclinations of labour historians, the existence of such difficulties has been hard to acknowledge, especially when socialist politicians or trade unionists appeared in less than democratic or ethically consistent lights. Yet, for the duration of the labour movement's history, socialists have set themselves virtuously apart from many features of working-class life, despite the abstract centring of collective working-class agency as the source of forward-moving historical change and progressive good. Self-improving or moralizing impulses in socialist outlook always validated certain kinds of workers – and certain attributes of working-classness – over others. Socialist imagery of class-conscious proletarians projected a manual worker in handicrafts or industry, formed by the dignity of labour and workplace cultures of skill, living by values of sobriety and self-improvement in settled working-class communities, with a respectable family life – all of which was heavily masculine-defined. An idealized image of the worker also omitted much negatively perceived working-class experience – notably, the roughness and disordered transience of much working-class living, with its dependence on informal economies, casualized labour markets, improvised domestic arrangements, and crime. Entire categories of workers barely figured in the imagery at all, including domestic servants, migrants, ethnic minorities, the religiously devout, and especially women.

Everyday working-class experience thus became the starting point for more complex appraisals of the potentials and difficulties of

---

University Press, 1986). For an incisive critique, see Margaret R. Somers, 'Class Formation and Capitalism: A Second Look at a Classic', *Archives européennes de sociologie* 37: 1 (1996), 180. See also Margaret R. Somers, 'Narrativity, Narrative Identity, and Social Action: Rethinking English Working-Class Formation', *Social Science History* 16 (1992).

progressive politics. Crucially, this was the *opposite* of any naively roman-
ticized construction of an 'alternative' or 'real' working class whose
authentic radicalism the labour movement had misrecognized or
betrayed. *Alltagshistoriker* certainly argued for the presence of needs
and desires – elementary structures of working-class solidarity – whose
democratic potentials were tragically neglected, whether during and
before 1914, in the German Revolution, or in the failure to head off
the rise of Nazism. Yet they also pointed to equally self-interested and
narrowly defensive aspects of working-class culture, including the short-
term calculus of survivalism and 'making it through', forms of collective
intolerance militating against the achievement of broadly based democratic unities, and the structural hierarchies of skill, age, region,
ethnicity, religion, and especially gender that divided the working class
and fragmented efforts at solidarity.[90]

Gendered cultures of patriarchal and work-related masculinity
proved the most persistent of these internal systems of difference. But if
Alltagsgeschichte and gender history had evident affinities, the actual
convergence was slow to occur. During the 1980s, few of the new practitioners noticed either the absence of women from their writing or the
masculinity of their working-class subjects; key gains in women's history
came from elsewhere.[91] Lüdtke's signature concept of *Eigensinn* showed
how complex practices of workplace self-affirmation, including pride in
skill and dignity of labour, could become a source of depoliticizing
consolation in times of fascist political repression, so that the best
resources for a positive working-class identity linked to democracy,
consistently celebrated by labour historians, could nurture acquiescence
and complicity in the anti-democratic values of the Third Reich. Yet this
analysis stopped short of the prerequisites of patriarchal and sexualized
masculinity these constructions of work-defined positive identity also

90   See especially Alf Lüdtke, 'What Happened to the "Fiery Red Glow"? Workers'
Experiences and German Fascism', in Lüdtke, *History of Everyday Life*, along with citations in
note 58, above.
91   One key exception was Wierling, 'History of Everyday Life and Gender Relations'. In
the meantime, see especially Kathleen Canning, *Languages of Labour and Gender: Female
Factory Work in Germany, 1850–1914* (Ithaca, NY: Cornell University Press, 1996); Kathleen
Canning, ed., *Gender History in Practice: Historical Perspectives on Bodies, Class, and Citizen-
ship* (Ithaca, NY: Cornell University Press, 2005); Belinda J. Davis, *Home Fires Burning: Food,
Politics, and Everyday Life in World War I Berlin* (Chapel Hill, NC: University of North
Carolina Press, 2000).

entailed. The coherence and efficacy of identities in the workplace might certainly be linked to egalitarian family relationships between women and men. More commonly, they presumed gendered inequalities of domestic and sexual power.

Across the intervening years, these neglects have markedly diminished. The hostile polemics of the first two decades have also mainly receded. Many of the everyday-life perspectives have won genuine recognition and generalized acceptance across both the discipline of history and the historian's broader range of collaborations, especially with regard to subjectivities, to the hidden meanings of an event or a political transaction, to the intimate histories of power and policy, to the default need for other disciplinary knowledges and methods, and to the value of microhistory and 'historical miniatures'.[92] A new journal, *Historische Anthropologie: Kultur, Geschichte, Alltag*, was launched in 1993, with Medick and Lüdtke on its masthead, creating a notable counterpart to *Geschichte und Gesellschaft*. The pertinent analyses have also been brought forward, through the Nazi time to the foundation years of the Federal and Democratic Republics and beyond, to the fractured moment of the 1950s and 1960s, when the later-twentieth-century configuration of West German society and politics was actually formed. The early proposals, notably the 1984 volume by Medick and Sabean on *Interest and Emotion* and Lüdtke's emphasis on a 'theory of needs', pioneered the study of the history of emotions, which since the early 2000s has been such a powerful trend in the German academy.[93]

In these ways, *Alltagsgeschichte* has acquired its legitimate place, becoming part of the discipline's accepted repertoire of historiographies, even joining its generalized common sense. Indeed, by their long and sustained advocacy, backed by patient and persuasive arguments grounded always in boldly empirical research, historians like von Saldern, Medick, and Lüdtke managed to break through the gratuitously built barriers separating 'social history' from the study of 'culture'. Once 'the social' was successfully freed from the narrowly prescribed

---

92 For stocktaking, see Paul Steege, Andrew Stuart Bergerson, Maureen Healey, and Pamela E. Swett, 'The History of Everyday Life: A Second Chapter', *Journal of Modern History* 80: 2 (2008); Davis et al., *Alltag, Erfahrung, Eigensinn*.

93 See Medick and Sabean, *Interest and Emotion*; *SOWI* editorial, 'Bedürfnisse, Erfahrung und Verhalten'. For current historiography in Germany, see Jan Plamper, *The History of Emotions: An Introduction* (Oxford: Oxford University Press, 2015), which either misses or un-remembers these earlier calls to histories of emotional life.

coordinates of the social-science historians, that false opposition could also be dismantled. There have always been ways of specifically *refusing* the polarized divisiveness of having to make a choice between approaches that prioritize the 'social' and those that foreground the 'cultural'. Recognizably social and political topics may be successfully invested with a cultural analytic, just as cultural topics can be grounded by all the contextualizing commitments social history had proposed. Social history is perfectly capable of responding to the incitements of cultural theory, just as cultural studies will benefit from the power of seeing structural regularities. The 'social' *versus* the 'cultural' was always a false categorical separation. In that sense, there is no need to choose.

7

Conjuncture and the Politics of Knowledge: The Centre for Contemporary Cultural Studies, 1968–1984

I begin with a discrepancy. On the one hand, the Birmingham Centre for Contemporary Cultural Studies (CCCS) has a recognized place in the cultural and intellectual histories of the last third of the twentieth century. Those histories embraced definite fields of inquiry (youth subcultures, popular cultural forms, ethnographies of working-class life); big new disciplinary areas (media, mass communications, cultural studies per se); long-evolving theories of language, ideology, and subjectivity; entire dimensions of social and cultural analysis (gender, class, above all race); and, last but not least, a particular reading of British political history during the early twentieth century. For the ferment of ideas in the 1970s and 1980s, CCCS was indispensable: notably, for debates within Marxist theory and everything covered by its eight anthologies, from *On Ideology* and *Women Take Issue* (both 1978), through *Working-Class Culture* (1979) to *The Empire Strikes Back* and *Making Histories* (both 1982), and finally *Crises in the British State* (1985).[1] This presence was crucial for the Left and its unresolved quest

---

1   See CCCS, ed., *On Ideology* (London: Hutchinson, 1978); Women's Studies Group, ed., *Women Take Issue* (London: Hutchinson, 1979); John Clarke, Chas Critcher, and Richard Johnson, eds, *Working Class Culture* (London: Hutchinson, 1979); CCCS, ed., *The Empire Strikes Back* (London: Hutchinson, 1982); CCCS, ed., *Making Histories* (London: Hutchinson, 1982); Mary Langan and Bill Schwarz, eds, *Crises in the British State 1880–1930* (London: Hutchinson, 1985). See also Stuart Hall and Tony Jefferson, eds, *Resistance through Rituals:*

for a politics to meet the needs of the transformed capitalist society then under construction. A history of the Left's debates and accomplishments in this period without the multiform contributions of the Birmingham Centre can hardly be imagined.

On the other hand, you would never know this from the steadily accumulating general histories of the times, where neither the Centre itself nor cultural studies as a body of thought ripple the surface. These general narratives of the 1970s and 1980s and the associated literatures on Anglo-British national identity simply ignore this exceptionally interesting collective contribution. So do the leading critics and intellectual historians of the period, including so centrally positioned and acutely perceptive an observer as Stefan Collini.[2] To take another example, CCCS proved a main source of debate around questions of Englishness/Britishness during the 1980s, particularly with respect to race, legacies of empire, and the reshaping of the twentieth-century state. Yet a prestigious contemporary historian like Peter Mandler could survey the 'English national character' between Edmund Burke and

---

Youth Subcultures in Postwar Britain (London: Hutchinson, 1976); CCCS, ed., *Unpopular Education* (London: Hutchinson, 1981). Stuart Hall, Chas Critcher, Tony Jefferson, John Clarke, and Brian Roberts, *Policing the Crisis: Mugging, the State, and Law and Order* (London: Macmillan, 1978) was a freestanding intervention. A final volume in the Hutchinson series, Sarah Franklin, Celia Lury, and Jackie Stacey, eds, *Off Center: Feminism and Cultural Studies*, London: Hutchinson (London: Hutchinson, 1991), came later. An anthology, Stuart Hall, Dorothy Hobson, Andrew Lowe, and Paul Willis, eds, *Culture, Media, Language: Working Papers in Cultural Studies, 1972–1979* (London: Routledge/CCCS, University of Birmingham, 1980) contains some additional work.

2   Popular histories include Dominic Sandbrook, *Seasons in the Sun: The Battle for Britain, 1974–1979* (London: Allen Lane, 2012); Andrew Marr, *A History of Modern Britain* (London: Pan, 2007); Andy Beckett, *When the Lights Went Out: What Really Happened to Britain in the Seventies* (London: Faber & Faber, 2009). None refer to Stuart Hall, cultural studies, or the Birmingham Centre. At the academic high end, neither Peter Clarke's *Hope and Glory: Britain 1900–2000* (London: Penguin, 2004) nor Brian Harrison's *Finding a Role? The United Kingdom, 1970–1990* (Oxford: Oxford University Press, 2010), pays any attention, although in a subsection ('University Growing Pains') of a chapter on 'Intellect and Culture', Harrison mentions 'cultural studies' in scare quotes (399). In Stefan Collini's oeuvre, Hall and cultural studies register in neither *Absent Minds: Intellectuals in Britain* (Oxford: Oxford University Press, 2006) nor *Common Reading: Critics, Historians, Publics* (Oxford: Oxford University Press, 2008). If in dismissive, supercilious tones, cultural studies does get a chapter, 'Grievance Studies: How Not to Do Cultural Criticism', in Stefan Collini, *English Pasts: Essays in History and Culture* (Oxford: Oxford University Press, 1999). Laurence Black's *Redefining British Politics: Culture, Consumerism and Participation, 1954–70* (Houndmills: Palgrave Macmillan, 2010) mounts an oblique attack on the CCCS version without ever naming it, invoking a caricatured rendition of 'New Left' ideas only as 'an unofficial foil to several [of his own] arguments' (209).

Tony Blair without even mentioning that discussion, except obliquely to confirm the 'perverse' wrongheadedness of 'left-wing intellectuals'.[3] As CCCS alumni dispersed across British higher education, an elaborate corpus continued to build around matters of Englishness, nationhood, race, and empire, without ever registering on Mandler's radar.[4] What is going on here? How do we make sense of this discrepancy?

At issue are those most basic of historiographical questions: Who writes history? And how is it authorized? When the past settles into the reliable patterns and normative stories taken to show how the present was shaped, inequalities of power, audience, and voice will always be in play. As I first composed these words (at the climax of the Labour Party leadership election in August 2015), public commentary dripped with references to '1983' and sometimes '1979', calling up an especially well-established story about how the present was shaped, one so successfully naturalized as to permeate the political common sense. This was a case, clearly, of victors' history: those complicated processes – some conscious, some not – that make certain events and ideas usable for history while leaving others on the cutting-room floor. How exactly the past is recalled or forgotten, how it is worked into arresting images and coherent stories, how it is ordered into reliable explanations, how it is celebrated and disavowed, suppressed and imagined, works in complicated ways to sanction the present as necessary, as the natural state of affairs, as an ending, in face of which 'There is no alternative'. From the conflicts of the 1970s and 1980s, some basic questions arise: Which narratives get to draw the commonly accepted contours of a society's collective understanding? How do they get composed? What goes into their making? Who is included, and who not? What is it that confers a place in the story, even if merely a paragraph or a sentence or two? Which ideas deserve to be noticed, and which can just be ignored? Who

---

3   See Peter Mandler, *The English National Character: The History of an Idea from Edmund Burke to Tony Blair* (New Haven, CT: Yale University Press, 2006), 234. A range of pertinent work is missing from Mandler's bibliography. One exception, Patrick Wright's *On Living in an Old Country: The National Past in Contemporary Britain* (London: Verso, 1985), is singled out for tendentious attack. Wright was at CCCS in 1979–80.

4   See especially Bill Schwarz, 'Englishness and the Paradox of Modernity', *New Formations* 1 (1987), and 'Night Battles: Hooligan and Citizen' and 'Black Metropolis, White England', both in *Modern Times: Reflections on a Century of English Modernity*, ed. Mica Nava and Alan O'Shea (London: Routledge, 1995). Bill Schwarz's *Memories of Empire, Vol. 1: The White Man's World* (Oxford: Oxford University Press, 2011), postdates the appearance of Mandler's *English National Character*, but builds on his many earlier essays.

decides, and how? If this is not exactly Brecht's worker who reads history, the thrust is surely the same.[5]

Stuart Hall, CCCS director from 1968 to 1979, was by any standard a significant British intellectual of the late twentieth century. Yet, in contrast to his predecessor and CCCS founder Richard Hoggart, who is routinely written into the narrative, Hall is missing from the presently materializing national histories. Hoggart authored *The Uses of Literacy*, a book that captured the national imagination when it was published in 1957, with a remarkably long-lasting resonance.[6] His post-Birmingham influence then took a very particular trajectory. From being primarily a teacher-intellectual, he entered a career in high-level public administration as, successively, assistant director-general of UNESCO (1971–75) and Warden of Goldsmiths (1976–84): 'Richard goes down the committee road, becomes one of the great and the good . . . and is very, very good at working behind the scenes, getting committees to take a progressive line on broadcasting, education, youth clubs, you name it, which did lead to substantial policy changes.'[7] The consummate outsider-turned-insider, experienced and adept at navigating the corridors of power, he joined the progressive establishment when it enjoyed particular leeway in cultural affairs.[8] But to authorize Hoggart's journey as part of the national story – rendering it visible – while effacing Hall's very different passage through the same strongly contested years, is to

5   See Bertolt Brecht, 'Questions from a Worker Who Reads', in *Poems*, ed. John Willett and Ralph Mannheim with Erich Fried (London: Eyre Methuen, 1976). Beginning with 'Who built Thebes of the seven gates?', the poem unfolds a litany of such questions. It ends: 'Every page a victory. / Who cooked the feast for the victors? / Every ten years a great man. / Who paid the bill? / So many reports. / So many questions.'

6   See Richard Hoggart, *The Uses of Literacy: Aspects of Working Class Life with Special Reference to Publications and Entertainments* (London: Chatto & Windus, 1957), and *An Imagined Life: Life and Times, Vol. III: 1959–91* (Oxford: Oxford University Press, 1992); Sue Owen, ed., *Richard Hoggart and Cultural Studies* (Houndmills: Palgrave Macmillan, 2008).

7   Christopher Pawling and Rosalind Brunt, 'Interview – 6 June 2011', *Cultural Studies* 27: 5 (2013), 702. Having famously testified in the landmark 1960 *Lady Chatterley's Lover* obscenity trial, Hoggart served on the Pilkington Committee on Broadcasting (1960–62) and the Arts Council (1976–81), as well as the earlier Albemarle Committee on Youth Services (1958–60); he chaired the Advisory Council for Adult and Continuing Education (1977–83) and the Broadcasting Research Unit (1981–91); and he was a governor of the Royal Shakespeare Company (1962–88).

8   The ür-text here – as reportage and affirmation – remains Noel Annan, 'The Intellectual Aristocracy', in *Studies in Social History: A Tribute to G. M. Trevelyan*, ed. J. H. Plumb (London: Longman, 1955), along with *The Dons: Mentors, Eccentrics and Geniuses* (Chicago: University of Chicago Press, 1999), and *Our Age: English Intellectuals between the World Wars – A Group Portrait* (New York: Random House, 1990).

write from a highly selective vantage-point, valorizing certain ideas and emplacements over others. The genuine importance of Hoggart's story – his justified place in contemporary history – makes that story no less partial and partisan in its presumption of entitlement, given the institutionally secured concentrations of cultural capital.

What follows is something of a counter-narrative – or at least a modest gesture in that direction. Why does this matter? From the earlier vantage-point of the mid 1960s, at the time of the Birmingham Centre's creation, and on the cusp of the tumults that launched its history, an official version of the national past seemed locked into place every bit as securely as the neoliberal mythology of our own time. As it unfolded in the 1940s and 1950s, the post-war consensus celebrating the much-vaunted British genius for compromise and gradualism proposed a politely complacent success story based on parliamentary evolution, expanding citizenship, and the welfare state. Key interventions commonly seen as foundational for cultural studies – Edward Thompson's *The Making of the English Working Class* (1963) and Raymond Williams's *Culture and Society* (1958) and *The Long Revolution* (1961) – joined the successive New Lefts in a critique of that consensus, acquiring an impressive reach across British intellectual culture.[9] This had various implications, including its most overtly political contribution: the reclaiming of past forms of popular democracy vitally challenged the reigning ideas of the time. The revelation that collective action, mass politics, and insurrectionary resistance had been needed to dislodge the coercive and corrupt practices of a narrowly based political system in the earlier nineteenth century helped fuel the emergent radicalisms in the present. But by attending to popular culture and popular beliefs, by exploring how ordinary people handled large-scale events through the ideas and practices available to them in everyday life, and by means of his distinctive ethnographic methods, Thompson delivered far wider resources for a very different construction of the modern British past.

Thompson's social histories – that were always already cultural – broadened the space for politics, requiring new theories and techniques of study. Political meanings appeared in all sorts of unexpected places.

---

9 E. P. Thompson, *The Making of the English Working Class* (London: Gollancz, 1963); Raymond Williams, *Culture and Society, 1780–1950* (London: Chatto & Windus, 1958), and *The Long Revolution* (London: Chatto & Windus, 1961).

Already powerfully present in *The Making*, this emerged still more clearly from 'The Moral Economy of the English Crowd in the Eighteenth Century' (1971) and his studies of criminality and the law conducted at the University of Warwick (1965–71), culminating in *Whigs and Hunters* and *Albion's Fatal Tree* (both 1975).[10] The freshly enhanced conception of 'the political' in these histories radically deinstitutionalized its possible locations. It shifted away from acknowledged arenas of parliaments, parties, and associations towards other settings and practices. These included neighbourhoods and streets, workplaces and informal economies, riots and criminality, youthful rebelliousness, expressiveness in style, sexual dissidence, and any of the ways in which a society's behavioural rules might be challenged or flaunted, including even the meanings of 'apathy' or indifference to politics as such.[11]

These were precisely where CCCS began much of its distinctive work after 1968. If some signature projects – on television and media, on broadcast news, on soap operas, on magazines and women, even *Policing the Crisis* in its earliest iteration as a study of media panic around a local incident of 'mugging' – were continuous with Hoggart's characteristic concerns, then others caught the Thompsonian momentum, especially the new focus on subcultures, but also emerging interest in work and cultural history.[12]

---

10   See E. P. Thompson, *Whigs and Hunters: The Origins of the Black Act* (London: Allen Lane, 1975); Douglas Hay, Peter Linebaugh, John G. Rule, E. P. Thompson, and Cal Winslow, *Albion's Fatal Tree: Crime and Society in Eighteenth-Century England* (Harmondsworth: Penguin, 1975).

11   See E. P. Thompson, ed., *Out of Apathy* (London: Stevens, 1960). See also Oxford University Socialist Discussion Group, eds, *Out of Apathy: Voices of the New Left Thirty Years On* (London: Verso, 1989).

12   In continuity with Hoggart were, for example, early works by Dorothy Hobson, David Morley, Charlotte Brunsdon, and Angela McRobbie. Stuart Hall's classic early text was 'Encoding and Decoding in the Television Discourse' (CCCS Stencilled Occasional Paper 7), extracted as 'Encoding/Decoding', in Hall, Hobson, Lowe, and Willis, *Culture, Media, Language*. Other early emphases mainly fizzled out, including popular sports and 'the western', D. H. Lawrence and related literary study around Matthew Arnold and F. R. Leavis, and the Frankfurt School as such. For the emergent ones, see especially Hall and Jefferson, *Resistance through Rituals*; Phil Cohen, *Rethinking the Youth Question: Education, Labour, and Cultural Studies* (Durham: Duke University Press, 1999); Paul Willis, *Learning to Labor: How Working-Class Kids Get Working-Class Jobs*, 2nd edn (New York: Columbia University Press, 1981). Cohen's book dated mostly from the 1970s, including the foundational 'Sub-Cultural Conflict and Working-Class Community'. Willis's book was one of the earliest works to be widely noticed, preceded by CCCS Stencilled Occasional Paper 43, 'How Working Class Kids Get Working Class Jobs', 1975.

A transition could be glimpsed at the end of 1971, with the demise of the Centre's General Theory Seminar, started in 1970. It was replaced by the famous and much-envied system of sub-groups, initially including 'Literature and Society' and 'Media Studies', then rapidly extended towards 'Sub-Cultures'. Hoggartian origins crossed with radicalized social histories and incipient Marxisms arriving through the excitements of 1968. Yet, no sooner had Thompsonian social history made its imprint than things were already moving on, driven intensely forward by commitment to theory as such – to linguistics and semiotics, to studies of ideology, to European critical theory, and above all to Marx.[13] Shooting far beyond any straightforwardly Thompsonian terrain, Centre discussions responded to the frenetic energy around wider Marxist debates of the time, compounded by the influx of students from the October 1975 launch of the MA.

This passage from 1971–72 to the middle of the decade occurred through an extraordinary concentration of debate, experiment, creative disagreement, and change, laying the ground for the Centre's influence over the next decade. But, in relation to Thompson, the Centre struggled with an ambivalence that was emblematic for tensions with an earlier New Left formation and its own wider support. If certain of the collective anthologies were heavily structured around critical dialogue with Thompson's ideas (*Working-Class Culture*, *Making Histories*), then from others he was almost entirely absent (*Women Take Issue*, *Empire Strikes Back*, *Crises in the British State*). Aside from migrating to zones of political urgency to which Thompson remained largely indifferent (notably, race and gender), CCCS developed strongly held differences over theory in general.[14] Though Thompson was always approached

---

13   See 'Introduction' in *Cultural Studies* 6 (Autumn 1974), where 'a theoretical shift in our approach to cultural studies' is flagged 'retrospectively, from an emerging Marxist perspective'. That entailed recognizing 'the theoretical and political limitations of the liberal radicalism from which "cultural studies" and the Centre emerged in the early sixties, and trying to clarify, in a preliminary way, the contemporary forces which shape us' (1). If this issue opened with a critique of Hoggart (Colin Sparks), a manifesto on 'The Politics of Popular Culture' (Bryn Jones), and an appreciation of Raymond Williams (Michael Green), it continued with a critique of 'Roland Barthes: Structuralism/Semiotics' (Iain Chambers), a three-way exchange on Louis Althusser's theory of ideology (Robin Rusher, John Mepham, Steve Butters), an exegesis of 'Marx's Notes on Method: A "Reading" of the "1857 Introduction"' (Stuart Hall), a critique of 'The Aesthetic Theory of the Frankfurt School' (Phil Slater), and a brief guide to the Frankfurt School (Chris Pawling).

14   These arrived with a vengeance in 'The Poverty of Theory or an Orrery of Errors', the principal essay (204 pages, roughly half the book) in E. P. Thompson, *The Poverty of Theory*

through a spirit of constructive and respectful critique, by the mid 1970s fissures were opening. Reacting initially against a 1976–77 Occasional Stencilled Paper, then against Richard Johnson's 1978 article in *History Workshop Journal*, Thompson unleashed his full polemical fury in a staged confrontation with Johnson and Hall at the Thirteenth Ruskin History Workshop in December 1979.[15]

Bringing together far broader disagreements within the Left among both intellectuals and activists, this confrontation seemed like a spectacular display of divisiveness – a severe crisis not just of civility, but of basic orientation. It queried the relationship of debates in theory to possible forms of political practice, bringing to a head conflicts that had been building over some years. It was also prefigured inside CCCS, where versions of the same discord attended each major discussion of the 1970s.[16] As it turned out, the Ruskin confrontation proved cathartic. The intellectual strife hardly melted immediately away. But the changed political climate after Margaret Thatcher's election the previous May combined with the Cold War's reboot in the early 1980s to relativize the severity of dissension among theorists, substantially containing its fallout.[17] Internal debates and trajectories of CCCS itself have been explicated many, many times, whether by participants themselves or by

---

and Other Essays (London: Monthly Review, 1978), an angrily polemical and intentionally divisive intervention.

15   The original paper, Richard Johnson, Gregor McLennan, and Bill Schwarz, 'Economy, Culture, and Concept: Three Approaches to Marxist History' (CCCS Occasional Stencilled Paper 50), considered the thought, respectively, of E. P. Thompson, Eugene Genovese, Maurice Dobb, Barry Hindess, and Paul Q. Hirst, engaging head-on with a range of bitterly adversarial debates across Britain's wider intellectual Left. Johnson then published a version of his part of that paper as 'Edward Thompson, Eugene Genovese, and Socialist-Humanist History', in *History Workshop Journal* 6 (1978), to a similarly divided response. For the December 1979 debate between Hall, Johnson, and Thompson, see Raphael Samuel, ed., *People's History and Socialist Theory* (London: Routledge & Kegan Paul, 1981).

16   See Kieran Connell and Matthew Hilton, 'The Working Practices of Birmingham's Centre for Contemporary Cultural Studies', *Social History* 40: 3 (2015), and 'Cultural Studies on the Margins: The CCCS in Birmingham and Beyond', in Kieran Connell and Matthew Hilton, *Cultural Studies 50 Years On: History, Practice, and Politics* (London: Rowman & Littlefield, 2016).

17   For the wider intellectual context and political developments, see Geoff Eley, *A Crooked Line: From Cultural History to the History of Society* (Ann Arbor, MI: University of Michigan Press, 2005), 48–60, 90–113, 115–33, and *Forging Democracy: The History of the Left in Europe, 1850–2000* (New York: Oxford University Press, 2002), 405–8, 384–404, 375–83. For the Ruskin drama, see especially Susan Magarey, 'That Hoary Old Chestnut, Free Will and Determinism: Culture vs Structure, or History vs Theory in Britain', *Comparative Studies in Society and History* 29 (1987).

the legion of commentators. The relationship of those Birmingham histories to the wider universe of cultural studies as it emerged from the 1980s – intellectually and institutionally, whether in Britain or internationally – is no less well known. But the CCCS's relationship to the wider political and intellectual radicalism of the time is often misread. Birmingham events were one particularly generative instance of similar histories proceeding in comparable ways elsewhere, whose character both grounds and illumines the course of the CCCS debates. Pinpointing their typicalities and convergences hardly diminishes the Birmingham Centre's importance. Rather, it deepens our grasp of the context.

The week-long student occupation of Birmingham University's Great Hall in November–December 1968 was a vital founding event, effecting the leadership transition from Hoggart to Hall. The sit-in and associated protests and debates energized Hall and the Centre's students into reimagining what CCCS might be. That led to 'a concerted attempt to initiate a democratization of its working practices' that would embrace all 'decisions relating to the day-to-day management of the Centre, its intellectual scope, and its future direction.'[18] The democratic collectivism that, with growing intensity, shaped the intellectual collaborations, production of knowledge, social relations, and the Centre's everyday institutional life are well described elsewhere.[19] But the politics of 1968–69 broke CCCS out of its Hoggartian cast into a different frame of theoretically driven analysis of cultural phenomena in their broadest historical contexts of social life. That change was traceable across the Centre's fifth and sixth annual reports, issued in October 1969 and December 1971, respectively.[20] One CCCS student active in the sit-in, Paul Willis, recalled a very direct relationship: it 'transformed how we would approach intellectual work.'[21] Hall was expansive in his own hopes for the outcome: CCCS could become a 'utopian enclave' capable of 'transcend[ing] the limits of what appears possible and natural within the existing limits of our situation'. It would 'challenge and modify the

---

18 Connell and Hilton, 'Working Practices', 296.

19 See the interviews collected in *Cultural Studies* 27: 5 (2013), including with Lucy Bland, Christopher Pawling and Rosalind Brunt, John Clarke, Paul Gilroy, Stuart Hall, Stuart Hanson, Andrew Tolson, Helen Wood, Richard Johnson, Gregor McLennan, Angela McRobbie, and David Morley.

20 Ibid., 880–6, 887–95.

21 Connell and Hilton, 'Working Practices', 296. See Willis, 'What Is News – A Case Study', *Working Papers in Cultural Studies* 1 (1971).

prevailing modes of knowledge and authority'. The goal was 'nothing less than the creation, within . . . the existing system, of a *collective* – an intellectual *foco*: a sort of advanced base'.[22]

This was the rhetoric of the headiest hopes of a particular grouping among the student movements of the late 1960s, including the International Socialists (IS, later the SWP), the International Marxist Group (IMG), and *New Left Review* (*NLR*), which in June 1968 formed the Revolutionary Socialist Students' Federation (RSSF), which flickered briefly across the map of student militancy in 1968–69. Espousing the neo-Maoist rhetoric of urban guerrillas and national liberation, along with a Marcusean sense of a deradicalized working class, RSSF proposed the building of 'red bases' in the universities to act as the 'growing points of revolutionary power' for society at large.[23] But if Hall's was a modified form of this language, it bespoke less any concrete expectation of controlling the university (or some space within it) than the generic militancy effervescing in students' political imagination in 1967–71. Some came to CCCS already energized elsewhere – Rosalind Brunt from Essex, Christopher Pawling from Frankfurt, for example; others, including Chas Critcher, Paul Willis, Larry Grossberg, as well as Pawling, were embroiled in Birmingham itself. The compelling *eventfulness* of the sit-in can never be gainsaid: the exceptional intensity and consequences of tasting direct action, whose charge came not just from the immediacy of local events, but also from links to everything else happening in the wider radicalized worlds of politics. Fuelled by events in other universities and colleges in Britain, Europe, and across the world, the soaring sense of possibility was inspired by countless other contexts of the late sixties (socially, nationally, globally) where popular actions were occurring. In the condensed unity of local and larger meanings, in the ramified directness of the relationship between immediate actions and wider realms of understanding, and in the breathtaking existential dramas of personal change, such times were exceedingly powerful. They conferred the rare privilege of learning one's politics – hectically,

---

22   Internal CSSS document by Hall (summer 1971), 'The Missed Moment', in Connell and Hilton, 'Working Practices', 296, 297. Emphasis in original.

23   In the Manifesto adopted at its second conference (November 1968), RSSF envisaged 'red bases in our colleges and universities'. For the Manifesto, see *New Left Review* I/53 (January–February 1969), 21–2, with a dossier of articles by James Wilcox (a.k.a. Robin Blackburn), David Triesman, David Fernbach, and Anthony Barnett, 23–53. 'Growing points of revolutionary power' was a phrase in Wilcox/Blackburn (26).

effectively, lastingly – in laboratories of practice. What was so memo-rable in such an experience (my own was an occupation in Oxford in February–March 1970) was the sheer excitement of being *inside* the event: the rush of joining direct action, the exhilarating novelty of so much collective discussion, the unprecedented ease of spontaneous communication, the rapidity of the political learning process, and of course the temporary high of success.[24]

The seeming ultra-leftism of Hall's thinking makes sense only in relation to these wider intensities and imaginative releases.[25] The inter-connectedness across Left intellectual initiatives – field by field, discipline by discipline, institution by institution, reaching beyond uni-versity precincts into sundry wider settings – was essential to their radicalism. CCCS can easily be credited with greater originality, van-guardism even, than it actually possessed; it takes nothing away from its achievements to find lots of equivalence elsewhere. Just as the sit-in's effects were replicated in many other places, so too was the drive to transform the university's interior relations, elements of which – in some version and degree, in particular units or disciplines or more widely across an institution – hit most of further and higher education in the late sixties and early seventies. Redefining the academic dis-ciplines and their boundaries; rethinking the structure and contents of curricula; challenging the given forms of pedagogy; democratizing faculty–student–staff relations – these were the oxygen of student life for anyone with left-wing inclinations at university in those years. Sometimes internal protests and pressures escalated into crises of an

---

24 Distribution of student activism across Britain is hard to summarize. Trevor Fisk, National Union of Students president in 1968–69, counted twenty-six cases of large-scale direct action in 1967–68; but this certainly understates the ferment, which further exploded in 1969–70. See Trevor Fisk, 'The Nature and Causes of Student Unrest', in *Protest and Discontent*, ed. Bernard Crick and William A. Robson (Harmondsworth: Penguin, 1970), 82. Major sit-ins occurred during 1968–70 at LSE, Hull, Essex, Leicester, Aston, Bristol, Keele, Leeds, Manchester, Birmingham, Warwick, Oxford, and elsewhere, including Hornsey and Guildford art colleges. Beneath the spectacular events was a thinner, spasmodic, and more dispersed, but constant activist current affecting most UK campuses. The flavour is conveyed best by Ronald Fraser, *1968: A Student Generation in Revolt* (New York: Pantheon, 1988), esp. 261–84.

25 See Christopher Pawling's remark in Pawling and Brunt, 'Interview', 'There was a sense where Stuart suggests, retrospectively . . . that we were trying to make the Centre into a place for revolutionaries in the university, when in actual fact there wasn't a basis for it at the time. He, maybe, thought the moment had been missed' (708). Pawling refers here to Colin McCabe, 'An Interview with Stuart Hall', *Critical Quarterly* 50: 1–2 (2008), esp. 21–7.

entire institution – at LSE (1967–69), Essex (1968–69), Hornsey (1968), Guildford (1968), Warwick (1968–70), Oxford (1970), and the Poly-technic of North London (1970–74).[26] More commonly, they energized particular departments and programmes in particular places, or flared more passingly. It was the *openness* to the possibility of radical change that became generalized across the student cohorts of the later 1960s, along with their few teacher allies. Unless we grasp the rapidity and extent of this generalized generational shift, the lines of indebtedness, impact, and affiliation will be obscured.[27]

If CCCS was a key point of confluence, others had their own demo-cratic collectivism, with working practices that may not have matched Birmingham's intensity but marked no less of a vital departure. Ideas and people travelled promiscuously between these nodes, wider con-nections always radiating outwards from Birmingham as well as originating elsewhere. Early on, there were two in particular. One was the National Deviancy Conference, founded in July 1968 by sociologists in their twenties as a breakaway from orthodox criminology, pressing theoretically driven social critique joined to political advocacy. Beside an array of monographs and three early conference anthologies (1971, 1972, and 1974), they produced the programmatic *New Criminology* (1973) and a companion anthology (1975), generating a ramified pattern of influence across the intellectual Left before disbanding in 1977–79.[28]

---

26 See also F. J. Campbell, *High Command: The Making of an Oligarchy at the Polytech-nic of North London, 1970–74* (London: Time Out, 1975). Colin Crouch, *The Student Revolt* (London: Bodley Head, 1970), is still a helpful overview.

27 All but one of the thirteen contributors to *Student Power* were in their twenties (Tom Nairn, fired from Hornsey in 1968, was thirty-one); only three others were older than twenty-five. The four slightly older contributors (Nairn, Perry Anderson, Robin Blackburn, Alexander Cockburn) each came from the 'second New Left', which controlled *New Left Review* from the early 1960s. See Andrew Cockburn and Robin Blackburn, eds, *Student Power: Problems, Diagnosis, Action* (Harmondsworth: Penguin, 1969). Other emblematic books were Trevor Pateman, ed., *Counter Course: A Handbook for Course Criticism* (Harmondsworth: Penguin, 1972), and Robin Blackburn, ed., *Ideology in Social Science: Readings in Critical Social Theory* (London: Fontana, 1972). Two later anthologies strikingly registered the intervening CCCS influence: Ann Marie Wolpe and James Donald, eds, *Is There Anyone Here from Education?* (London: Pluto, 1983), four of whose contributors came from CCCS, and Janet Finch and Michael Rustin, eds, *A Degree of Choice? Higher Education and the Right to Learn* (Harmondsworth: Penguin, 1986), which includes Bill Schwarz, 'Cultural Studies: The Case for the Humanities'.

28 The seven founders were Kit Carson, Stanley Cohen, David Downes, Mary McIntosh, Paul Rock, Ian Taylor, and Jock Young. See Stanley Cohen, ed., *Images of Deviance* (Harmond-sworth: Penguin, 1971); Ian Taylor and Laurie Taylor, eds, *Politics and Deviance* (Harmondsworth: Penguin, 1971); Paul Rock and Mary McIntosh, eds, *Deviancy and Social*

In conducting this work, they developed a collective esprit and working practices based on intensive collaboration.

Ties within CCCS were extremely close. Stanley Cohen published an early essay in the Centre's journal (1974). Stuart Hall coedited *Situating Marx: Evaluations and Departures* (1973) with Paul Walton, another member of the group, from a conference on David McLellan's selections from *Marx's Grundrisse* (1971) held at CCCS and organized by Ian Taylor. Both Phil Cohen's benchmark 'Sub-Cultural Conflict and Working Class Community' (1972) and *Resistance through Rituals* (1975/76) were heavily indebted to conceptual work by Stanley Cohen, Laurie Taylor, and Jock Young. Hall gave a key paper on 'Reformism and the Legislation of Consent' to the last-but-one Deviancy conference in 1977, whose proceedings were coedited by John Clarke (1980).[29]

Partly through shared concepts of 'media amplification' and 'moral panic', radical criminology became linked to mass communications and media studies, the second early stream running through CCCS. It included the Centre for Mass Communication Research (CMCR), established in 1966 at Leicester University under James Halloran, whose trajectory closely mirrored Hoggart's own (each worked at Leicester from 1957 and 1958, in Adult Education and English respectively). CMCR's signature study, an exhaustive analysis of the remarkably successful public delegitimizing of the 27 October 1968 anti–Vietnam War demonstration, converged with Birmingham's own emergent interests, but from different political, methodological, and theoretical perspectives.[30] Later, these links were apparent in two Open University anthologies on Mass Communication and Society edited by James Curran, Michael Gurevich, Tony Bennett, and Janet Woollacott (1977,

---

Control (London: Tavistock, 1974); Ian Taylor, Paul Walton, and Jock Young, *The New Criminology: For a Social Theory of Deviance* (London: Routledge & Kegan Paul, 1973) and Ian Taylor, Paul Walton, and Jock Young, eds, *Critical Criminology: For a Social Theory of Deviance* (London: Routledge & Kegan Paul, 1973). Key monographs included: Jock Young, *The Drugtakers: The Social Meaning of Drug Use* (London: Paladin, 1972); Stanley Cohen, *Folk Devils and Moral Panics* (London: Paladin, 1973).

29 See Stanley Cohen, 'Breaking Out, Smashing Up, and the Social Context of Aspiration', *Working Papers* 5 (1974); Stuart Hall and Paul Walton, eds, *Situating Marx: Evaluations and Departures* (London: Human Context, 1973); Stuart Hall, 'Reformism and the Legislation of Consent', in *Permissiveness and Control: The Fate of the Sixties Legislation*, ed. National Deviancy Conference (London: Macmillan, 1980). Interestingly, direct citations of this sociology of deviancy no longer accompanied *Resistance through Rituals*.

30 See James D. Halloran, Philip Elliott, and Graham Murdock, *Demonstrations and Communication: A Case Study* (Harmondsworth: Penguin, 1970).

1982), including magisterial commentaries by Hall on the re-theorizing of ideology then in progress across the Left's many sectors.[31] Both patterns of cross-area and cross-institutional conversation (sociology of deviance, mass communications) converged in a 1973 anthology edited by Stanley Cohen and Jock Young, *The Manufacture of News: Social Problems, Deviance, and the Mass Media*, where CCCS was also present, including an excerpt from *Policing the Crisis* (1978) added for the second edition (1980).[32]

How distinctive was the CCCS institutional culture? Unlike the National Deviancy Conference, CCCS had the advantage precisely of being a centre – of having a single institutional location, in a freestanding physical space that proved both autonomous and resilient, despite all the university's efforts to constrain and undermine it. There were other examples, of which I will cite two, each from direct experience. Neither exactly mirrored CCCS circumstances. They were smaller, more dispersed, in different relations with their institutional contexts, lacking either the same autonomies or longer-term theoretical legacies. But each revealed the wider fields of intellectual and political influence and conversation. Some embraced other universities and areas of inquiry. Some involved larger theoretical debates and departures. But others reached beyond seminar rooms and conference halls altogether to non-academic settings in more direct relation to social movements, the arts and aesthetics, public culture, and politics.

The first case was the interdisciplinary 'Women in Society' course at the University of Cambridge, created in 1973 under the auspices of the Social and Political Sciences Committee (SPS) by a mixed collective of faculty, graduate students, non-academic professionals, and community workers – some with university affiliation, others not. Avowedly interdisciplinary not just in the collective's composition but in the basic

---

31   Stuart Hall, 'Culture, the Media, and the "Ideological Effect"', in *Mass Communication and Society*, ed. James Curran, Michael Gurevitch, and Janet Woollacott (London: Edward Arnold, 1977) – reprinted in *Essential Essays, Vol. 1*, ed. David Morley (Durham: Duke University Press, 2019); Stuart Hall, 'The Rediscovery of "Ideology": The Return of the Repressed in Media Studies', in Michael Gurevich at al., *Culture, Society, and the Media* (London: Meuthen, 1982).

32   Stanley Cohen and Jock Young, eds, *The Manufacture of News: Social Problems, Deviance, and the Mass Media* (London: Constable, 1973). New criminology also converged with Thompson-influenced social histories of crime at the Warwick Centre for Social History, culminating in *Whigs and Hunters* and *Albion's Fatal Tree* (both 1975).

epistemology of its approach to knowledge and curriculum, the group assembled an entire array of disciplines, from anthropology, history, semiotics, and psychology, through medicine, genetics, and history of science, to economics, sociology, politics, and feminist theory. The collective esprit grew from the same intensity of reading, talking, and writing that characterized the democracy of CCCS working practices. Reflecting the same commitment to breaking down teacher–student hierarchies of knowledge, this was far more than a working method or set of protocols for approaching an academic study. It involved an ethically driven and socially motivated willingness to rethink what a democracy of knowledge might mean, whether in the micropolitics of the classroom or in wider arenas of political action in university, community, and society at large. Like CCCS, it encouraged 'an entire outlook, an ethos, a common acceptance that thinking, learning, writing, personal life, and politics all belonged axiomatically together'. Separations between these elements could be boldly refused.[33]

This Cambridge initiative evinced the wider impact of the new women's movement, which showed insistently by example how teaching and learning practices could be remade. A similar dynamic moved the SPS Marxism Seminar, likewise run by a teacher–student collective largely beneath the radar of the tenured university faculty. Launched in 1975 without History Faculty support, the Cambridge Social History Seminar was another such site, where the radicalism of changes in the discipline conjoined with various oppositional experience, from generational difference to a certain marginal or subaltern status, represented by graduate students, research fellows, part-time teachers, and non-tenured lecturers, all in their twenties and early thirties, with no official standing in the Faculty's eyes. For speaking across these various milieus, politics supplied the binding ties – in the Tawney Society, for example, the public face of a Left faculty group that sponsored occasional political lectures; or the Cambridge branch of the Communist Party, whose modest but energizing presence enabled a highly theoreticist Marxism. More than simply overlapping, these contexts were porous beyond the university too. If tilted towards the metropolitan Oxbridge–London triangle, the thickening of the Left's public sphere was also important,

---

33   See 'Stuart Hall, 1932–2014' (Chapter 11 below). See Cambridge Women's Studies Group, ed., *Women in Society: Interdisciplinary Essays* (London: Virago, 1981).

with new journals, academic and professional networks, some access to national media, and major annual gatherings like the Ruskin History Workshops in Oxford or the summertime Communist University of London (CUL).[34]

My second instance is from University College, Swansea, where I spent 1973–74, immediately before going to Cambridge. In an early stage of what became a general critique of orthodoxies in German historiography, I gave my arguments a first outing in spring 1974, in a freshly formed Radical Humanities group with barely half a dozen members. At first glance this was a very small, embattled outpost of Left-intellectual life, the very opposite of CCCS. But tilting the angle reveals another picture. Swansea was the home to the Coalfield History Project, supported in 1971–74 by the Social Science Research Council (SSRC) and the National Union of Mineworkers (NUM) South Wales Area, devoted to salvaging what remained of the old Miners' Institute Libraries after the calamitous colliery closures of 1959–71. From that process came the South Wales Miners' Library, opened in October 1973. During its inaugural calendar, the library galvanized intense interest and activity, drawing on the coalfield radicalization surrounding the 1972 and 1974 national strikes. Here, the fulcrum of intellectual radicalism was much different from Birmingham's, with a pedagogy and cultural politics more akin to those associated with Hoggart and Raymond Williams in the early CCCS years.[35] The permeable quality of this endeavour, in the transfers back and forth between academic work and aspirations beyond the university, was very apparent – although CCCS likewise had projects that were community-based and linked to the city's cultural life. As it happens, 1973–74 also saw the climax of a three-year student campaign in Swansea to reform curriculum and pedagogy in the Philosophy Department, escalating into full-scale

---

34   In 1976–79 the Cambridge CPGB branch published at least five issues of *Red Shift*. For annual CULs, see Geoff Andrews, *End Games and New Times: The Final Years of British Communism, 1964–1991* (London: Lawrence & Wishart, 2004).

35   Williams had close affinities with the South Wales project. See Raymond Williams, 'The Social Significance of 1926', *Llafur* 2: 2 (1977); Raymond Williams, *Who Speaks for Wales? Nation, Culture, Identity*, ed. Daniel Williams (Cardiff: University of Wales Press, 2003); Dai Smith, *Raymond Williams: A Warrior's Tale* (Cardigan: Parthian, 2008). For the Coalfield History Project, funded further by SSRC in 1980–83, see Hywel Francis, 'The Origins of the South Wales Miners' Library', *History Workshop Journal* 2 (1976). The Library became a major archive depository, research centre, and adult education hub.

confrontation when the chair, D. Z. Phillips, sought dismissal of sympathetic lecturers and mass student expulsions.[36] If Swansea lacked the same 'red base' ethos as CCCS, then a different set of radicalisms could still be found, one no less significant for what ensued during the 1980s.[37]

In judging the place of CCCS in late-twentieth-century British history, we should widen our perspective in this way. Its legacies can be tracked not just in the diffusion of cultural studies as an academic discipline, but in much ampler domains. Other academic fields – the sociology of deviance, mass communications, social history – saw the emergence of a very similar politics of knowledge, in terms of both working practices and cross-disciplinary collaboration. Other examples include the Conference of Socialist Economists (CSE), formed in January 1970, along with its *Bulletin* (December 1971), which became the journal *Capital and Class* (1977); the Radical Philosophy Group (January 1972), with its journal *Radical Philosophy* and an extensive network of groups and meetings, including its Philosophy Festival, held in Oxford in January 1976, and the Radical Science Collective around Robert M. Young in Cambridge and London and its *Radical Science Journal* (1974), feeding directly into Free Association Books and its journal *Free Associations* (1984).[38] These groups were always in mutual conversation. 'United by a recognition of the need to take an integrated approach' while marking 'the convergence of interests of Marxists working in a wide range of areas' (sociology of law, jurisprudence, industrial relations, political theory, social history, and deviancy theory), the National Deviancy Conference

---

36   See *Radical Philosophy* 9 (Winter 1974), 1–3, and 10 (Spring 1975), 1–2. These events involved bizarrely manipulative and authoritarian behaviour by Phillips and the college administration. An Industrial Relations Court ruled a senior academic's targeted dismissal unfair.

37   One trajectory linking various nodes was that of Kim Howells. Born in 1946 from South Wales working-class Communist origins, with battle spurs from Hornsey in 1968 and a BA from Cambridge College of Arts and Technology (1971–74), he wrote a Warwick PhD dissertation (1979) on the South Wales coalfield, 1937–57. While living in Cambridge he joined the Social History Seminar. Back in South Wales, he helped run the 1980–83 SSRC Coalfield History project, worked for the NUM, and coordinated the 1984–85 strike in South Wales. He was elected to parliament for Labour in 1989, serving in various junior posts in New Labour governments during 1997–2008.

38   Other examples include *Critique: Journal of Marxist Theory and Soviet Studies*, founded in Glasgow by Hillel Ticktin (1973), and *Review of African Political Economy* (1974). For the Radical Science Collective, see Les Levidow and Bob Young, eds, *Science, Technology and the Labour Process: Marxist Studies*, 2 vols (London: Free Association, 1981/84, 1985). Vol. 2 includes Bill Schwarz, 'Re-Assessing Braverman: Socialization and Dispossession in the History of Technology'.

and CSE joined forces in January 1979 for a conference on 'Capitalist Discipline and the Rule of Law'.[39] The best-known coalescence of this kind – combining disciplinary insurgency, interdisciplinary desire, and extramural ambition – was the History Workshop Movement and its journal (1976), at its height between the early 1970s and later 1980s. Whether in the pages of its journal, its annual meetings, or the many other local and issue-oriented activities, it was in the History Workshop Movement that other networks most evidently converged.[40]

History Workshop, as a ramified movement reaching far beyond the academic world, brings us directly to the extramural dimension. Raymond Williams always defined cultural studies in terms of histories that preceded CCCS, in the experiments in adult education going back to the later 1930s that bound him, Hoggart, and Thompson together: 'That shift of perspective about the teaching of arts and literature and their relation to history and contemporary society began in Adult Education, it didn't happen anywhere else.'[41] If the South Wales Miners' Library offers one continuity in this regard, then another runs through the Federation of Worker Writers and Community Publishers (FWWCP) founded in 1976, through which Ken Worpole brought together initiatives in London, Manchester, Liverpool, Brighton, Bristol, Bradford, Birmingham, Edinburgh, Newcastle, and elsewhere. FWWCP was further linked to Comedia (formerly the Minority Press Group), founded in 1978, where David Morley (then writing his dissertation attached to CCCS) was an instigator.[42] Yet another link came via radical

---

39 Conference proceedings were published as Bob Fine et al., eds, *Capitalism and the Rule of Law: From Deviancy Theory to Marxism* (London: Hutchison, 1979), and included an essay by Phil Cohen, 'Policing the Working-Class City'.

40 See Ian Gwinn, '"A Different Kind of History Is Possible": The History Workshop Movement and the Politics of British and West German Historical Practice', PhD dissertation, University of Liverpool, 2015. See also Raphael Samuel, ed., *History Workshop: A Collectanea, 1967–1991: Documents, Memoirs, Critique, and Cumulative Index to 'History Workshop Journal'* (Oxford: History Workshop, 1991); Eley, *Crooked Line*, 51–3, 124–5.

41 Raymond Williams, 'The Future of Cultural Studies', in *The Politics of Modernism: Against the New Conformists* (London: Verso, 1989), 162. See also John McIlroy and Sallie Westwood, eds, *Border Country: Raymond Williams in Adult Education* (Leicester: National Institute of Adult Continuing Education, 1993); W. John Morgan and Peter Preston, eds, *Raymond Williams: Politics, Education, Letters* (Houndmills: Macmillan, 1993). More generally, see Tom Steele, *The Emergence of Cultural Studies 1945–65: Cultural Politics, Adult Education and the English Question* (London: Lawrence & Wishart, 1997).

42 See David Morley and Ken Worpole, eds, *The Republic of Letters: Working Class Writing and Local Publishing* (London: Comedia, 1982). Stephen Yeo, centrally active in QueenSpark, FWWCP's Brighton affiliate, chaired the December 1979 Ruskin panel.

caucuses forming inside the teaching and social work professions. Coalescing around journals, these included *Libertarian Education* (1973) and *Radical Education* (founded 1974) for teachers, and *Hard Cheese, Humpty Dumpty*, and *Case-Con* (all early 1970s) for psychologists and social workers.[43] On another key front, Counter Information Services (CIS) was formed by a collective of anti-capitalist journalists who produced thirty-six 'Anti-Reports' during 1970–84, providing critical analysis of particular companies and economic sectors, areas of economic and social policy, taxation, industrial relations, and other aspects of British capitalism.[44]

This history conveyed the unity of theory and practice so essential to the excitements of the 'long '68' (say, 1967–75) and its aftermaths. At CCCS, that unity worked severally: in the democratic intensities of its own working practices; in its relationship to the politics and cultural life of the city; in its desire to produce methodologies, analyses, and theories capable of making a difference to public policy (media and news, social policy and youth, crime and policing, schooling and education, racism and race, gender and the equality of women); and in its conviction that theory offered the best chance of producing really useful knowledge. This decisively recast the boundaries of politics. In David Morley's words, 'it was one of the key institutions that changed the definition of politics'. He continues: 'The invention of *cultural* politics, the fact that these days it's only commonsensical to think of the cultural dimension of politics, was a form of the remaking of common sense to which the Centre contributed enormously.'[45]

I have three final observations. First, the exhilarating *catholicity* of Left intellectual work in the earlier 1970s contrasted with the divisiveness later in the decade: an overarching solidarity that only slowly acknowledged its differences. Partly, the new cohorts of students recruited through the expansion of higher education were testing their mettle: amid dissertations and first jobs, they formed left caucuses discipline by discipline, field by field, institution by institution, profession

---

43   See Mike Smith, *The Underground and Education: A Guide to the Alternative Press* (London: Methuen, 1977).

44   For details of CIS and *Anti-Reports*, see anti-report.com. See also the 'Noticeboard' section of *History Workshop Journal*, from 1976 to the early 1990s, when the feature began petering out.

45   David Morley, 'Interview – 6 June 2011', Cultural Studies 27: 5 (2013), 836. Emphasis in original.

by profession. Most texts of European Marxism and other social theory, including Max Weber, were only then being translated, invariably by New Left Books/Verso in its self-consciously programmatic way. Influences and emphases changed extraordinarily quickly: individuals assayed a bewildering successions of thinkers and bodies of thought, eagerly inhaling the latest 'ideas from France' (as it seemed) and working them through, before moving on.[46] This teeming profusion of access – Lukács, Sartre, and the Frankfurt School; Merleau-Ponty, Barthes, and Goldmann; Althusser and Poulantzas; Gramsci, of course; Kristeva, Irigary, and Cixous; Lacanian psychoanalysis; Saussurian linguistics; the philosophy of science of Bachelard and Canguilhem; the aesthetics of Macherey; semiotics and theories of film; then Derrida and Foucault – initially obscured the places of tension and difficulty, the serious conflicts and downright incompatibilities contained in this broad coalition of critical thought. The divisiveness that exploded later in the 1970s was in that way already inscribed by the manner of early reception of these texts and traditions. Stuart Hall's 1980 retrospective on the Centre's trajectory brilliantly recapitulates the local version of that heady collective autodidacticism.[47]

Second, the discrepancy that began this chapter is vividly present throughout this history. These intellectual and political intensities helped shape not just the outlook of the Left but the national story in general. They deserve to be rescued from 'the enormous condescension of posterity'.[48] While the reigning silence of historians suggests amnesia, at the time their liberal and right-wing intellectual predecessors found a good deal to say.[49] In September 1977, CCCS held a conference on 'Left Intellectual Work', attended by several hundred representatives of the various journals and networks. The closing plenary was dominated by

---

46   Lisa Appignanesi, ed., *Ideas from France: The Legacy of French Theory – ICA Documents* (London: Free Association, 1989). The Institute of Contemporary Arts (ICA) became another key node of interdisciplinarity oriented towards cultural studies. Erica Carter, at CCCS in the late 1970s, was an ICA events coordinator.

47   Stuart Hall, 'Cultural Studies and the Centre: Some Problematics and Problems', in Hall, Hobson, Lowe, and Willis, *Culture, Media, Language*.

48   E. P. Thompson, *Making of the English Working Class*, 12.

49   Another striking illustration: Anthony Seldon and Stuart Ball, eds, *Conservative Century: The Conservative Party since 1900* (Oxford: Oxford University Press, 1994), an 842-page all-but-official history, contains no single mention of Stuart Hall in an otherwise full bibliography for Thatcherism (766–7). CCCS contributions more generally are absent, including a contribution by Bill Schwarz on Baldwinian Conservatism (758–62).

the hot-off-the-press publication of *The Attack on Higher Education: Marxist and Radical Penetration* (the so-called Gould Report), the latest in a series of 'Black Papers on Education' spearheading the assault on progressive education. A survey of Marxism in the universities, complete with lists of participants in the various networks and their meetings, this text certainly found the ideas to be very threateningly influential.[50] In that light, by contextualist protocols alone, it makes no sense to ignore the battles of ideas around which the political shifts of the 1970s revolved. Too many accounts of what is taken to be '1968' or 'the New Left' seek mainly to delegitimize or dismiss – to show the actors as naive and failed, as producing only a backlash or reaction formations, while ultimately enabling a set of 'bourgeois' logics and values (individualism, hedonism, consumption, excess). We can surely revisit the departures of the 1970s less crudely than this – not to resurrect them as alternative histories, as the path not taken in some simple-minded counterfactual way, but to recover the open and unfinished fields of incompleteness, as the complicated ground from which histories of the present can be written. Taking the victor's viewpoint alone is just bad history, the eerie sound of one hand clapping.[51]

How, finally, should we best summarize the CCCS contribution? From the beginnings of critical distance, in the 1992 *Cultural Studies* mega-volume, Stuart Hall called cultural studies 'a discursive formation, in Foucault's sense': 'we were trying to find an institutional practice . . . that might produce an organic intellectual' in the complicated sense meant by Gramsci.[52] My own summary would run something like this: after the inception years of 1956–68, cultural studies was predicated on a cross-disciplinary ferment of self-consciously innovative ambition, schooled by theoretical work and its political applications, with a collectivist ethos and an anti-hierarchical, collaborative method of working. Binding it together was the conviction that *culture* – as theory and as life – is vital for the Left's practice of democracy. Culture matters not just for capitalism's securing of stabilities, but for the

---

50   The report became known by its editor, conservative Nottingham sociologist Julius Gould. See Julius Gould, *The Attack on Higher Education: Marxist and Radical Penetration – Report of a Study Group of the Institute for the Study of Conflict* (London: Institute for the Study of Conflict, 1977). The Birmingham conference met on 17 September 1977.

51   See McCabe, 'Interview with Stuart Hall', 22–7.

52   Stuart Hall, 'Cultural Studies and Its Theoretical Legacies', in *Cultural Studies*, ed. Larry Grossberg, Cary Nelson, and Paula Treichler (New York: Routledge, 1992), 278, 281.

practice of critique and political resistance too. By taking popular culture seriously, Hall argued in *NLR*'s founding editorial in 1960, we honour 'the imaginative resistance of people who have to live within capitalism – the growing points of social discontent, the projections of deeply felt needs'.[53] With Raymond Williams, he brought cultural matters to the centre-ground of the Left's concerns – as questions of ideology, meaning, identity, and subjectivity, whose pertinence for political change could become the ground of analysis and action. This unity of intellectual and political work captured the imagination in cultural studies during the classic CCCS years. Cultural studies tried to make a place where important intellectual work, matters of the highest public concern, the political common-sense of ordinary people, and the pressing political demands of the present conjuncture – in other words, ideas, politics, popular culture, and the movements of history – could all come together. Using the concept of *conjuncture*, this was Stuart Hall's guiding question. As Suzanne Moore so crisply put it, 'He was not one for revolutionary politics. Instead he was always trying to discuss the circumstances or events that would precipitate change. For that he used the word conjuncture. What joins together to make the big shifts in consciousness?'[54]

---

53   Stuart Hall, 'Introducing NLR', *New Left Review* I/1 (January–February 1960), 1. A decade later, the idea of 'growing points' remained an active referent. See note 23, above.

54   Suzanne Moore, 'Stuart Hall Was a Voice for Misfits Everywhere. That's His Real Legacy', *Guardian*, 13 February 2014.

PART III
Thinking Globally

8

Imperial Imaginary, Colonial Effect: Writing the Colony and the Metropole Together

Empire as a Cultural Presence

In the unfinished effort at gathering the history of the empire and the history of Britain into a common analytical field, popular culture and everyday life have become key tests of that approach. The pervasiveness of the empire's presence – its tangible consequences for ordinary life, from the spectacular to the commonplace – has been emphasized again and again. Anyone interested in the making of national culture from the mid nineteenth century to the present is now likely to stress the empire's vital relevance, both palpable and obscure, for working-class formation. Yet this was not always the case. In keeping with the prevailing political temper and broad populist identifications of the time, social historians' first impulse in the 1960s and 1970s was more commonly *scepticism* about the quality and extent of working-class sympathies for the empire, whether in relation to specific imperial policies or as more diffuse enthusiasm for the colonial idea and interests overseas.

Emblematic for that earlier time was Richard Price's pioneering study of working-class reactions to the South African War of 1899–1902, keenly greeted by social historians on its appearance in 1972.[1] In

---

1 Richard Price, *An Imperial War and the British Working Class: Working-Class Attitudes and Reactions to the Boer War, 1899–1902* (Toronto: University of Toronto Press, 1972).

querying conventional wisdom about working-class jingoism, Price made some of the classic methodological moves of the social historian, pitting received assumptions about working-class attitudes against newly assembled contexts of evidence. These included the world of working men's clubs as an institutional arena of working-class sociability and opinion; the actual content of campaigning in the 'Khaki' election of 1900; the sociology of volunteering during the war; and use of George Rudé's work on 'the crowd in history' to identify the actual composition of the crowds on Mafeking Night, as well as the organized rowdyism involved in disrupting anti-war meetings. On these bases, Price advanced a forthrightly sceptical thesis of working-class imperial indifference, whether in relation to the urgencies of imperial defence or to more generalized appeals to patriotism. But moralizing appeals by anti-war and pro-Boer campaigners left workers likewise unmoved. Anti-war rhetoric gained purchase mainly when linked with the more 'practical demands of social reform' or some aspect of day-to-day experience, such as a death or the return of a disabled soldier.[2] Otherwise, 'working-class objections to imperialism were based upon what was a typical working-class characteristic: a concern for the immediate and the material':

> It was this essential irrelevance of imperialism which explains the working-class reaction to volunteering: a reaction based generally more upon economic and social circumstances than upon the ethos of patriotism and desire to serve the mother-country. It also explains the rejection of good imperialists at the 1900 election. The imperialism embodied in a candidate like Sir Alfred Newton had little or no meaning to working-class life and society.[3]

Several decades later, historiography has strikingly changed. For some, empire now has an axiomatic ubiquity, one both insidious and overt, making it ever harder during the nineteenth century for Britons to evade either its material or ideological reach. For anyone encountering the overseas by the turn of the twentieth century, empire suffused any possible relationship to a wider-than-British world. In *At Home with the*

---

2   Ibid., 238, 239.
3   Ibid., 237, 241.

Empire, another emblematic volume, the editors aim to 'assess how people thought imperially, not in the sense of political affiliations for or against empire', though these also mattered, 'but simply assuming it was there, part of the given world that had made them who they were'. They ask what the empire meant 'for those located, physically or imaginatively, "at home"', ranging from its 'impact on constructions of womanhood, masculinity and class to its influence in shaping literature, sexuality, visual culture, consumption, and history-writing'. They examine how the empire 'was lived through everyday practices – in church and chapel, by readers at home, as embodied in sexualities or forms of citizenship, as narrated in histories – from the eighteenth century to the present'.[4]

That earlier social historian's reflex, claiming empire's essential *unimportance* for the lives of metropolitan populations, is far harder to find. Impetus comes instead from analysing the manifold forms of the empire's domestic embeddedness. This has various sources. One is certainly the desire to see British history in the global setting of its far-flung colonial and diasporic geographies. J. G. A. Pocock set the ball rolling, calling for a 'new British history' that reached from the British Isles themselves through an 'Atlantic archipelago' to the Australasian settler colonies further beyond. But discussion has long left this behind. So far from dislodging the nation from its explanatory primacy, Pocock even sealed its exorbitant prominence. As Tony Ballantyne remarks, while 'the cultural, institutional and linguistic continuities that tied the colonies to the United Kingdom' remained clear, the 'fundamental differences in the demographic, economic and ecological frameworks of the "new" societies' ran counter to any framework still centred on Britain itself. For all its heuristic energy, Pocock's 'global Britishness' offers only 'an impoverished and reductive model for the history of multi-ethnic and polyglot colonial societies far removed from the United Kingdom', leaving 'older traditions of metropolitan-focused imperial history' effectively intact. [5]

---

4   Back cover description, Catherine Hall and Sonya O. Rose, eds, *At Home with the Empire: Metropolitan Culture and the Imperial World* (Cambridge: Cambridge University Press, 2007).

5   Tony Ballantyne, *Orientalism and Race: Aryanism in the British Empire*, 2nd edn (Palgrave Macmillan, 2002), 3. For the relevant writings, the earliest dating from 1974, see J. G. A. Pocock, *The Discovery of Islands: Essays in British History* (Cambridge: Cambridge University Press, 2005).

Still more vitally, the nation was itself 'an imperialized space – a political territory which could not, and still cannot, escape the imprint of empire'. Rather than simply presupposing Britain's place 'as the centripetal origin of empire', Antoinette Burton 'insist[s] on the interdependence . . . of national/imperial formations in any given historical moment' – what Marxists called their uneven and combined development. That perspective 'materializes the traffic of colonial goods, ideas and people across metropolitan borders and indeed throws into question the very Victorian distinction between Home and Away that defined the imagined geography of empire in the nineteenth century'.[6] Rather than forming an unbroken linear continuity for which empire became a further expression, 'national' history revealed unfinishedness and indeterminacy. The nation was made only *through* its imperial entanglements, not as their precursor.

Reading histories of empire and nation together is now a commonplace of discussion among advocates of the 'new imperial history', whether for the 'first' or 'second' British empire. Only by bringing 'metropole and colony, colonizer and colonized, British and indigenous peoples into one frame, into a single analytical field' would 'whole configurations, general processes, an entire interactive system, one vast interconnected world' come properly into view.[7] Early empire and the slave trade's complex imbrications inside Britain itself have become incontestable, involving not only trade, statecraft, and national aggrandizement, but everything from religion, gender relations, literary pleasure, and the fantasy life of intellectuals to manners, taste, sociability, and the new craze for drinking tea.[8] By the eighteenth century, this was far more than a British story, one where many kinds of voyagers, sailors and soldiers, scientists, map-makers, writers, philosophers,

---

6   Antoinette Burton, 'Who Needs the Nation? Interrogating British History', in *Cultures of Empire – A Reader: Colonisers in Britain and the Empire in the Nineteenth and Twentieth Centuries*, ed. Catherine Hall (Manchester: Manchester University Press, 2000), 140.

7   Philip D. Morgan, 'Encounters between British and "Indigenous" Peoples, c.1500–c.1800', in *Empire and Others: British Encounters with Indigenous Peoples, 1600–1850*, ed. Martin J. Daunton and Rick Halpern (London: Routledge, 1999), 68.

8   See Kathleen Wilson, *The Island Race: Englishness, Empire and Gender in the Eighteenth Century* (London: Routledge, 2002); Kathleen Wilson, ed., *A New Imperial History: Culture, Identity, and Modernity in Britain and the Empire* (Cambridge: Cambridge University Press, 2004); Nicholas Canny, *Making Ireland British, 1580–1650* (Oxford: Oxford University Press, 2001); Philip Lawson, *A Taste for Empire and Glory: Studies in British Overseas Expansion, 1600–1800* (London: Routledge, 1997).

and sundry adventurers – including, as Linda Colley reminds us, many who were captured in the lands and seas they traversed – brought reports of overseas worlds that helped define European differences against those many versions of a non-European elsewhere.[9]

Looking forward into the nineteenth and twentieth centuries, the growing corpus dealing with empire's complex reciprocities – the many kinds of relays, some very evident, others quite indirect and submerged, back and forth between Britain's overseas and the dynamics of national life at home – continues to accumulate. Missionary societies' contribution to the production of colonial knowledge, whether as popular perceptions or colonial governmentality, conditioning imperial rule on the ground while diffusing its imagery at home, has long been recognized, as have imperial involvements of the sciences and academic disciplines. Women's involvement has been intensively researched, whether in the religious missions, the efforts of feminists and other reformers, or avowedly imperialist agencies like the Girls' Friendly Society, the Primrose League, the British Women's Emigrant Association, and the Victoria League. Empire's relationship to working-class formation, whether in colonial 'periphery' or metropolitan 'core', is increasingly accepted. So too is the importance of popular culture, which was suffused before 1914 with the traces and imprints of empire The spectacle of empire – its monumental architecture and the burgeoning 'exhibitionary complex', its commodified representations in consumption and entertainment, its heroics and disasters, its pomp and ceremony, its vast and variegated cultures of display – attracts the interest of scholars across a wide variety of disciplines.[10] Impetus has come, last but not least, from the new attentiveness to the salience of 'race'.[11]

Running through these approaches is a cultural materialism that makes not only the tangible advantages and proceeds of empire but also

---

9   See Linda Colley, *Captives: Britain, Empire and the World 1600–1850* (New York: Pantheon, 2003).

10   The quoted reference is to Tony Bennett's 'The Exhibitionary Complex', in *Culture/Power/History*, ed. Nicholas B. Dirks, Geoff Eley, and Sherry B. Ortner (Princeton: Princeton University Press, 1994).

11   See especially Stuart Hall, 'Ethnicity: Identity and Difference', in *Becoming National: A Reader*, ed. Geoff Eley and Ronald Grigor Suny (Oxford: Oxford University Press, 1996); 'Negotiating Caribbean Identities', *New Left Review* I/209, (January–February 1995); Paul Gilroy, *The Black Atlantic: Modernity and Double-Consciousness* (Cambridge: Harvard University Press, 1993).

their symbolic meanings – thus the sugar in the coffee, the tea-leaves in the tea – vital to the bases of social cohesion, the character of popular culture, and the dominant values inside Britain itself.[12] Empire's presence in British society settled into the practicalities of ordinary lived experience, sedimenting over time into a reserve of instinctually held beliefs. Paul Gilroy underscores 'the less obviously purposeful ways' in which 'material culture and technological developments – new objects, commodities, devices, and procedures including postcards, cigarette cards, the revolution in cheap colour printing and packaging – afforded exciting new communicative opportunities and cultural vehicles for an imperial phantasmagoria'. Distinctive to the new imperialism after the 1880s 'was an especially rich visual culture that disseminated the militaristic and patriotic imagery of empire and colony on a vast scale celebrating and creating a stimulating world of signs to which racial difference was absolutely fundamental'. In these ways empire acquired a social and cultural ontology. As a regime of politics, it *required* such grounding:

> [Its] stability and continuity depended upon the organized transmission of key cultural motifs, habits, and mentalities to distant colonizers, to a new public at home who would develop a relationship to the imperial project as supporters and potential colonizers, and, of course, to a measured and significant proportion of the colonized who had to be given a stake in the workings of manifestly brutal and exploitative arrangements.[13]

Amid this profusion, both the inevitability and the primacy of empire's impact may too easily come to be taken for granted, encouraging the view that it was always and everywhere a decisive underlying explanation for main features of the British story. Common to the best of these historiographies, however, is a presumption of relative contingency and process, the degree to which acceptance of the empire and its

---

12   In that sense the racial imaginary of empire remains a deeply embedded cultural formation: 'It is in the sugar you stir; it is in the sinews of the famous British "sweet tooth"; it is in the tea-leaves at the bottom of the next "British" cuppa.' Stuart Hall, 'Racism and Reaction', in *Five Views of Multi-Racial Britain: Talks on Race Relations Broadcast by BBC TV* (London: Commission for Racial Equality, 1978), 25.

13   Paul Gilroy, *Against Race: Imagining Political Culture Beyond the Color Line* (Cambridge MA: Harvard University Press/Belknap, 2000), 139.

mechanisms of rule revealed less the automatic and overpowering ease of imperial understandings – the rolling causality of the 'one big thing' – than the unfinished local narratives of fraught legitimacy, negotiated consent, and continuing contestation.[14]

Overt and direct knowledge about the empire, whether as support or opposition, popular enthusiasm or popular indifference, supplies only one way of detecting its presence.[15] Just as importantly, the everyday experience of empire became 'the vital, enabling counterpoint to institutional practices' as encountered in the military and bureaucratic machinery of colonial rule: 'at home the fact of empire was registered not only in political debate and economic and foreign policy, but entered the social fabric, intellectual discourse, and the life of the imagination'.[16] Thus, Bill Schwarz considers equally the metropolitan histories of politics and culture inside Britain itself and the histories of the colonial overseas, from the British Caribbean to the major settler colonies of Australia and southern Africa. Diverse human migrancy, colonial circuits of labour power, the transnationalizing of ideas, or the career paths of imperial policy and colonial administration – this was the multiform traffic between the metropole and the colony. From Disraeli and Chamberlain to Baldwin and Churchill, Schwarz brilliantly aligns the intellectual history and political sensibilities of British Conservatism with two fields of global Britishness – on the one hand, all aspects of migration from the Caribbean; on the other, the resonance for the British public of certain authoritative political voices from the white settler elsewhere, who became vital in defining the 'colour line' for Britain during the twentieth century. Through the racializing of British politics since the 1960s – via the scandal of apartheid, the drama of UDI, and the spectacle of Powellism, shadowed by the stop-go ambivalences of the relationship with Europe – these histories sutured decolonizing Britain into a new political imaginary. *White Tribunes*, the first volume of Schwarz's *Memories of Empire*, compellingly demonstrates the

---

14   In 'One Big Thing: Britain and Its Empire', *Journal of British Studies* 45 (2006), Richard Price cautions against the appeal of the new imperial history as a new master narrative.

15   This was the dichotomous framework employed heuristically by Richard Price in *An Imperial War*.

16   Benita Parry, 'Overlapping Territories and Intertwined Histories: Edward Said's Postcolonial Cosmopolitanism', in *Edward Said: A Critical Reader*, ed. Michael Sprinker (Oxford: Basil Blackwell, 1992), 24.

salience of the empire's presence in the cultural and political life of the home society, both in popular-cultural terms and in the shaping of the social, cultural and political horizons of the political class.[17]

Similarly, Jonathan Hyslop shows how, before 1914, politics 'took place not within local political boundaries' defined by this or that particular colony, but in a larger transnational realm of imperial interconnectedness. Those global circuits of the empire bound colonies not only into reciprocities with the metropole, but also laterally into relations with one another. Hyslop cites Keir Hardie's world tour of India, Australasia, and southern Africa in 1907–08, and the intellectual trajectory of the Scottish-born trade unionist, ex-soldier, and Johannesburg labour leader James Thomas Bain. Each exemplifies an imperial working class increasingly displaying a common outlook of 'white labourism' during the early twentieth century, 'which fused elements of racism and xenophobia with worker militancy and anti-capitalism'. Rather than inhabiting 'nationally discrete entities' dispersed across a colonial periphery, in other words, white British migrants became 'bound together into an international working class by flows of population across the world'.[18] Thus the provenance of the iconic text of British literary socialism, Robert Tressell's *Ragged Trousered Philanthropists*, is located in its author's travels from his youth in Dublin to an early adulthood working in Cape Town and Johannesburg between 1890 and 1901. An avatar of the early-twentieth-century English workingman, Robert Noonan (Tressell's real name) was actually an Irishman who was formed as a socialist, Irish nationalist, and worker in South Africa.[19] In light of stories like this, Richard Price's title might well be transposed as 'A British War and the Imperial Working Class'.

In a third instance, James Vernon shows how new thinking about the social problem during the later nineteenth century proceeded from intense and intimate relays back and forth between the empire and

17   Bill Schwarz, *Memories of Empire, Vol. I: The White Man's World* (Oxford: Oxford University Press, 2011).

18   Jonathan Hyslop, 'The World Voyage of James Keir Hardie: Indian Nationalism, Zulu Insurgency, and the British Labour Diaspora 1907–1908', *Journal of Global History* 1 (2006), 344, and 'A Scottish Socialist Reads Carlyle in Johannesburg Prison, June 1900: Reflections on the Literary Culture of the Imperial Working Class', *Journal of Southern African Studies* 29 (2003).

19   Jonathan Hyslop, 'A Ragged Trousered Philanthropist and the Empire: Robert Tressell in South Africa', *History Workshop Journal* 51 (Spring 2001).

home. If in the colonial contexts of hunger and famine a concerned humanitarianism acquired its impetus, then in the metropolitan setting of Britain itself a slow political realignment eventually allowed social-democratic ideas of the welfare state to coalesce. Between the Great Exhibition and the 1940s, the colonial laboratory vitally shaped the change inside Britain itself: 'The humanitarian discovery of hunger during the second half of the nineteenth century' helped prize open the political dilemmas of liberalism and assemble the case for public intervention. Hunger delivered the ground for a new political critique:

> In the wake of the New Poor Law and the Irish famine, journalists and social innovators developed new techniques to represent the innocent suffering of the hungry. By giving it a human face, they ensured that hunger, both at home and abroad, became a focus for humanitarian concern before the Great War. Colonial nationalists in Ireland and India, together with suffragettes and unemployed protestors in Britain, mobilized this newfound sympathy for the hungry by turning hunger into a symbol of the failure of British liberalism and Britain's colonial states.[20]

As Vernon shows in the course of his book, the languages of public policy, social administration, and political mobilization helping shape this modern form of the social problem were assembled in constant dialogue with varieties of knowledge produced in the colonial elsewhere. The colony and the metropole formed a common field in that regard.

No less than Schwarz or Hyslop, Vernon places India and Africa in a decisive imperial matrix. The resulting back-and-forth of multiform interchange proved every bit as generative as the global histories emphasized in Atlantic studies. Here Mrinalini Sinha's study of the political fallout surrounding the publication of Katherine Mayo's 1927 journalistic exposé of India's social ills, *Mother India*, powerfully vindicates the promise of a transnational analytic. Not only did the international resonance of the scandal of that book's reception help shape the political subjectivities available to women in India, but it

---

20 James Vernon, *Hunger: A Modern History* (Cambridge, MA: Harvard University Press, 2007).

circulated simultaneously across the British and North American contexts too.[21] In transnationalizing the imperial imaginary in this way,
Srinha shows the spaces of interconnectedness themselves: not just the
diverse origins of historical processes (any history is usually made in
more than just a single place), but their very construction through the
movement between and across the pertinent localities, sites, and regions.
Her analysis is triangulated through the Indian, British, and US contexts
of imperial security, international relations, anticolonial nationalism,
women's suffrage, and changing languages of citizenship. Pushing
beyond the established understanding of a political history territorially
bounded within the Indian colonial and later national states, she also
tracks the dispersal of South Asians across all parts of the British Empire,
from South Africa through the Pacific to the Caribbean. Histories of
empire have invariably been written from a highly centred global geography, running from core to periphery, centre to margins, metropole to
colony. The recent complicating of that directional logic therefore contains the real force of Srinha's idea of an 'imperial social formation.'[22]

The question of popular attitudes towards the empire, including the
susceptibilities of working-class culture, was being complicated even as
Price published his pioneering book. Thus Gareth Stedman Jones's
'Notes on the Remaking of a Working Class' was already directly in
dialogue with Price, while Anna Davin's 'Imperialism and Motherhood'
appeared in 1978.[23] All the ramified ways in which the empire 'came
home' are exhaustively charted in the volume edited by Catherine Hall
and Sonya Rose.[24] Not the least of these returns was the impact of
colonial violence – not just the brutalities and destructiveness directly
experienced by its perpetrators in the field, but their generalized trans-
fer into the assumptions and representations shaping an imperialist
imaginary, everything entailed in the complicated trajectory from the
reportage of Rorke's Drift in January 1879 to the cinema spectacle of
Cy Endfield's *Zulu* in 1964.

---

21   Mrinalini Sinha, *Specters of Mother India: The Global Restructuring of an Empire*
(Durham, NC: Duke University Press, 2006).
22   See especially Mrinalini Sinha, 'Mapping an Imperial Social Formation: A Modest
Proposal for Feminist Historiography', *Signs* 25 (2000).
23   Gareth Stedman Jones, 'Working-Class Culture and Working-Class Politics in London,
1870–1900: Notes on the Remaking of a Working Class', *Journal of Social History* 7 (1974); Anna
Davin, 'Imperialism and Motherhood', *History Workshop Journal* 5 (Spring 1978).
24   Hall and Rose, *At Home with the Empire*.

In his more recent book, a study of the conquest of the Xhosa in what became the South African Eastern Cape between the 1820s and the later nineteenth century, Richard Price dissects the making of colonial rule on the ground. He shows in compelling detail how informal or indirect rule structured around the practices of 'the humanitarian ideology of missionary evangelicalism' and the local governance of chiefs came to be supplanted by a coercive regime of direct colonial annexation.[25] Under Sir George Grey, Cape Colony governor from 1854 to 1861, enabled by the millenarian catastrophe of the cattle killings of 1856–58, the standing of the chiefs was brutally broken, the Xhosa population decimated, their land expropriated, and the society thoroughly subjugated. For Price this violent consummation of the cumulative encroachment of the British on Xhosa autonomies supplies the key to 'how a culture of imperial rule grows.'[26] It profoundly vitiated the empire's official self-representation as 'a force for liberal progressivism around the globe', a discourse acquiring at various levels an insidious political potency by the end of the nineteenth century. This discourse included a capacity for enlisting the popular imagination, while penetrating deep into the collective consciousness of metropolitan society.[27]

As Price argues, 'the implosion of missionary culture as it confronted Xhosa culture and politics' combined with 'the emergence of settler politics' and Grey's activist governorship to override the missionary outlook with a new system of colonial knowledge that no longer saw the savagery of Africans as redeemable through the civilizing process:

Colonial culture had to be *created* and *constructed* out of the interaction between the metropolitan culture that the colonizers brought with them and the culture they found at the frontier of empire. This was the foundation on which the knowledge system of empire was built. The knowledge that was produced in empire then had to be fitted into the culture of the metropole.[28]

---

25   Richard Price, *Making Empire: Colonial Encounters and the Creation of Imperial Rule in Nineteenth-Century Africa* (Cambridge: Cambridge University Press, 2008), 163.

26   Ibid., 4.

27   Ibid., 9.

28   Ibid., 163, 179–81, 154. Emphasis in original.

The prevailing imperial discourse 'portrayed [Britain's] empire as a "liberal empire", as a humanitarian "trust" and not as a brutal instrument of domination'.[29] The colonial functionaries on the ground, who perpetrated 'the deeds and actions that undid the chiefs and gutted civil society in British Kaffraria', were indeed 'upstanding Victorian gentlemen. They were exemplars of the culture of Britain's *liberal* empire.'[30] But fully to grasp the character of the imperial imaginary, the role of the violence also needs to be faced, for otherwise 'the practices of denial, of silence, of forgetting' will remain 'deeply ingrained in the history of Britain'. The 'empire *as it was known in Britain*', Price concludes, 'was an artifice, a fiction, a creation from events that were filtered and silenced and denied to produce a version of empire that fitted the cultural expectations and aspirations of the British themselves.'[31]

Colonialism, Comparatively Speaking

Removed from contemporary political meanings, these current approaches would not be imaginable. Anxieties about foreignness, cultural belonging, migration, and race; the problematizing of 'the West' in the wake of Edward Said's *Orientalism* and the wider impact of postcolonial theory; the wildly proliferating discourse of 'globalization' in its market-driven and militarized forms – all these converge on an interest in empire. For two decades now, intensively grounded arguments about the importance of imperialism have been slowly transforming the questions British, French, and now German and Italian historians bring to their national history.[32] This applies par excellence to the United States, where American studies entirely presupposes a recognition of empire's importance.[33] Contemporary advocates of globalization are likewise busily reappropriating pre-1914 colonialisms as grist to their mill, as in the

---

29   Ibid., 9.

30   Ibid., 271. Emphasis in original.

31   Ibid., 355–6. Emphasis in original.

32   In general: Antoinette Burton, ed., *After the Imperial Turn: Thinking With and Through the Nation* (Durham, NC: Duke University Press, 2003).

33   Foundationally, see Amy Kaplan and Donald E. Pease, eds, *Cultures of United States Imperialism* (Durham, NC: Duke University Press, 1993); and, most recently, Ann Laura Stoler, ed., *Haunted by Empire: Geographies of Intimacy in North American History* (Durham, NC: Duke University Press, 2006).

French law of February 2005 affirming the positive legacies of French colonialism.[34] A redeployed metanarrative of pre-1914 world history centred on the progressive directionality of 'empire' has been circulating through the public sphere ever more insistently, gaining momentum from the new world dynamics since 9/11. The gist of this simplified high-Victorian analogy is a sort of developmentalist realism that joins a theory of economic modernization to sanitized versions of the 'civilizing mission' and the inevitable consequences of European military superiority.[35]

That some of Europe's sovereign states possessed colonial empires of impressive longevity dating from the sixteenth century clearly helped shape national imaginaries later on, whether in official, popular, or intellectual terms. Such deeper patterning notwithstanding, contemporary genealogies come more from the so-called 'new imperialism' of the later nineteenth century, which dramatically accelerated the world economy's global integration.[36] After the 1880s, the military, administrative, and technological superiority of the industrializing capitalist countries bore down on the defenceless and less developed parts of the globe in a restless and rapacious onslaught of exploitative, coercive, and civilizationist power. This was qualitatively different in its consequences from the much older structures of thought and relations symbolized by 1492. Thus the imposing territorial extent of the Spanish Empire in the Americas was largely a thing of the past after the independence revolutions of 1776–1825; the Portuguese colonial presence was a byword for administrative and cultural decrepitude by the time of the so-called 'scramble for Africa'; and, after the Napoleonic Wars, the French colonial empire only experienced a partial and faltering renewal, until the general imperialist upsurge in the 1880s. Rather than such direct colonial rule, by the nineteenth century it was the wider commercial and missionary penetration of the rest of the world that was the more decisive factor. From *those* histories alone, the British Empire was already coalescing into a significant territorial colonialism.

---

34 See Julio Godoy, 'Recasting Colonialism as a Good Thing', *Global Policy Forum*, 5 July 2005, archive.globalpolicy.org.

35 These phrases are taken from Niall Ferguson, 'America: An Empire in Denial', *Chronicle of Higher Education*, 28 March 2003, B7–B10. See also Niall Ferguson, *Empire* (London: Allen Lane, 2002), xxv–xxix.

36 See Francis Barker et al., eds, *Europe and Its Others: Proceedings of the Essex Conference on the Sociology of Literature* (Colchester: University of Essex, 1985), including Edward Said, 'Orientalism Reconsidered'.

Thus, the more pervasive cultural impact of colonialism inside Europe really dated from the renewed colonial encounters of the later nineteenth century, when the intensified Great Power rivalries precipitated the territorial division of the globe, whether through direct colonial annexation or the securing of indirect spheres of dominance. How this expansionism exactly occurred, empire by empire, had consequences for how colonial legacies would later be processed. But in a more fundamental convergence, the cultural effects exceeded such national distinctions, seeping into the societies of the European metropole whether or not colonies were seized. Thus, it scarcely mattered whether the empire was dramatically expanding (like the British), making more modest advances (like the French), consolidating older trading outposts and circuits into a territorial dominion (like the Dutch in Southeast Asia), had produced a single spectacular land grab (such as the Belgian Congo), or persisted as the mainly moribund remnant of an older imperium (like the Spanish and Portuguese).

The German and Italian cases were distinguished both by the spectacular novelty of the two national states themselves, unified only in the 1860s, and by the subsequent loss of their newly acquired colonies in 1918 and 1943. These two colonialisms were more patently imbricated with the very making of the nation itself, whether viewed in state-institutional terms, culturally and ideologically, or in the place now imagined for the national economy in the world market. Given the established presence of the older 'world empires' and the degree to which available territories had already been seized, nationalist agitations for a German or Italian 'place in the sun' acquired an edge of unrequited aggression. Finally, the loss of colonial possessions meant that Germany and Italy avoided the particular violence and divisiveness of the decolonizing process and its longer-lasting legacies in Britain, France, Belgium, the Netherlands, and Portugal.

Whether as bare acquisition of land overseas or as wider systems of direct governance, colonies per se were a contingent aspect of an expansionism taking various other forms. By 1900, a far more pervasive patterning of unequal and exploitative relations bound together the societies of the European metropole with those of an exotic and exploitable overseas, whose logics unfolded beneath and beyond any formal colonial rule. The consequences of European expansionism might inveigle and entrap the peoples of foreign lands into relations of imperialist domination, whether those territories were governed formally from Europe or not. Conversely, the citizens of the metropole acquired the mark of the privilege of that relationship, regardless of any direct colonial-imperialist encounter.

The sheer density of the material traces of the colonized overseas in the lived environment of the metropole was an essential feature of the pre-1914 decades. The expanding commercial penetration of extra-European markets since the boom years of 1849–73; the growth of mass production and the associated machineries of advertising and packaging; the new 'exhibitionary complex' of colonial museums and colonial expositions; entertainment spectacles like circuses, forms of minstrelsy, and *Völkerschauen* (ethnographic performances and exhibitions of exotic peoples); writings on travel and exploration; adventure stories and other pulp fictions; a new visual landscape of posters, postcards, advertisements, and collectors' picture cards; all kinds of bric-a-brac, photographs, and moving pictures – all of these produced a generic and brutally simplified field of images, ideas, and assumptions increasingly divorced from their indebtedness to any particular colonial event, colonial relationship, or colonial commodity. The Scandinavian countries, which barely joined the colonial scrambles of the late nineteenth century were just as susceptible in these terms to the power of colonial discourse as were Britain, Germany, and France, with their substantial territorial possessions.[37] Whether concretely or practically connected to this reservoir of experience or not, ordinary Europeans could hardly set themselves outside it, whatever their social background, gender, or age.

These wider cultural consequences of colonialism – of colonial relations in the widest sense – pervaded the twentieth century. From an accumulating wealth of finely grained empirical histories, the degree to which racialized discourses of European cultural superiority produced in the colonies migrated back into the metropolitan societies to permeate them becomes ever more apparent. With particular intensity between the 1880s and 1914, European citizens came to know themselves – their national self-identifications, their emplacement in society and national

---

37 As the evidence assembled by Allan Pred compellingly shows. See Allan Pred, *The Past Is Not Dead: Facts, Fictions, and Enduring Racial Stereotypes* (Minneapolis: University of Minnesota Press, 2004), and *Even in Sweden: Racisms, Racialized Spaces, the Popular Geographical Imagination* (Berkeley: University of California Press, 2000).

culture, their claims to national citizenship, their access to varieties of personhood – through representations of the wider-than-European overseas world as they encountered them in the newly commodified and mass-mediated public spheres of the time. Sometimes these ideas might be explicitly promulgated by governments or disseminated by parties and pressure groups, often in highly manipulative or demagogic ways, whether in an election campaign, in mobilizations behind a particular policy or piece of legislation, or simply as generalized propaganda. Far more insidiously, they permeated the general texture of public discourse, worming into the basic architecture of public belief.

As an enormous weight of scholarship makes ever clearer, this new machinery of representation and understanding was becoming explicitly racialized through uneven temporalities in each country, accelerating from the 1850s and 1860s.[38] By the *fin de siècle*, this disorderly profusion of Europe's relations with non-European colonial worlds was being shaped into an evidently racial matrix. Racialized assumptions included not just formal ideas and easily legible prejudices about colonial peoples. They also coexisted with semi-consciously or unconsciously internalized patterns of belief, structured by terms of distinction, both sophisticated and crude, defining the British, French, Germans, Italians, and other Europeans against the patent inferiority of their colonial or neocolonial subjects. Inside metropolitan social life, particular elements of political subjectivity were made from these complicated relations linking Europeans through webs of ideas to the overseas worlds of the colony. This 'colonial effect' was the sum of the transference and translation of meanings made far away from European homelands during the course of the relentless drives of European expansionism. Such meanings were spun from an entire complex of perceptions and encounters, including disorderly and heterogenous knowledge; idioms of thought; direct and vicarious experiences; spectacular events; arresting and seductive images; compelling arguments about economics, prosperity, and global survival; a visual repertoire of fantasy and desire; manifold forms of everyday consumption; and all the relevant registers of government action. Over time, that aggregative, malleable, and extraordinarily

---

38   For a general reflection, see Christian Geulen, 'The Common Grounds of Conflict: Racial Visions of World Order 1880–1940', in *Conceptions of World Order: Global Moments and Movements, 1880s–1930s*, ed. Sebastian Conrad and Dominic Sachsenmaier (Basingstoke: Palgrave Macmillan, 2007).

ramified discursive presence could acquire an interpellative coherence deserving the name *colonialism*. Deployed in the domestic arenas of European politics, it revealed sustained capacities for producing active forms of political agency with a lasting presence and a multiplicity of results.

The Colonial and the Transnational

A notably clear instance of the colonial effect was the later-nineteenth-century fixation on the rivalries of 'world empires', whose terms rapidly enlisted opinion in each of the Great Powers. Thinking that passed from Charles Dilke's *Greater Britain* in 1867 to John Robert Seeley's *Expansion of England* in 1883, with its re-centring of national destiny around imperial reach, paralleled both the emergent discourse of 'Greater France' and the German preoccupation with the national state's global competitiveness [39] Decisive in each case were the perceived stakes of global economic and strategic competition in a time of intensified domestic anxieties around the 'social question' of industrializing capitalism. Caught in this dialectic – between fears of democracy and challenges to Britain's global supremacy – advocates of a Greater Britain imagined varieties of imperial union linking Britain itself to the white-settler colonies of Australia, New Zealand, Canada, and southern Africa. Projecting a 'vast "Anglo-Saxon" political community' of dispersed global Britishness, these efforts 'ranged from the fantastically ambitious – creating a globe-spanning nation-state – to the practical and mundane – reinforcing existing ties between the colonies and Britain'. They drew on a rich reservoir of received visions of how an imperial polity might be organized, ranging across Greece, Rome, and the Americas, while mobilizing emergent attitudes towards 'the state, race, space, nationality, and empire'.[40] If this discourse coalesced most overtly after the 1860s, it was presaged by realignments of liberal thought in

---

39   See Gary Wilder, *The French Imperial Nation-State: Negritude and Colonial Humanism Between the Two World Wars* (Chicago: University of Chicago Press, 2005); Charles Wentworth Dilke, *Greater Britain: A Record of Travel in English-Speaking Countries During 1866 and 1867* (London: Macmillan, 1867); J. R. Seeley, *The Expansion of England: Two Courses of Lectures* (London: Macmillan, 1883).

40   See the jacket description of Duncan Bell, *The Idea of Greater Britain: Empire and the Future of World Order* (Princeton: Princeton University Press, 2007).

both Britain and France in the middle decades of the century around affirmative visions of imperial expansion embracing the conquest of non-European peoples.[41]

The dramatic rapidity and imbricated simultaneity of two processes that in British history lasted over several centuries – national state formation and global expansionism – made the German case especially charged. The wider global coordinates for the making of German nationhood even *preceded* the territorial state itself. Well in advance of unification in 1866–71, the German nation had already acquired a prefigurative existence – a functioning political, cultural, and institutional actuality in myriad practical ways. In a European geopolitical environment shaped by the emergent post-Napoleonic norm of the national state, nationalist ideas were circulating with ever more resonance through those Central European lands shortly to be remapped into the German Empire. While social movements were so vehemently pressing its claims, 'Germany' was already present as an active political horizon. Germany composed a social and political imaginary long before German statehood was attained. Nor was that imaginary confined to the state-territorial sovereignty ratified in the 1871 Constitution. In this 'pre-state' era, wider relations overseas linked the peoples of German-speaking Europe to sundry non-European worlds, whose importance was increasingly processed within an avowedly *national* framework of aspiration. The resulting representatives of 'Germandom' elsewhere – German migrants to the south of Brazil, German merchants in Chile and Venezuela, German commercial representatives in the Ottoman Empire, German travellers in central Africa, German missionaries in southern Africa – proved an advance guard for a national-state project in Europe itself still waiting to be realized. German patriots learned from their counterparts in that regard too, for the existing imperial powers were already treating their own scattered overseas outposts as the heterogeneous attachments of a globalized sovereignty. In a global setting of distributed nationhood, sovereignty could no longer be contained on its historic European ground.

---

41 Jennifer Pitts, *A Turn to Empire: The Rise of Imperial Liberalism in Britain and France* (Princeton: Princeton University Press, 2005). This argument was pioneered early in the new imperial history. See, for example, Bill Schwarz, 'Introduction: The Expansion and Contraction of England', in *The Expansion of England: Race, Ethnicity, and Cultural History* (London: Routledge, 1996).

By the later nineteenth century, nationhood in Europe was fast becoming imperial.[42] Between the 1840s and 1870s, Germany's emergent national intelligentsia – writers, journalists, travellers, academics, economists, businessmen, political activists – used the visionary landscape of a putative colonial imaginary to do much of the ideological work of elaborating a programme for what they assumed a future national government could be expected to do. To secure its popular legitimacy, that government would have to be capable of defending Germany's interests on the world stage of international competition, as well as sustaining the power of German culture overseas and creating a framework of ties strong enough to retain the affiliations of the migrants who were leaving the German-speaking lands in such prodigious and disquieting numbers. But this mid-century discourse was also no mere preamble or backstory for the later main narrative of the Bismarckian colonial policy of the mid 1880s: it was an integral part of the main story itself. 'Germany' was being realized transnationally in advance of the creation of the national state. Even before Bismarck's wars of unification, the 'boundaries of Germanness' were already being fashioned into place.[43]

This construction of a German national imaginary that was expansive and far-flung rather than confined to contiguous German-speaking Europe itself – one that encompassed German interests, influences, and populations in the world at large rather than simply the European heartlands of German nationality, while looking past the core territories of 1871 to the dispersed topography of German settlement further to the east – paralleled the process of imagining a Greater Britain. Many advocates of German expansion into the world now saw the already acquired statehood as painfully insufficient. The very terms of national unification in the 1860s had themselves been hotly contested, as Bismarck's small-German solution vied with versions of a larger-German

---

42   See especially Kevin Grant, Philippa Levine, and Frank Trentmann, eds, *Beyond Sovereignty: Britain, Empire, and Transnationalism, c. 1880–1950* (Basingstoke: Palgrave Macmillan, 2007); Ann Laura Stoler, 'Degrees of Imperial Sovereignty', *Public Culture* 18 (Winter 2006).

43   See Bradley D. Naranch, 'Beyond the Fatherland: Colonial Visions, Overseas Expansion, and German Nationalism, 1848–1885', PhD dissertation, Johns Hopkins University, 2006; Matthew P. Fitzpatrick, *Liberal Imperialism in Germany: Expansionism and Nationalism* (Oxford: Berghahn, 2008); Susanne Zantop, *Colonial Fantasies: Conquest, Family, and Nation in Precolonial Germany, 1770–1870* (Durham, NC: Duke University Press, 1997).

programme that included Austria. Almost from the very start, the Wilhelmine Empire's national sufficiency was brought under contention, as diverse patriotisms lamented this or that area where the new state seemingly fell short. Certainly, that empire barely approximated to the idealized unity of lands, language, institutions, high-cultural traditions, and customary heritage that nationalist discourse loved to presume. Both the linguistically defined German populations beyond the 1871 borders and the dispersal of German-speakers to settlements overseas easily encouraged ethno-cultural assumptions about German nationhood that were necessarily irredentist and diasporic. By the end of the empire's first decade, moreover, the dynamics of European colonial expansion were giving further edge to these frustrated nationalist hopes. As classic works by Hans-Ulrich Wehler, Klaus Bade, and others showed, the early construction of a wider global imaginary for Germany's national self-determination now came to be reprocessed into a powerful consensus behind the new state's need for colonies.[44]

Under intensifying imperialist rivalries, that consensus became further articulated through arguments about the mutually adversarial competition between the 'great world empires'. The 'scramble for Africa' and other instances of the new imperialism were only the spectacular manifestations of a more general shift in the drive towards global integration, which brought the Great Powers into worsening contention over resources, markets, communications, spheres of influence, and worldwide geopolitical space. The neo-mercantilist conviction that a nation's global competitiveness had become the vital condition not only of Great Power standing, but also of the expanding prosperity needed for social peace, acquired ever greater impetus across German-speaking Europe after the 1880s, suffusing the public realms of business, journalism, academic life, and politics. In its discursive architecture, this thinking had become the common sense of German foreign policy-making by 1900, mixing hard-headed geopolitical calculation, economic projections, and much visionary social and political thought.

Such 'empire talk' explicitly forged connections across the putatively interlinked priorities of several distinct domains in the life of the nation.

---

44   Klaus J. Bade, *Friedrich Fabri und der Imperialismus in der Bismarckzeit: Revolution – Depression – Expansion* (Freiburg: Atlantis, 1975); Hans-Ulrich Wehler, *Bismarck und der Imperialismus* (Cologne: Kiepenheuer & Witsch, 1969).

Most obvious was the sphere of foreign policy and international conflict per se, defined by the arms drive and a diplomacy of aggressive interventions once *Weltpolitik* was proclaimed in the late 1890s. Just beyond was the burgeoning discourse of national efficiency in the economy. Harnessed to projections of future economic growth, this encompassed everything deemed necessary to secure Germany's competitiveness in the world market, including the aggressive deployment of tariffs, bilateral trading treaties, and state-aided export offensives.[45] Then came the entire domain of social welfare, likewise conceived under the sign of national efficiency. While any particular social policy only ever emerged from complicated interactions between economic, sociopolitical, ethico-religious, institutional, and short-term political motivations, sometimes strategically conceived and woven together, but as often discretely undertaken out of expediency, most major initiatives were at some level consciously framed as being in the cause of social cohesion and political stability.[46] Between the 1880s and 1914, the urgency of world-political advocacy developed symbiotically across each of these domains.

Once Germany had become organized into a sovereign territorial space understanding itself as a national state – once Germany had become unified into the Empire of 1871 – the terms of its transnational projection necessarily shifted. The object of ambition and anxiety transmuted from the 'not yet national' into the 'not yet national enough'. The idea of an 'imperial imaginary' then becomes a good way of conceptualizing the expansionist dynamic so vital to German history from 1871 to 1945, linked to the aggressively iterated ideological consensus that Germany's future prosperity and survival necessarily presupposed some basis for effectively competing with the rival world empires of Britain, Russia, and the United States. That thinking was hardwired around a

---

45 Wehler, *Bismarck und der Imperialismus*, 112–42, 423–53; Willfried Spohn and Bernd Rabehl, *Weltmarktkonkurrenz und Industrialisierung Deutschlands 1870–1914: Eine Untersuchung Nationalen und Internationalen Geschichte der Kapitalistischen Produktionsweise* (Berlin: Olle & Wolter, 1977); Cornelius Torp, *Die Herausforderung der Globalisierung: Wirtschaft und Politik in Deutschland 1860–1914* (Göttingen: Vandenhoeck & Ruprecht, 2005); Sebastian Conrad, *Globalisierung und Nation im Deutschen Kaiserreich* (Munich: C. H. Beck, 2006), 32–73.

46 See here Geoff Eley, 'Social Imperialism in Germany: Reformist Synthesis or Reactionary Sleight of Hand?', in Geoff Eley, *From Unification to Nazism: Reinterpreting the German Past* (Boston: Allen & Unwin, 1986).

grand project of continental integration under German hegemony usually called *Mitteleuropa* (Central Europe); it was always bound integrally to a global projection of expanding trade and cultural influence; and it was permanently edged with a deep history of emigrationist anxieties, which saw the loss of population to non-German parts of the world as a debilitating drain on national vitality. This bundle of insistently and repeatedly voiced arguments about Germany's strengths and vulnerabilities in a dangerously rivalrous world then became aggressively condensed in the accelerating debates after the turn of the century.[47]

~

This chapter has been chiefly concerned with the complicated definitional field surrounding, on the one hand, the terms *empire*, *nation*, and *state*, and on the other hand the categories of the *global* and the *transnational*. Whereas the former carry strong institutional and jurisdictional meanings concerning the definitions of sovereignty and the boundaries of a polity, the whole point of the latter is deliberately to transgress such boundedness or limitations, consciously prioritizing other ways of thinking about political space. The two sets of terms usefully call one another into question. Thus, while the 'colony–metropole' binary can map very easily onto extremely conventional ways of understanding the ordering of political space, with a system of two-way flows between 'cores and peripheries' or 'centres and margins', as soon as we introduce the terms *global* and the *transnational*, we can begin to complicate those given approaches and open up other ways of seeing how political space might be imagined. In that case the pay-off will come with the successful concretizing of such claims.

While very large-scale frameworks are needed for questions of empire and imperialism, such arguments need always to be brought down to the ground. However big the larger-scale impact of colonial rule or the metropolitan imperial presence, the relationship between 'the local' and 'the imperial' was always secured in very practical micro-political settings. On the one hand, 'the local' signified all those specifics of time and place, custom and law, gender, sexualities, and family forms, economy and social relations, institutional recalcitrance and cultural differences, that colonizers needed to navigate once they entered the

---

47   See Chapter 9, below.

putative space of the making of imperial rule. On the other hand, 'the local' was a metonym for all those spaces from which public powers, regulatory interventions, the machineries of welfare and policing, and all the intrusions of governmentality might be deflected or even kept out, whether those spaces were physical, institutional, and geographic or cultural, existential, imaginary, and imagined. This understanding of 'the local' implies a cultural condition as much as a physical place. It alerts us to all those areas of life seldom allowed a secure and acknowledged role inside the available practices of a polity or the accessible political relations of a society. They include everything from forms of everyday life, realms of subjectivity, and protected personal spaces to informal economies, official and dissident sexualities, practices of communal self-regulation, and areas of fantasy, pleasure, and disavowal.

Such meanings of 'the local' may be found in the metropole no less than the colony. In fact, the most creative experiments with transnational history reveal that the relations between the local and the national, or the local and the imperial, can be made in some very unexpected places. Just as lives made and lived 'out on the borderlands' may physically be found in the geopolitical heartland of a society, and vice versa, so will the rhythms and architecture of metropolitan living be laid down and assembled in many other places too.[48] Deciding how best to track these connections has become more challenging and interesting than ever.

---

48   The quoted phrase is taken from Carolyn Steedman, *Landscape for a Good Woman: A Story of Two Lives* (London: Virago, 1986), 5.

9

Empire by Land or Sea? Germany's Imperial Imaginary, 1840–1945

From Imperialism to Empire

After something of a hiatus in the 1980s, interest in imperialism is booming.[1] Yet the language has changed. We prefer the sanitized usage of 'empire'. In the 1960s, 'imperialism' described the coercive domination and exploitative relations imposed by metropolitan countries on the more vulnerable parts of the world. Imperialist expansion was attributed to compulsions from inside the imperialist societies, whether economic, more specifically mercantile, more narrowly strategic, or more grandiosely geopolitical. Usually, this was linked to arguments about dominant interests too, variously located among military and naval strategists as well as foreign policy-makers, colonial administrators and civil servants, entrepreneurial and business interests, freebooters and visionaries, or simply 'the official mind'. Yet, these days, 'empire' often shrinks back to international politics, more narrowly understood: foreign policy-making, national security concerns, geopolitical strategy, international monetary policy, trade agreements,

1   This chapter began at the Midwest German History Workshop in Urbana-Champaign in October 2003, and has evolved through many iterations since. I am grateful to each of the audiences concerned. I am especially indebted to Sebastian Conrad, Jessica Dubow, Julia Hell, Jennifer Jenkins, Wendy Lower, A. Dirk Moses, Bradley D. Naranch, Robert L. Nelson, Roberta Pergher, Hartmut Pogge von Strandmann, George Steinmetz, Ronald Grigor Suny, Dennis Sweeney, Lenny Urena-Valerio, Andrew Zimmerman, and Jürgen Zimmerer.

international policing, the deployment of military force. That earlier structural or systemic unity linking power abroad to pressures at home seems far less evident.[2]

Yet, for *popular* involvement in imperialism, the contrast cuts the other way. Treatments of empire seem *more* capacious rather than less. Social historians' first impulse in the 1960s and 1970s was often to query the extent of working-class identification with colonies, locating imperialist enthusiasm mainly elsewhere, whether among the prosperous educated and propertied bourgeoisie or the self-employed and white-collar lower middle class. From anti-imperialist sentiments or sheer parochialism and indifference to the wider overseas worlds, historians argued, working people remained stubbornly uninvolved. On the evidence of elections and nationalist campaigning groups, workers proved much harder to win for patriotic causes.[3] Now, however, the contrast could hardly be greater. In the wake of cultural history, scholarship shows the penetration of colonial ideas into all possible areas of popular culture and everyday life. Today, we emphasize not the marginality or insignificance of empire for ordinary life, but rather its pervasiveness and presence.

This dichotomy, between stressing the thinness of colonialism's impact inside the home society and seeing its depth, describes most national historiographies. But scepticism had been all the stronger in

2   For the high tide of earlier interest, see Roger Owen and Bob Sutcliffe, eds, *Studies in the Theory of Imperialism* (London: Longman, 1972); and for the tide's receding, Wolfgang J. Mommsen and Jürgen Osterhammel, eds, *Imperialism and After: Continuities and Discontinuities* (Boston: Allen & Unwin, 1986). For current writing, see Antoinette Burton, ed., *After the Imperial Turn: Thinking With and Through the Nation* (Durham, NC: Duke University Press, 2003); Charles Maier, *Among Empires: American Ascendancy and Its Predecessors* (Cambridge, MA: Harvard University Press, 2006); Alexei Miller and Alfred J. Rieber, eds, *Imperial Rule* (New York: Central European University Press, 2005); Craig J. Calhoun, Frederick Cooper, and Kevin Moore, eds, *Lessons of Empire: Imperial Histories and American Power* (New York: New Press, 2006); and Ann Laura Stoler, Carole McGranahan, and Peter C. Perdue, eds, *Imperial Formations* (Oxford: Oxford University Press, 2007). For conceptual guidance, see George Steinmetz, 'Imperialism or Colonialism? From Windhoek to Washington, by Way of Basra', in Calhoun, Cooper, and Moore, *Lessons of Empire*, and 'Return to Empire', *Sociological Theory* 23: 4 (December 2005). Paul A. Kramer, 'Power and Connection', *American Historical Review* 116: 5 (December 2011), is a magisterial survey.

3   For my own earliest work, see Geoff Eley, 'Defining Social Imperialism: Use and Abuse of an Idea', *Social History* 1: 3 (October 1976), and 'Social Imperialism in Germany: Reformist Synthesis or Reactionary Sleight of Hand?', in *Imperialismus im 20. Jahrhundert*, ed. Joachim Radkau and Imanuel Geiss (Munich: C. H. Beck, 1976). In British history, see Richard Price, *An Imperial War and the British Working Class: Working-Class Attitudes and Reactions to the Boer War, 1899–1902* (Toronto: University of Toronto Press, 1972).

the German field, given the colonial empire's transitory duration. Because German colonialism lasted only from 1884 to 1919, the argument runs, it makes no sense for German historians to copy the British and French by taking the 'imperial turn'. By any criteria, German colonialism was a marginal phenomenon, at best a sideshow. For Jürgen Osterhammel, 'the social histories above all of Great Britain, Portugal, and the Netherlands, and in some respects of Russia and France, have to remain incomplete or incomprehensible once divorced from their imperial-colonial context', whereas in Germany that is not the case.[4] David Blackbourn agrees: 'One could hardly argue that the German colonies possessed the same centrality for domestic political debate as the far larger empires of the British and French', or for that matter the Belgians and Dutch.[5] Under a 'transnational' perspective, moreover, the colonies become recalibrated into just one instance of Germany's growing embeddedness in a larger set of global relations.[6] By relativizing the colonies in this way, the transnational perspective as often shrinks their significance as asserting it.

As recent scholarship makes abundantly clear, though, knowledge about the colonies reached far down into German society in manifold ways.[7] From propaganda of Colonial Society and Navy League, through the literary and visual landscapes of newspapers, magazines, pulp literature, postcards, schoolbooks, and all the new paraphernalia of advertising and mass marketing, to the public spectacles of museums, *Völkerschauen*, films, slide shows, exhibits, and congresses, the public sphere of the late *Kaiserreich* was saturated with citations of colonialism overseas. Here, the patriotic intensities unleashed in December

---

4   Jürgen Osterhammel, 'Transnationale Gesellschaftsgeschichte: Erweiterung oder Alternative?', *Geschichte und Gesellschaft*, 27: 3 (2001), 468.

5   David Blackbourn, 'Das Kaiserreich transnational: eine Skizze', in *Das Kaiserreich Transnational: Deutschland in der Welt 1871–1914*, ed. Sebastian Conrad and Jürgen Osterhammel (Göttingen: Vandenhoeck & Ruprecht, 2004), 321.

6   See especially Sebastian Conrad, *Globalisation and the Nation in Imperial Germany*, transl. Sorcha O'Hagan (Cambridge: Cambridge University Press, 2012), and 'Transnational Germany', in *Imperial Germany 1871–1918 (The Short Oxford History of Germany)*, ed. James Retallack (Oxford: Oxford University Press, 2008), esp. 221–3. Significantly, there is no separate chapter or subentry in Retallack's volume for colonies per se. In contrast, Andrew Zimmerman, 'Race and World Politics: Germany in the Age of Imperialism, 1878–1914', in *Oxford Handbook of Modern German History*, ed. Helmut Walser Smith (Oxford: Oxford University Press, 2011), brilliantly integrates treatment of colonies and imperialism together.

7   Bradley Naranch and Geoff Eley, eds, *German Colonialism in a Global Age* (Durham, NC: Duke University Press, 2015).

1906–January 1907, during the 'Hottentot elections', afford a telling illustration. By the first day of polling, on 25 January 1907, the Navy League central office, acting as a clearinghouse for the government's electioneering, had dispatched 21 million leaflets highlighting Germany's colonial interests. The most numerous included *Arbeiter, Kolonien und Flotte* (5 million copies), *Für die Kämpfer in Südwest Afrika* (3.5 million), *Die Wahrheit über unsere Kolonien* (2.4 million), *Deutsches Volk, wie sorgt der Reichstag* (2.3 million), and *Warum ist der Reichstag aufgelöst?* (2 million).[8] The use of Gustav Frenssen's 1906 popular novel *Peter Moors Fahrt nach Südwest – Ein Feldzugsbericht* is especially well documented. Embraced immediately by radical nationalists, Frenssen's account of a young Schleswig-Holstein artisan's experience of the Herero War brought the violent romance of the colonial frontier home vividly, selling 180,000 copies by 1914; during the 1907 elections the Navy League purchased a thousand copies for distribution through its regional sections.[9] A bestselling popular novelist from Schleswig-Holstein commonly associated with regionalist *Heimatkunst* but actually far more outward-looking, Frenssen epitomized the colonial world's new allure. Inspired by friendship with Friedrich Naumann, he constructed his fictions around the neo-Nietzschean idealism of his youthful protagonists as they passed from family and farm into the scenes of national grandiosity that, by the 1900s, were patently placed on a global-cum-imperial scale.[10]

Frenssen's novel conveyed the German colonies' long afterlife. Never out of print, the book was produced by the Third Reich in numerous editions for schools and the army; during the Second World War it surpassed half a million copies; in 1952 in appeared once again.[11]

---

8   As itemized in August Keim's report to the Reich Chancellery, 22 January 1907, cited in Geoff Eley, 'The German Navy League in German Politics, 1898–1914', PhD dissertation, University of Sussex, 1974, 420.

9   See Frank Oliver Sobich, '*Schwarze Bestien, rote Gefahr*': Rassimus und Antisozialismus im Deutschen Kaiserreich (Frankfurt: Campus Verlag, 2006); Sibylle Benninghoff-Lühl, *Deutsche Kolonialromane 1884–1914 in ihrem Entstehungs – und Wirkungszusammenhang* (Bremen: Im Selbstverlag, 1983), 111; Geoff Eley, *Reshaping the German Right: Radical Nationalism and Political Change after Bismarck* (London: Yale University Press, 1980).

10   For Frenssen, see above all Roy Pascal, *From Naturalism to Expressionism: German Literature and Society, 1880–1918* (London: Weidenfeld & Nicolson, 1973), esp. 38–41, 100; Rita Thalmann, *Protestantisme et nationalisme en Allemagne de 1900 à 1945* (Paris: Librairie Klincksiech, 1976).

11   The English translation appeared almost immediately: Gustav Frenssen, *Peter Moor's Journey to Southwest Africa: A Narrative of the German Campaign* (London: Forgotten Books, 2019).

Contrasting with the other old-imperial western European countries, (West) Germany faced none of the violence and divisiveness of decolonization, although the large-scale labour migrancy from the late 1950s had similar displaced effects. If British and French reactions to immigrants signalled a postcolonial return of the repressed, then so too did West German reactions to *Gastarbeiter*, especially once earlier German imperialisms are brought to mind – from *Mitteleuropa*, Berlin-Baghdad, and the Balkan entanglements of the *Kaiserreich* to the south-east European and Mediterranean theatres of expansionism under the Nazis. Colonialism not only seared long-lasting legacies into the public cultures of Britain, France, Belgium, the Netherlands, and Portugal, but left their viral traces in German popular memory too, where they flared every so often into life.[12]

In October 1966, at the height of the Fischer Controversy, West German television broadcast a polemical documentary by Ralph Giordano called *Heia Safari*, subtitled *The Legend of the German Colonial Idyll in Africa*. Its audience of some 9 million confirmed German colonialism's ability to continue troubling the political unconscious of the nation. The right-wing press was outraged. Eugen Gerstenmeier and Franz Joseph Strauss telephoned Klaus von Bismarck, head of Westdeutsche Rundfunk, to demand that the documentary's second part be shelved and replaced with a more sympathetic film instead. As a compromise, the channel agreed to a studio discussion, aired in February 1967.[13] While German society lacked the permanent reserves of love for the colonies found in Britain, France, and elsewhere, a constructed memory of colonial benevolence continued to resurge on occasions like this, goading the defenders of Germany's civilizing mission into vociferous voice. In these ways 'colonial fantasies' continued to echo.[14]

---

12   See Geoff Eley, 'The Trouble with "Race": Migrancy, Cultural Difference, and the Remaking of Europe', in *After the Nazi Racial State: Difference and Democracy in Germany and Europe*, ed. Rita Chen, Heide Fehrenback, Geoff Eley, and Atina Grossmann (Ann Arbor, MI: University of Michigan Press, 2009).

13   Eckard Michels, 'Geschichtspolitik im Ferhsehen. Die WDR-Dokumentation "Heia Safari" von 1966/67 über Deutschlands Kolonialvergangenheit', *Vierteljahrshefte für Zeitgeschichte* 56: 3 (2008). I first learned of this in 1969–70, from the consultant to the documentary, Hartmut Pogge von Strandmann, who joined the studio discussion.

14   Susanne Zantop, *Colonial Fantasies: Conquest, Family, and Nation in Precolonial Germany, 1770–1870* (Durham, NC: Duke University Press, 1997).

So, we have a paradox, setting longstanding tendencies to play down the importance of Germany's formal empire, whether in its duration or its domestic penetration, against a current insistence on its thorough-going pervasiveness. Here, Hans-Ulrich Wehler offers a revealing example. In Wehler's mature works – whether his multi-volume *magnum opus*, the *Gesellschaftsgeschichte*, or the collections of essays and reviews – colonialism plays virtually no part.[15] This silence seems deafeningly ironic because Wehler's 1969 classic, *Bismarck und der Imperialismus*, made such a compelling case for taking colonies seriously.[16] It also stood so plainly alone. There were only Helmut Bley's and Karin Hausen's case studies, a smattering of works by Africanists, and monographs from the DDR. One work that did tackle German colonialism on a broader front was Klaus Bade's study of Friedrich Fabri.[17]

Yet once we begin broadening the contexts for colonialism by setting our sights beyond direct colonial rule towards German expansion into the wider extra-European world – as soon as we make the conceptual moves of Sebastian Conrad's *Globalisation and Nation* – older literatures

---

15   See Hans-Ulrich Wehler, *Deutsche Gesellschaftsgeschichte. Dritter Band, Von der 'Deutschen Doppelrevolution' bis zum Beginn des Ersten Weltkrieges (1849–1914)* (Munich: C. H. Beck, 1978), 977–90, 1137–41, where colonialism remains confined within two perfunctory subsections, with no cross-referencing to economy, culture, or social life. Concepts of imperialism and empire are absent from the successor volume, Hans-Ulrich Wehler, *Deutsche Gesellschaftsgeschichte. Vierter Band, Vom Beginn des Ersten Weltkriegs bis zur Gründung der Beiden Deutschen Staaten, 1914–1949* (Munich: C. H. Beck, 1987), and his volumes of collected essays, *Politik in der Geschichte* (Munich: C. H. Beck, 1998), *Umbruch und Kontinuität* (Munich: C. H. Beck, 2000), and *Notizen zur deutschen Geschichte* (Munich: C. H. Beck, 2007). This isolating of colonialism also characterizes Thomas Nipperdey's general history, which briefly notices the topic under foreign policy and *Weltpolitik*. See Thomas Nipperdey, *Deutsche Geschichte 1866–1918. Zweiter Band: Machtstaat vor der Demokratie* (Munich: C. H. Beck, 1992), 445–53, 629–70. The companion volume dealing with social, economic, and cultural history omits any mention. See Thomas Nipperdey, *Deutsche Geschichte 1866–1918. Erster Band: Arbeitswelt und Bürgergeist* (Munich: C. H. Beck, 1990).

16   Hans-Ulrich Wehler, *Bismarck und der Imperialismus* (Cologne: Kiepenheuer & Witsch, 1969). See also Hans-Ulrich Wehler, 'Industrial Growth and Early German Imperialism', in Owen and Sutcliffe, *Studies in the Theory of Imperialism*. Wehler barely mentions imperialism in his recent interview reflections. See Hans-Ulrich Wehler, '*Eine lebhafte Kampfsituation': ein Gespräch mit Manfred Hettling und Cornelius Torp* (Munich: Beck, 2006).

17   Helmut Bley, *South-West Africa under German Rule, 1894–1914*, transl. Hugh Ridley (London: Heinemann, 1971); Karin Hausen, *Deutsche Kolonialherrschaft in Afrika: Wirtschaftsinteressen und Kolonialverwaltung in Kamerun vor 1904* (Freiburg: Atlantis, 1970); Klaus J. Bade, *Friedrich Fabri und der Imperialismus in der Bismarckzeit. Revolution, Depression, Expansion* (Freiburg: Atlantis, 1975). For an exhaustive critical review of the historiography of German colonialism and its wider contexts, see Bradley Naranch, 'Introduction: German Colonialism Made Simple', and the associated bibliography, in Naranch and Eley, *German Colonialism*, 1–18, and 347–406.

provide far more help.[18] While not formally addressing colonialism, certain earlier works become extremely suggestive once viewed in that light: Mack Walker's study of German emigration; William Hagen's *Germans, Poles, and Jews*; Kenneth Barkin's *Controversy over German Industrialization*; Alfred Vagt's older study of German–US relations in the context of *Weltpolitik*; Fritz Fischer's two great classics; Wolfgang Mommsen's *Max Weber and German Politics*.[19] Each proves very illuminating once colonialism is approached in a more broadly contextualized set of ways.

Where these older works offer little help is with the less direct, less perceptible, and more diffuse consequences of colonialism inside German society at home – all those questions now gathered under the sign of the 'cultural turn'. Here the decisive contemporary departure was certainly the volume edited by Sara Friedrichsmeyer, Sara Lennox, and Susanne Zantop called *The Imperialist Imagination*.[20] If that volume came almost entirely from *literary* studies, moreover, the intervening historical work has now transformed that disciplinary picture, opening German historians in the process to the pertinence of race, gender, and sexuality.[21] In consequence, the salient questions, methodologies, types

---

18   Conrad, *Globalisation and the Nation in Imperial Germany*. See also Conrad and Osterhammel, *Das Kaiserreich transnational*.

19   Mack Walker, *Germany and the Emigration: 1816–1885* (Cambridge: Harvard University Press, 1964), esp. 197–227; William Hagen, *Germans, Poles, and Jews: The Nationality Conflict in the Prussian East, 1772–1914* (Chicago: University of Chicago Press, 1980); Kenneth D. Barkin, *The Controversy over German Industrialization 1890–1902* (Chicago: University of Chicago Press, 1970); Alfred Vagts, *Deutschland und die Vereinigten Staaten in der Weltpolitik* (New York: Macmillan, 1935); Fritz Fischer, *Germany's Aims in the First World War* (London: Chatto & Windus, 1967), and *War of Illusions: German Policies from 1911 to 1914* (London: Chatto & Windus, 1975); Wolfgang J. Mommsen, *Max Weber and German Politics 1890–1920* (Chicago: University of Chicago Press, 1997). See also, Ekkehard Böhm, *Überseehandel und Flottenbau: Hanseatische Kaufmannschaft und Deutsche Seerüstung 1879–1902* (Düsseldorf: Bertlesmann, 1972).

20   Sara Friedrichsmeyer, Sara Lennox, and Susanne Zantop, eds, *The Imperialist Imagination: German Colonialism and Its Legacy* (Ann Arbor, MI: University of Michigan Press, 1998).

21   The plenitude of current research was captured in two major conferences in Sheffield (September 2006) and San Francisco (September 2007) – proceedings later published as Michael Perraudin and Jürgen Zimmerer, with Katy Heady, eds, *German Colonialism and National Identity* (London: Routledge, 2011), and Volker Max Langbehn and Mohammad Salama, eds, *German Colonialism: Race, the Holocaust, and Postwar Germany* (New York: Columbia University Press, 2011), respectively. See also Volker Max Langbehn, ed., *German Colonialism, Visual Culture, and Modern Memory* (New York: Routledge, 2010); A. Dirk Moses and Dan Stone, eds, *Colonialism and Genocide* (London: Routledge, 2006); A. Dirk Moses, ed. *Empire, Colony, Genocide: Conquest, Occupation, and Subaltern Resistance in World History* (New York: Berghahn, 2011).

of archive, and grounds of inquiry look profoundly different from those inspiring Bley and Hausen forty years before. The complicated passages between 'the social' and 'the cultural' experienced by historians during the intervening time are nowhere more evident than in the history of colonialism.[22] Indeed, it is exactly the bringing of the cultural and the political together that makes possible the most challenging recent work on the history of German empire-making before 1918.

From 'Social Imperialism' to What?

There seems far less interest today than during the 1970s in drawing connections from the domestic environment of politics to foreign policy. From the perspective of the 'primacy of domestic politics' (*Primat der Innenpolitik*) the new histories seem decoupled from an interest in the societal grounding of German foreign expansionism as more tradition-ally understood.[23] In the wake of the Fischer Controversy, the continuity thesis originally took its cachet primarily from foreign policy and the similarities linking the war aims of 1914–18 with the later imperialism of the Nazis. At the outset, the continuity argument involved Germany's 'grab for world power', after all. In those discussions of the 1960s and 1970s, it was the *compulsion towards empire* that, in the first instance, defined the postulated continuity.[24]

Conceptually speaking, the sharpest contrast between then and now concerns the idea of 'social imperialism', which in the 1970s had been pivotal for new approaches to the *Kaiserreich*. In Wehler's formulation, this denoted a 'defensive ideology' against the 'disruptive effects of industrialization on the social and economic structure of Germany', one that enabled 'the diversion outwards of internal tensions and forces of change in order to preserve the social and political status quo'.[25] In a

---

22 See Geoff Eley, *A Crooked Line: From Cultural History to the History of Society* (Ann Arbor, MI: University of Michigan Press, 2005).

23 The reference here is to Eckart Kehr, *Der Primat der Innenpolitik ges. Aufsätze Preuss –dt. Sozialgeschichte im 19. u. 20 Jh.* (Frankfurt: Ullstein, 1976), transl. Grete Heinz as *Economic Interest, Militarism, and Foreign Policy* (Berkeley: University of California Press, 1977).

24 See Fritz Fischer, *World Power or Decline: The Controversy over Germany's Aims in the First World War* (New York: Norton, 1974), and *From Kaiserreich to Third Reich: Elements of Continuity in German History, 1871–1945* (London: Allen & Unwin, 1986).

25 Wehler, 'Industrial Growth and Early German Imperialism', 89, 87, 88.

more recent iteration, 'It was only beneath this perspective that Wilhelmine "Weltpolitik" revealed its real meaning, its deeper driving force.'
By 1914 it was a permanently embedded pattern of politics: 'Only this
technique of rule seemed to make it possible to continue blocking the
reformist modernization of the social and political constitution in
the necessary degree.'[26] Beginning with Bismarck and continuing from
the later 1890s with growing recklessness and escalating results, a fateful
pattern was projected into the future: 'If there is a continuity in German
imperialism', Wehler argued, then it consists in 'the primacy of social
imperialism from Bismarck to Hitler'.[27]

Much of the historiographical excitement then surrounding the
Kaiserreich came from an insistence that the imperialist drives of
the two world wars possessed direct and compelling equivalence. That
is, those successive waves of foreign expansionism needed to be understood in relation to the persistence of a domestic political power
structure, a definite constellation of dominant class interests and their
associated anti-democratic politics. For the Nazi period, the analogue
to this 'Fischerite' approach to the July Crisis was Tim Mason's interpretation of the outbreak of the Second World War – a more pointed
version of the widely shared view that the essential principle of the
Third Reich's social system was the drive for war.[28]

Neither of these viewpoints – the centrality of 'social imperialism' for
historiography of the *Kaiserreich*; Mason's thesis about Nazi expansionism – retains much influence. Yet there are other ways of continuing to
connect imperialist expansion to life inside Germany itself: the 'racial
state' clearly links the drive for Nazi foreign expansion to the logics of

26 Wehler, *Deutsche Gesellschaftsgeschichte. Dritter Band*, 1139.
27 See, respectively, Hans-Ulrich Wehler, 'Bismarck's Imperialism 1862–1890', *Past and Present* 48 (1970), 161, and 'Probleme des Imperialismus', *Krisen-Herde des Kaiserreichs 1871–1918: Studien zue Deutschen Sozial- und Verfassungsgeschichte* (Göttingen: Vanden-hoeck & Ruprecht, 1970), 131.
28 See Tim Mason, 'The Legacy of 1918 for National Socialism', in *German Democracy and the Triumph of Hitler: Essays in Recent German History*, ed. A. J. Nicholls and E. Matthais (London: Allen & Unwin, 1971): 'National Socialism appears as a radically new variant of the social imperialism of Bismarck and Wilhelm II . . . foreign expansion would legitimize not an inherited political and social system but an entirely new one' (218). For the more diffuse view of the Third Reich as 'a regime inherently geared to war', see Jeremy Noakes and Geoffrey Pridham, eds, *Nazism 1919–1945, Vol. 3: Foreign Policy, War, and Racial Extermination. A Documentary Reader* (Exeter: University of Exeter Press, 1988), 751; Ian Kershaw, *The Nazi Dictatorship: Problems and Perspectives of Interpretation*, 4th edn (London: Arnold, 2000), 134–60.

domestic policy-making, while cultural histories of the salience of the colonial relationship for the life of the German metropole could hardly enjoy greater influence. What *has* been lost is the strong conceptual unity that Wehler's generation constructed between the drive for empire, government strategies of rule, dominant class interests, and the structural persistence of authoritarianism. Current work on colonialism is concerned less with the persistence of authoritarian forms of rule than with the broader impact of German interactions with a non-European set of worlds. Rather than being interested mainly in *origins* (in colonial policy as an expression of conflicts and pressures coming from inside German society), recent work focuses on the *consequences* and impact of the colonial encounter. One obvious priority, therefore, would be to find ways of re-establishing concrete linkages from 'colonialism' into the mainstream of German politics and policy-making in the early twentieth century.

We get furthest in tackling that question by adopting a far more capacious concept of colonialism.[29] Formal colonial rule might be deemed just one instance in a wider repertoire of Germany's expansionist relations with an exploitable world. 'German expansionism' might then encompass everything from colonial policy as such to all the other ways in which German interests began to seek global penetration: the arms race and the big navy; export drives and trading policy; the competitiveness of the German economy in world markets; questions of migration and maintenance of ties with Germans overseas; the 'civilizational' impetus behind German culture; German diplomacy and the wider realm of *Weltpolitik*; and, finally, the July Crisis and Germany's aims in the First World War.

Current talk of 'empire' in our own time makes it easier to see this wider field of expansionary meanings. In contemporary globalization

---

29 George Steinmetz properly ties colonial rule to the *colonial state*, defining modern colonialism as 'the annexation of a territory by people with ties to a foreign state who perceive the conquered population as culturally distant and inferior'. The colonial relationship then presumes both a state apparatus and a regime of cultural inequality that work to fix the subject people's inferiority, by what Partha Chatterjee calls the 'rule of colonial difference'. Broadening the concept of colonialism risks occluding these specificities, but the heuristic gains outweigh the drawbacks. See George Steinmetz, '"The Devil's Handwriting": Precolonial Discourse, Ethnographic Acuity, and Cross-Identification in German Colonialism', *Comparative Studies in Society and History* 45: 1 (2003), 42; Partha Chatterjee, *The Nation and Its Fragments: Colonial and Postcolonial Histories* (Princeton: Princeton University Press, 1993), 14, 20.

talk, interestingly, pre-1914 colonialism is now being reclaimed across a wide political spectrum in exactly this way, whether in Britain, France, or the United States.[30] Such arguments bespeak grandiose historical claims about the distinctive global order made by the Soviet Union's collapse and the end of the Cold War; they link to concepts of 'failed' or 'collapsed' states; they redeploy older liberal-imperialist arguments for new versions of the civilizing mission; and they urge the advanced states like the United States, or prospectively the European Union (EU), to embrace 'their responsibilities in the world' by realizing 'a vision of cooperative empire'.[31] In such discussion the nineteenth-century *Pax Britannica* is invariably invoked as a guide. Epitomized by the lionizing of Niall Ferguson, a recharged metanarrative of pre-1914 world history centring on the progressive directionality of 'empire' began circulating through the public sphere with ever greater insistence.[32]

For new interest in colonialism and empire before 1914, these contemporary languages of politics have been decisive. Recent historical discussions are simply not thinkable without present anxieties about borders, cultural belonging, migrancy, and race; without post-Saidian critiques of 'the West'; or without the wildly burgeoning discourse of 'globalization'.[33] For some scholars, the concept of 'empire' seems even to acquire analytical, or perhaps epistemological, equivalence with the older category of 'society'.[34] From the early 1990s, a set of intensively grounded arguments about the importance of imperialism – meaning

---

30   For the French law of February 2005 affirming French colonialism's positive legacies, see Julio Godoy, 'Recasting Colonialism as a Good Thing', *Global Policy Forum*, 5 July 2005, at globalpolicy.org. For Nicolas Sarkozy's related speech at the University of Dakar on 28 July 2007, see Mialy Andriamananjara, 'Senegal: Africa According to Nicolas Sarkozy', at globalvoicesonline.org.

31   Phrases are taken from Robert Cooper, 'The New Liberal Imperialism', *Guardian*, 7 April 2002. An advisor to British prime minister Tony Blair, Robert Cooper became EU director-general for external and politico-military affairs in 2002. For his longer essay, see 'Post-Modern State', in *Reordering the World: The Long-Term Implications of September 11*, ed. Mark Leonard (London: Foreign Policy Centre, 2002).

32   Niall Ferguson, 'America: An Empire in Denial', *Chronicle of Higher Education*, 28 March 2003, and *Empire: The Rise and Demise of the British World Order and the Lessons for Global Power* (New York: Basic Books, 2003).

33   See Chapter 8 above and Chapter 10 below.

34   See here Michael Hardt and Antonio Negri, *Empire* (Cambridge: Harvard University Press, 2000); Gopal Balakrishnan, ed., *Debating Empire* (London: Verso, 2003); Paul A. Passavant and Jodi Dean, eds, *Empire's New Clothes: Reading Hardt and Negri* (New York: Routledge, 2004); Stephen Howe, *Empire: A Very Short Introduction* (Oxford: Oxford University Press, 2002).

both the acquiring of colonies and the informal dynamics of the West's coercive and exploitative impact in the rest of the world –slowly transformed the questions British and French historians bring to the study of national history, and the same became true par excellence for the United States.[35] American studies programmes became entirely suffused with recognitions of empire's importance.[36]

The Nation's Urgent Needs: An Expanding Imaginary

What are the larger contexts that best illuminate German colonialism? Current historiography suggests a wealth of possible answers, but here I consider four.

Competitive globalization?

How should we read talk of the 'great world empires' acquiring evergreater impetus after the 1880s across German-speaking Europe? Such talk suffused the public realms of business, journalism, academic life, and politics, enlisting the imaginations of the Wilhelmine intelligentsia into another version of the 'ideological consensus' Wehler found behind the drive for colonies in the earlier 1880s.[37] In its discursive architecture, such talk uncannily resembles the progress of the languages of globalization today. As a deep-lying context of economic projection, hard-headed geopolitical calculation, and visionary thought, it likewise foreshadows one strand of current expectations for European integration.

---

35 In general, see Burton, *After the Imperial Turn*. For Britain, see Catherine Hall, ed., *Cultures of Empire: Colonizers in Britain and the Empire in the Nineteenth and Twentieth Centuries: A Reader* (Manchester: Manchester University Press, 2000); Antoinette Burton, *Empire in Question: Reading, Writing, and Teaching British Imperialism* (Durham, NC: Duke University Press, 2011). For France, see Gary Wilder, 'Unthinking French History: Colonial Studies beyond National Identity', in Burton, *After the Imperial Turn*, and *The French Imperial Nation-State: Negritude and Colonial Humanism between the Two World Wars* (Chicago: University of Chicago Press, 2005). For Germany, see Lora Wildenthal, 'Notes on a History of "Imperial Turns" in Modern Germany', in Burton, *After the Imperial Turn*.

36 A foundational text was Amy Kaplan and Donald Pease, eds, *Cultures of United States Imperialism* (Durham, NC: Duke University Press, 1993). For current discussion, see Ann Laura Stoler, ed., *Haunted by Empire: Geographies of Intimacy in North American History* (Durham, NC: Duke University Press, 2006); and Kramer, 'Power and Connection'.

37 See Wehler, *Bismarck und der Imperialismus*, 112–93. See also Bade, *Friedrich Fabri*, 67–79, 80–135.

This 'empire talk' explicitly forged connections across the presumptively interlinked priorities of several distinct domains in the life of the nation. The first of these encompassed national efficiency in the economy, including the general projection of continuing economic growth; deployment of tariffs, bilateral trading treaties, and export offensives to ensure the conditions of market viability; and the aggressive securing of Germany's competitiveness in the world economy.[38] Second came the entire domain of social welfare, likewise conceived increasingly under the sign of national efficiency. While social policy was always complexly overdetermined by a plethora of economic, sociopolitical, ethico-religious, institutional, and short-term political considerations, sometimes strategically conceived, but as often undertaken for reasons of expediency, most major initiatives were at some level consciously framed to further the cause of social cohesion and political stability, commonly again under the sign of Germany's national competitiveness.[39] Last came the sphere of foreign policy and international conflict per se, increasingly defined after the proclamation of *Weltpolitik* in the late 1890s by the arms drive and a diplomacy of aggressive interventions. The urgency of world-political advocacy developed symbiotically across each of these domains.

As a consensus of imposing breadth came together during the *Kaiserreich*, it travelled through perhaps four distinct phases. Each was marked by an intense concentration of public discussion across the press, associations, and wider journalistic domain, intersecting with the business and government worlds, and finding powerful resonance in parties and Reichstag. If each was then followed by a relative lull, the political climate had been fatefully ratcheted forward.

---

38   Wehler, *Bismarck*, 112–42, 423–53, remains the best overall guide, together with Willfried Spohn, *Weltmarktkonkurrenz und Industrialisierung Deutschlands 1870–1914. Eine Untersuchung zur nationalen und internationalen Geschichte der kapitalistischen Produktionsweise* (Berlin: Olle & Wolter, 1977). See also Cornelius Torp, *Die Herausforderung der Globalisierung. Wirtschaft und Politik in Deutschland, 1860–1914* (Göttingen: Vandenhoeck & Ruprecht, 2005); and Conrad, *Globalisation and the Nation in Imperial Germany*, 27–76.

39   See here Eley, 'Social Imperialism in Germany'; Erik Grimmer-Solem, *The Rise of Historical Economics and Social Reform in Germany 1864–1894* (Oxford: Oxford University Press, 2003), 89–168, 171–245, and 'Imperialist Socialism of the Chair: Gustav Schmoller and German *Weltpolitik*, 1897–1905', in *Wilhelminism and Its Legacies: German Modernities, Imperialism, and the Meanings of Reform, 1890–1930*, ed. Geoff Eley and James Retallack (New York: Berghahn, 2003); James J. Sheehan, *The Career of Lujo Brentano: A Study of Liberalism and Social Reform in Imperial Germany* (Chicago: University of Chicago Press, 1966).

- The first phase, from late 1870s to mid 1880s, was described by Wehler's 'ideological consensus' in the third part of his *Bismarck* book: here, the first surge of colonialism was matched by conventional strategic and diplomatic concerns for stabilizing the new Germany's geopolitical security in central Europe.[40]
- A second spurt occurred in the mid 1890s with the naval expansion, the end of the depression in 1895–96, and the huge fanfare of the Kaiser's proclaiming of *Weltpolitik* in January 1896.[41] But concurrent with this new assertiveness about Germany overseas was an equally marked drive for a politically secured and state-guaranteed central European economic trading region, galvanized by the impact of the Caprivi commercial treaties of 1892–94. The most serious attempt to hold these goals politically together came from the Pan-German League, founded in 1890–91.[42]
- A third phase was sparked by the 1902 tariff settlement, the standard of living agitation behind the SPD's 1903 electoral landslide, and the economic recovery after the brief depression of 1900–02. While enthusiasm for *Weltpolitik* continued apace (dramatized around the first Moroccan Crisis and the radicalizing of naval agitation), the most notable initiative was the founding of the *Mitteleuropäischer Wirtschaftsverein* in 1904, again strongly inflected by Pan-German thinking. It was now that the characteristic oscillation between 'world policy' and 'continental policy' began to be named.
- The fourth phase immediately preceded 1914, introduced by the watershed of the second Moroccan Crisis and the reversion to a military, as opposed to a naval, arms drive in 1911. The intensifying public discussion was classically demonstrated in

---

40 See Wehler, *Bismarck*, 112–93; Bade, *Friedrich Fabri*; Bascom Barry Hayes, *Bismarck and Mitteleuropa* (Cranbury, NJ: Associated University Presses, 1994).

41 Vagts, *Deutschland und die Vereinigten Staaten*; Böhm, Überseehandel und Flottenbau; Torp, *Die Herausforderung der Globalisierung*; Conrad, *Globalisiation and the Nation in Imperial Germany*.

42 Roger Chickering, *We Men Who Feel Most German: A Cultural Study of the Pan-German League, 1886–1914* (Boston: George Allen & Unwin, 1984), is silent on this front. But see Dirk Stegmann, *Die Erben Bismarcks. Parteien und Verbände in der Spätphase des Wilhelminischen Deutschlands: Sammlungspolitik 1897–1918* (Cologne: Kiepenheuer & Witsch, 1970), 54–8; Dennis Sweeney, 'Pan-German Conceptions of Colonial Empire', in Naranch and Eley, *German Colonialism in a Global Age*.

Fischer's second book, *Krieg der Illusionen*, together with the key supporting works of Dirk Stegmann, Peter-Christian Witt, and Klaus Wernecke.[43]

Running through this discourse from the start was the idea of three existing 'world empires', namely the British, American, and Russian (plus occasionally the French as a fourth), against whose global dominance (economically, demographically, geo-strategically) Germany would need comparable resources to compete. German unification and French military defeat had already prized open this global constellation of the existing 'world nations', but now the urgency of further securing Germany's claims to parity was severe. As Paul Rohrbach succinctly put it, 'The fourth nation – that is ourselves.'[44] Indeed, a fundamental condition of Great Power standing under the pressures of intensifying world economic rivalry, which put into question not just a society's future prosperity but its very longer-term survival, would be Germany's ability to assemble an equivalent basis for 'world imperial' expansion, usually conceptualized as some version of *Mitteleuropa*, but in its wider

---

43   Fischer, *War of Illusions*; Stegmann, *Erben Bismarcks*; Peter-Christian Witt, *Die Finanzpolitk des Deutschen Reiches von 1903 bis 1913. Eine Studie zur Innenpolitik des Wilhelminischen Deutschland* (Lübeck: Mattheisen, 1970); Klaus Wernecke, *Der Wille zur Weltgeltung: Außenpolitik und Öffentlichkeit im Kaiserreich am Vorabend des Ersten Weltkrieges* (Düsseldorf: Droste, 1970).

44   Paul Rohrbach, 'Das Kriegsziel im Schützengraben', quoted by Fischer, *Germany's Aims in the First World War*, 160. A Baltic German who came to Germany to escape Russification and complete his PhD in Protestant theology, Paul Rohrbach (1869–1956) was an emblematic figure of the Wilhelmine nationalist intelligentsia. Protégé of Hans Delbrück and Adolf von Harnack, early associate of Friedrich Naumann, regular contributor to *Preußische Jahrbücher*, *Christliche Welt*, and *Die Hilfe*, and sometime secretary of the *Evangelisch-Sozialer Kongreß*, he defies easy categorization. An inveterate Russophobe, his travels across Central Asia, Persia, and Turkey during 1897–1902 made him an expert advocate of the Baghdad Railway. Serving in 1903–06 as Commissioner for Settlement in South-West Africa, he produced a spate of associated writings, including the two-volume *Deutsche Kolonialwirtschaft*. Teaching from 1912 in the Berlin *Handelshochschule*, with numerous commissions from the Colonial Office and Foreign Office, he was linked to Bethmann Hollweg's circle through Delbrück and Ernst Jäckh. Editor of *Das Größere Deutschland* (from early 1914) and *Deutsche Politik* (from 1916), he was instrumental in Germany's strategy of destabilizing the Russian Empire, helping in 1918 to form the German-Ukrainian Society. His writings on Germany's arrival as a 'world nation' included *Deutschland unter den Weltvölkern: Materialien zur auswärtigen Politik* (Berlin: Fortschritt, 1903), *Die Bagdadbahn*, 2nd edn (Berlin: Wiegandt & Grieben, 1902), *Der deutsche Gedanke in der Welt* (Düsseldorf: K. R. Langewiesche, 1912), and *Weltpolitisches Wanderbuch, 1897–1915* (Königstein im Taunus: K. R. Langewiesche, 1916). See also his autobiography, *Um die Teufels Handschrift. Zwei Menschenalter erlebter Weltgeschichte* (Hamburg: Dulk, 1953).

webs of dominance extending (as Fischer said) 'from Spitzbergen to the Persian Gulf'.[45]

On the outbreak of war, German chancellor Theobald von Bethmann Hollweg embraced this idea in the form of a customs union between Germany and Austria-Hungary, which Belgium and France would be compelled to join. Crystallizing from earlier discussions with Walter Rathenau and others into the core of his September Programme, *Mitteleuropa* hardwired Bethmann's thinking about war aims. During the intensive ministerial discussions of September 1914, Bethmann's main collaborator, Interior Secretary Clemens von Delbrück, projected a single customs unit stretching 'from the Pyrenees to Memel, from the Black Sea to the North Sea, from the Mediterranean to the Baltic'.[46] This characteristic imagery of the globalized struggle for existence among rival 'world nations' or 'world empires' had become the default language of international politics in German policy-making circles, organized around the dialectics of prosperity and survival.[47] This was how powerful nations – expanding economies, prosperous societies, dynamic cultures, strategically dominant Great Powers – *had* to develop to avoid sinking into stagnation, poverty, decadence, and marginality. The terms of success under the competitive world system required such a logic.

Before 1914, such thinking was necessarily more speculative. Sometimes France was part of the projected union, sometimes not; sometimes it was deemed a fourth world empire, sometimes marked as irremediably

---

45   Fischer, *Germany's Aims in the First World War*, 160.

46   Ibid., 248. This is how Under-Secretary Friedrich von Falkenhausen of the Ministry of Agriculture saw the goal: 'To match the great, closed economic bodies of the United States, the British, and the Russian Empires with an equally solid economic bloc representing all European states, or at least those of Central Europe under German leadership, with a twofold purpose: (1) of assuring the members of this whole, and particularly Germany, the mastery of the European market, and (2) of being able to lead the entire economic strength of allied Europe into the field, as a unified force, in the struggle with those world powers over the conditions of the admission of each to the markets of the others' (250).

47   Delbrück's assistant von Schoenebeck repeated the argument: 'Difficulties of procedure should not make us forget the "great final aim" of creating a great Central European economic unit to enable us to hold our place in the economic struggle for existence of the peoples and to save us from shrinking into economic impotence against the ever-increasing solidarity and power of the economic World Powers, Great Britain with her colonies, the United States, Russia, and Japan with China.' Ibid., 251, 247–56. See also Hartmut Pogge von Strandmann, ed., *Walther Rathenau: Industrialist, Banker, Intellectual, and Politician – Notes and Diaries 1907–1922* (Oxford: Oxford University Press, 1985), 183–91.

decadent. In Gustav Roloff's *Kolonialpolitscher Führer*, produced for the 1907 elections, *Mitteleuropa* was a German-centred confederation of states capable of 'produc[ing] all modern necessities as successfully as any of the giant empires' of Britain, France, the United States, and Russia: 'At the top of a union to which Holland, Belgium, Scandinavia, Austria, perhaps also Italy and a few extra-European states such as Mexico and Chile could accede, Germany would have nothing to fear from the four others.'[48] This continental projection of necessary economic security was always bound integrally to a global imaginary of expanding trade and cultural influence, inflected by a history of emigrationist anxieties descending from the early nineteenth century. Here is Gustav Schmoller during the agitation for the 1900 Navy Law, invoking the familiar exclusionary threat from the three 'conquering and colonizing empires' of Russia, the United States, and Britain:

> [Germany] no longer wishes to be the nursery and schoolroom of the rest of the world, a land that sends out millions of its sons abroad so that they cease being Germans in the next generation. Its state, its energy, its scholarship and its technology, its trade and its reputation in the world are so great [and] its moral and intellectual qualities, its affective life, its fine arts, its diligence, its institutions, stand so high that it can demand in the interests of the *Kultur* of humanity to assert, on the basis of its own law, its own colonies, its own stations, its own influence of power, its place in the world economy next to . . . the three great world empires.[49]

As Rohrbach said in *Der Deutsche Gedanke in der Welt* in 1912, 'For us there can be no standing still or stopping, not even a temporary renunciation of the expansion of our sphere of life; our choice is either to

---

48 Roloff extolled the virtues of this centred cultural heterogeneity: 'This coalition of territory would have the enormous cultural advantage over the giant empires in that not one nation, not one language dominates, but instead that almost all nations that have created modern *Kultur* would be represented and protected from decline'. See Kolonialpolitisches Aktionskomité, ed., *Kolonialpolitischer Führer: Herausgegeben* (Berlin: Verlag Dr. Wedekind, 1907), cited by Erik Grimmer-Solem, 'The Professors' Africa: Economists, the Elections of 1907, and the Legitimation of German Imperialism', *German History* 25: 3 (2007), 333.

49 G. Schmoller, 'Die wirtschaftliche Zukunft Deutschlands und die Flottenvorlage', in *Zwanzig Jahre Deutscher Politik (1897–1917)* (1920), cited in Grimmer-Solem, 'The Professors' Africa', 320.

decline again . . . or to struggle for a place alongside the Anglo-Saxons . . . Our growth is a process of elemental natural force.'[50] That was partly what Weber had meant in 1895 when he worried caustically that the unification of Germany was starting to seem like a 'costly extravagance' and frivolous 'youthful spree', which 'would have been better left undone if it was meant to be the end and not the starting point of a German policy of world power'.[51] Just as Germany's unification had required war, so too might its future survival. Here is Rohrbach again in 1913:

> *Whether we shall obtain the necessary territorial elbow room to develop as a world power or not* without use of the old recipe of 'blood and iron' is anything but certain . . . Our situation as a nation today is comparable to that before the wars of 1866 and 1870 which it was necessary to fight to settle the national crisis. At that time, it was Germany's political unification which was at stake, today it is Germany's admittance to the circle of World Nations or its exclusion from it.[52]

How are we to judge the effects of this discourse in politics? What was its relationship not only to the making of wartime policy, but also over the longer term to the ideas, projects, and ambitions shaping German expansionism under the Third Reich? For that matter, what legitimate lines might be drawn from these earlier projections of *Mitteleuropa* to later images of more peaceful commercial and industrial penetration, including the prospects opened by 1989–90?

Global Germany?

Historians are drawn increasingly to 'transnationalism' as a 'way of seeing' that allows us to think 'beyond the nation' or outside the framework of the nation-state. Without diminishing states, empires, and other forms of bounded sovereignty, this stresses a different field of connections defined more by 'networks, processes, beliefs, and institutions that transcend these politically defined spaces'.[53] Isabel Hofmeyr amplifies

---

50   Fischer, *War of Illusions*, 264.

51   Mommsen, *Max Weber and German Politics*, 69. See Weber's Freiburg inaugural address in May 1895, 'The National State and Economic Policy (Freiburg Address)' together with Keith Tribe's 'Introduction to Weber', in *Economy and Society* 9: 4 (1980).

52   Fischer, *War of Illusions*, 264. Emphasis in original.

53   Sven Beckert in C. A. Bayley, Sven Beckert, Matthew Connelly, Isabel Hofmeyr, Wendy Kozol, and Patricia Seed, '*AHR* Conversation: On Transnational History', *American Historical Review* 111: 5 (December 2006), 1459, 1446.

the point: 'The key claim of any transnational approach is its central concern with movements, flows, and circulation, not simply as a theme or motif, but as an analytic set of methods which defines the endeavor itself.' Citing Arjun Appadurai, she calls this a concern with the 'space of the flows', which insists not only on the diverse origins of historical processes (any 'national' history will usually be made in more than a single place), but also that 'they are constructed in the movement between places, sites, and regions.'[54]

A transnational perspective has many dimensions. The complicated interconnectedness of nationality and territoriality will not always map easily onto Europe's actual national-state sovereignties of the period between, say, 1859 and 1973. People, goods, and ideas circulated *across* the national frontiers, both actual and imagined, of any particular time. The permeability of geographical borderlands and state-territorial frontier lines allowed the porousness and mobility of both cultures and all kinds of personal affiliations. Parochialism could break down in 'non-national' or 'pre-national' ways. National affiliations might be shaped from margins and across distances markedly separated from the physical heartland of the nation itself, subtly complicating relations of inclusion and exclusion. Any period in a society's history contains a complex repertoire of processes – economic, social, cultural, political – that cut across the main patterns of nation-forming, whether in state-territorial or culturalist terms. Such processes work against the grain of either the actually consummated histories or the imagined realizations of the nation form. A transnational history proposes regional contexts for exploring questions a national frame might otherwise obscure.

A transnational optic calls attention to the extra-European and colonial theatres of Germany's metropolitan history. It illumines the earlier nineteenth-century settings in which the *national* itself was yet to be properly formed – before a 'national' had arrived that could yet become 'trans'. Between *Vormärz* and the 1860s, nationhood and national belonging had attained a prefigurative presence even in advance of statehood per se. In a geopolitical environment already occupied by older-established national states, where nationalist ideas were palpably

---

54   Hofmeyr, in ibid., 1444. See Arjun Appadurai, *Modernity at Large: Cultural Dimensions of Globalization* (Minneapolis: University of Minnesota Press, 1996).

circulating through those central European lands soon to be remapped into a new state-bounded entity of Germany, and where the urgency of nationalist advocacy saturated the emergent public sphere, the language of the transnational already makes sense. As Bradley Naranch has shown, expansionary relations were already binding the inhabitants of German-speaking Europe into a set of larger-than-European worlds within an avowedly national frame of aspiration, yet *in advance* of the national state's actual foundation.

Between the 1840s and 1870s, well ahead of the coming unification, Germany's emergent national intelligentsia – writers, journalists, academics, economists, businessmen, political activists – used the visionary landscape of a putative colonial imaginary to do much of the ideological work of describing what the future national government would be expected to do. To secure its popular legitimacy, that government should be capable of defending Germany's interests on the world stage of international competition, as well as sustaining the power of German culture overseas and creating organized ties strong enough to retain the affiliations of those who were leaving German-speaking Europe in such prodigious and disquieting numbers. No mere preamble to the later narrative of the Bismarckian colonial policy of the mid 1880s, this was an integral part of the story itself. It was vital to the process through which the making of the German nation was accomplished.[55] By thinking transnationally in advance of the national state's creation, we can observe the 'boundaries of Germanness' already being fashioned into place.[56]

In this mid-nineteenth-century context, a transnational approach unsettles our thinking about where exactly 'Germany' was to be found. Before unification itself, the nation coalesced around an imagined topography of European and global locations far larger and more dispersed than the lands to which the political entity fashioned in 1864–71 then became attached. Once Germany had become organized into the 'small-German' territorial sovereignty that understood itself as a national state – once Germany was unified into the *Kaiserreich* of 1871 – the stakes radically changed. The transnational object radically shifted its

---

55   Bradley D. Naranch, 'Beyond the Fatherland: Colonial Visions, Overseas Expansion, and German Nationalism, 1848–1885', PhD dissertation, Johns Hopkins University, 2006.

56   See Krista O'Donnell, Renate Bridenthal, and Nancy Reagin, eds, *The Heimat Abroad: The Boundaries of Germanness* (Ann Arbor, MI: University of Michigan Press, 2005).

aspirational ground. One horizon, the 'not yet national,' was exchanged for another, the 'not yet national enough'. For German nationalists, the language of what I am calling 'competitive globalization' – the constant invoking of the circle of the 'great world empires' to which Germany needed admittance – became a principal means through which that lack was to be bridged.

Andrew Zimmerman's study of the Tuskegee expedition to German Togo in the early 1900s offers a fascinating demonstration of this point. To examine the complex interrelations between ideas of free labour, race, and social science, Zimmerman tracks their journeying back and forth along the Atlantic circuits of influence, ideas, and political economy that joined Germany, Africa, and the United States.[57] By proceeding transnationally, he brings previously separated histories compellingly together. In venturing outside the well-beaten paths of national history, he reconstructs the complex channels that brought a series of paired histories unexpectedly into cross-cutting dialogue. The first of these couplets sets Booker T. Washington's speech at the Atlanta Cotton States and International Exposition of 1895 alongside Max Weber's Freiburg inaugural address of the same year; the second joins the politics of internal colonization in the Prussian east with the political economy of plantation agriculture in the post-slave South; and a third juxtaposes the structure of the agricultural labour market in eastern Germany with the range of agrarian labour relations encountered in North America, including the sharecropping system, the various regimes of post-emancipation labour coercion, and the 'Negro question' in the US New South. In pondering the problem of East Elbian backwardness, seemingly so intractably linked to the co-dependent inefficiencies of Prussian Junkers and Polish peasants, German economists looked to the labour regimes and models of agricultural economy prevalent in Canada and the United States. The late nineteenth century saw significant traffic of German agronomists to the Canadian Prairies, the Great Plains, and the plantation South. Attracted by Washington's Tuskegee experiments, percipient German policy-makers saw opportunities for colonial development potentially adaptable for the East Elbian

---

57   Andrew Zimmerman, 'A German Alabama in Africa: The Tuskegee Expedition to German Togo and the Transnational Origins of West African Cotton Growers', *American Historical Review* 110: 5 (2005), and *Alabama in Africa: Booker T. Washington, the German Empire, and the Globalization of the New South* (Princeton: Princeton University Press, 2010).

home. Borne by the Tuskegee expedition, these transatlantic links came to be convened in the German colony of Togo, where Washington's ideas inspired an ambitious programme for the *Erziehung des Negers zur Arbeit* ('Education of the Negro for Work'). By situating the Tuskegee expedition in the complex circuitry of influences inside a 'German Atlantic', Zimmerman shows how a history located in Germany's 'East' disclosed far more complex genealogies that can be tracked back and forth across some unexpected places between Europe, Africa, and the Americas.[58]

Several particulars arise. First, by following Weber in 1904 to his meetings with Washington in Tuskegee and W. E. B. Du Bois in Atlanta, Zimmerman shows how Weber's thinking about ethnicity, labour, and agricultural proletarianization in the Prussian-Polish east came to be shaped by his understanding of race, land, and agricultural labour across the Atlantic in the United States. German thinking about settlement policies for eastern Europe relied on a reservoir of knowledge about the relative efficiencies of farming on the Canadian Prairies, in the Midwest, and in the plantation economies of the slave and post-slave South. German overseas colonialism and German landward expansionism to the east were always in a complex exchange before 1914, involving traceable relays of ideas, influences, and people.[59]

Second, Zimmerman shows how the freshly racialized category of the 'Negro' supplanted older anthropological designations of the *Naturvölker* ('natural peoples') or the *Eingeborenen* ('natives') by constructing 'an individual capable of improvement, in contrast to the so-called "natural person", who was doomed either to extinction or to a travestied approximation of civilization'.[60] Under the spell of Tuskegee, German colonial theorists 'hoped to make Africans just like US "Negroes", only more so – more productive, more docile, more rational and free, and more

---

58   See Robert L. Nelson, ed., *Germans, Poland, and Colonial Expansion to the East: 1850 through the Present* (New York: Palgrave Macmillan, 2009); Sven Beckert, 'From Tuskegee to Togo: The Problem of Freedom in the Empire of Cotton', *Journal of American History* 92: 2 (2005). More broadly, see Conrad, *Globalisation and the Nation in Imperial Germany*, 77–143.

59   See Mommsen, *Max Weber and German Politics*, 68–90; Oliver Grant, *Migration and Inequality in Germany 1870–1913* (Oxford: Oxford University Press, 2005), 181–252; Keith Tribe, 'Prussian Agriculture – German Politics: Max Weber 1892–97', *Economy and Society* 12 (1983); John A. Perkins, 'The Agricultural Revolution in Germany, 1850–1914', *Journal of European Economic History* 10 (1981).

60   Zimmerman, 'German Alabama in Africa', 1377–8.

obedient and constrained'.[61] Zimmerman likewise shows how racialized thinking forged in the colonies simultaneously subsisted on social experience back in the metropole – in this case, a body of social thought preoccupied with the property relations of eastern Prussian agriculture: 'The concept of the "Negro" buttoned together a number of ideological discourses about race and ethnicity, free labor, and agricultural production in the United States, Africa, and Germany.'[62]

Third, this production of ideas about the 'Negro' in an apparently unimportant Togolese colonial margin shows racialized categories possessing a *contingency*, a *constructedness*, and a *mobility* that belie our assumptions about national peculiarities, allowing us to track their effects into unexpected places. The transnational perspective encourages us not only to follow the genealogies of racialized ideas back and forth across the Atlantic rather than just into the deeper nineteenth-century mists of specifically German time, but also to understand the fallout from the 'colonial effect' inside the German metropole as far more pervasive than older dismissals of Germany's colonial history could allow. As Zimmerman says, the Tuskegee expedition 'stitch[ed] together and thus permanently transform[ed] three powerful networks: German social science, New South race politics, and African cash cropping. At their points of intersection, these three networks produced objects whose apparent stability both conceals and results from a dynamic and transnational history: blackness, peasants, and cotton.'[63]

---

61   This was further linked to a Christian ideal of household structure and family life, and to an economic postulate of the free peasant farmer. On the ground, as Zimmerman compellingly shows, these ideas could only be practised via the most brutal forms of coercion. His account acutely captures this basis of German colonial practice in ideals of family relations and household production linked to a cotton-based economy and *Volkskultur* rooted in 'a patriarchal, monogamous domesticity'. Such a model was predicated on a violent reordering of Togolese social relations. The Germans 'imagined that this [reordering] would result in cultural transformations that would bring the normal bourgeois Christian family to Togo. Indeed, their actions may have revealed an uncomfortable truth about the normal bourgeois Christian family. Germans could call this attempt to radically restructure the Togolese economy *Volkskultur* only because they identified Africans with the imaginary "Negroes" concocted by New South ideologues – inherently pathological agents requiring outside force to become what they purportedly had always, essentially, been' (ibid., 1388).

62   Ibid., 1378.

63   Ibid., 1362–3.

Empire by sea or by land?

Within the commonly agreed 'world-imperial' frame of reference, radical nationalists hotly debated the preferred direction for Germany's interests before 1914. Was this to be *Überseepolitik oder Festlandspolitik?* ('overseas policy or continental policy?'), to invoke a keynote debate at the 1905 Pan-German Congress between the editor of the Essen-based *Rheinisch-Westfälische Zeitung*, Theodor Reismann-Grone, and the former Governor of German East Africa and head of the *Reichsverband gegen die Sozialdemokratie* (Imperial League Against Social Democracy), Eduard von Liebert.[64]

Yet, as Sweeney shows, this public exchange only staged a longer-standing Pan-German debate – one that explicitly refused any such conflict between landward empire and *Weltpolitik*.[65] Under Ernst Hasse's presiding tutelage, that discussion ambitiously reconceived Germany's imperialist future as a new type of complex macropolity or 'imperial formation', whose spatial reach went far beyond unambiguous colonial government of the direct kind. Instead it embraced not only 'blurred genres of rule and partial sovereignties', but also varying modalities of cultural influence and economic penetration, whether inside Europe or in the wider extra-European world.[66] Within a federated European structure linked to variegated global dominion, this empire would combine gradated sovereignties arranged around a dominant German core with integrated economic planning linked to grandiose biopolitical

---

64   See Theodor Reismann-Grone and Eduard von Liebert, 'Überseepolitik oder Festlandspolitik?', *Alldeutsche Flugschriften 22* (Munich: Lehmann, 1905). A charter signatory of the Pan-Germans' founding manifesto in 1891, Reismann-Grone (1863–1949) eventually broke with the leadership around Heinrich Claß during the First World War. After serving several years as general secretary of the Ruhr Mineowners' Association, he devoted himself fulltime to his newspaper, making it a leading organ of pro-industrial and overtly radical nationalist opinion. Backing Hitler from the 1920s, he ended his career after 1933 as the first Nazi mayor of Essen. A career officer of bourgeois provenance, von Liebert (1850–1934) served in the Russian section of the General Staff, became interested in colonies, and was appointed in 1897 governor of German East Africa, before being ennobled and retired in 1900–01. In 1904 he headed the Imperial League in the aftermath of the SPD's success in the 1903 elections, and in 1907 entered the Reichstag as a Free Conservative. An early Pan-German, he joined its national leadership before 1914. He entered the Reichstag as a Nazi in 1928. See Eley, *Reshaping the German Right*, 54–7, 108–11, 229–35; Stefan Frech, *Wegbereiter Hitlers? Theodor Reismann-Grone: Ein völkischer Nationalist (1863–1949)* (Paderborn: Schöningh, 2009); Eduard von Liebert, *Aus einem bewegten Leben: Erinnerungen* (Munich: J. F. Lehmann Verlag, 1925).

65   Sweeney, 'Pan-German Conceptions of Colonial Empire', 270–3.

66   Ann Laura Stoler, 'On Degrees of Imperial Sovereignty', *Public Culture* 18: 1 (2006).

schemes for social engineering and large-scale population transfers. Pan-German visions of a 'Greater Germany' specifically held these European and extra-European logics of imperial policy-making together, binding the prospects for colonial expansion overseas to the securing of Germany's dominance inside the continent at home. If the resulting co-prosperity zone, a 'Greater German Federation', would have to include far more heterogeneous populations, it would still be 'exclusively ruled' by ethnic Germans.[67] For Pan-Germans, European empire-making also presumed an active social policy at home, one profoundly technocratic and hostile to democracy. As Sweeney argues, it was the racialized logic of this emergent biopolitical programme for the management of populations, intensifying on the eve of 1914, that allowed a recognizably fascist conception of the *Volkskörper* ('national body') to form.[68]

Pan-German visions were the most radical of the efforts at imagining, consistently and programmatically, how Germany might take its place among the vaunted 'world empires'. As international tensions escalated towards 1914, others found the simultaneity of overseas and landward expansionism harder to sustain. The government found itself constrained to choose one over the other. The abrupt reversion in 1911–12 to the more orthodox primacy of an army-based armaments policy, after the navy's long dominance ushered in by the call to *Weltpolitik* in 1896, formed the most obvious context for this. The debacle of the second Moroccan Crisis during the summer of 1911, the government's policy-making disarray, and the associated breakthrough of the national opposition (right-wing anti-democratic coalition) combined with Germany's deteriorating trading position and the 1913–14 recession to tarnish the appeal of overseas colonialism and bring *Mitteleuropa* strongly back to the fore. Only further confirmed by the projected drive through the Balkans, Asia Minor, and the Caucasus along the direction of Berlin-Baghdad, the war years then necessarily endorsed those priorities, with the practical effacement of any overseas colonial goals.[69]

---

67   Ernst Hasse, *Großdeutschland und Mitteleuropa um das Jahr 1950* (Berlin: Thormann & Goetsch, 1895), 47 – cited in Sweeney, 'Pan-German Conceptions of Colonial Empire', 269.

68   Sweeney, 'Pan-German Conceptions of Colonial Empire', 278–9.

69   Volker R. Berghahn sees this as a 'Retreat to the European Continent'. See *Germany and the Approach of War in 1914*, 2nd edn (Houndmills: Macmillan, 1993), 136–55, plus the preceding discussion, 97–135. See also Fischer, *War of Illusions*, 71–159, 291–329, 355–69, 439–58.

As I have argued, expansionist policies in Europe and colonialism in the rest of the world contained definite logics of equivalence. It was no accident that an infrastructure was being created for internal colonization of eastern Prussia's Polish enclaves just as the 1884 Congress of Berlin laid the foundations for Germany's overseas empire. In the event, the Prussian Settlement Commission cemented Polish solidarities as much as it promoted the German presence.[70] Yet this self-defeating quality of the Germanization measures mattered less than the radical nationalist ambitions they incited or the German–Polish tensions they inflamed. Lack of success diminished neither their place in the colonizing imagination nor their cumulative relation to the more determined policies applied against occupied Poland and the Baltic during 1914–18. Nor was the scale negligible: the 120,000 German-speakers settled in the eastern provinces before 1914 exceeded by five times the aggregate numbers who settled in colonies overseas.[71]

There remained distinctions. In projecting eastern mastery, German nationalists did not remotely approach the mass killing and other colonial violence all too prevalent on African land. In that sense, the genocidal ruthlessness of Nazi expansion certainly presupposed the brutalizations of 1914–18. But the character of Germany's impact on the extra-European world was actually no less heterogeneous: German migrants to the south of Brazil, German commercial representatives in Chile and Venezuela, and German consular officials in the Ottoman Empire comported themselves very differently from German settlers in south-west Africa or German administrators in Dar-es-Salaam. Once we broaden our perspective beyond the colonial empire per se, we can see how easily Polish policy fits into the larger repertoire of practice associated with the pre-1914 colonial ordering of the world. Those practices included settlement policies and property regimes; regional planning and infrastructural investment; the dynamics of labour markets and 'education for labour'; schooling and language policies; family relations, sexuality, and miscegenation; and, finally, all the

---

70   See Scott M. Eddie, 'The Prussian Settlement Commission and the Activities in the Land Market, 1886–1918', in Nelson, *Germans, Poland, and Colonial Expansion to the East*; Hagen, *Germans, Poles, and Jews*, 159–287; Richard Blanke, *Prussian Poland and the German Empire 1871–1900* (New York: Columbia University Press, 1981).

71   A point made by Sebastian Conrad, *Deutsche Kolonialgeschichte* (Munich: C. H. Beck, 2012), 98.

discursive machinery associated with the construction and elaboration of colonial hierarchy and difference.[72] It is precisely when anti-Polish policies are viewed in this way that the relevance of the Pan-Germans' racialized biopolitical ambitions becomes most apparent.

What else was at stake in the couplet opposing 'overseas Policy' with 'continental policy'? In what precise ways might the overseas colonial contexts of 'Germanness' before 1914 and the eastern European territories into which Germany expanded during 1915–18 be given equivalence? How should we think about this comparison? Whereas German nationalist ideas of the eastern frontier grew from deeply embedded antagonisms going back several centuries, after all, the dynamics of African colonialism involved more novel encounters with foreignness. But the congruence and reciprocities have recently been prompting attention. The possibilities only increase as treatments of the 'racial state' and 'racialization' under Nazism get pushed back into the *Kaiserreich*. Approaching such questions from each of the respective 'peripheries', recent works by Paul Weindling and Pascal Grosse seek to recast the interrelations between race, science, public health, eugenics, social engineering, and the larger complex of modernizing reform before 1914.[73] Similarly, the most recent debates over Nazi 'modernity' have unsettling implications for how we approach questions of planning, technology, population, and national efficiency in the earlier period – not only in Germany itself

---

72 Ibid., 100. In the radicalizing of German nationalism against the Poles from the early 1900s, we can see a cumulative realization of Steinmetz's definition, in which colonialism required the ruthless abrogation of Polish rights: 'The core of colonial policy is an image of the native's essential distance from, or proximity to, the culture of the colonizer. Colonial policy organizes its stabilizing projects around this image of the sociocultural essence of the colonized. Native policy can thus be defined as an attempt to lock the colonized into a single, stable position somewhere along a spectrum ranging from absolute difference to absolute identity, but not encompassing either of those extremes. Complete identity, or genuine assimilation, was incompatible with the rule of colonial difference.' By 1914, as far as the Polish east was concerned, Pan-Germans had crossed the Rubicon of the colonial wish. By 1915, as the annexationist logic of the war aims unfolded, government had joined them. See Steinmetz, '"Devil's Handwriting"', 47.

73 Paul Weindling, *Epidemics and Genocide in Eastern Europe, 1890–1945* (Oxford: Oxford University Press, 2000); Pascal Grosse, *Kolonialismus, Eugenik und bürgerliche Gesellschaft in Deutschland 1850–1918* (Frankfurt: Campus, 2000). See also Lenny Urena Valerio, *Colonial Fantasies, Imperial Realities: Race Science and the Making of Polishness on the Fringes of the German Empire, 1840–1920* (Athens, OH: Ohio University Press, 2021); Nelson, *Germans, Poland, and Colonial Expansion to the East*; Kristin Kopp, 'Constructing Racial Difference in Colonial Poland', in *Germany's Colonial Pasts*, ed. Eric Ames, Marcia Klotz, and Lora Wildenthal (Lincoln, NE: University of Nebraska Press, 2005).

but also with respect to the developmentalist futures projected into the colonial sphere.[74]

How far does it make sense to consider the eastern territories as a *colonial* frontier in these ways? Should we think of the eastern borderlands and the overseas colonies on a plane of equivalence, or do the specificities undermine the usefulness of that comparison? How far should the period between the 1880s and the 1940s be treated as a single entity in this regard? Is there a single chain of equivalence linking, first, the ideologies of overseas settlement and colonization feeding from the 1880s into the later radical nationalism of the Wilhelmine Pan-Germans; second, the colonization and settlement projects invented for the occupied east during 1915–18; and third, the further radicalization of such thinking about the east under the Third Reich? How do we position the experience of the First World War in this overall story? Is there a coherent strand of continuity tying languages of racialization under the Third Reich into the earlier race thinking of the *Kaiserreich*, or are the breaks and disjunctures more decisive?

Social imperialism once more?

Is there a case for revisiting the explanatory usefulness of Wehler's 'social imperialism' thesis of thirty years ago? In that argument the drive for overseas empire was connected to the desire to contain or divert social and political tensions at home.[75] But Wehler focused on the manipulative and directly propagandistic aspects of colonialism and other nationalist enthusiasms from a specifically governmental point of view; only recently have historians turned to its wider cultural effects. Via many complicated fields of indebtedness, we now appreciate, forms of social relations, patterns of culture, and increasingly racialized

---

74 See especially Bradley Naranch, "'Colonized Body', 'Oriental Machine'": Debating Race, Railroads, and the Politics of Reconstruction in Germany and East Africa, 1906–1910', *Central European History* 33: 3 (2000); Juhani Koponen, *Development for Exploitation: German Colonial Policies in Mainland Tanzania, 1884–1914* (Helsinki/Hamburg: Lit Verlag, 1995); Thaddeus Sunseri, *Vilimani: Labor Migration and Rural Change in Early Colonial Tanzania* (Portsmouth: Heinemann, 2002); Dirk van Laak, *Imperiale Infrastruktur: Deustche Planungen für eine Erschließung Afrikas 1880 bis 1960* (Paderborn: Schöningh, 2004); Zimmerman, '"What Do You Really Want in German East Africa Herr Professor?" Counterinsurgency and the Science Effect in Colonial Tanzania', *Comparative Studies in Society and History* 48: 2 (2006), 'A German Alabama in Africa'.

75 See Wehler, 'Bismarck's Imperialism'; Wehler, 'Industrial Growth and Early German Imperialism'; Eley, 'Defining Social Imperialism' and 'Social Imperialism'.

discourses of national superiority fashioned in the colonies came to be powerfully reinserted into the metropolitan social world. Forms of colonial representation in literature, museums and exhibitions, commercial entertainments, marketing and advertisements, and the widest domain of popular culture all now come into view.[76] The re-gendering of national identity in this period also acquired colonial dimensions.[77]

We now see more clearly the relays back and forth between the colonial worlds and the German metropole. Diverse categories of German-speakers came to define themselves – their 'German-ness' in its social and cultural dimensions, their claims to citizenship, their access to varieties of personhood – through representations of the wider-than-German overseas world, as those ideas circulated ever more profusely through the commodified and mass-mediated public spheres of the new German state. It was more these discursive materials that assembled the real ground of 'social imperialism', and less the conscious manipulations Wehler ascribed to governing elites. More insidious ideological restructuration was at work, reorientating nationalist assumptions in manifold ways. Yet, while many such relays exactly correspond to the connectedness addressed by Wehler – the relationship between domestic prosperity and overseas expansion, or the political proceeds of artfully mobilized popular nationalism, or the propaganda value of foreign adventures and diplomatic coups, or the unifying feedback of patriotic rhetorics on popular opinion – any interest in 'social imperialism' per se has disappeared.[78]

---

76   See David Ciarlo, 'Mass-Marketing the Empire: Colonial Fantasies and Advertising Visions', Jeff Bowersox, 'Classroom Colonialism – Race, Pedagogy, and Patriotism in Imperial Germany', and Brett van Hoesen, 'The Rhineland Controversy and Weimer Postcolonialism', all in Naranch and Eley, *German Colonialism in a Global Age*. See also Ciarlo, *Advertising Empire: Race and Visual Culture in Imperial Germany* (Cambridge, MA: Harvard University Press, 2011); John Phillip Short, *Magic Lantern Empire: Colonialism and Society in Germany* (Ithaca, NY: Cornell University Press, 2012); Langbehn, *German Colonialism, Visual Culture, and Modern Memory*.

77   See Lora Wildenthal, '"She Is the Victor": Bourgeois Women, Nationalist Identities, and the Ideal of the Independent Woman Farmer in German Southwest Africa', in *Society, Culture, and the State in Germany, 1870–1930*, ed. Geoff Eley (Ann Arbor, MI: University of Michigan Press, 1996), and her important book *German Women for Empire 1884–1945* (Ann Arbor, MI: University of Michigan Press, 2001). See also Ann Laura Stoler, 'Sexual Affronts and Racial Frontiers: European Identities and the Cultural Politics of Exclusion in Colonial Southeast Asia', in *Becoming National: A Reader*, ed. Geoff Eley and Ronald Grigor Suny (New York: Oxford University Press, 1996).

78   As a concept, 'social imperialism' appears nowhere in the new works on German imperialism.

Irrespective of the *term* 'social imperialism', however, we surely need some means of theorizing the long-term domestic consequences of empire – everything generated from the colonial encounter that became assimilated into the metropolitan society's self-understanding with sufficiently potent and pervasive continuity to have helped the later implanting of the 'racial state'. These discursive consequences of empire included not just formal ideas and easily recognizable prejudices about the colonial world. They worked through insidiously internalized, culturally perduring patterns of belief. Such patterns embraced many transferential conflations from overseas colonial populations to colonized territories inside Europe itself, as well as all the racialized systems of distinction, both sophisticated and crude, defining Germans against their 'others'. Inside metropolitan social life were produced particular elements of political subjectivity complexly structured around ideas of the colony, forming a metropolitan version of the 'colonial effect'. By this I mean the sum of the transference and translation of complex and heterogeneous knowledge; idioms of thought; direct and vicarious experiences; spectacular events; arresting and seductive images; compelling arguments about economics, prosperity, and global survival; a visual repertoire of fantasy and desire; manifold forms of everyday consumption; and all the relevant registers of governmentality – in other words, the aggregative, adaptable, and coherent discursive presence we call *colonialism*, whose availability for deployment in the domestic arenas of politics then enabled the production of active forms of political agency and particular active effects.[79]

~

Any firm and fast distinction between colonizing expansionism overseas and landward colonialism inside Europe seems hard to sustain. Colonialism, in established usage, begins from the seizure and settlement of lands or trading posts and coaling stations overseas, joined to exploitation of resources and people, in a framework of imperial rule and political dispossession. Most working definitions stress destruction of indigenous social relations; imposition of the colonizers' own systems of law, economy, and political rule; denial of rights of all kinds, whether in the form of citizenship, protections under law, and the franchise, or

---

79   See Chapter 8 above.

human dignity and access to livelihood; and finally, of course, the exercise of coercion and violence embracing extremes of mass incarceration, mass killing, and ultimately genocide. Racialized forms of the overseas colonial encounter come next, with their obsessiveness about skin colour and the dangers of race mixing, practices of exoticizing, logics of 'othering', and the essentializing of human differences. That describes colonial rule during the period of intensified imperialist competition between the industrializing countries before 1914. Yet it likewise offers a compelling inventory of everything the Nazis pursued in the east after 1939. These planes of equivalence between colonialism overseas and twentieth-century expansionism inside Europe itself are too clear to ignore.

Scholars such as Jürgen Zimmerer, from the overseas vantage-point before 1914, and Wendy Lower, writing on the 1940s, have convincingly thought these histories together.[80] That need not require us to posit oversimplified causal or explanatory continuities from one to the other, whether biographically, ideologically, or in some other way. Birthe Kundrus writes instead about specific 'chains of influence, transfers, and situational parallels', treating earlier colonial histories as a future reservoir of models and policies, ideas and attitudes, dreams and fantasies, usable practices, modalities of planning, and available blueprints, including those paths *not* to be followed.[81] Nazi expansionism also had its own terrible specificities, never subsumable within such larger-scale frameworks. But the basic case for placing Nazi empire inside a framework of colonialism, whether in the abstract or for purposes of comparison, seems uncontroversial.

If structures of rule, systems of exploitation, and patterns of expansionism allow colonialism to be historicized across varying contexts of *Kaiserreich* and Third Reich, so too does 'civilizationism': the claim to

---

80   See Jürgen Zimmerer, 'The Birth of the "Ostland" out of the Spirit of Colonialism: A Postcolonial Perspective on Nazi Policy of Conquest and Extermination', *Patterns of Prejudice* 39: 2 (June 2005), and 'Colonialism and the Holocaust: Towards an Archaeology of Genocide', in *Genocide and Settler Society: Frontier Violence and Stolen Indigenous Children in Australian History*, ed. A. Dirk Moses (New York: Berghahn, 2004); Wendy Lower, *Nazi Empire-Building and the Holocaust in Ukraine* (Chapel Hill, NC: University of North Carolina Press, 2005). See also David Furber, 'Near as Far in the Colonies: The Nazi Occupation of Poland', *International History Review* 26: 3 (2004); Pascal Grosse, 'What Does German Colonialism Have to Do with National Socialism?', in Ames, Klotz, Wildenthal, *Germany's Colonial Pasts*.

81   Birthe Kundrus, 'Kontinuitäten, Parallelen, Rezeptionen. Überlegungen zur Kolonialisierung des Nationalsozialismus', *WerkstattGeschichte* 43 (2006).

German national superiority based in the empowerment of science and reason, the compulsion to bring progress to the non-European peoples, and the projection outward of a German national mission.[82] In the two arenas of overseas colonialism and Nazi empire in the east, cultural dominion over the foreign elsewhere converged. Again, theorizing these affinities in an overarching framework of colonialism implies no simplified and linear causal chains.

Finally, each of these concluding propositions – the meaningful equivalence linking colonialism overseas and landward expansionism; the commonalties binding Nazi expansionism and pre-1914 colonialism; the convergence of 'civilizationist' ideologies – suggests an argument running throughout this discussion. In recovering the genealogies of Nazism, it is to the connective dynamics of the period between the 1890s and the 1930s that we should turn.

---

82 Marcia Klotz, 'Global Visions: From the Colonial to the National Socialist World', *European Studies Journal* 16 (1999), and 'The Weimar Republic: A Postcolonial State in a Still-Colonial World', in Ames, Klotz, and Wildenthal, *Germany's Colonial Pasts*.

10

Historicizing the Global, Politicizing Capital: Giving the Present a Name

Politics in Command

First, a simple quotation, from a proclamation issued to the people of Baghdad: 'Our armies do not come into your cities and lands as conquerors, but as liberators.'[1] These words were spoken by British commander Lieutenant-General Stanley Maude on the occasion of the military occupation of Baghdad in March 1917. They were mirrored almost exactly by the address to British troops on the eve of the more recent invasion in 2003 by Lieutenant-Colonel Tim Collins, who said: 'We go to liberate, not to conquer.' The mirroring of these two stories does not end there. Within three years of Maude's proclamation, 10,000 had died in an Iraqi uprising against the British rulers, who gassed and bombed the insurgents. It was likewise entirely predictable that a new military occupation of Iraq would face determined guerrilla resistance long after

1   These thoughts began in conferences on globalization at the University of Nevada, Reno (April 2006), and the Institute for the Transnational History of the Americas in Tepoztlán, Mexico (late July–early August 2006). I am indebted to audiences and colleagues on those occasions, along with the following: Charles Bright, Vinayak Chaturvedi, Jessica Dubow, Dennis Dworkin, Julia Hell, Young-son Hong, Jennifer Jenkins, Paul Kramer, Gina Morantz-Sanchez, Dirk Moses, Ken Pomerantz, Moishe Postone, Carolyn Steedman, George Steinmetz, Ron Suny, Dennis Sweeney, Charles Tshimanga-Kashama, and Jeff Wasserstrom. Jessica Dubow got me started with the overarching arguments. Carolyn Steedman inspired me to think differently about the histories of capitalism and working-class formation. Young-sun Hong and Dennis Sweeney supplied especially careful readings.

Saddam Hussein had gone. In 2003 the British military headquarters in Baghdad's Green Zone was named 'Maude House'.[2]

'History' not only casts the current geopolitical catastrophe of the Middle East and Central Asia into a necessary longer context of colonialism, military pacification, improvised state formation, and anticolonial insurgency. It was also constantly called into service by the architects of recent US and British policies in the region to explain their decision to invade. I am thinking here not so much of the debased comparisons of Saddam Hussein and his dictatorship with Hitler and the Third Reich, nor the associated loose analogies with the processes of economic and political reconstruction in Europe after the Second World War. I want to consider instead the larger historical rationales powering the two principal and partially competing visions of a 'new world order' that underpinned the recent US and British intervention in the Middle East.

The first is the British government's more 'liberal' version, along with its wider chorus of support. The latter ranged from mavericks like Christopher Hitchens to human-rights pundits like Michael Ignatieff and more equivocating circles of public intellectuals, who accepted the rationale for regime change without quite bringing themselves to endorse the Bush administration. In its advocates' common rhetoric, this standpoint was a 'new internationalism' or a 'new doctrine of humanitarian intervention', what Tony Blair called in February 2003 a necessary redefinition of 'centre-left politics to cope with a more insecure world'.[3] This view postulated a cooperative international system. Among practitioners, one of the most influential was British diplomat Robert Cooper (director-general for external and politico-military affairs at the EU), who presented it in an essay on 'The Post-Modern State' in a 2002

---

2   For 'The Proclamation of Baghdad', issued to the city on 19 March 1917 by Lt. Gen. Sir Stanley Maude on the occasion of the British military occupation, see harpers.org, May 2003. Lt. Col. Tim Collins was commanding officer of the 1st Battalion, Royal Irish Regiment of the British Army. For his speech, see 'UK Troops Told: Be Just and Strong', news.bbc.co.uk, 20 March 2003.

3   Tony Blair, 'The Left Should Not Weep if Saddam Is Toppled', carried the subtitle 'We have to redefine Centre-Left politics to cope with a more insecure world', *Guardian*, 10 February 2003. See also the interview reported in Jackie Ashley, 'No Moving a Prime Minister Whose Mind Is Made Up', *Guardian*, 1 March 2003. For Michael Ignatieff, see his 'Human Rights as Politics', in *Human Rights as Politics and Idolatry*, ed. Amy Gutmann (Princeton: Princeton University Press, 2001), and, in elegantly equivocating mode, 'Empire Lite', *Prospect* 83 (February 2003). See also Michael Walzer, *Arguing About War* (New Haven, CT: Yale University Press, 2004).

volume from the Foreign Policy Centre.[4] Its arguments presuppose a
large historical claim about the distinctive international order left by the
Soviet Union's collapse at the end of the Cold War; they are linked to
concepts of 'failed' or 'collapsed' states; they redeploy liberal-imperialist
rhetorics of the civilizing mission; and they urge advanced actors like the
United States and the EU to rise to the occasion by accepting 'their
responsibilities in the world'. These are the concluding paragraphs:

> The post-modern EU offers a vision of cooperative empire, a common
> liberty and a common security without the ethnic domination and
> centralised absolutism to which past empires have been subject, but
> also without the ethnic exclusiveness that is the hallmark of the nation
> state – inappropriate in an era without borders and unworkable in
> regions such as the Balkans. A cooperative empire might be the
> domestic political framework that best matches the altered substance
> of the post-modern state: a framework in which each has a share in
> the government, in which no single country dominates and in which
> the governing principles are not ethnic but legal. The lightest of
> touches will be required from the centre; the 'imperial bureaucracy'
> must be under control, accountable, and the servant, not the master,
> of the commonwealth. Such an institution must be as dedicated to
> liberty and democracy as its constituent parts. Like Rome, this
> commonwealth would provide its citizens with some of its laws, some
> coins and the occasional road.
>
> That perhaps is the vision. Can it be realized? Only time will tell.
> The question is how much time there may be. In the modern world
> the secret race to acquire nuclear weapons goes on. In the premodern
> world the interests of organised crime – including international
> terrorism – grow greater and faster than the state. There may not be
> much time left.[5]

---

4   Mark Leonard, ed., *Reordering the World: The Long-Term Implications of September 11*
(London: Foreign Policy Centre, 2002). The Foreign Policy Centre was launched by Tony
Blair and Robin Cook in 1998 to develop a 'vision of a fair and rule-based world order'. See
fpc.org.uk. An extract from Robert Cooper's essay appeared in the print edition of the
Observer, 7 April 2002, but the full text may be accessed as 'The New Liberal Imperialism' at
observer.guardian.co.uk. For Robert Cooper, see also *The Post-Modern State and the World
Order* (London: Demos, 2000), *The Breaking of Nations: Order and Chaos in the Twenty-First
Century* (New York: Grove, 2003), and 'Grand Strategy', *Prospect* 81 (December 2002).
5   Cooper, 'New Liberal Imperialism'.

The second vision of new world order was the one motivating the Bush administration in the United States. Explicitly inspired by the new global circumstances of the end of the Cold War, its advocates asserted from the beginning a unique opportunity for the United States as the sole remaining superpower, which it would be irresponsible to forgo. In contrast to the Blair version, this has always been avowedly unilateralist, extending from non-ratification of the Kyoto accords, through rejection of the International Criminal Court and withdrawal from international nuclear agreements to general disregard for the United Nations. In one of its main statements, the 2002 National Security Strategy report rejected older policies of deterrence, containment, and collective security, asserting instead the principles of offensive military intervention, pre-emptive first strikes, and proactive counter-proliferation measures against rogue states and other enemies. As George W. Bush stated in presenting this strategy document, 'The only path to peace and security is the path of action.'[6] As a new grand design, it was presaged in the Defence Policy Guidance document written in 1992 by Paul Wolfowitz (later deputy secretary of defense) and I. Lewis Libby (later Vice-President Dick Cheney's chief of staff). It was expounded in great detail in the Report on *Rebuilding America's Defences: Strategy, Forces, and Resources for a New Century* issued by the Project for a New American Century (PNAC) in advance of the 2000 presidential elections.[7]

That report's authors, whose signatories included Wolfowitz, Libby, Cheney, Donald Rumsfeld, Richard Perle, Zalmay Khalilzad, and Jeb Bush, embraced US mastery of the globe for the coming age. They spoke of 'full spectrum dominance', meaning American invincibility in every field of warfare (land, sea, air, and space) in a world where no two nations' relationship with each other would trump their relationship with the United States. There should be no place on earth, or the

---

6 See *The National Security Strategy of the United States* (Washington, DC: White House/United States Government, 2002).

7 Chaired by William Kristol, PNAC was established in Washington, DC, in spring 1997 under aegis of the New Citizenship Project as 'a non-profit, educational organization whose goal is to promote American global leadership'. Its report, *Rebuilding America's Defenses* (principal author Thomas Donnelly), was released in September 2000. For the 1992 Defense Policy Guidance document, see Barton Gellman, 'Keeping the US First: Pentagon Would Preclude a Rival Superpower', *Washington Post*, 11 March 1992, A1. See especially Tom Barry, 'Rise and Demise of the New American Century', *International Relations Center Special Report*, 28 June 2006.

heavens for that matter, where Washington's writ did not run supreme. To that end, a ring of US military bases would surround China, the latter's containment being the proximate goal and its liberation the ultimate prize.

What should we make of this body of thought?[8] First, there is unmistakeable continuity between this pre-2000 policy discussion and what the Bush administration actually did. This overall coherence of the programmatic discourse emanating from the dense constellation of policy institutes, think tanks, research foundations, advisory committees, lobbying networks, journals, and other organs of opinion ringing the Bush administration was palpable. Whatever the precise relationship to big oil and other corporate interests, or to the new techno-military complex of defence industries in the privatized contract economy, the direct lobbying was far less vital than the larger strategic vision binding this all together.[9] In that Eldorado dream-world of full-scale global integration, the post–Cold War hubris of wanting to be the benign hegemon worked harmoniously with the dogma of untrammelled free-market capitalism and the self-serving rhetoric of supposedly expanding democracy. The geopolitical remaking of the whole of the Middle East and Central Asia was crucial not only in its immediate terms, but also for the longer-term containment of China. Responding to Brent Scowcroft's warnings that a war against Iraq could 'turn the whole region into a cauldron', Michael Ledeen countered in August 2002 with exactly that goal:

> One can only hope that we turn the region into a cauldron, and faster, please. If ever there were a region that richly deserved being cauldronized, it is the Middle East today. If we wage the war effectively, we will bring down the terror regimes in Iraq, Iran, and Syria, and either bring down the Saudi monarchy or force it to abandon its global assembly line to indoctrinate young terrorists. That's our mission in the war against terror.[10]

---

8   For greater detail, see George Steinmetz, 'The State of Emergency and the Revival of American Imperialism: Toward an Authoritarian Post-Fordism', *Public Culture* 15: 2 (2003); Perry Anderson, 'Casuistries of Peace and War', *London Review of Books*, 6 March 2003, 12.

9   This argument is brilliantly developed in RETORT (Iain Boal, T. J. Clark, Joseph Matthews, and Michael Watts), *Afflicted Powers: Capital and Spectacle in a New Age of War* (London: Verso, 2005) – esp. Chapter 2, 'Blood for Oil?'.

10   Michael Ledeen, 'Scowcroft Strikes Out', *National Review*, 6 August 2002.

'Change toward democratic regimes in Tehran and Baghdad would unleash a tsunami across the Islamic world', claimed Joshua Muravchik that same month.[11] On 4 September 2002, Ledeen called on the United States to launch 'a vast democratic revolution to liberate all the peoples of the Middle East . . . It is impossible to imagine that the Iranian people would tolerate tyranny in their own country once freedom had come to Iraq. Syria would follow in short order.'[12] Or, as one enthusiast for *Rebuilding America's Defences* concisely put it: 'After Baghdad, Beijing.'[13]

Second, we can only grasp the import of globalization if we situate it within one authorizing political framework or another.[14] The current languages and processes of 'globalization' are not legible outside their specific relations to a variety of political projects, whose coherence and genealogies need to be carefully reconstructed. Among radical commentators of the past two decades, globalization claims have prompted many diverse reactions. Some are avowedly 'for' or 'against' the 'new global order'. Others take 'globality' as the increasingly universal ground, the given or 'objective' historical circumstances, from which political thinking will now have to begin. Among the more abstractly affirmative defenders of globalization as a new master-concept have been Anthony Giddens, Zygmunt Bauman, Ulrich Beck, and David Held. Joining them are the sociologists of particular 'globalizing' phenomena like migration, diasporas, 'global cities', borderlands, transnational social movements and forms of politics, cross-border networks and regions, new electronic media and their consequences, and the vaunted emergence of a 'global civil society'. Qualified critics of the excessive neoliberalism of globalization in its current form, and advocates of greater degrees of international regulation, include Joseph Stiglitz and George Soros. Among globalization's more fundamental root-and-branch critics, we can separate those like David Harvey, who accept its demonstrated actuality, from those who remain sceptical in principle about the

11 Joshua Muravchik, 'Democracy's Quiet Victory', *New York Times*, 19 August 2002.

12 Michael Ledeen, 'The War on Terror Won't End in Baghdad', *Wall Street Journal*, 4 September 2002.

13 Unnamed PNAC source, quoted by Jonathan Freedland, 'Decisions, Decisions', *Guardian*, 26 February 2003. The best access to biographies and standing of Ledeen, Muravchik, and other right-wing intellectuals around the Bush administration's inner edges is via the website of the American Enterprise Institute, at aei.org/scholars, and cognate websites and available links.

14 See Steinmetz, 'State of Emergency'.

novelties it involves, such as Immanuel Wallerstein and Fred Cooper. Beyond them all lies the spectrum of downright adversarial rejectionism associated with parts of the anti-globalization movement.[15]

Here, we can distinguish between globalization as a category of ordinary language, or a descriptive term in 'plain speech', and globalization as a category of analysis, which aims to capture the specificities of change in the actually existing worlds of capitalism and their social formations at the turn of the twenty-first century. On one side are the late-twentieth-century intellectual histories shaping this particular way of conceptualizing contemporary change; on the other are the unfolding histories – economic, sociological, cultural, institutional, political – to which it brings both coherence and further impetus. In that sense, 'globalization' is both symptom (as the language generated around a particular set of powerful contemporary histories) and diagnosis (as the processes requiring description). Contemporary change both constructs globalization talk and is further constructed by it.

So, we are dealing with that familiar dialectical reciprocity between, on the one hand, the purchase of a particular language of social understanding as it circulates through the public sphere, and, on the other hand, the actually existing phenomena, events, and transformations such language purports to describe and explain. In other words, 'globalization' as a socioeconomic, cultural, and political postulate (as a set of powerful claims about changes in the existing world) is just as crucial to the process of globalization as its existence as a demonstrable social fact

---

15   See Anthony Giddens, *Runaway World: How Globalization Is Reshaping Our Lives*, 2nd edn (New York: Routledge, 2003); Will Hutton and Anthony Giddens, *Global Capitalism* (New York: New Press, 2000); Zygmunt Bauman, *Globalization: The Human Consequences* (New York: Columbia University Press, 1998) and *Wasted Lives: Modernity and Its Outcasts* (Cambridge: Polity, 2003); Ulrich Beck, *What Is Globalization?* (Cambridge: Polity, 1999) and *World Risk Society* (Cambridge: Polity, 1999); David Held, Anthony McGrew, David Goldblatt, and Jonathan Perraton, *Global Transformations: Politics, Economics, and Culture* (Cambridge: Polity, 1999); George Soros, *The Crisis of Global Capitalism: Open Society Endangered* (New York: Public Affairs, 1998); Joseph E. Stiglitz, *Globalization and Its Discontents* (New York: Norton, 2003) and *Making Globalization Work* (New York: Norton, 2006); David Harvey, *The New Imperialism* (Oxford: Oxford University Press, 2003) and *Spaces of Global Capitalism: Towards a Theory of Uneven Geographical Development* (London: Verso, 2006); Frederick Cooper, 'Globalization', in *Colonialism in Question: Theory, Knowledge, History* (Berkeley, CA: University of California Press, 2005); Immanuel Wallerstein, *The Decline of American Power: The US in a Chaotic World* (New York: New Press, 2003). For the full breadth of debate, see Anthony Barnett, David Held, and Caspar Henderson, eds, *Debating Globalization* (Cambridge: Polity Press/openDemocracy, 2005).

(the supposed structural primacy of global integration). The *ideology* or *discourse of globalization* is, arguably, a better starting point for analysis than either economics or sociology in the structural or materialist sense, because it is at this discursive level that the operative purchase of globalization on public understanding has been constituted and secured. That includes the terms under which ideas and policies are admitted into its frame. Who gets to speak in its languages? Who gets to set the dominant tone? By the 'ideology or discourse of globalization' I mean both the insistence on globalization as the organizing reality of the emerging international order and the crystallizing of specific practices, policies, and institutions around that insistence. In other words, the history of globalization has become inseparable from the history of the category. Globalization has emerged during the past quarter-century as a set of discursive claims about the international world seeking aggressively to reorder that world in terms of itself.[16]

Locating the Difference of the Present

This is the import of 'historicizing the global'. Among many of its critics, globalization remains a highly disputed term, given its annoying lack of historical specificity and frequently inflated claims about the radical novelty of the present. For critics like Paul Hirst and Grahame Thompson, the world economy is far less completely integrated today than true-believing globalists would claim. Indeed, by some measures it falls

---

16 Globalization now covers a bewildering profusion of relevant literatures from wildly diverse disciplines and public sources, some of which (in sociology, economics, anthropology, communications, literature, history, cultural studies, and postcolonial studies) barely worry about one another's existence. One key starting point is now Ania Loomba, Suvir Kaul, Matti Bunzl, Antoinette Burton, and Jedd Esty, eds, *Postcolonial Studies and Beyond* (Durham: Duke University Press, 2005). The following have especially shaped my thinking: Roger Rouse, 'Mexican Migration and the Social Space of Postmodernism', *Diaspora* 1 (1991); Stuart Hall, 'When Was the "Postcolonial"? Thinking at the Limit', in *The Post-Colonial Question: Common Skies, Divided Horizons*, ed. Iain Chambers and Lidia Curti (New York: Routledge, 1996); Fredric Jameson and Masao Miyoshi, *The Cultures of Globalization* (Durham: Duke University Press, 1998); Pheng Cheah and Bruce Robbins, eds, *Cosmopolitics: Thinking and Feeling Beyond the Nation* (Minneapolis: University of Minnesota Press, 1998); Fernando Coronil, 'Beyond Occidentalism: Towards Non-Imperial Geohistorical Categories', *Current Anthropology* 1 (1996), and 'Towards a Critique of Globalcentrism: Speculations on Capitalism's Nature', *Public Culture* 12: 2 (2000); Saskia Sassen, 'Spatialities and Temporalities of the Global: Elements for a Theorization', *Public Culture* 12: 1 (2000).

well behind the degree of integration before 1914. By some key indi-
cators, the scale and pace of pre-1914 change were strikingly more
impressive – as measured by the degree of integration of world capital
markets, the interdependence of national and regional economies, the
expansion of international trade, and the scale of transnational and
intercontinental labour migrations.[17] Other sceptics make the argument of 'Nothing New Under the Sun'. There is no shortage of voices
among historians of colonialism, slavery, and capitalism's creation of the
world economy, for whom globalism has been a constant for a very long
time. Recent international actions, with their confusing mélange of
self-interested, altruistic, and aggrandizing rationalizations, are hardly
a surprise to historians of decolonization, of the high imperialism before
1914, of the nineteenth-century civilizing mission, or of 1492. Marxists
have long studied global capital flows and their social and political
effects, which free capacities for progress only in the most contradictory
and rebarbative of ways. If we are all global now, these critics aver, we
need far more precise analytics to clarify what exactly that condition
might mean. We need better means of specifying the originality of the
present.[18]

Fred Cooper, in particular, pours withering scepticism on 'globalization' as a useful category of analysis. If we concede the longevity and
depth of the processes involved by taking globalization to mean 'the
progressive integration of different parts of the world into a singular
whole' going back to the fifteenth century, he insists, then 'the argument
falls victim to linearity and teleology'. If we argue that 'the global age is
now' by sharply separating it from any deeper past, then the concept of
'the global' ceases to distinguish the present from earlier periods in that
sense. 'Communications revolutions, capital movements, and regulatory
apparatuses all need to be studied and their relationships, mutually

---

17   See Paul Hirst and Grahame Thompson, *Globalization in Question: The International
Economy and the Possibilities of Governance*, 2nd edn (Cambridge: Polity, 1999); Paul
Hirst, 'The Global Economy: Myths and Realities', *International Affairs* 73 (1997); Kevin H.
O'Rourke and Jeffrey G. Williamson, *Globalization and History: The Evolution of a Nine-
teenth-Century Atlantic Economy* (Cambridge, MA: Harvard University Press, 1999); Paul
Bairoch, 'Globalization Myths and Realities: One Century of External Trade and Foreign
Investment', in *States against Markets: The Limits of Globalization*, ed. Robert Boyer and
Daniel Drache (London: Routledge, 1996).

18   For some thoughts on periodization, emphasizing early nineteenth century and early
modern contexts of global integration, see Adam McKeown, 'Periodizing Globalization',
History Workshop Journal 63 (Spring 2007).

reinforcing or contradictory, explored', but the language of 'globalization' badly oversimplifies the tasks of analysing 'the variety and
specificity of cross-territorial connecting mechanisms in past and
present'. In Cooper's view, 'From the sixteenth-century slave trade
through the nineteenth-century period of imperialism in the name of
emancipation, the interrelation of different parts of the world was essential to the histories of each part of it. But the mechanisms of interrelation
were contingent and limited in their transformative capacity – as they
still are.' But if that earlier 'Atlantic system' was not systemic enough to
be called 'an eighteenth-century "globalization"', then nor, in its own
ways, is the early-twenty-first-century present. Each needs a more
exactly constructed analytical term than the simplifying rhetorics of
'globalization' can provide. What we need, Cooper argues, is 'precision
in specifying how such commodity circuits are constituted, how connections across space are extended and bounded, and how large-scale,
long-term processes, such as capitalist development, can be analyzed
with due attention to their power, their limitations, and the mechanisms
that shape them'.[19]

If much globalization talk lacks specificity of 'depth' in Cooper's
sense, then it also flattens out geographical unevenness. The most facile
versions accept the programmatic advocacy of global integration
straightforwardly on its own terms. On the one hand, they flatly presume
neoliberalism's 'powerful cultural and economic ideology of the world
market as naturally operating within neoliberal terms, which will try to
enforce one world with one cultural framework of reference, one pattern
of consumption, without significant cultural differences'.[20] Such versions presume an overriding logic to the contemporary functioning of
the world economy, to which no viable alternative may be posed. To the
degree that particular states, regions, or economies drop out of the
frame, they become emptied of significance as 'failed' or 'collapsed'
cases. On the other hand, these versions efface the *political* centrality
for the ascendant market order of an elaborate and usually coercive

---

19 Cooper, *Colonialism in Question*, 111, 110, 104. For globalization's deeper history in
the long nineteenth century, emphasizing the role of 'great accelerations', see Christopher A.
Bayly, *The Birth of the Modern World 1780–1914: Global Connections and Comparisons*
(Oxford: Blackwell, 2004), esp. 'Conclusion: The Great Acceleration, c.1890–1914'.
20 Roy Boyne, 'Cosmopolis and Risk: A Conversation with Ulrich Beck', *Theory, Culture
and Society* 18 (2001), 49.

complex of regulative international interventions. Those interventions can sometimes be financial, as in the Mexican default of 1982–84 and the many other national debt crises of the 1980s, which finally ushered in the crucial IMF shift from a broadly Keynesian frame of thinking to the monetarist orthodoxies of 'structural adjustment'; they can sometimes be institutional, as most obviously in the creation of the new regulative complex of North American Free Trade Agreement (NAFTA) and the World Trade Organization (WTO) since 1994–95; they can sometimes be diplomatic; if necessary, they can certainly be military.[21] Particularly for weaker or thinly specialized economies without any viable world-market niche, this political machinery of globalization tends to produce destructive and subordinated lines of connectedness to the world economy, whose chronically selective, segmented, and exclusionary forms militate brutally against those types of organized social solidarity and societal cohesion that a well-functioning polity normally requires.

This is calamitously true for Africa, where any 'global' links occur predominantly 'in a selective, discontinuous, and point-to-point fashion'.[22] Whether in relation to capital flows or the increasingly salient political agency of non-governmental organizations (NGOs), each of which in effect transnationalizes the bases for policy-making in sub-Saharan Africa, accountability in conventional political terms has all but disappeared. In James Ferguson's words, those networks 'hop over (rather than flowing through) the territories inhabited by the vast majorities of the African population', who thereby gain 'only a tenuous and indirect connection' to any wider global economy.[23] As an actual set of processes affecting the world (as against the idealized claims of the globalizing grand narrative), globalization presumes and produces, indeed specifically feeds off, dynamics of destabilizing and destructive

21   For this regulative history of the reconfiguring of the 'Dollar-Wall Street Regime' during the 1980s to produce the 'Washington Consensus' of the mid 1990s, see Peter Gowan, *The Global Gamble: Washington's Faustian Bid for World Dominance* (London: Verso, 1999); Robert Brenner, *The Boom and the Bubble: The US in the World Economy* (London: Verso, 2003); Ben Fine, ed., *Development Policy in the Twenty-First Century: Beyond the Post-Washington Consensus* (London: Routledge, 2001); David Harvey, 'Neoliberalism and the Restoration of Class Power', in *Spaces of Global Capitalism*.

22   James Ferguson, *Global Shadows: Africa in the Neoliberal World Order* (Durham, NC: Duke University Press, 2006), 14.

23   Ibid.

unevenness and inequality. From an African standpoint, as Ferguson puts it, the global

> is not a seamless, shiny, round, and all-encompassing totality (as the word seems to imply). Nor is it a higher level of planetary unity, interconnection, and communication. Rather, the 'global' we see in recent studies of Africa has sharp, jagged edges; rich and dangerous traffic amid zones of generalized abjection; razor-wired enclaves next to abandoned hinterlands. It features entire countries with estimated life expectancies in the mid-thirties and dropping; warfare seemingly without end; and the steepest economic inequalities seen in human history to date. It is a global where capital flows and markets are at once lightning fast and patchy and incomplete; where the globally networked enclave sits right beside the ungovernable humanitarian disaster zone. It is a global not of planetary communion, but of disconnection, segmentation, and segregation – not a seamless world without borders, but a patchwork of discontinuous and hierarchically ranked spaces, whose edges are carefully delimited, guarded, and enforced.[24]

Given these various kinds of well-grounded scepticism, how should we approach the extremely large-scale claims advanced by globalization talk? How should we render the concept usable? My own rough-and-ready response to this conundrum follows, grouped into four areas of definition, each resting on a particular historicizing argument.

The Din of Globalization

Our first move should be to register the inescapable discursive noise. The easiest demonstration is to find a particularly vociferous loudmouth, such as Thomas L. Friedman – bestselling, Pulitzer Prize–winning op-ed columnist for the *New York Times*, and author of *The Lexus and the Olive Tree: Understanding Globalization*.[25] If, as an analytical term,

---

24 James Ferguson, 'Globalizing Africa? Observations from an Inconvenient Continent', in ibid.

25 See Thomas L. Friedman, *The Lexus and the Olive Tree: Understanding Globalization* (New York: Random House, 1999) and *The World Is Flat: A Brief History of the Twenty-First*

'globalization' has more extensive genealogies from the early 1990s, with finer-tuned origins between the 1960s and early 1980s, there can be no question that Friedman launched it into general public currency.[26] 'The driving idea behind globalization', he said in 'A Manifesto for a Fast World', published in the *New York Times Magazine* in March 1999 to accompany his book, 'is free-market capitalism.' His brash and fervent advocacy was organized around three axioms. To begin with, globalization provides the main, inescapable logic of development and prosperity in the present: 'The more you let market forces rule and the more you open your economy to free trade and competition, the more flourishing and efficient your economy will be. Globalization means the spread of free-market capitalism to virtually every country in the world.'[27] Next, the present of globalization was produced by the world-historical defeat of socialism and the new vistas opened by the end of the Cold War: 'Unlike the cold-war system, which was largely static, globalization involves the integration of free markets, nation-states and information technologies to a degree never before witnessed, in a way that is enabling individuals, corporations and countries to reach around the world farther, faster, deeper, and cheaper than ever. It is also producing a powerful backlash from those brutalized or left behind.'[28]

Precisely because of that backlash, finally, this 'emerging global order' requires ruthless political guarantees: quite aside from the underlying discipline of market efficiencies, the new 'globalization system' needs militarized protection. Or, as Friedman puts it: if 'the [new] super-markets can destroy you by downgrading your bonds', then 'the United States can destroy you by dropping bombs':

> That is why sustainable globalization still requires a stable, geopolitical power structure, which simply cannot be maintained without the active involvement of the United States. All the technologies that Silicon Valley is designing to carry digital voices, videos, and data around the world, all the trade and financial integration it is

Century (New York: Picador, 2005).

26 For pioneering discussions going back to the early 1980s, see Roland Robertson, *Globalization: Social Theory and Global Culture* (London: Sage, 1992).

27 Thomas L. Friedman, 'A Manifesto for a Fast World: From Supercharged Financial Markets to Osama bin Laden, the Emerging Global Order Demands an Enforcer. That's America's New Burden', *New York Times Magazine*, 28 March 1999, 42.

28 Ibid.

promoting through its innovations and the wealth this is generating, are happening in a world stabilized by a benign superpower, with its capital in Washington, DC.[29]

In Friedman's thinking, economics, politics, and culture all work seamlessly together: 'In most countries, people can no longer distinguish between American power, American exports, American cultural assaults, American cultural exports, and plain old globalization.'[30] But the military guarantee is crucial: 'The hidden hand of the market will never work without a hidden fist – McDonald's can never flourish without McDonnell Douglas, the builder of the F-15. And the hidden fist that keeps the world safe for Silicon Valley's technologies is called the United States Army, Air Force, Navy and Marine Corps.'[31] In the words of his concluding sentence, 'Without America on duty, there will be no America Online.'[32]

The point here is very straightforward: in a public environment defined so pervasively and aggressively – so noisily – by globalization talk of this kind, in which the talk is so completely embedded in an expanding repertoire of process and policy, it becomes naive and ineffectual to continue insisting primarily on the historical imprecisions of the term itself. Something is happening here, and as a matter of intellectual and political urgency we need to capture what it is.

Histories of Capitalism

A workable grand periodization can help crucially in allowing the distinctiveness of the present to emerge. This is where Cooper's critique seems most useful. It is easy enough here to see the primary logics of globalization in Friedman's rendition as a belated vindication of the predictions of *The Communist Manifesto*, even as a rather vulgar paraphrase. At the very time Marxist thought was consigned so effectively to the dumpster, the forms of capitalist power in the world were coming

---

29   Ibid., 43, 84, 96. Friedman had a long-standing predilection for bombing: 'Stop the Music: Give the Air War a Chance', *New York Times*, 23 April 1999, A25.
30   Ibid., 43.
31   Ibid., 96.
32   Ibid., 97.

closer than ever to vindicating a powerful feature of classical Marxist critique. If the latter had been more or less driven from the public field, the celebratory tones of pro-market advocacy ironically confirmed a key set of Marxist claims. The near-universal triumph of market principles – not just as the ideas denoting an untrammelled capitalist economy, but as the precepts for all areas of public policy and social life – became the fundament for a brutally frank materialist theory of politics based on the movement of the economy. Indeed, our remarkable contemporary conjuncture, in which the public values, dominant ideas, and range of accessible politics were all tied so consistently to an overriding logic of capital accumulation and the ruling dictates of the economy, seems eerily reminiscent of the triumph of capitalism on a world scale imagined by Karl Marx and Friedrich Engels in *The Communist Manifesto*, first published in 1848.

As it happens, in its 1996 *World Development Report*, entitled *From Plan to Market*, the World Bank summarized the transition of the former socialist countries to a 'market orientation' in precisely these terms, describing the momentousness of the changes of the 1990s with the *Manifesto*'s famous phrase: 'all that is solid melts into air'.[33] Indeed, this image of the victorious free-market order prevailing on a genuinely global scale, dissolving any anti-capitalist recalcitrance and sweeping away the impediments to expansion, became an extraordinarily apposite one for the early twenty-first century. As Eric Hobsbawm observed in his 'Modern Edition' of the *Manifesto*, published to mark its 150th anniversary, Marx and Engels offered insights of 'startling contemporary relevance', including 'the recognition of capitalism as a world system capable of marshalling production on a global scale; its devastating impact on all aspects of human existence, work, the family, and the distribution of wealth; and the understanding that, far from being a

---

33   The Report's blurb expressed this: 'Between 1917 and 1950, countries with one-third of the world's population seceded from the market economy and launched an experiment in constructing alternative systems of centrally planned economies. This transformed the political and the economic map of the world. World Development Report 1996, the 19th in this annual series, is devoted to the transition of these countries – in particular, those in Central and Eastern Europe, the newly independent states of the former Soviet Union, China, and Vietnam – back to a market orientation.' See World Bank, *World Development Report: From Plan to Market* (Oxford: Oxford University Press, 1996). See also Sheila Rowbotham, 'The Tale that Never Ends', in *The Socialist Register 1999: Global Capitalism Versus Democracy*, ed. Leo Panitch and Colin Leys (New York: Monthly Review, 1999), 354.

stable, immutable system, it is, on the contrary, susceptible to enormous convulsions and crisis'.[34] Events that, at one level, are taken to have refuted Marxism's validity as a theory of the direction of history – Communism's ending, the collapse of viable alternatives to capitalism, the obstacles to a politics centred around class – at another level precisely instantiate Marxism's analysis of the dynamism of capitalist accumulation. Similarly, neoliberal thinking has now made the possibilities for democracy so strictly dependent on a particular conception of the economy as to put the most vulgar of all vulgar Marxists to shame. The space for any realistic or accessible politics – meaningful actions of government in society – became strictly demarcated in this way of thinking by the needs of the economy conceived in terms of the market.

This is how I would begin to elaborate my grand-scale periodization: by structuring it around the histories of the development of capitalism and its distinctive social formations as we encounter them on a global scale. I would build that framework not around the classical understanding of industrialization and the Industrial Revolution to which we normally repair, nor around those deeper arguments about the passage from feudalism to capitalism we associate with the so-called 'transition debates' of the 1950s and 1970s, but by bringing two other bodies of contemporary thought into play.[35] One of these comprises the increasingly rich historiographies of slavery, postemancipation societies, and the Black Atlantic, which continue to challenge us into rethinking the origins of the modern world. The other draws on what we know about the distinctive conditions of accumulation and exploitation that now define the new globalized division of labour of the present, particularly in the deregulated migrant and transnationalized labour markets being generated at an ever-accelerating pace. The latter highlights some contrasts with the

---

34 Jacket description to Karl Marx and Friedrich Engels, *The Communist Manifesto: A Modern Edition*, 'Introduction' by Eric Hobsbawm (London: Verso, 1998). The 150th anniversary attracted widespread attention in the daily and periodical press. New editions were also introduced by John Toews (Boston: Bedford, 1999), Martin Malia (New York: Signet, 1998), and Mark Cowling (New York: New York University Press, 1998).

35 For the so-called transition debate, see Rodney Hilton, ed., *The Transition from Feudalism to Capitalism* (London: Verso, 1976); Trevor Aston and C. H. E. Philpin, eds, *The Brenner Debate: Agrarian Class Structure and Economic Development in Pre-Industrial Europe* (Cambridge: Cambridge University Press, 1985); Robert Brenner, 'The Origins of Capitalist Development: A Critique of Neo-Smithian Marxism', *New Left Review* I/104 (July–August 1977).

previous accumulation regime, established after 1945 and lasting until the fresh changes of the mid 1970s.

Histories of capitalism on a world scale both *precede* and *postdate* those more specific accounts of industrial manufacturing that commonly define the rise of capitalism. Much of the 'Black Atlantic' argument has been formulated around questions of citizenship and personhood focused by the impact of the French Revolution – most classically in the Haitian Revolution and the wider insurrectionary aspirations to freedom in the Caribbean – rather than around the *modernity of capitalism* as such.[36] The turning from social to cultural history may have occluded our ability to grasp this primary form of 'the social', or even to engage the origins of capitalism in the manner of the 1960s and 1970s. New historiographies of the societal transformations accompanying the end of New World slavery tend to foreground the countervailing logic of the drive to secure the generalized norm of the free labour contract, which worked inexorably *against* the longed-for ideals of civic liberty and emancipated personhood. The conceptual focus tends to be on the securing of the new relations required by the capitalist labour contract, even as elaborate machineries for the recruitment and deployment of indentured and 'semi-free' labour power persisted, so that the promised meanings of freedom and citizenship, which were in any case vitally conditioned by race and labour during the transition out of slavery, necessarily became compromised. But the already-formed place of slavery itself in a capitalist system of production is brought less easily into thought. The coding of slavery as an essentially *precapitalist* formation, or at best an anomaly once 'the wage labor-driven capitalist system [began] maturing on a global scale', remains tacitly intact.[37]

---

36   The reference here is to Paul Gilroy's *The Black Atlantic: Modernity and Double Consciousness* (Cambridge: Harvard University Press, 1993). More generally, see Stuart Hall, 'Breaking Bread with History: C. L. R. James and *The Black Jacobins*', *History Workshop Journal* 46 (Autumn 1998); Michel-Rolph Trouillot, *Silencing the Past: Power and the Production of History* (Boston: Beacon, 1997); Laurent Dubois, 'The Citizen's Trance: The Haitian Revolution and the Motor of History', in *Magic and Modernity: Interfaces of Revelation and Concealment*, ed. Birgit Meyer and Peter Pels (Stanford: Stanford University Press, 2003); Laurent Dubois, *Avengers of the New World: The Story of the Haitian Revolution* (Cambridge: Harvard University Press, 2004).

37   Frederick Cooper, Thomas C. Holt, and Rebecca J. Scott, *Beyond Slavery: Explorations of Race, Labor, and Citizenship in Postemancipation Societies* (Chapel Hill, NC: University of North Carolina Press, 2000), 23. These three authors' monographs superbly address the

What becomes increasingly clear from monographic work on slave economies of the Caribbean, as well as from Robin Blackburn's magnum opus *The Making of New World Slavery* and the oeuvre of Sidney Mintz, is that slavery was not some archaic or precapitalist social formation in anomalous relationship to the rise of capitalism as such, but, on the contrary, produced the first modern proletariat of large-scale, highly organized, and integrated capitalist production.[38] Thinking of the New World plantation economies in relation to capitalist regimes of production, exploitation, and accumulation in this way vitally destabilizes our more familiar teleologies of capitalist industrialization. It resituates our understanding of working-class formation in a set of social relations that both preceded and starkly differed from those normally attributed to capitalist industry. Organized on the most global of scales, the labour regime in question continued to overlap and coexist with the latter well into the epoch of the Industrial Revolution, classically understood. To the modernity of the enslaved mass worker, moreover, we may further add the analogous importance of domestic servitude for the overall labour markets and regimes of accumulation prevailing inside the eighteenth-century Anglo-Scottish national economy at home.[39]

---

complexities of the transitions between slavery and wage labour. See, respectively, Frederick Cooper, *From Slaves to Squatters: Plantation Labor and Agriculture in Zanzibar and Coastal Kenya, 1890–1925* (New Haven, CT: Yale University Press, 1980); Rebecca J. Scott, *Slave Emancipation in Cuba: The Transition to Free Labor, 1860–1899* (Princeton: Princeton University Press, 1985); Thomas C. Holt, *The Problem of Freedom: Race, Labor, and Politics in Jamaica and Britain, 1832–1938* (Baltimore: Johns Hopkins University Press, 1992); Rebecca J. Scott, *Degrees of Freedom: Louisiana and Cuba after Slavery* (Cambridge: Harvard University Press, 2005). For use of indentured labour, see Hugh Tinker, *A New System of Slavery: The Export of Indian Labour Overseas, 1830–1920* (Oxford: Oxford University Press, 1974); David Northrup, *Indentured Labor in the Age of Imperialism, 1834–1922* (Cambridge: Cambridge University Press, 1995). For the historically determinate processes working to produce the nineteenth-century version of 'free labor', see Robert J. Steinfeld, *The Invention of Free Labor: The Employment Relation in English and American Law and Culture, 1350–1870* (Chapel Hill, NC: University of North Carolina Press, 1991) and *Coercion, Contract, and Free Labor in the Nineteenth Century* (Cambridge: Cambridge University Press, 2001). Dennis Sweeney pointed me to these works.

38   See Robin Blackburn, *The Making of New World Slavery: From the Baroque to the Modern* (London: Verso, 1997) and *The Overthrow of Colonial Slavery 1776–1848* (London: Verso, 1988); Sidney W. Mintz, *Sweetness and Power: The Place of Sugar in Modern History* (New York: Viking, 1985); David Scott, 'Modernity that Predated the Modern', *History Workshop Journal* 58 (Autumn 2004).

39   My thinking here is hugely indebted to Carolyn Steedman. See her *Master and Servant: Love and Labour in the English Industrial Age* (Cambridge: Cambridge University Press, 2007) and *Labours Lost: Domestic Service and the Making of Modern England* (Cambridge: Cambridge University Press, 2009).

If we put these two social regimes of labour together – that of the enslaved mass workers of the New World and that of the servile labourers of the households, workshops, and farms of the Old – then we have the makings of a radically different account of the dynamics of the rise of capitalism and the modes of social subordination that allowed it to occur.[40] In the most basic social-historical terms, servants in their many guises formed one of the very largest and most essential working categories of the later eighteenth and early nineteenth centuries (that is, precisely in the core period of industrialization); yet they seldom figure anywhere in the established general accounts of either the capitalist economy or working-class formation. So, if we seriously take on board this centrality of non-industrial work and the fundamental importance of service, domestic labour, and everything accomplished in households, while adding it to the driving importance of enslaved mass production, then our conventional understanding of the histories of political economy and working-class formation will surely have to change.[41]

Our perspective shifts again when we consider capitalism's history in the present. Once we revise our understanding of the early histories of capital accumulation by integrating the generative contributions of slavery and servitude, the presumed centrality of waged work in manufacturing, extractive, and other forms of modern industry already becomes less obvious for the metanarrative of the rise of capitalism.

---

40   For reasons of brevity and space, I focus here on the transatlantic circuits of extraction, production, and accumulation between the seventeenth and nineteenth centuries. In a fuller treatment, the Indian Ocean and Pacific circuits would need to be added.

41   To the labour regimes of slavery and servitude, Linebaugh and Rediker have added a third, namely that of the sailing ship, which they claim as the site of production characteristic of the Atlantic arena of globalization in the seventeenth and eighteenth centuries. See Peter Linebaugh and Marcus Rediker, *The Many-Headed Hydra: Sailors, Slaves, Commoners, and the Hidden History of the Revolutionary Atlantic* (London: Verso, 2002). Linebaugh first developed this argument in an essay of 1982: 'By the end of the seventeenth century we may distinguish four ways by which capital sought to organize the exploitation of human labor in its combination with the materials and tools of production. These were first, the plantation, in many ways the most important mercantilist achievement; second, petty production such as the yeoman farmer or fortunate artisan enjoyed; third, the putting-out system which had begun to evolve into manufacture; and the mode of production which at the level of circulation united the others, namely the ship.' In Linebaugh's argument, ships 'carried not only the congealed labour of the plantations, the manufactories, and the workshops' in their holds, but also the 'living labour . . . of transported felons, of indentured servants, above all, of African slaves'. See Peter Linebaugh, 'All the Atlantic Mountains Shook', in Geoff Eley and William Hunt, *Reviving the English Revolution: Reflections and Elaborations on the Work of Christopher Hill* (London: Verso, 1988), 207, 208. The essay was first published in *Labour/Le Travail* 10 (Autumn 1982).

That shift of perspective relativizes wage labour's place in the social histories of working-class formation. It opens our accounts to other regimes of labour. Waged work's claim to analytical precedence in the developmental histories of capitalism grows less secure. Indeed, the de-skilling, de-unionizing, de-benefiting, and de-nationalizing of labour through the processes of metropolitan deindustrialization and trans-nationalized capitalist restructuring in our own time have undermined that claim from the opposite end of the chronology. Social relations of work in Europe and North America today are being drastically trans-formed towards the new low-wage, semi-legal, and deregulated labour markets of a mainly service-based economy increasingly organized in complex transnational ways. In light of that radical re-proletarianizing of labour under today's advanced capitalism, the preceding salience of socially valued forms of organized labour prevalent after 1945, regarded so confidently as normative by post-war social democrats, re-emerges as an extremely transitory phenomenon. That now-defeated redistributive social-democratic vision of the humanizing of capitalism becomes reduced to a strictly finite and exceptional project, one mainly confined to the years linking the post-war settlement to its long and painful dismantling after the mid 1970s.

Considering that contemporary re-proletarianization, the time of labour's recognition – both collectively organized and socially valued via trade unions, public policy, wider common sense, and the acceptable ethics of a society's shared collective life – becomes a striking inter-ruption in the longer history of capitalist social formations between the eighteenth century and the present. Those societies' ordering principles have otherwise been quite differently institutionalized and understood, whether at the beginning (in the eighteenth century) or at the end (today). Their interruption may be located historically inside Eric Hobsbawm's 'golden age' of the unprecedented post-1945 capitalist boom, whose forms of sociopolitical democratization (through plan-ning, full employment, social services, redistributive taxation, recognition of trade unions, public schooling, collectivist ideals of social improvement, a general ethic of public goods) were subjected steadily from the mid 1970s to brutally effective political attack.[42] At most, the

---

42 I refer here to the argument in Eric Hobsbawm, *The Age of Extremes: A History of the World, 1914–1991* (New York: Pantheon, 1994), esp. 225–400. See also Geoff Eley, *Forging*

labour movement's rise and political validation were confined to the first three quarters of the twentieth century, albeit in trajectories that varied markedly from country to country.

Two features of this argument deserve extra clarification. First, treating both slaves and servants as categories of workers implies an abandonment of the well-established definition of the working class by the wage relationship. Yet, once located in the history of capitalism as a whole, the classic wage-earning proletariat becomes a transitory and sectorally specific formation produced in quite delimited historical circumstances. Under any particular capitalism, moreover, wage work has in any case always continued to coexist with various types of unfree and coercive labour. The salience of such simultaneities – of the temporal coexistence inside a particular capitalist social formation of forced, indentured, enslaved, and unfree forms of work along with the free wage relationship, strictly understood – needs to be honestly acknowledged. Such simultaneities become all the more striking once we begin to see capital accumulation on a properly global scale by integrating the forms of surplus extraction occurring in the colonial, neocolonial, or underdeveloped worlds. The West's privileged prosperity, including precisely the possibility of the social-democratic betterment affixed to the three decades after 1945, was founded constitutively on horrendous repertoires of extraction and exploitation on a world scale. Other forms of labour coercion have likewise been characteristic of even the most advanced capitalist economies in their time, as for instance during the two world wars, or under the racialized New Order of the Third Reich. In these terms, the search for a 'pure' working-class formation, from which enslavement, servitude, indenturing, impressment, conscription, imprisonment, and coercion have been purged, remains a chimera. Once we define working-class formation not through the creation of the wage relationship in the strict sense alone, therefore, but through labour's contributions to the wider variety of accumulation regimes we encounter in the histories of capitalism since the eighteenth century, we can see the multiplicity of possible labour regimes more easily.

Second, I am proposing neither a 'cyclical' history of labour, through which forms of labour exploitation in the twenty-first century somehow

Democracy: The History of the Left in Europe, 1850–2000 (New York: Oxford University Press, 2002), esp. Chapter 23: 'Class and the Politics of Labor'.

loop back or revert to those prevailing in the early phases of capitalism, nor an equivalency between today's 'deskilled' or 're-proletarianized' labourers, on one hand, and eighteenth-century servants and slaves, on the other. Rather, by focusing on those two largest categories of workers during the earliest processes of accumulation, we can see the extremely varied labour regimes sustaining those processes, including those based on coercion. This argument has some affinities with earlier critiques of the classical narratives of the Industrial Revolution, which emphasized instead proto-industrialization, small-scale rural industry, new forms of non-industrial manufacturing, and the wide range of 'alternatives to mass production'.[43] Clearly, the distinctions between forms of 'free' and 'coercive' labour need to be retained, because otherwise certain specificities of the labour contract under industrial capitalism would become far harder to see, particularly those requiring new domains of power and exploitation beyond the immediate labour process and workplace themselves.

To summarize: on the one hand, servitude and slavery were the social forms of labour foundational to the capitalist modernity forged during the eighteenth century; on the other hand, since the late twentieth century a new and radically stripped-down version of the labour contract has been shaped. Those new forms of labour exploitation have been accumulating around the growing prevalence of minimum-wage, dequalified and deskilled, disorganized, and deregulated semi-legal and migrant labour markets, through which workers are systemically stripped of most forms of security and organized protections. This is what characterizes the circulation of labour power in the globalized and post-Fordist economies of the late-capitalist world, and this is where the distinctiveness of the present can be found. Whether from the standpoint of the 'future' of capitalism or from its 'origins', the centring of capitalism and its social formations around industrial production in manufacturing begins to seem like an incredibly partial and potentially distorting understanding. It describes a phase found overwhelmingly in

---

43   The heyday of those critiques was the early 1980s. See Charles Sabel and Jonathan Zeitlin, 'Historical Alternatives to Mass Production: Politics, Markets, and Technology in Nineteenth-Century Industrialization', *Past and Present* 108 (1985); Charles Tilly, 'Flows of Capital and Forms of Industry in Europe, 1500–1900', *Theory and Society* 12 (1983) and 'The Demographic Origins of the European Proletariat', in *Proletarianization and Family History*, ed. David Levine (Orlando, FL: Academic, 1984); Geoff Eley, 'The Social History of Industrialization: "Proto-Industry" and the Origins of Capitalism', *Economy and Society* 13 (1984).

the West, in ways that specifically presupposed its absence from the rest of the world. The very functioning of the golden age – its material conditions of possibility – was the continuing impoverishment of the rest of the world. And it lasted for a remarkably brief slice of historical time.[44]

The Demise of Anti-Imperialist Sovereignty

There is a further dimension to my proposed periodization. As argued above, the architects of the post-1945 settlement in western Europe mistook its transitory and exceptional circumstances of regulated capitalism, collectivist social policy and redistributive betterment for an indefinite future, for a kind of permanently unfolding present. In the event, that settlement started falling apart in the new conjuncture after 1968–73. Moreover, the heft of that post-war system of politics had also rested on the pressures of the Cold War. From the strategic thinking behind the Marshall Plan through the logics of trade-union corporatism and the building of the post-war welfare states to the general social policy regimes of the 1950s and 1960s, the desire to solidify a broad societal consensus against the 'Second World' of socialism was always crucial.

There were two key dimensions, one concerning the advanced capitalist West, the other involving the former Third World, each with direct bearing on our globalized present. Thus, there can be little doubt that the Soviet Union's collapse removed a vital constraint previously shaping the political cultures of the capitalist West. Quite aside from the West's interior dynamics of deindustrialization and capitalist restructuring after the 1970s and their consequences for politics, the public triumphalism at the end of Communism in 1989–91 decisively damaged the future plausibility of socialist ideas. Both the crimes of Stalinism and

---

44   Between the later 1940s and the mid 1970s, Western Europe's period of relatively humanized capitalism was no less beholden to systems of globalized exploitation of natural resources, human materials, and grotesquely unequal terms of trade than the periods before or since. The privileged metropolitan prosperity in which social-democratic gains were embedded rested (systemically, constitutively) on historically specific repertoires of extraction and exploitation operating on a world scale. Amid all contemporary talk of colonialism and postcoloniality, of globalization and 'empire', a workable theory of *imperialism* remains urgently in need of recuperation. For one starting point, see Alain Lipietz, 'Towards Global Fordism?' and 'Marx or Rostow?', both in *New Left Review* I/132 (March–April 1982).

the manifold exhaustion of Soviet-style planning had long undermined socialism's resources of legitimacy, severely compromising the ground of socialist argument between the 1950s and 1980s. But, however manifestly 'actually existing socialism' was already discredited, the ultimate denouement decisively compounded the difficulty. Any socialist advocacy became marginalized and constrained. That space became all but closed down.[45]

The long-running analogue in the former Third World has been the disappointments and steady exhaustion of the welfare populism and progressive nationalist aspiration towards 'development in one country' that once formed the main scaffolding for the politics of independence after decolonization. This is what Samir Amin and others have called the Bandung Era, during which the combined project of national developmentalism, anti-imperialist sovereignty, and international non-alignment became focused after the Bandung Conference of April 1955 around regimes like Nehru's India, Nasser's Egypt, Sukarno's Indonesia, and Nkrumah's Ghana.[46] That intense valorizing of anti-imperialist sovereignty around rhetorics of economic self-sufficiency, popular governance, social equity, and cultural pride then acquired further momentum from projects like Salvador Allende's Chile, Julius Nyerere's Tanzania, and Michael Manley's Jamaica. The coalescence of Left-nationalist aspirations around that progressivist project of decolonization gained continuing impetus from the successful liberation of the Portuguese colonies, from US defeat in Southeast Asia, and from radical nationalist departures, from the Horn of Africa to Afghanistan. Left-nationalist projects of one kind or another attained considerable purchase in both the popular and intellectual imaginations, until they unevenly collapsed beneath the conflicts of the 1970s and 1980s.[47]

---

45   See Geoff Eley, 'Reviewing the Socialist Tradition', in *The Crisis of Socialism in Europe*, ed. Christiane Lemke and Gary Marks (Durham, NC: Duke University Press, 1992).

46   See Samir Amin, *Re-Reading the Postwar Period: An Intellectual Itinerary* (New York: Monthly Review, 1994). See also David Scott, *Refashioning Futures: Criticism after Postcoloniality* (Princeton: Princeton University Press, 1999), 143–9, and *Conscripts of Modernity: The Tragedy of Colonial Enlightenment* (Durham: Duke University Press, 2005).

47   For an essential starting point, see the Forum on the Bandung era in *Radical History Review* 95 (Spring 2006), including: Antoinette Burton, Augusto Espiritu and Fanon Che Wilkins, 'Introduction: The Fate of Nationalism in the Age of Bandung'; Antoinette Burton, 'Cold War Cosmopolitanism: The Education of Aantha Rama Rau'; Augusto Espiritu, '"To Carry Water on Both Shoulders": Carlos P. Romulo, American Empire, and the Meanings of Bandung'; and Fanon Che Wilkins, 'Beyond Bandung: The Critical Nationalism of Lorraine

Amid the resulting turmoil, a decisive international realignment came to be engineered. The World Bank's 'structural adjustment' programmes came to supply the new principles of global reordering. In this extra-European global context, too, the persuasiveness and workability of socialist ideas met drastic defeats, well ahead of the Soviet collapse. Again, the discursive space still adumbrated during the 1970s by a politics of 'feasible socialism' disastrously disappeared.[48] In precisely that sense, the socialist part of the world had functioned as a vital ideological resource for the emergent Third World societies: less as a practical model of social administration and the planned economy, let alone any concretely realized utopia, than as a space of non-capitalist experimentation. However unappealing and compromised under Stalinism, that source of alternative potentials at least allowed liberalism's bid for the one universal and necessary path to be contested. Since Communism's end, that horizon of alternative thinking has effectively gone. As Arno J. Mayer argued over sixty years ago in *Wilson versus Lenin*, the Bolshevik Revolution opened a distinct period of world history, which reached from 1917 to 1991. At its close, the global option of a nationally conceived anti-imperialist sovereignty had finally been taken off the agenda. It was removed from the colonial, neocolonial, and postcolonial non-Western world by a complex convergence of many histories. But the most brutally determinative remains the neo-liberal triumphalism made possible by the collapse of the Soviet Union.[49]

Hansberry, 1950–1965'. See also 'Beyond What? An Introduction', in Loomba et al., *Postcolonial Studies and Beyond*; Penny von Eschen, *Race Against Empire: Black Americans and Anti-Colonialism, 1937–1957* (Ithaca, NY: Cornell University Press, 1997).

48   Alec Nove, *The Economics of Feasible Socialism Revisited* (London: Routledge, 1983).

49   See Arno J. Mayer, *Wilson vs Lenin: Political Origins of the New Diplomacy, 1917–1918* (New York: World, 1964) and *Dynamics of Counter-Revolution in Europe, 1870–1956: An Analytical Framework* (New York: Harper & Row, 1971). This is the framework adopted in Hobsbawm, *Age of Extremes*. For critical commentary, see Perry Anderson, 'The Vanquished Left: Eric Hobsbawm', in Perry Anderson, *Spectrum: From Right to Left in the World of Ideas* (London: Verso, 2005).

How Is the Present Globalized?

In what ways has our present become 'globalized'? The concept of post-Fordist transition supplies one historically grounded means of theorizing the contemporary process of capitalist restructuring.[50] Prefigurations and longer continuities notwithstanding, the period since the 1970s has brought a qualitative acceleration and intensification of the world's integration in three directions: 'a marked *reduction in the barriers* between societies and states, an *increasing homogeneity* of societies and states, and an *increase in the volume of interactions* between societies – be this in terms of trade, capital, volumes of currency traded or movements of tourists and migrants.'[51] In Anthony Giddens's rendition, globalization rests on a new 'time-space distantiation', historically replacing sociology's 'classical emphasis upon the analysis of "societies"' or discretely demarcated and sovereign 'social systems'.[52] Under the logic of globalization, an unprecedented 'spatio-temporal' dynamic of sped-up interdependence has produced both a shrinkage of the world and the rearranging of its earlier divisions towards growing interconnectedness on a cross-regional, transoceanic, or transcontinental scale. That reordering then links the 'intimate self' to 'social processes of a worldwide reach' in dramatic new ways.

In the words of one of Giddens' principal followers, David Held, globalization signifies

a significant shift in the spatial reach of social action and organization towards the interregional or intercontinental scale. This does not

---

50   See Alain Lipietz, *Towards a New Economic Order: Post-Fordism, Ecology, and Democracy* (Oxford: Oxford University Press, 1992); Robin Murray, 'Fordism and Post-Fordism', in *New Times: The Changing Face of Politics in the 1990s*, ed. Stuart Hall and Martin Jacques (London: Lawrence & Wishart, 1991); David Harvey, *The Condition of Postmodernity* (Oxford: Blackwell, 1989); Ash Amin, 'Post-Fordism: Models, Fantasies, and Phantoms of Transition', and Bob Jessop, 'Post-Fordism and the State', in *Post-Fordism: A Reader*, ed. Ash Amin (Oxford: Blackwell, 1994).

51   Fred Halliday, *The World at 2000* (New York: Red Globe, 2000), 61. Emphases in original.

52   The quoted phrases and the ones that follow are taken from Justin Rosenberg's summarizing critique in *The Follies of Globalization Theory: Polemical Essays* (London: Verso, 2000), 89–90. For the key work in question, see Anthony Giddens, *The Consequences of Modernity* (Stanford: Stanford University Press, 1990), along with his later overall statement in *Runaway World*.

mean that the global necessarily displaces or takes precedence over local, national, or regional orders of social life. Rather, the latter can become embedded within more expansive sets of interregional relations and networks of power. Thus, the constraints of social time and geographical space, vital coordinates of modern social life, no longer appear to impose fixed barriers to many forms of social interaction or organization, as the existence of the World Wide Web and round-the-clock trading in global financial markets attests. As distance 'shrinks', the relative speed of social interaction increases too, such that crises and events in distant parts of the globe . . . come to have an immediate worldwide impact involving diminishing response times for decision-makers. Globalization engenders a certain cognitive shift expressed in a growing public awareness of the ways in which distant events can affect local fortunes (and vice versa) as well as public perceptions of shrinking time and geographical space.

Held continues: 'Simply put, globalization denotes the expanding scale, growing magnitude, speeding up, and deepening impact of interregional flows and patterns of interaction. It refers to a shift or transformation in the scale of human organization that links distant communities and expands the reach of power relations across the world's major regions and continents.'[53]

Beyond this more abstract systemic definition, at least three key political effects need especially to be marked: first, the consequences for organizing sovereignty within national states; second, new forms of transnational or transregional social and political mobilization; and third, the profoundly ramified and volatile social, cultural, and political consequences of the new patterns of transnational migration, through which millions of workers, asylum-seekers, and refugees are moving across the territorial borders of nationally conceived sovereign states.

Each of these topics requires full-scale treatment in its own right. With respect to nation-state sovereignty, diverse logics and counter-logics have been distinguished by contending schools of thought in international relations. On the one hand, new modalities of supra-national governance

---

53   David Held and Anthony McGrew, 'The Great Globalization Debate: An Introduction', in *The Global Transformations Reader: An Introduction to the Globalization Debate* (Cambridge: Polity, 2000), 3–4.

have clearly compromised and reconfigured the earlier capacities of states as defined by an established national-territorial model of sovereignty. Linked to an inter-state system descending from the territorialized sovereignties ratified through the 1648 Peace of Westphalia, that model broadly prevailed in Europe and the Americas after the early nineteenth century, and elsewhere in the world since the early twentieth, with sustained culmination in Europe between the 1860s and the 1930s. For one school of thought on globalization, the distinctive late-twentieth-century world order may then become the end of that 'Westphalian system' of sovereign state actors. As Held puts it,

In short, boundaries between states are of decreasing legal and moral significance. States are no longer regarded as discrete political worlds. International standards breach boundaries in numerous ways. Within Europe, the European Convention for the Protection of Human Rights and Fundamental Freedoms and the European Union create new institutions and layers of law and governance, which have divided political authority. Any assumption that sovereignty is an indivisible, illimitable, exclusive, and perpetual form of public power – entrenched within an individual state – is now defunct.[54]

On the other hand, the completeness of this supersession has been exaggerated, especially for the penetration of new institutional arrangements into the social relations and everyday practices of those pre-constituted nationally bounded societies. The evolving and reversible unevenness – the complex ledger of claims, jurisdictions, and capacities – also requires analysis. The duress, undermining, and systematic dismantlement of one historically particular form of territorialized sovereignty – the Keynesian national welfare state, normalized

---

54 David Held, 'Violence, Law, and Justice in a Global Age', in *Understanding September 11*, ed. Craig Calhoun, Paul Price, and Ashley Timmer (New York: New Press, 2002), 96. For a succinct rendition of the 'Westphalian model', see David Held, *Democracy and the Global Order: From the Modern State to Cosmopolitan Governance* (Stanford: Stanford University Press, 1995), 74–83; and for full-scale critique, Benno Teschke, *The Myth of 1648: Class, Geopolitics, and the Making of Modern International Relations* (London: Verso, 2003). For additional commentaries, Rosenberg, *Follies of Globalization Theory*, 27–43; Andrew Linklater, 'Citizenship and Sovereignty in the Post-Westphalian European State', in *Re-Imagining Political Community: Studies in Cosmopolitan Democracy*, ed. Daniele Archibugi, David Held, and Martin Köhler (Stanford, CA: Stanford University Press, 1998).

in north-western Europe from later 1940s to the late 1960s – can certainly be tracked. But despite the latter's patent demise, the embedded territorialized jurisdictions attaching to the national state have scarcely atrophied or disappeared in some overall and final sense. In Bob Jessop's view, 'a restructured national state remains central to the effective management of the emerging spatio-temporal matrices of capitalism and the emerging forms of post- or transnational citizenship.'[55]

Back to Politics Again

Globalization is a contested political project. One progressivist antinomy pits 'global governance' against 'global civil society', as two principal rubrics for conceptualizing political accountability or control. If the former bears the signature of a Blairite, centrist programme, the latter suggests a democratic version of the new global order. In neither case have existing gains been exactly compelling. If 'global governance' remains in complicated tension with older bases of nationally organized political rule and governmentality, then the much-vaunted emergence of a new 'global civil society' grounded by social movements remains inchoate, spasmodic, and malformed.[56] Nonetheless, between these two programmatic descriptions lies the field of possibility for an innovative politics of globalization.[57]

---

55 Bob Jessop, 'The Future of the State in an Era of Globalization', *Internationale Politik und Gesellschaft* 3 (2003), 46. See also Bob Jessop, 'Globalization and the National State', in *Paradigm Lost: State Theory Reconsidered*, ed. Stanley Aronowitz and Peter Bratsis (Minneapolis: University of Minnesota Press, 2002); Hirst and Thompson, *Globalization in Question*, 256–80.

56 See esp. Mary Kaldor, *Global Civil Society: An Answer to War* (Cambridge: Polity, 2003); Akira Iriye, *Global Community: The Role of International Organizations in the Making of the Contemporary World* (Berkeley, CA: University of California Press, 2002); Held, *Democracy and the Global Order*; Archibugi, Held, and Köhler, *Re-Imagining Political Community*. See John Rennie Short, *Global Dimensions: Space, Place and the Contemporary World* (London: Reaktion, 2001), 84–5, for 'an example of good globalization [the campaign for eradication of polio initiated by Rotary International in 1990], a case where a combination of international civil society, international organizations and nation-states combined to produce good things'. For 'global governance', see the website of the Policy Network launched in December 2000 by Tony Blair, Gerhard Schröder, Giuliano Amato, and Göran Persson following the Progressive Governance summits originally hosted by Bill Clinton in New York in April 1999, policy-network.net. See also Aseem Prakash and Jeffrey A. Hart, eds, *Globalization and Governance* (London: Routledge, 1999).

57 For measured and persuasive advocacy of a transnationally conceived legal order or *Rechtstaat*, a specifically global or cosmopolitan model of democracy, see David Held, 'The

The primary political logic since the 1990s has powerfully *immunized* the globalizing economy from either kind of political accountability, whether aggregated through forms of international coalition-building among progressive governments and guaranteed by a transnational legal order, or imagined via the limiting checks created by the participatory activism of social movements. In contrast with either of these putative democratic imaginaries, neoliberalism specifically enthrones capital as the sovereign force for the organizing of society. The sole agencies ever recognized by neoliberalism for the purposes of the polity are the property-owning individual or corporation, who are 'free' to engage in a competitive quest for improvement, and the market as regulator of that quest. In other words, the dominant neoliberal programme of globalization deliberately, aggressively, and dogmatically *brackets off* the economy from the sphere of available political choice.

In the early 2000s, one very specific political project of globalization captured leadership of the neoliberal logic, namely, the ruthlessly ambitious geopolitical strategy of the Bush administration: remaking the global political order under the aegis of the United States as the sole hyperpower or hegemon. That strategy may be found in the programme presented with tremendous conviction in the Report on *Rebuilding America's Defences* issued by the PNAC, discussed at the start of this chapter.

As that unilateralist programme became implemented, it remained extremely unclear how any effective opposition might occur. As already suggested, the degree to which economic globalization has superseded the nation-state framework is easily exaggerated. Even if national Keynesianism has been decisively undermined, great latitude remains for political action at the national legislative and policy-making levels, where checks on neoliberal globalization can still realistically occur, however sticky the impediments. Under the aegis of movements for global justice, much creativity has developed around new types of transnational mobilization. Those new forms of action – from NGOs and trans-border advocacy networks to transnational citizens' movements and the social-movement activism pioneered in Seattle and Genoa,

---

Transformation of Political Community: Rethinking Democracy in the Context of Globalization', in *Democracy's Edges*, ed. Ian Shapiro and Casiano Hacker-Cordón (Cambridge: Cambridge University Press, 1999). For well-founded scepticism, Chantal Mouffe, 'Cosmopolitan Democracy or Multipolar World Order?', *Soundings: Frontier Markets* 28 (2005).

together with the organized activity of the World Social Forum (WSF) –
quickly became a source of optimism. Measured by past forms of
democratic political action, they also seemed quite dramatically distinct.[58] What are the new political imaginaries inscribed in the present
conjuncture of globalization?

Talk of an emergent global Left – a Left whose forms of thought and
organized action are prospectively realigning, slowly and unevenly, in
larger than national-state ways – remained speculative and cautious.
One front was turn-of-the-century anti-globalization activism, with its
intersections in protests against G8 and IMF summits, growth of the
WSF and its regional equivalents, and the massed transnational protests
against the Iraq War, with its associated slogans: 'We Are Everywhere', 'A
Movement of Movements', and 'Another World Is Possible'. A corollary
was the coalescence of a revived anti-capitalist discourse, evidenced in a
wave of post-Seattle publication, including anthologies assembled by
Joel Schalit, Emma Bircham and John Charlton, Notes from Nowhere,
and Tom Mertes, plus a variety of popularizing guides to analysis and
action by John Carter and Dave Morland, Simon Tormey, Alex Callinicos, and others.[59] An acknowledged founding event of this recharged
anti-capitalist politics – one called into being by precisely the transnational framing of globalization described in this chapter – was the
Zapatistas' response to the inauguration of NAFTA on 1 January 1994.
We can add campaigns of the 1990s against globalized sweatshop

58   See Margaret E. Keck and Kathryn Sikkink, *Activists Beyond Borders: Advocacy
Networks in International Politics* (Ithaca, NY: Cornell University Press, 1998); Matthew
Evangelista, *Unarmed Forces: The Transnational Movement to End the Cold War* (Ithaca, NY:
Cornell University Press, 1999); John A. Guidry, Michael D. Kennedy, and Mayer N. Zald,
eds, *Globalizations and Social Movements: Culture, Power, and the Transnational Public Sphere*
(Ann Arbor, MI: University of Michigan Press, 2000); Valentine M. Moghadam, *Globalizing
Women: Transnational Feminist Networks* (Baltimore: Johns Hopkins University Press, 2005);
Peter Steven, *The No-Nonsense Guide to Global Media* (London: New Internationalist, 2003);
Tom Mertes, ed., *A Movement of Movements: Is Another World Really Possible?* (London:
Verso, 2004); William F. Fisher and Thomas Ponniah, eds, *Another World Is Possible: Popular
Alternatives to Globalization at the World Social Forum* (London: Verso, 2003).
59   Joel Schalit, *Anti-Capitalism Reader: Imagining a Geography of Opposition* (New
York: Akashic Books, 2001); Emma Bircham and John Charlton, *Anti-Capitalism: A Guide to
the Movement* (London: Bookmarks, 2001); Notes from Nowhere, ed., *We Are Everywhere:
The Irresistible Rise of Global Anticapitalism* (London: Verso, 2003); Mertes, *Movement of
Movements*; John Carter and Dave Morland, *Anti-Capitalist Britain* (Cheltenham: New
Clarion, 2004); Simon Tormey, *Anti-Capitalism: A Beginner's Guide* (Oxford: Oneworld,
2004); Alex Callinicos, *An Anti-Capitalist Manifesto* (Cambridge: Polity, 2003).

labour;[60] broader anti-corporate activism;[61] and emblematic texts like Naomi Klein's *No Logo* and Noreena Hertz's *Silent Takeover*, which helped crystallize emergent radical democratic and critical-liberal publics in the metropolitan West, or Arundhati Roy's *Cost of Living*, which spoke across North–South divides.[62]

This anti-capitalist discourse notably revived a general societal critique, whose meaning can hardly be gainsaid given the banishing from public visibility of socialist advocacy, always the earlier source of oppositional talk. This is the kind of critique (as Fredric Jameson observed) whose terms 'could not be fulfilled or satisfied without transforming the system beyond recognition, and which would at once usher in a society structurally distinct from this one in every conceivable way, from the psychological to the sociological, from the cultural to the political'.[63] By now, even the barest ameliorative demand bespeaks such practical utopianism, including 'full employment, universal full employment around the globe', whose pursuit and possible terms of realization have come to acquire the most revolutionary entailments. We need to ask, again with Jameson. What is the utopia of globalization? More practically: What are globalization's distinctive social relations? What forms of culture and belief are being generated. What forms of politics might crystallize around them? What remains the most formidable strategic challenge is the building of links from intermittent explosions of concentrated and spectacular transnationalized protest like Seattle and Genoa, and from the dispersed, localized, and decentred activity we mainly know as anti-globalization to sustained and organized action at the level of states and their new supranational governing equivalents. In principle that goal seems not so dissimilar from earlier tasks of organizing society-wide labour movement–centred democratic parties inside

---

60   See in particular Andrew Ross, ed., *No Sweat: Fashion, Free Trade, and the Rights of Garment Workers* (London: Verso, 1997) and *Low Pay, High Profile: The Global Push for Fair Labor* (New York: New Press, 2004).

61   For example, Kevin Danaher and Jason Mark, *Insurrection: Citizen Challenges to Corporate Power* (New York: Routledge, 2003).

62   Naomi Klein, *No Logo: Taking Aim at the Brand Bullies* (New York: Picador, 1999); Noreena Hertz, *The Silent Takeover: Global Capitalism and the Death of Democracy* (New York: Free Press, 2001); Arundhati Roy, *The Cost of Living* (New York: Modern Library, 1999). See also Arundhati Roy, *The Checkbook and the Cruise Missile: Conversations with Arundhati Roy by David Barsamian* (Cambridge, MA: South End, 2003).

63   Fredric Jameson, 'The Politics of Utopia', *New Left Review* II/256 (January–February 2004), 37.

national states, which most fundamentally meant the 'effort at continuity in working-class culture', as an old article in labour history once called it.[64] Yet, under the globalized equivalent of those conditions, both the logistics and the theoretical arduousness of tackling that question on a transnational scale have become immeasurably more difficult.[65]

In one widely resonant intervention, Michael Hardt and Antonio Negri specifically refused those questions of organized coordination on grounds expounded in their two books *Empire* and *Multitude*.[66] Those works issued hyper-abstracted claims about the transformation of political sovereignty under neoliberal globalization ('Empire'), without ever clarifying the concrete steps required for focused and future-directed democratic practice. Hardt and Negri recognize a place for revolutionary transformation in implicitly institutional terms linked to the idea of 'a strong event, a radical insurrectionary demand' that seems assimilable to the political category of revolution as classically understood.[67] But they eschew any concretization of how 'the constituent power of the multitude' (theorized only 'ontologically' and 'sociologically') might pass politically into the desired 'moment of rupture'.[68] Beyond the elusive claims of ontological 'commonalty', they do situate the multitude's presence inside 'the cooperative and communicative networks of social labor'. But the crucial *political* questions of 'What Is to Be Done?' – of how 'a world beyond sovereignty, beyond authority, beyond every tyranny' is to be practically organized, within an institutional field of 'guarantees and constitutional motors' – are wilfully evaded.[69]

When pressed, they concede only the most starkly dichotomized of political choices, one that pits the most limited kind of reformism, institutionally bounded by national constitutionalist politics, against the most maximalist of grassroots activisms, conceived in kaleidoscopic and shape-shifting localist terms: 'either one can work to reinforce the

64   Peter N. Stearns, 'The Effort at Continuity in Working-Class Culture', *Journal of Modern History* 52 (1980).

65   Strikingly, this issue of the institutionalizing of protest was omitted from the terms of discussion in Calhoun, Price, and Timmer, *Understanding September 11*.

66   Michael Hardt and Antonio Negri, *Empire* (Cambridge, MA: Harvard University Press, 2000) and *Multitude: War and Democracy in the Age of Empire* (New York: Penguin, 2004).

67   Hardt and Negri, *Multitude*, 358.

68   Ibid., 357.

69   Ibid., 354.

sovereignty of nation-states as a defensive barrier against the control of foreign and global capital; or one can strive towards a non-national alternative to the present form of globalization that is equally global'.[70] Yet that missing question of 'articulation' – the practical and strategic difficulties of how to negotiate back and forth between different scales of action, different forms of demand, different sites of political pressure, different geopolitical locations, different institutional concentrations of power, whether nationally, globally, or locally – has precisely the greatest urgency.[71]

The dangers of ignoring such practical exigencies of organized, strategic, and discursive articulation become all the clearer once we turn to the opposing end of the political spectrum and consider the effects of globalization on the cultural politics of the Right, where the main logic has become a kind of involution. For large sectors of opinion in the advanced capitalist or metropolitan societies, the new transnational liquidities have inspired xenophobia, cultural racism, and general ideological retrenchment, particularly in response to mass labour migrations, the movements of asylum-seekers and refugees, and the growing porousness of borders. These consequences of the globalization process are being driven deep into the everyday politics of the metropole, as events in France so dramatically showed, in both the urban insurrection of autumn 2005 and the subsequent turmoil that blocked the proposed youth employment legislation. But, in these respects, even if we take Hardt and Negri's ontological and sociological claims on their own terms, globality's generative logic is assembling a kind of 'multitude' whose forms of presence, incitements to thought and action, and discernible political effects have no single direction or bundle of potentials, but on the contrary require both careful analysis and hard political labour. In this respect, certain aspects of the grandiose ideological or discursive consequences of globalization inside the European political space deserve particular attention.

During the early 2000s, a strong politico-cultural imaginary of 'Europe' was often counterposed against the unilateralism of the Bush

---

70   Michael Hardt, 'Today's Bandung?', in Mertes, *Movement of Movements*, 232.
71   For critical symposia around Hardt and Negri's proposals, see Gopal Balakrishnan, ed., *Debating Empire* (London: Verso, 2003) and Paul A. Passavant and Jodi Dean, eds, *Empire's New Clothes: Reading Hardt and Negri* (New York: Routledge, 2004). See also Antonio Negri with Anne Dufourmantelle, *Negri on Negri* (New York: Routledge, 2004).

administration in the United States, whether construed narrowly in terms of the EU, hitched to some future attainment of a more strongly federated Europe, or postulated in some distinct and superior civilizational terms. Both affirmatively inside Europe itself and pejoratively in the Rumsfeldian rhetoric of 'Old Europe', these constructions acquired great political urgency in the build-up to the Iraq War. Thus, the urgent plea for a common European vision grounded in shared cultural goods ('the consciousness of a shared political fate and the prospect of a common future') issued during that time by Jürgen Habermas and Jacques Derrida not only bespoke the codified heritage of 'Western civilization'; it was also filtered through some enduring assumptions about popular culture.[72]

But in the circumstances of the early 2000s, in the new social landscapes being shaped by capitalist restructuring, with their deindustrialized ruins, class decomposition, and post-Fordist disarray, European popular cultures no longer contained the earlier resources and more familiar potentials from which democratic meanings might be made. The old and resilient political cultures of the Left, which from the late nineteenth century to the 1970s had proved so effective in allowing society's dominant values to be contested in collective and organized ways, no longer commanded the democratic capacities they had in the past. The 'ordinariness' of culture could no longer be imagined in the earlier registers of a socialist and class-based collectivism, which still retained extensive social purchase in the 1950s and 1960s.[73] From a contemporary

---

72   See Jürgen Habermas and Jacques Derrida, 'February 15. Or, What Binds Europeans Together. Plea for a Common Foreign Policy, Beginning in a Core Europe', in *Old Europe, New Europe, Core Europe: Transatlantic Relations after the Iraq War*, ed. Daniel Levy, Max Pensky, and John Torpey (London: Verso, 2005), 7. In Umberto Eco's contribution to the initiative proposed by Habermas and Derrida, 'An Uncertain Europe between Rebirth and Decline', he itemized Western civilization's characteristics as follows: 'the fundamental principles of the so-called Western world, the Greek and Judeo-Christian heritage, the ideas of freedom and equality born out of the French Revolution, the heritage of modern science that started with Copernicus, Galileo, Kepler, Descartes, and Francis Bacon, the capitalistic form of production, the secularization of the State, Roman or Common Law, the very idea of justice achieved through class struggle (all typical products of the European Western world, and we could cite many more) are nowadays no longer the exclusive domain of Europe. On the contrary, they have spread and become popular in America, Australia, and – although not everywhere – in many parts of Asia and Africa'. Levy, Pensky, and Torpey, *Old Europe, New Europe, Core Europe*, 15.

73   I take the notion of the 'ordinariness' of culture from Raymond Williams. See especially his essay 'Culture Is Ordinary', in his *Resources of Hope: Culture, Democracy, Socialism* (London: Verso, 1989).

vantage-point, in fact, culture's 'ordinariness' needs to be engaged on at least two other fronts: that of a multicultural or multi-ethnic hetero-geneity, which poses unresolved challenges to progressive political culture; and that of an introspectively nationalist populism, which takes the presence of 'foreigners' or ethnically isolable minorities as incite-ments to violent boundary-drawing and cultural demarcation. In neither of those contexts did the imagining of a European future in the way envisioned by Habermas and Derrida carry much appeal.[74]

The invocation of a 'common European home', as Mikhail Gorbachev once called it, usually rests upon the claim to a distinctive and coherent history. This is what Adolf Muschg, in his contribution to the Habermas–Derrida initiative, called 'sharing a common destiny':

> What holds Europe together and what divides it are at heart the same thing: common memories and habits, acquired step by step through the process of distancing itself from fatal habits. Europe is what Europe is becoming. It is neither the Occident nor the cradle of civi-lization; it does not have a monopoly on science, enlightenment, and modernity. It shouldn't attempt to ground its identity in any other way than through its own experiences: any claims for exclusivity can only lead into the same delusion and pretension through which Europe of the nineteenth century believed itself to represent the rest of the world, and entitled to dominate it.[75]

But, for all the new modesty and affected humility of its terms, this claim to a common culture is predicated on a silence. Europe's actually existing diversity of contemporary populations, whether considered via the bare-bones demography of migrancy, ethnicity, language, and reli-gious affiliation, or through more complex sociologies and cultural formations, radically exceeds such appeals to discretely unfolding his-tories held in common. In fact, far more than a mere silence is entailed here: such advocacy for the vaunted political community of 'Europe' requires an active *disremembering* or *repression* of certain vital histories before the hoped-for 'official memory' of liberal or social-democratic

---

74 Nor, we might add, do they provide much evidence for the practical realization of the political fantasy of the Multitude.

75 Adolf Muschg, '"Core Europe": Thoughts About the European Identity', in Levy, Pensky, and Torpey, *Old Europe, New Europe, Core Europe*, 26.

intellectuals like Habermas can become enabled. Instantiating this
'Europe' as a widely agreed object of political aspiration, no less than
earlier political and cultural constructions of the nation, actively presupposes such a work of forgetting and repression.

This emerged with unfailing clarity from Hans-Ulrich Wehler's
response to the Habermas–Derrida manifesto. For Wehler, whose
impeccably liberal advocacy had helped define the historical grounded-
ness of (West) German political debates across four decades, one of the
key problems left unresolved by Habermas and Derrida was the issue of
'Europe's borders'. More specifically, this was a problem of Europe's
opening to 'the east and southeast':

> White Russia [sic], the [sic] Ukraine (which has already introduced a
> parliamentary and governmental resolution to join the EU by 2011),
> Moldova, Russia itself, and Turkey in particular have never been part
> of a historic Europe. They do not live off the legacy of Judaic, Greek,
> or Roman antiquity that is present in Europe to this day. They have
> not fought their way through the far-reaching separation of state and
> church, and have even returned, as they did after the Bolshevik or
> Kemalist intermezzo, to a symbiotic relationship between the two.
> They have not experienced any Reformation and, even more import-
> antly, hardly any 'Enlightenment'. They have produced no European
> bourgeoisie, no autonomous European bourgeois cities, no European
> nobility, and no European peasantry. They have not participated in
> the greatest achievement of European political culture since the late
> nineteenth century: the construction of the social welfare state.
> Cultural divergences are deeply engraved in Europe. Orthodox Chris-
> tendom still differs greatly from a Protestant and Roman Catholic
> Europe that also remains separated from the Islam of Turkey by an
> obvious cultural barrier.[76]

In its guileless iteration of the most classical of Eurocentrisms, this was
a remarkable statement, which spoke as much to an exclusionary logic
of cultural centredness *inside* German society as it did to the maintenance of Europe's boundaries against any particular state. Wehler had

---

76 Hans-Ulrich Wehler, 'Let the United States Be Strong! Europe Remains a Mid-Size
Power: A Response to Jürgen Habermas', in ibid., 121.

ignited controversy several years before with an article in *Die Zeit* arguing unambiguously against Turkey's putative accession to the EU. In an associated interview, he insisted that 'peaceful coexistence' with Germany's Turkish immigrants 'really does not work': 'The Federal Republic does not have a foreigner problem, it has a Turkish problem. The Muslim diaspora is essentially not capable of integration.' Germany had dealt successfully with its various immigrations since the Republic's foundation, 'but at some point a boundary is reached'.[77] This standpoint was further embedded in an orientalist outlook of startling simplicity, questioning the Islamic world's capacity for democracy, invoking many centuries of a 'clash of civilizations' between the Ottoman Empire and Christendom, and generalizing its arguments onto a European scale ('Everywhere in Europe Muslim minorities are showing themselves not assimilable, huddling defensively in their subculture').[78] Wehler painted a lurid picture of the great Anatolian unwashed, massing on the frontier in their millions, awaiting only the opening of the EU's labour market. As Rita Chin remarks, 'he even revived one of the Enlightenment's oldest tropes of absolute difference, comparing 65 million contemporary Turks to Ottoman hordes at the gates of Vienna.'[79]

The most striking feature of western European debates such as these was the degree to which the racialized terms of so many contemporary anxieties about the workability of received and emergent political arrangements, and the stability of their social bases, were at the same time so profoundly embedded in the discursive architecture of political debate while still remaining unspoken. In fact, 'race' was speaking itself with troubling volubility, in a cacophony of conflicting and frequently violent ways. Both the overt racisms of the far Right and the collective actions of beleaguered minorities had been marking out the social and cultural space of racialized political understanding for some three or

---

77   Hans-Ulrich Wehler, interviewed by Ralph Bollmann, *TAZ* 6849 (10 September 2002), 6.

78   Hans-Ulrich Wehler, 'Das Türkenproblem', *Die Zeit* 38 (12 September 2002). See also Hans-Ulrich Wehler, 'Verblendetes Harakiri. Der Türkei-Beitritt zerstört die EU', *Aus Politik und Zeitgeschichte* B 33-34 (2004), 6–8. My reference to Samuel P. Huntington, *The Clash of Civilizations and the Remaking of World Order* (New York: Simon & Schuster, 1998), is deliberate, as Wehler invokes this book at the outset of his interview with Ralph Bollmann. See note 77, above.

79   Rita Chin, *The Guest Worker Question in Postwar Germany* (Cambridge: Cambridge University Press, 2007), 273.

four decades, varying country by country and locality by locality. But how this particular part of the European political unconscious might be brought productively and democratically into voice remained anything but clear.[80]

End-Point

Ending a chapter on the political framing of globalization, and the importance of historicizing its character, without mentioning 9/11 would be perverse. My own first reaction to that event, given the extraordinary spectacle of the attacks themselves, was to fear a powerfully concerted backlash against the nascent global justice movement – one that would wield the iconic imagery of the destruction of the Twin Towers as a means of delegitimizing future activism. Much of that backlash has indeed occurred, although, after the initial shock, the elements of the global justice movement rather successfully regrouped, not least under the aegis of opposition to the war.[81] Moreover, when the representational repertoire surrounding 9/11 became so crassly commodified, when the commemorative politics became so easily mired in the wrangling of competing commercial, propertied, municipal, civic, victimological, and public claims, and when a right-wing polemicist like Ann Coulter could accuse four 9/11 widows of luxuriating narcissistically in their own bereavement, it became clear that the public sphere had passed beyond any straightforward forms of conservative *Gleichschaltung*, or coordination.[82]

Fred Halliday, in one useful conspectus, outlined three clear dimensions to 9/11's impact on the world: the consequences for US public

---

80   See Geoff Eley, 'The Trouble with "Race": Migration, National Belonging, and Citizenship in Europe', in Rita Chin, Heide Fehrenbach, Geoff Eley, and Atina Grossmann, *After the Nazi Racial State: Difference and Democracy in Germany and Europe* (Ann Arbor, MI: University of Michigan Press, 2009), 137–81, 227–42. For a valuable overview of the politics of migration in Europe, see Gallya Lahav, *Immigration and Politics in the New Europe: Reinventing Borders* (Cambridge: Cambridge University Press, 2004). For radicalized far-right politics during the 2010s, see Geoff Eley, 'What Is Fascism and Where Does It Come From?', *History Workshop Journal* 91 (Spring 2021).

81   Here I deliberately substitute 'global justice' for 'anti-globalization', as this seems a far more productive umbrella designation, whether politically or descriptively.

82   See Ann Coulter, *Godless: The Church of Liberalism* (New York: Crown Forum, 2006).

opinion; the unleashing of an aggressive new dynamism in US foreign policy; and the reconfiguring of US relations with the rest of the world.[83] Common to each were elements of tension relating to Muslims, Arabs, and Islamic political activism which ran increasingly counter to any benignly transnationalizing logics of globalization. By enabling older political boundaries to be reconstituted, the effects were the opposite. They emphasized the power disparities between the advanced capitalist countries and the rest, which in military, diplomatic, and fiscal terms were still organized mainly in older national-state ways. By harnessing the fearful and angry patriotisms focused on the permanent emergency of the 'war against terror', they allowed the older national-state identifications to be re-soldered back together. As those forms of highly mobilized patriotic defensiveness became driven ever deeper into the 'homelands' of national political consciousness, they formed the focus for general political realignment. Inside the United States, those dynamics of patriotic rallying were palpable enough, both licensing and strengthening the 'security state' and hardening intolerance against difference and dissent. In 'fortress Europe', they threatened to converge, country by country and with ever greater logics of equivalence, on the possibility of an in-turned and re-centred pan-European anti-Islamic racism. Whatever the strength of the superordinate transnational political arrangements imagined by the advocates of 'global governance', in other words, any transference of popular political loyalties in such directions had a very long way to go.

The power of globalization as a discursive formation – as the demonstrated unity of talk and practice suggested at the start of this chapter – does have a vital political consequence. That very return of political allegiance to a dangerous and fearful ground of national-state patriotism is hard-wired to a ruthlessly compelling claim on the part of governments in power that the severity of the crisis both licenses and requires their *non-accountability*. And that immunity from constitutional oversight is consistently defended by the exigencies of a state of emergency presented explicitly in *global* terms. On the one hand, the 'global war against terror' is justified by a conception of 'freedom'

---

83   Fred Halliday, 'Letter from Ground Zero', *openDemocracy*, 26 May 2006, at open-Democracy.net. For the best guidance, see Steinmetz, 'State of Emergency'. See also the various essays in Calhoun, Price, and Timmer, *Understanding September 11*.

deemed to be global in its mainsprings and reach. On the other hand, the sovereignty of decision-making is resituated beyond the established constitutional lines of referral. That logic of emphatic non-accountability is unfolding at a time when the historic infrastructures of democratic citizenship under advanced capitalism – from mass-membership parties and associational solidarities to community-based structures of national political affiliation and the very exercise of citizenship through the vote – have sunk into advanced states of dissolution. Even as the largest transnational massed demonstrations of democratic citizenship ever recorded in the history of the integrated world were occurring in February 2003, the locus of political decision-making was shifting further and further away from accountability. Secure in the higher necessities of global security, governments could simply sit the protests out.

11

Stuart Hall, 1932–2014

A Devastating Loss

One of the most brilliant and significant intellectuals of his times, Stuart Hall was an outstanding social and cultural theorist, a gifted teacher and communicator, and a person of extraordinary generosity, wisdom, and largeness of vision. Though not a historian by either training or formal affiliation, he wrote and thought historically as an axiom of effective understanding. For several generations of historians, on either side of the Atlantic, he was a vital inspiration. Over a long lifetime he made so many rich and various contributions in so many areas that any pared-down summary is out of the question. He touched an astonishing number of lives – as friend and political comrade, as teacher and intellectual mentor, as organizer and collaborator, as author and editor, as broadcaster and public intellectual, or simply as the speaker of brilliance at countless conferences, seminars, workshops, and public meetings. He had an active intellectual and political presence of international proportions that reached far beyond any direct in-person encounters. At a time when resources for hope began dwindling to a distressingly short supply, he was not just an inspiration, but a kind of cement.

Hall was one of the most significant voices of the Left in Britain during the second half of the twentieth century. No one did more to mark out the ground where the contemporary politics of race would need to be thought through and faced. With acute prescience, his writings on Thatcherism from the late 1970s analysed the dissolution of the post-war settlement and the triumph of neoliberalism. In the academic world, he played a singular role in the cross-disciplinary ferment that came to be called cultural studies, notably between 1964 and 1979 as research fellow and then director at the University of Birmingham Centre for Contemporary Cultural Studies (CCCS). Framing each of these purposes and their attendant politics of knowledge were the elements of a personal history which, over time, he wrestled into a theoretically shaped ethico-political outlook of remarkable clarity and coherence. These included everything contained in the turbulence of '1968'; in the no less powerful meanings of '1956'; in all the Caribbean experiences that went into 'the formation of a diasporic intellectual'; and in his lifelong partnership with the feminist historian Catherine Hall (then Barrett), whom he met and married in 1964.

Binding all of it together was the conviction that *culture* – both as theory and as life, as literature, the arts, and aesthetics, and as the ordinary places where people find or make meaning and enjoyment in their lives – is vital for the Left's practice of democracy. Culture matters, not just for how capitalism secures its stabilities, but also for how critique and political resistance will need to be conducted. The point of taking popular culture and its forms seriously, he argued in *New Left Review*'s founding 1960 editorial, was that these were 'directly relevant to the imaginative resistance of people who have to live within capitalism – the growing points of social discontent, the projections of deeply felt needs'. Together with the slightly older Raymond Williams (1921–88), he insisted on bringing cultural questions into the centre-ground of the Left's primary concerns – as questions of ideology, meaning, identity, and subjectivity whose pertinence for the chances of political change could then be made into objects of analysis and action.

My intellectual biography was mapped by Hall's influence and writings. I began reading him in 1972–73, when I stumbled on the Birmingham Centre's *Working Papers in Cultural Studies*. I next happened on a volume coedited with Paul Walton called *Situating Marx: Evaluations and Departures*, published from a Centre conference around David

McLellan's early selections from the *Grundrisse*.[1] By then, I was delving into early issues of *NLR* and *Universities and Left Review*, so I found him there as well. He cropped up in anthologies on aspects of the history of the press and media, likewise the sociology of deviance and radical criminology, fields each undergoing an exciting boom. His pioneering essays on 'The Social Eye of Picture Post' and 'The Determination of News Photographs' first appeared at this time (in *Working Papers* 2 and 3), as did 'Encoding and Decoding in the Media Discourse' (as Stencilled Paper 7). Each utilized a still unfamiliar European resource of theory (semiotics and structuralism, Roland Barthes, Claude Lévi-Strauss, Louis Althusser) for reading media texts in less transparently common-sensical ways. References to the writings and ideas of both Hall himself and the CCCS seemed everywhere.

His early work on popular culture continued apace – on television and violence, news and current affairs, journalism and the press, media power and its effects – in an array of journals, anthologies, conference proceedings, and working papers. The renowned studies of youth subcultures appeared first as *Working Papers* 7 and 8, and then immediately in book form as the first of Hutchinson's CCCS series, *Resistance through Rituals: Youth Subcultures in Postwar Britain* (1976), coedited with Tony Jefferson. The earliest versions of parts of the 'Mugging Study' appeared as Stencilled Papers 27 and 36, before eventually culminating as the famous multi-authored book.[2] Hall was also producing his remarkable readings of Marx, a sustained exercise in theoretical reflection central to the Marxist renaissance of the time.[3] Emblematic here was the CCCS volume *On Ideology*, initially as *Working Papers* 10 (1977), then the following year as a Hutchinson volume, guided editorially by Bill Schwarz

---

1   Paul Walton and Stuart Hall, eds, *Situating Marx: Evaluations and Departures* (London: Human Context, 1973); David McLellan, ed., *Marx's Grundrisse* (London, Macmillan, 1971).

2   Stuart Hall, Chas Critcher, Tony Jefferson, John Clarke, and Brian Roberts, *Policing the Crisis: Mugging, the State, and Law and Order* (London: Macmillan, 1978).

3   Especially the following: 'Marx's Notes on Method: A "Reading" of the "1857 Introduction"', in *Working Papers in Cultural Studies* 6 (Birmingham: University of Birmingham, 1974) – reprinted in *Cultural Studies* 17: 2 (2003); 'Rethinking the "Base and Superstructure" Metaphor', in *Class, Hegemony, and Party*, ed. Jon Bloomfield et al. (London: Lawrence & Wishart, 1977) – reprinted in *Essential Essays, Vol. 1*, ed. David Morley (Durham: Duke University Press, 2019); 'The "Political" and the "Economic" in Marx's Theory of Classes', in *Class and Class Structure*, ed. Alan Hunt (London: Lawrence & Wishart, 1978); 'The Problem of Ideology: Marxism without Guarantees', in *Marx: A Hundred Years On*, ed. Betty Matthews (London: Lawrence & Wishart, 1983).

with Hall's support. Hall's own direct part, a co-authored essay on Antonio Gramsci, tracked his own intellectual progression. This striking intensity of writing and publication confirmed him as a leading voice of the Left, forging connections from ideas to practice, theory to politics, and back. If the resonance was at this stage mainly inside the Left itself, it was a time of huge energy and excitement, with the Left expanding outward, not recoiling into defeat.

This unity of intellect and politics in the heady years between the mid 1960s and the late 1970s became ever more pronounced. Hall continued forging it for three further decades. His death left a devastating absence in that most vital of political ways. He stunningly succeeded in claiming an exceptionally difficult space: one where important intellectual work, matters of the highest public concern, the political common-sense of ordinary people, and the pressing political demands of the present all come together. Complicated theory, the established patterns of politics, the shape of popular culture, and the logics of contemporary history assemble at that difficult intersection in combinations of great danger and great possibility. That was where Hall did his thinking. Trying to understand how ideas, politics, popular culture, and the movements of history all join with each other, as a basis for the most effective intervention, was an abiding theme of his life. This shuttling back and forth between the *space of experience* (all the given practices, structures, and relations that can potentially enable us, yet so often hold us in place) and a moving *horizon of expectation* (where we can imagine living differently) was how he thought. It was less a movement back and forth, in fact, than an active simultaneity, an effort at thinking those things together: space of experience, horizon of expectation; weight of history, vision of possible futures. That is what Hall meant by *conjuncture*. He asked: 'What joins together to make the big shifts in consciousness?'[4]

---

4   These are Suzanne Moore's words in her obituary, 'Stuart Hall Was a Voice for Misfits Everywhere. That's His Real Legacy', *Guardian*, 13 February 2014. See the closing paragraph of Chapter 7 above.

A Travelling Life

Stuart McPhail Hall was born in Kingston, Jamaica on 3 February 1932, into what he called 'a lower-middle-class family that was trying to be an upper-middle-class family trying to be an English Victorian family'.[5] In reflecting on this origin, as he did with growing frequency from the later 1980s, he found both formative strengths and the source of much unease and pain. The first non-white in a senior position at the United Fruit Company, his father Herman came from a poor shopkeeper family of patchwork ethnicity – African, East Indian, Portuguese, Scottish, Jewish – living deferentially inside the given racial and colonial hierarchies. His mother Jessie ('an overwhelmingly dominant person') came from the better-off middle class: very light-skinned, with a profoundly conservative outlook, she identified both with England as 'the mother country' and with 'that old plantation world . . . as a "golden age"'.[6] On the one hand, Hall received what by any criteria was a fine academic schooling. At Kingston's Jamaica College, with its entirely English and imperial curriculum, he ended by reading 'T. S. Eliot, James Joyce, Freud, Marx, Lenin, and some of the surrounding literature and modern poetry'. A number of his teachers, attuned to the emergent Caribbean nationalism, broadened his access to reading, ideas, and current affairs at a time (middle and late 1940s) when big events were in train.

The family was highly race-conscious in severely self-damaging ways. In his final years at school, his parents vetoed his elder sister's love relationship with a black Barbadian medical student, ruled inadmissible by his skin. Through the resulting conflict, his sister had a catastrophic psychic collapse, was treated with ECT, and never recovered. Witness to this family drama, by his own much later accounting, Hall was pitched into a different understanding: 'I was suddenly aware of the contradiction of a colonial culture, of how one lives out the color-class-colonial dependency experience and of how it could destroy you, subjectively.' At

---

5   Stuart Hall, 'Minimal Selves', in Lisa Appingnanesi, *Identity: The Real Me, ICA Documents* 6 (London: Institute of Contemporary Arts, 1988), 45 – reprinted in *Black British Cultural Studies: A Reader*, ed. Houston A. Baker Jr, Manthia Diawara, and Ruth H. Lindeborg (Chicago: University of Chicago Press, 1996).

6   Kuan-Hsing Chen, 'The Formation of a Diasporic Intellectual: An Interview with Stuart Hall', in *Stuart Hall: Critical Dialogues in Cultural Studies*, ed. David Morley and Kuan-Hsing Chin (London: Routledge, 1996), 489, 485.

a lifetime's distance, composed with intervening languages of theory, this story acquired formative coherence: 'It broke down forever, for me, the distinction between the public and the private self. I learned about culture, first, as something which is deeply subjective and personal, and at the same moment, as a structure you live.'[7]

In his later telling, the story became paradigmatic. It impelled him outwards. His sister's life became 'a complete tragedy, which I lived through her, and I decided I couldn't take it; I couldn't help her, I couldn't reach her, although I understood what was wrong.' It 'crystallized my feelings about the space I was called into by my family. I was not going to stay there, I was not going to be destroyed by it. I had to get out.' By 1951, he was gone, borne by a Rhodes Scholarship, escorted to Merton College, Oxford by his mother. The direction was finally set later, by 1957, but he never went back. Learning about his politics, his mother kept him away too. By the 1980s, Hall made this story foundational. It described the in-betweenness of the diasporic condition – the necessary unfinishedness of making a new home (the permanent ambivalence of being in England), yet the impossibility of being able to 'go home again'. The late twentieth century had now universalized this experience, he thought, turning it 'archetypal'. His story's power could only be reclaimed later, enabled by Hall's own writing about race, colonialism, diaspora, and postcoloniality, along with the wider thinking he helped inspire, in which Paul Gilroy was such a key pioneer.[8] Capturing his Jamaican starting point 'in that way' – personally rather than just analytically, and from inside the position of 'a black West Indian, just like everybody else' – took him 'a very long time'. As he said in 1992, 'I am able to write about it now because I'm at the end of a long journey . . . In that sense, it has taken me fifty years to come home.'

Hall read English at Oxford, moving directly in 1954 to a dissertation on Henry James, which political urgencies led him to set aside. Two parallel times defined these Oxford years. He moved first in expatriate circles of fellow students from the Caribbean, whose encounter with students from Africa made them 'West Indians' in a new way. 'We were passionate about the colonial question', he later said. 'We followed the

---

7   These and the following quotations are taken from Chen, 'Formation of a Diasporic Intellectual', 484–91.

8   Paul Gilroy, *The Black Atlantic* (Cambridge, MA: Harvard University Press, 1993).

expulsion of the French from Indochina with a massive celebration dinner.' He 'was very much formed' inside this 'first generation, black, anti-colonial or postcolonial intelligentsia, who studied in England, did graduate work, trained to be economists'.[9] When most went back, he stayed. His second scene, overlapping slightly with the first via friend-ships with classicist Alan Hall and fellow Rhodes Scholar Charles Taylor, was the Oxford Left. Little more than a loose conversation between student Communists ('the Balliol Reds' – Raphael Samuel, Peter Sedg-wick, Gabriel Pearson), the 'Cole Group' (the politics seminar of G. D. H. Cole), and a few independents like the two Halls and Taylor, it revived the moribund Socialist Club. When 1956 arrived, this nascent network supplied one of the New Left's main strands. As Hall recalled, it included 'more than its fair share of exiles and migrants, which reinforced its cosmopolitanism': they were from Trinidad, Jamaica, Quebec, Sudan, Syria, and from one kind of British margin or another – provincial or working-class; or Scottish, Welsh, Irish, or Jewish.[10]

1956

The story of 1956 as the crucible of the New Left has been well told, many times. From the cataclysmic political shocks of the year – first the reports of Nikita Khrushchev's indictment of Stalin at the Twentieth Congress of the CPSU in February, then the invasions of Egypt and Hungary in October–November – came a vital shift in the Left's pros-pects in Britain. If there were no massed ranks of a full-fledged popular movement, it unlocked the existing fronts of expectation. As Hall later reflected, the events broke through 'the climate of fear and suspicion' that prevailed during those years, when 'the "Cold War" dominated the political horizon, positioning everyone and polarizing every topic by its remorseless binary logic'. The combined spectacle of Hungary and Suez dramatized the bankruptcy of each of the Left's primary traditions, Communism and social democracy. It 'unmasked the underlying violence and aggression latent in the two systems which dominated

---

9   Chen, 'Formation of a Diasporic Intellectual', 492.
10   Stuart Hall, 'The "First" New Left: Life and Times', in *Out of Apathy: Voices of the New Left Thirty Years On*, ed. Oxford University Socialist Discussion Group (London: Verso, 1989), 19–20.

political life at that time – Western imperialism and Stalinism'. It promised 'the break-up of the political Ice Age'. It pointed the way forward to
an exciting, unanticipated opportunity, a 'third' political space where a
'New Left' could form.[11]

This was Hall's defining political experience. It posed challenges
which he continued to engage throughout his life. They included the
very idea of a 'third space' per se. In our own time, after Communism's
1989 demise, when the vast weight of official and media commentary
began dragooning any permissible opinion into the crude polarity of
socialism's definitive failure versus market capitalism's triumph, he
refused to be unnerved. Anyone inspired by the breaks of 1956 should
feel no embarrassment about the ending of the state-socialist model, he
argued sardonically, because 'we have been waiting for it to happen for
three decades'. New Left positions of 1956–57 were fully continuous
with democracy talk in 1989.[12]

That new space lay beyond any given models of leadership – whether
vanguardist and sectarian, democratic-centralist, Fabian and expert-
derived, or based in the machine-style Labourism of parliament,
elections, conference, and the trade-union block vote. The politics
arising from the crisis year's frenetic disarray had two main strands. One
was a new generation's critique of the reconstructed capitalist society
observably changing around them – younger intellectuals, still mainly
in their twenties, for whom Hall and the Oxford group wanted to
speak ('an alternative – not to say beleaguered – intellectual minority
culture').[13] They hatched a new journal in early 1957, *Universities and
Left Review*, with a Samuel–Pearson–Taylor–Hall editorial team. Concurrently, dissident Communists and their allies, famously grouped
around Edward Thompson, John Saville, and *The Reasoner*, drew passionately on an older set of Anglo-British socialist and popular radical
traditions, now recharged as 'socialist humanism'. This grouping
launched *The New Reasoner* (*NR*). The two networks were matched in a
common conversation. Some organized initiatives ensued – New Left
Clubs around the country (twenty in 1960, a year later forty-one, by
1963 still thirty-eight); the Partisan coffee house in Soho; the Campaign

---

11   Ibid., 16–17, 13.
12   Stuart Hall, 'Coming Up For Air', *Marxism Today* 34 (March 1990), 25.
13   Hall, '"First" New Left', 19.

for Nuclear Disarmament (launched 1957–58) – as a key New Left arena. But the movement was avowedly one of ideas – of non-sectarian networking, of debates across the old dividing lines, of ideas as such (against 'the conventional anti-intellectualism of the British labour movement'). It spelled a participatory politics within an ethics of 'commitment', what Hall dubbed 'our missionary phase'.[14]

The journals merged by the close of 1959 to form New Left Review, with an unmanageably expanded board and Hall as editor – a role he discharged until the end of 1961, bringing the 'first' New Left to a finish. The latter remained entirely innocent of the gender issues exploding around the second New Left ten years later. If not absent, race questions remained embedded in contexts formally about something else, such as poverty, welfare, housing. But three decisive recognitions moving the ULR part of this story stayed vital for the coming six decades. Hall was an active intelligence in each. The first addressed contemporary capitalism and its new corporate organization, fresh dynamics of accumulation, and burgeoning consumerism. Social structure, labour markets, patterns of residence, spending habits, educational chances, mass leisure and entertainment – in short, the entire given meanings of class in their relation to politics – were made open to question. Hall's 1958 article on 'A Sense of Classlessness' was fundamental here.[15] Second, any narrow definition of politics was blown apart. The political domain became radically redefined. While work and its social relations remained vital, politics moved away from the 'point of production' towards other places too. The boundaries were changing:

We raised issues of personal life, the way people live, culture, which weren't considered the topics of politics on the left. We wanted to talk about the contradictions of this new kind of capitalist society in which people didn't have a language to express their private troubles, didn't realize that these troubles reflected political and social questions which could be generalized.[16]

14   In his opening editorial, 'Introducing NLR', for New Left Review I/1 (January–February 1960).
15   Stuart Hall, 'A Sense of Classlessness', Universities and Left Review 1: 5 (1958).
16   Stuart Hall in Ronald Fraser, 1968: A Student Generation in Revolt (New York: Pantheon, 1988), 30.

That points precisely to the third decisive recognition: the centrality of culture. For the *ULRers*, 'it was in the cultural and ideological domain that social change appeared to be making itself most dramatically visible'. That 'cultural dimension seemed to us not a secondary, but a constitutive dimension of society', signifying a key part of 'the New Left's long-standing quarrel with the reductionism and economism of the base–superstructure metaphor'. Most vitally of all, it was through cultural analysis that the most empowering critique of the 'new capitalism' would be mounted – by tracing 'the impact of "commodification" in areas of life far removed from the immediate sites of wage-labor exploitation'. By these means, the traditional framing of debate as 'high culture versus popular culture' could be transcended. In Hall's words, 'the discourse of culture seemed to us fundamentally necessary to any language in which socialism could be redescribed'. And then, crucially: 'No one expressed the fundamental and constitutive character of this argument for and within the New Left more profoundly than Raymond Williams'.[17]

On the very eve of Suez-Budapest, in the summer of 1956, Stuart had gone with Alan Hall and two other friends for a summer's working vacation to 'sketch out a book on the new contours of cultural change in "Contemporary Capitalism"'. With them went a small library of reading that included 'two typescript chapters of what was to become Raymond Williams' *Culture and Society*'. Hall had just met Williams in the Oxford seminar of F. W. (Freddy) Bateson (1901–78), an older socialist and eighteenth-century literary scholar, who launched the quarterly *Essays in Criticism* in 1951 as an alternative to F. R and Q. D. Leavis's *Scrutiny*.[18] Williams, still a little-known figure, now came to the heart of New Left circles, particularly once *Culture and Society* was published in 1958. That was a momentous conjunction. Coming fast after Richard Hoggart's *The Uses of Literacy* in 1957, Williams's thinking converged powerfully with discussions in *ULR* and *NR*, whose pages dripped with allusions to his and Hoggart's impact. It was only natural that, for his first issue of the freshly merged *NLR*, Hall should feature a dialogue on 'Working-Classic Attitudes' between Williams and Hoggart – the first time the two had met.[19]

---

17 Hall, '"First" New Left', 25, 27.
18 Dai Smith, *Raymond Williams: A Warrior's Tale* (Cardigan: Parthian, 2008), 398–9.
19 Richard Hoggart and Raymond Williams, 'Working Class Attitudes', *New Left Review* I/1 (January–February 1960).

Having taught in South London secondary schools during 1957–59, Hall now took a lectureship in media, film, and popular culture at Chelsea College of the University of London, one of the earliest teaching positions of its kind. From that experience, and collaboration with Paddy Whannel at the British Film Institute, came the jointly authored study of contemporary popular culture, which along with Denys Thompson's anthology, *Discrimination and Popular Culture*, remains the defining book of its kind from that time.[20] When Richard Hoggart moved universities in 1964, from Leicester to Birmingham, and created CCCS, he asked Hall to take the Centre on. Hoggart 'thought that, with my combination of interests in television, film, and popular literature, my knowledge of the Leavis debate and my interest in cultural politics, I would be a good person. I went to Birmingham in 1964 and got married to Catherine – who transferred to Birmingham from Sussex – the same year.'[21]

From 1968 to New Times

If Hall's links to Hoggart, personally and intellectually, proved fleeting, ending effectively when Hoggart left for UNESCO in 1968–69, those to Williams were lasting and close. Separated in years by a decade (and generationally by the wartime), as well as by origin and race, they shared a very great deal. They each travelled the journey of a scholarship boy, the one from colony and colour, the other from region and class. Williams pitched his tent in the border country of nation and class, Hall in the margins of race, gender, and the postcolonial. They lived a complex, if differently grounded commitment to thinking through a post-Leavisite conception of the importance of culture for democratic nationhood. Their common route was through a sustained encounter with Gramsci. They each spent the 1970s and 1980s systematically exploring the widest body of European theoretical Marxism (though Williams, interestingly, mostly stopped short of Foucault). Closer to home, they each pioneered critical analysis of television: while Hall was

20   Hall and Paddy Whannel, *The Popular Arts* (London: Hutchinson, 1964) – reprinted by Duke University Press (2008); Denys Thompson, ed., *Discrimination and Popular Culture* (Harmondsworth: Penguin, 1964).
21   Chen, 'Formation of a Diasporic Intellectual', 498.

honing his own highly original methodology, Williams delivered his
monthly column for *The Listener* (1968–72) and wrote *Television: Technology and Cultural Form*.[22] In retrospect, this was a fascinating set of
convergences, emblematic for an entire slice of later-twentieth-century
intellectual life. Their work brilliantly established the necessity of culture
for social and political analysis, not just for the Left or people in cultural
studies directly, but for anyone seeking to render that contemporary
world intelligible. To find them at the core of the *May Day Manifesto* in
1967–68 was no surprise.[23]

Hall's years at CCCS were uniquely productive. His leadership was
inspirational and charismatic, yet democratic and enabling. He was
intellectually rigorous and exacting, yet generous, patient, calming. By
the time he left in 1979 for the Open University (OU) chair of sociology, cultural studies had uncertainly coalesced as an acknowledged
cross-disciplinary field. In the course of the 1980s, former CCCS students fanned out across academic and allied employment, not often
with immediate security or high-end recognition, most commonly in
what were then polytechnics, where cultural studies gained early institutional footholds. New journals were launched. Stronger programmatic
initiatives developed, especially during the 1990s. Calling this straightforwardly a Birmingham story inflates not only the degree of its
influence, but also its intellectual cohesion (Hall habitually deflected
talk of 'the Birmingham school'), as if CCCS was the sole active origin.
Yet, between *Resistance through Rituals* (1976) and *Crises in the British
State 1880–1930* (1985), with trailblazing originality, the Centre led a

---

22   Hall, 'Encoding and Decoding in the Television Discourse', Stencilled Occasional
Paper 7: Centre for Contemporary Cultural Studies, University of Birmingham (1973),
128–38. In a 2007 republication, 'Television' was substituted for the original 'Media' in the
title. See also Stuart Hall, 'The Determination of News Photographs', *Working Papers in
Cultural Studies* 3 (Centre for Contemporary Cultural Studies, Birmingham: University of
Birmingham, 1972) and 'The Social Eye of Picture Post', *Working Papers in Cultural Studies*
3 (Centre for Contemporary Cultural Studies, Birmingham: University of Birmingham,
1972). Williams's TV columns are collected in Alan O'Connor, ed., *Raymond Williams on
Television: Selected Writings* (London: Routledge, 1989). See also David Lusted, ed., *Raymond
Williams: Film, TV, Culture* (London: National Film Theatre/British Film Institute Educa-
tion, 1989).
23   Originally issued the previous year and greatly expanded in 1968, *May Day Manifesto* (London: Penguin, 1968) was drafted by a committee headed by Williams, Hall, and
Edward Thompson. See Stephen Woodhams, 'The 1968 *May Day Manifesto*', in *About
Raymond Williams*, ed. Monika Seidl, Roman Horak, and Lawrence Grossberg (London:
Routledge, 2010).

series of very major discussions, with echoes across many fields and countries.[24] During the 1980s, that resonance became fully international. Hall's ideas and writings were at its beating heart, registered by a summer institute he taught at University of Illinois, Urbana-Champaign in June–July 1983. By the time of the successive mega-conferences hosted there (1983 and 1990) and the volumes they left behind – Old Testament and New – that centrality was plain.[25]

This wider influence flourished during the OU period, in 1979–98. Hall's Birmingham time had been extraordinarily intense. In several dimensions, he thrived there. With no resources from the university, in an institutional climate at best indifferent and mostly adversarial, he enabled a collaborative way of working that broke the usual mould, especially the barriers separating teachers and students. But, as imagined at CCCS, this collective ideal was far more than a working method or an approach to one's academic studies. It was an effort at radically reconceiving what a socially responsible and ethically driven commitment to higher education might mean – an entire outlook, an ethos, a common acceptance that thinking, learning, writing, personal life, and politics all belonged axiomatically together. From person to person, among students and teachers at the Centre, the exact balance varied, some tending more to intellectual work, some to community-based activism, some to the socialisms that became so energizing at the time, some to a cultural politics of identity and style. From the Labour and Communist Parties, through the International Marxist Group, the Socialist Workers Party, and Big Flame, to various unaffiliated anarchisms and Marxisms – and, cutting across all of these and increasingly against them, the emergent feminisms – most groups and tendencies were present. But belonging to one or another of these was beside the point. The *collective* quality of the Centre's ethos came from a common involvement in the unities of ideas, politics, and practice. To call that 'the politics of intellectual work' would also be a misnomer, an import from a different time, as its practitioners deliberately refused the

---

24   For complete citations, see above, Chapter 7, note 1.
25   Cary Nelson and Lawrence Grossberg, eds, *Marxism and the Interpretation of Culture* (New York: Routledge, 1988); Lawrence Grossberg, Cary Nelson, and Paula Treichler, eds, *Cultural Studies* (New York: Routledge, 1992). Hall's 1983 lectures have been published in Daryl Slack and Lawrence Grossberg, eds, *Cultural Studies 1983: A Theoretical History* (Durham: Duke University Press, 2016).

implied separation. It was also the ground from which Hall's Gramscian commitments could unfold.

Hall's own intellectual work at CCCS, along with the research and
writing he helped inspire, on media, deviance, race, class, history (especially of Britain's early twentieth century), politics, and critical theory,
radically shifted the terms of debate and understanding across a large
swathe of intellectual life in Britain and elsewhere. But there were costs.
He found the necessary turbulence of the collectivist culture – the
entailments of trying to make knowledge democratically – exhausting.
The conflicts around feminism were painfully hard, making Hall's
situation, as an avowedly feminist man but the responsible director of an
institution, less and less tractable. He was caught structurally in what he
knew to be 'an impossibly contradictory position'. However patiently
non-hierarchical his vision of the Centre's practices and procedures,
certain conflicts and dilemmas could not be escaped. 'It wasn't a personal thing', he later reflected: 'I'm very close to many of the feminists of
that period. It was a structural thing. I couldn't any longer do any useful
work, from that position. It was time to go.'[26]

The OU offered a less fraught and more orthodox teaching situation,
yet one different enough – a more flexible interdisciplinary setting,
collaborative teaching, media-related pedagogy, non-traditional students, an ethos of expanding access to higher education still connected
to the sixties – to give politics scope. For Hall, it was the chance to
translate the Centre's theory-driven vision of cultural studies into forms
more available to wider audiences. Amid the resulting accomplishments, four bodies of work especially stand out. The first two centred on
the OU courses 'State and Society' (D209) and 'Beliefs and Ideologies'
(DE354). The first produced anthologies Hall edited with Gregor
McLennan and David Held on *The Idea of the Modern State* (OU Press,
1984) and *State and Society in Contemporary Britain: A Critical Introduction* (Polity, 1984); the second, a reader edited with James Donald on
Politics and Ideology (OU Press, 1986). Later came 'Culture, Media and
Identities' (D318), with six collectively produced original readers, includ-
ing Hall's own *Representation: Cultural Representations and Signifying
Practices* (Sage, 1997); and, finally, 'Understanding Modern Societies'
(D213), with four edited volumes, later imposingly anthologized into a

---

26   Chen, 'Formation of a Diasporic Intellectual', 500.

single-volume sociology textbook, *Modernity: An Introduction to Modern Societies* (Blackwell, 1996), coedited with David Held, Don Hubert, and Kenneth Thompson. Immeasurably more than just codifying the already familiar, each brilliantly realized the purposes of a politically engaged and theoretically formed pedagogy. Partly via the OU's use of TV and radio for teaching, he also became more active in broadcasting, developing documentaries, for example, on the Caribbean for BBC television, on W. E. B. DuBois for radio.

In these years, Hall acquired a vital presence in the Left's national politics. That began in the notorious stand-off between Edward Thompson and Richard Johnson at the Thirteenth Ruskin History Workshop on 1 December 1979, when Hall, as third speaker, tried in vain to mediate the fight and contain Thompson's grandiosity. The impulse came from CCCS discussions of historiography, with previews in key debates of the mid 1960s. With Thompson on one side, Perry Anderson and Tom Nairn on the other, these centred on the New Left's contested intellectual and political legacy. The Ruskin event was the nadir of the increasingly embittered divisiveness surrounding precisely the theory work that defined Hall's importance. But, in the event, it proved cathartic. Six months before, Margaret Thatcher's government had been elected, with consequences that rapidly changed the stakes of political argument. A little earlier, Hall had proposed his category of Thatcherism in 'The Great Moving Right Show' (*Marxism Today*, January 1979), itself prefigured in *Policing the Crisis*, which now framed the terms of the Left's response to this new right. Published mainly in *Marxism Today* and *New Socialist*, written avowedly for the widest readership, these essays showed Hall at his pellucidly accessible and communicative best. First in *The Politics of Thatcherism* (Lawrence & Wishart, 1983), edited with Martin Jacques, then in his own *The Hard Road to Renewal: Thatcherism and the Crisis of the Left* (Verso, 1988), he mapped the new terrain. *This* was the vital return on all of that arduous theory work. He showed, in the course of political commentary intended to be useful, how readings of Marx, Althusser, Poulantzas, feminist theory, theories of language and discourse, Laclau and Mouffe, Foucault, and above all Gramsci, could all really help. In the related project of *New Times: The Changing Face of Politics in the 1990s* (Lawrence & Wishart, 1989), edited with Martin Jacques, he turned to the constructive question of the possible political strategies that might now be opening.

The optimism moving *New Times* failed to win through. It outlasted to some extent the shock of the 1992 elections and the Conservatives' fourth term. But the abrupt disappointment of New Labour after 1997, followed by the Blair years' relentless attrition of public and social goods, left little intact. While remaining highly active and inspiring public figures, two of Hall's leading New Left comrades, Marxist historians Edward Thompson and Raphael Samuel, had each immersed themselves in historical work with very different directions from his own. The tragically early death of Raymond Williams in 1988 stole one vital interlocutor; Thompson followed in 1993, and then Samuel in 1996. With a third historian, another key voice of *New Times*, Eric Hobsbawm (who died in 2013), differences were always plain. But Hall continued patiently on, deploying not only the arguments forged from the 1980s, but the perduring insights of the 1950s too.

The New Left already saw that people no longer live their relation to society through just a single identity (if they ever had), he pointed out, however salient such 'big' identities as class might sometimes become. Rather, 'there were different identities, different forms of social subjectivity, which had to be mobilized in any kind of contemporary political movement'.[27] Under not only Thatcher but also John Major and again, since 2010, David Cameron, the Tories 'are sitting on top of a society without commanding even a normal electoral, popular majority'. To stay there, 'they must constantly adapt, absorb, translate, and transform. They are constantly buying in from society, whether it is ecology or consumer needs, and transforming ideas into their own language'.[28] If New Labour succeeded only by mimicking a modified version of this reigning post-Thatcherite script, then another new Left needed to build its own popular-democratic leadership, speaking across differences with some compelling political appeal. Nor can issues and causes be merely patched together in some additive or rhetorically aggregating fashion. A new vision for reclaiming the popular high ground, with moral-political persuasiveness in the Gramscian way, required something more. 'I could give you a whole range of arenas around which I think one ought now to organize and mobilize, but still there would always be in my mind the

27   Stuart Hall in 'Then and Now: A Reevaluation of the New Left', in Oxford University Socialist Discussion Group, *Out of Apathy*.
28   Stuart Hall, 'Opening Up Our Vision', in *Talking About Tomorrow: A New Radical Politics*, Stuart Wilks (London: Pluto, 1993), 158.

larger question of how those particular struggles connect with a larger socialist project.'[29]

Identity, Difference, Articulation

However dispirited by the managerial gutting of public life, he never gave up. He continued seeking new ways to have an effect. In 1995, from the ruins of *New Times*, along with Doreen Massey, Michael Rustin, and a wider circle of co-thinkers, he launched a new journal called *Soundings*. Together, in spring 2013, they began issuing the Kilburn Manifesto, intended to prepare the ground for a post-neoliberal politics. At the same time, he had long committed his main energies to questions of race, to radicalizing and democratizing the discourse of multiculturalism, and to campaigning for racial justice. Descending from his earliest London years and the Notting Hill riots, followed by the climate of fear in Birmingham surrounding Enoch Powell's 'rivers of blood' speech in 1968, those questions were never very far away. But, from the mid 1970s and *Policing the Crisis*, they gained ever greater immediacy. Though he had left CCCS by the time it appeared, the landmark volume *The Empire Strikes Back: Race and Racism in 70s Britain* (1982) eloquently bore his imprint. A wide variety of his essays marked the 1980s, some directly on race per se – paradigmatically with 'The Whites of their Eyes' and 'Race, Articulation, and Societies Structured in Dominance'.[30] Other writings threaded that problem through wider discussions of ideology, politics, and increasingly diaspora and post-colonialism. Later, in the 1990s, he was active in the Stephen Lawrence campaign and other settings, including a variety of public bodies, official and unofficial. In 1997 he joined the Runnymede Trust Commission on the Future of Multi-Ethnic Britain, whose findings were published in October 2000.

---

29   Hall in 'Then and Now', 168.

30   Stuart Hall, 'The Whites of Their Eyes: Racist Ideologies and the Media', in *Silver Linings: Some Strategies for the Eighties*, ed. George Bridges and Rosalind Brunt (London: Lawrence & Wishart, 1981) – reprinted in *Gender, Race, and Class in Media*, 4th edn, ed. Gail Dines and Jean M. Humez (London: Sage, 2015), 'Race, Articulation, and Societies Structured in Dominance', in *Sociological Theories: Race and Colonialism*, ed. UNESCO (Paris: UNESCO, 1980) – reprinted in *Black British Cultural Studies: A Reader*, ed. Houston A. Baker Jr, Manthia Diawara, and Ruth H. Lindeborg (Chicago: University of Chicago Press, 1996).

Across these same years, intensifying from the later 1980s, Catherine Hall made her own travels through histories of the Caribbean, beginning from a family trip to Jamaica in the summer of 1988. Having earlier pioneered the study of gender, family, and capital formation in the making of the English middle class, she now moved that thinking onto the global stage, placing 'the imagined nation' firmly 'within a wider frame of empire'.[31] Essays on the colonial relation soon followed, and by May 1993 she had joined Stuart in dissecting the 'the post-colonial' in a major conference in Naples.[32] They worked in brilliant counterpoint. While Stuart argued patiently and insistently that race and legacies of empire be brought finally into the open, so that the English might actually face up to their whiteness (and lose what James Baldwin called the 'jewel of [their] naiveté'), Catherine showed in compelling detail how colonialism worked its effects, whether 'at home' in the remaking of metropolitan society or 'away' through its impact on the colonized worlds.[33] Catherine's books followed in rapid succession: a benchmark anthology on *Cultures of Empire* (2000); an analysis of the political conjuncture of the 1860s, *Defining the Victorian Nation* (also 2000), co-authored with Keith McClelland and Jane Rendall; her magnum opus, *Civilising Subjects* (2002); an outstanding volume coedited with Sonya Rose, *At Home with the Empire* (2006); and a dual biography of the Macaulays, father and son (2012).[34] While Stuart brought the empire's continuing presence under his finely focused theoretical lens, Catherine gave theory its history. Their

---

31 Leonore Davidoff and Catherine Hall, *Family Fortunes: Men and Women of the English Middle Class, 1780–1850* (Chicago: University of Chicago Press, 1987); Catherine Hall, 'The Nation Within and Without', in *Defining the Victorian Nation: Class, Race, Gender, and the Reform Act of 1867*, ed. Catherine Hall, Keith McClelland, and Jane Rendall (Cambridge: Cambridge University Press, 2000), 179.

32 Stuart Hall, 'When Was "the Post-Colonial"? Thinking at the Limit', and Catherine Hall, 'Histories, Empires, and the Post-Colonial Moment', both in *The Post-Colonial Question: Common Skies, Divided Horizons*, ed. Iain Chambers and Lidia Curti (London: Routledge, 1995).

33 James Baldwin, 'Stranger in the Village', quoted in Catherine Hall, *Civilising Subjects: Metropole and Colony in the English Imagination, 1830–1867* (Chicago: University of Chicago Press, 2002), 5–6.

34 Catherine Hall, ed., *Cultures of Empire: Colonizers in Britain and the Empire in the Nineteenth and Twentieth Centuries* (Cambridge: Cambridge University Press, 2000); Hall, McClelland, and Rendall, *Defining the Victorian Nation*; Hall, *Civilising Subjects*; Catherine Hall, *Macaulay and Son: Architects of Imperial Britain* (New Haven, CT: Yale University Press, 2012); Catherine Hall and Sonya Rose, eds, *At Home with the Empire* (Cambridge: Cambridge University Press, 2006).

collaboration modelled the reciprocal inspiration any lifelong intellectual partnership would hope to attain.

On retiring from the OU in 1998, Hall gave himself energetically to
the black arts movement, opening conversation with younger cohorts
of artists, photographers, and filmmakers, with diverse writings in
catalogues, journals, and anthologies. He was active in creating Rivington Place in Shoreditch, opened in 2007 as a centre for public education
and exhibition in the contemporary visual arts around multiculturalism and global diversity. He chaired both Iniva (Institute of International
Visual Arts) and Autograph (Association of Black Photographers),
each attached to Rivington Place, where the Stuart Hall Library is
housed. While exploring the politics of black subjectivity through 'the
"writing" of the postwar history of the black diaspora through the optic
of its visual arts', he connected this interest brilliantly to underlying
problems.[35] He further disturbed the available master narrative of
British national history. He pushed on another long-lasting problem:
'the difficulty of trying . . . to make connections between works of art
and wider social histories without collapsing the former or displacing
the latter'.[36]

That brings us full circle. Hall had journeyed as a young person
from the edges of an empire into its core, helping perhaps more than
anyone else to expose and explore the continuing effects of that colonial and postcolonial history. He exchanged in the process one James
for another – the Henry of that discarded dissertation for the C. L. R.
who inspired his thinking for the coming decades. John Akomfrah's
gallery installation, *The Unfinished Conversation*, and the associated
film *The Stuart Hall Project* (2013), beautifully captured that cultural
itinerary, through which the politics emerged. By 1990, Hall was
approaching questions of identity and subjectivity using diaspora and
the postcolonial as primary analytics, while critically reworking post-
Althusserian French thought into a major battery of essays.[37] He engaged
more directly with Caribbean histories too, as a 1998 interview and a

35   Stuart Hall, 'Black Diaspora Artists in Britain: Three "Moments" in Postwar History',
History Workshop Journal 61 (2006), 22.
36   Ibid., 23.
37   These included 'Cultural Identity and Diaspora', in *Identity: Community, Culture,
Difference*, ed. Jonathan Rutherford (London: Lawrence & Wishart, 1990), 'The Question of
Cultural Identity', in *Modernity and Its Futures*, ed. Stuart Hall, David Held, and Anthony
McGrew (Cambridge: Polity Press, 1992), and 'When Was "the Post-Colonial"?'

reflection on Franz Fanon each eloquently confirmed.[38] Catherine's studies of Jamaica and the imperial relationship worked vitally with this thinking. The ingrained assumptions of racial difference around which British identity (and the 'Englishness' within) was structured were a recurring preoccupation. Contemporary national identity was centred around an unmarked and unspoken whiteness, he argued, which kept other populations in Britain on the margin. This was the red thread through all of Hall's biography, certainly from the middle 1960s. It made him the most eloquent architect, advocate, and practitioner of what could be British multiculturalism. It shaped his writings and influence on race, identity, politics, diaspora, difference, and then the movement for black arts. From the 1970s forward, he pioneered new understandings of 'race' and its centrality for contemporary social, cultural, and political life.

Stuart Hall's role as founding architect of cultural studies remains essential to his legacy: he insisted that popular culture be taken seriously; he advocated patiently for cross-disciplinary intellectual collaboration. He believed passionately in a democracy of the intellect. Among his countless publications over a fifty-year period, there were no books in his own name only. As a critical theorist, he combined a lucidly accessible grasp of the most difficult areas of high theory, an equally brilliant attentiveness to the common sense of popular beliefs, a visionary breadth and precision of contemporary political analysis, and an exceptional clarity of communication. Somehow, he could think simultaneously with and inside many distinct bodies of contemporary thought – western Marxism, structuralism and semiotics, literary theory, ethnography and cultural anthropology, communications and media studies, psychoanalysis, theories of language, feminist theory, poststructuralism, postcolonial theory, and more – while modelling such a widely based non-sectarian conversation for others. He was an extraordinary teacher – not just in the seminar room, the lecture theatre, and the institutional world of the university, but in the very fullest sense of public and political pedagogy, including of course the media programming of the Open

---

38   See 'Breaking Bread with History: C. L. R. James and *The Black Jacobins*', interviewed by Bill Schwarz, *History Workshop Journal* 46 (1998); 'The After-Life of Franz Fanon: Why Fanon? Why Now? Why *Black Skin, White Masks?*', in *The Fact of Blackness: Franz Fanon and Visual Representation*, ed. Alan Read (London: Institute of Contemporary Arts/Institute of International Visual Arts, 1996).

University and his many TV appearances. He was a brilliant communicator. When he lectured, he brought light into the room.

Hall's final years were impeded by ill health, burdening him with
intensive dialysis and eventually a kidney transplant. Inevitably, that
began affecting his ability to work. Increasingly, it kept him from speaking in public, and certainly from serious travelling. He received many
honours, including election to the British Academy in 2005. In 2007 at
the University of Michigan, to our own immense delight, he was to
receive an honorary degree, but had to forgo the trip. He was survived
by Catherine, his daughter Rebecca and son Jess, two grandchildren, his
sister Patricia, and an immense multitude of friends and admirers.

The loss of his warmth of presence and guiding intelligence was
simply not bearable. At the end of their obituary in the *Guardian*, David
Morley and Bill Schwarz described Hall's appearance on *Desert Island
Discs*, when he talked about his lifelong passion for Miles Davis. He
explained that the music represented for him 'the sound of what cannot
be'. 'What was his own intellectual life', they asked, 'but the striving,
against all odds, to make "what cannot be" alive in [thought and] the
imagination?' He was the source of extraordinary wisdom and generosity.
One of the best lights of the world had gone.

Index